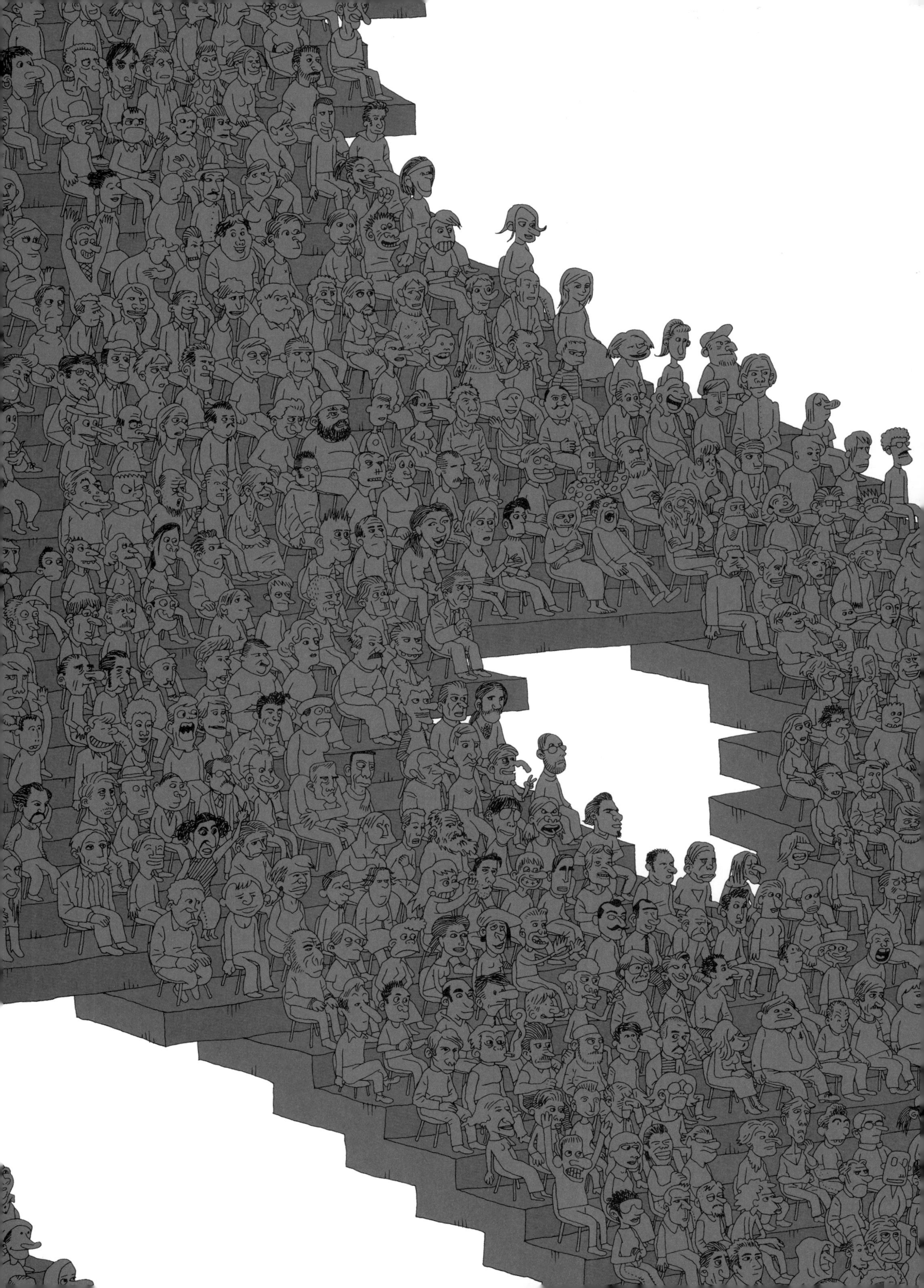

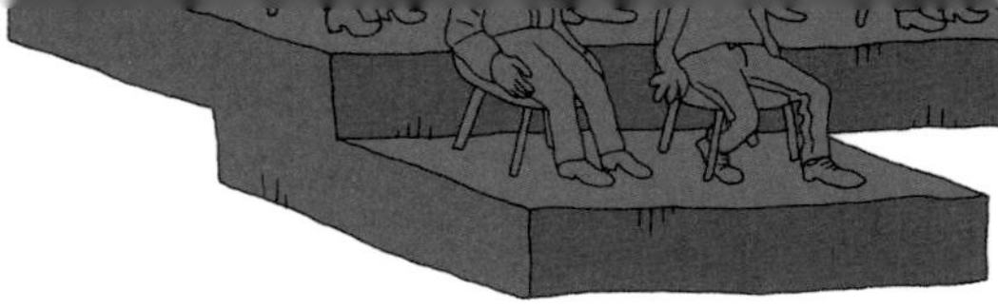

FROM WONDERL

DANISH COMICS IN T

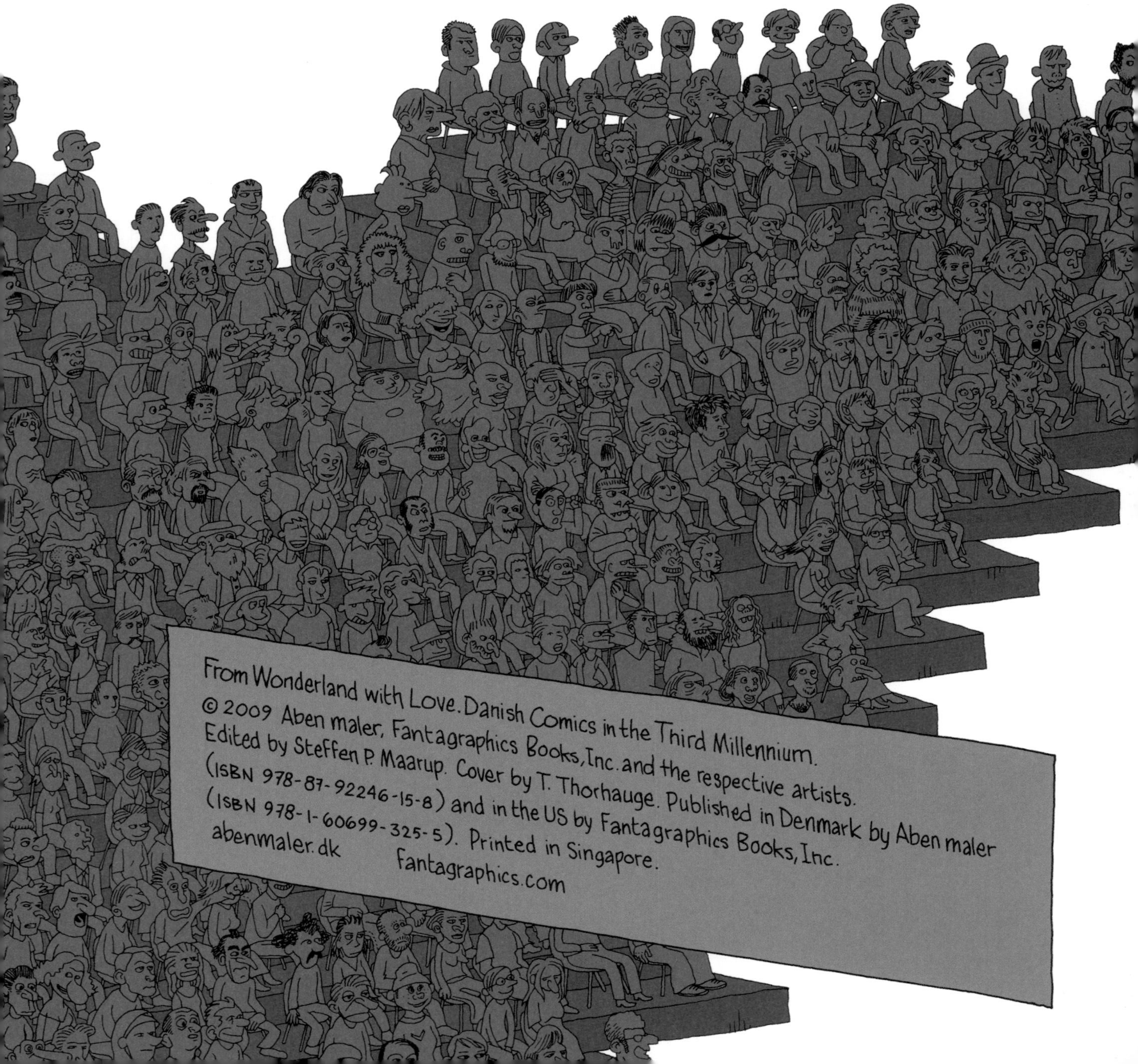

From Wonderland with Love. Danish Comics in the Third Millennium.

Edited by Steffen P. Maarup. Cover by T. Thorhauge. Published in Denmark by Aben maler
(ISBN 978-87-92246-15-8) and in the US by Fantagraphics Books, Inc.
(ISBN 978-1-60699-325-5). Printed in Singapore.
abenmaler.dk fantagraphics.com

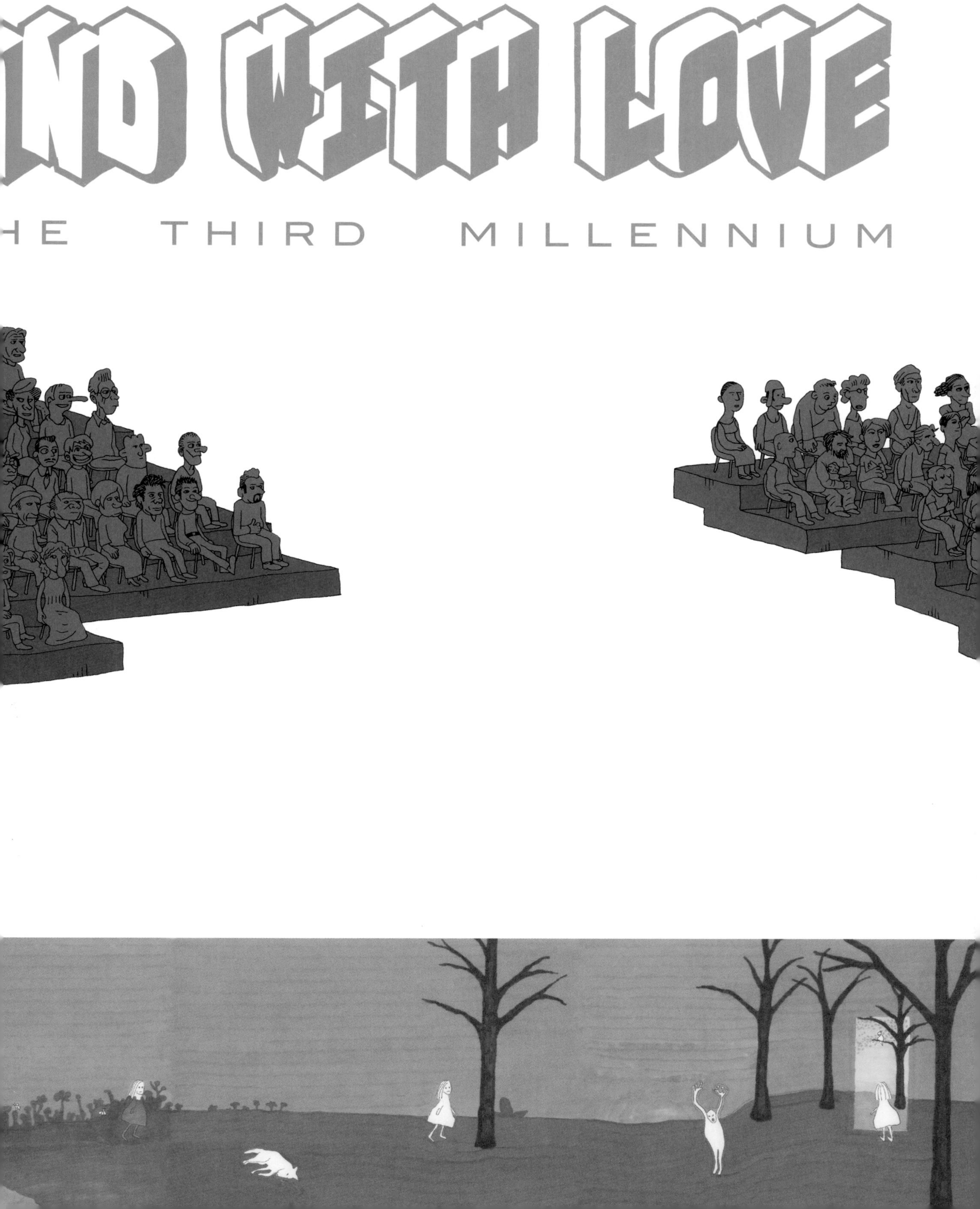
ND WITH LOVE
HE THIRD MILLENNIUM

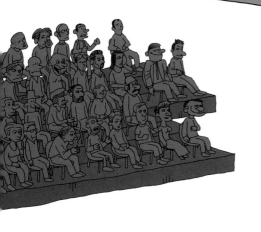

BALL USA
MARC O POLO
KAPPA
BALL
LEVI'S
CLAUDIO
EVERLAST
CONVERSE
LINDEHØJ SCHOOL 8A 1989
CHICAGO BULLS
BALL

I was the only one who hadn't gotten a logo shirt from my parents but fortunately I got to hold the sign.

NOW, FIRST WE GO TO THE GREENGROCER MR. MØLLER, THEN TO THE BAKERY AND AFTERWARDS TO INGEBORG THE HAIRDRESSER. WE ALSO HAVE TO STOP BY THE POST OFFICE AND LASTLY WE'RE GOING DOWN TO FEED THE NICE DUCKS
YES, MOM
YES, MOM

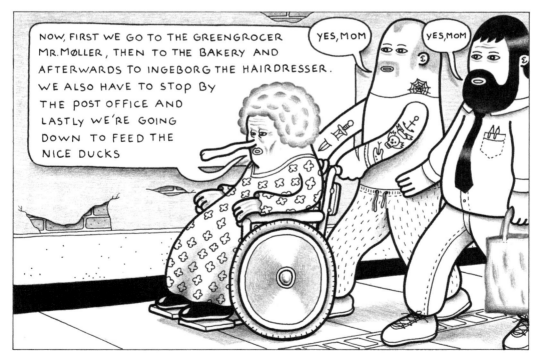

Adults are children too.

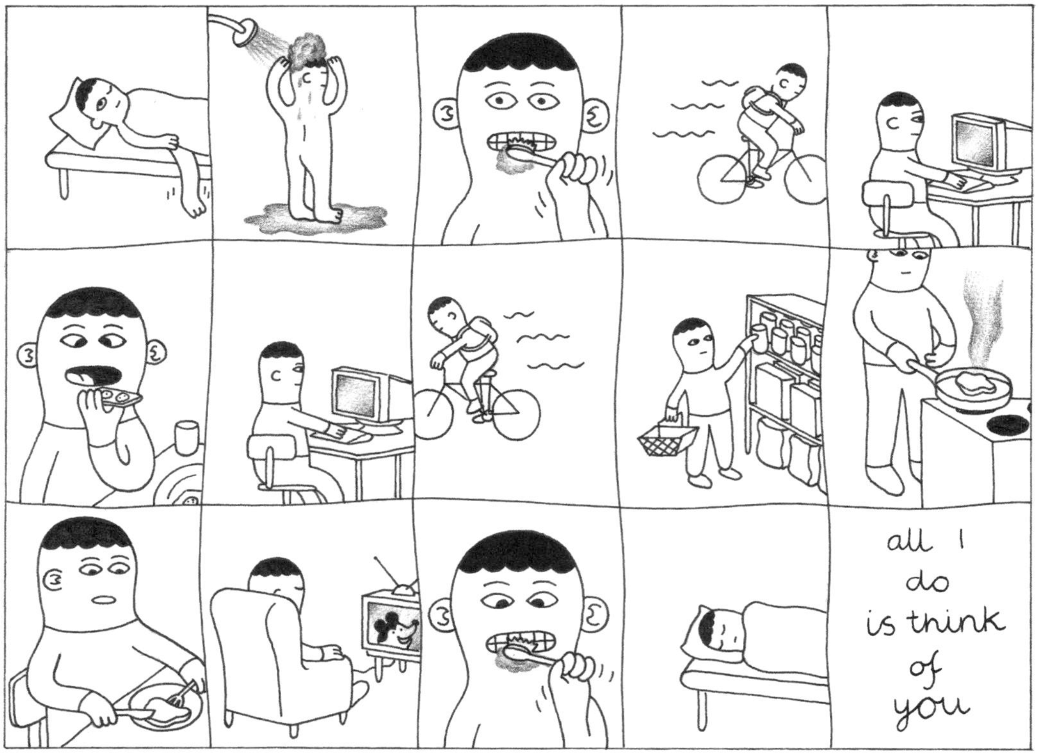
all I do is think of you

8

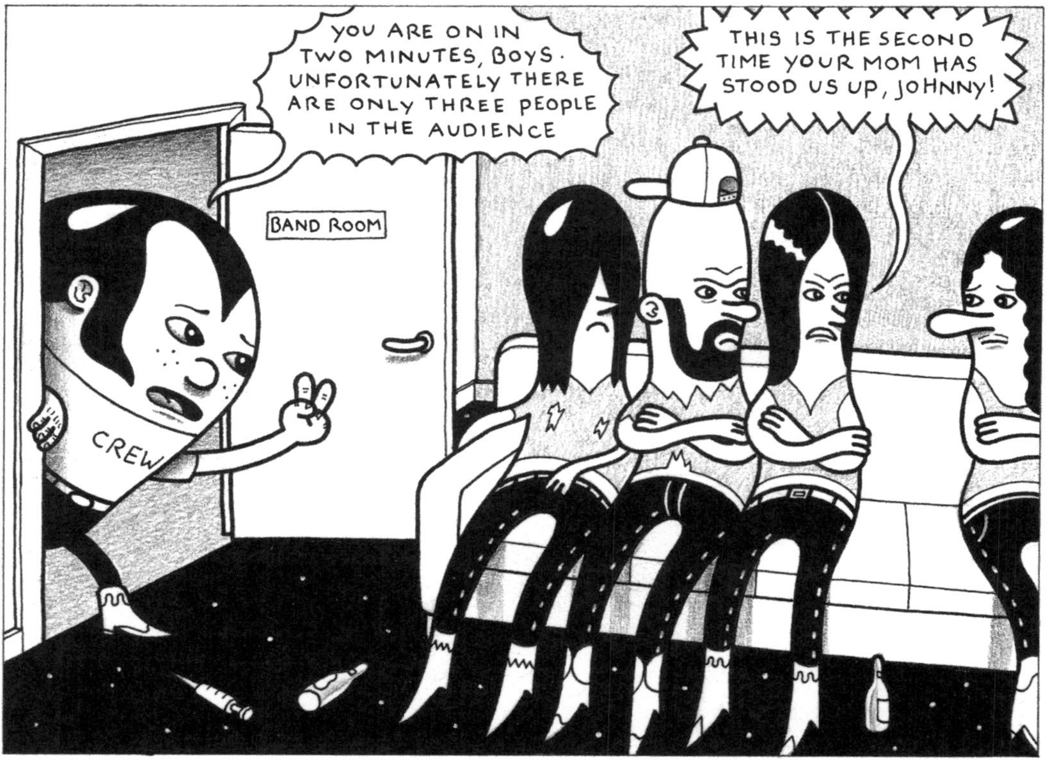
YOU ARE ON IN TWO MINUTES, BOYS. UNFORTUNATELY THERE ARE ONLY THREE PEOPLE IN THE AUDIENCE
THIS IS THE SECOND TIME YOUR MOM HAS STOOD US UP, JOHNNY!
BAND ROOM
CREW

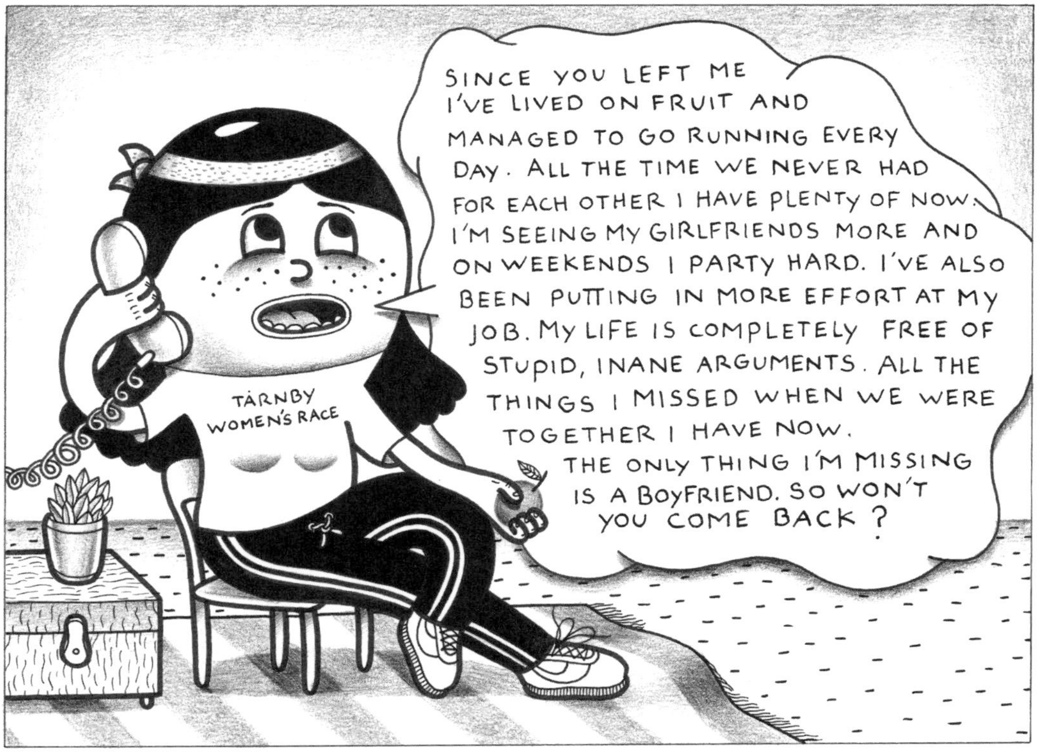
SINCE YOU LEFT ME I'VE LIVED ON FRUIT AND MANAGED TO GO RUNNING EVERY DAY. ALL THE TIME WE NEVER HAD FOR EACH OTHER I HAVE PLENTY OF NOW. I'M SEEING MY GIRLFRIENDS MORE AND ON WEEKENDS I PARTY HARD. I'VE ALSO BEEN PUTTING IN MORE EFFORT AT MY JOB. MY LIFE IS COMPLETELY FREE OF STUPID, INANE ARGUMENTS. ALL THE THINGS I MISSED WHEN WE WERE TOGETHER I HAVE NOW. THE ONLY THING I'M MISSING IS A BOYFRIEND. SO WON'T YOU COME BACK?
TÅRNBY WOMEN'S RACE

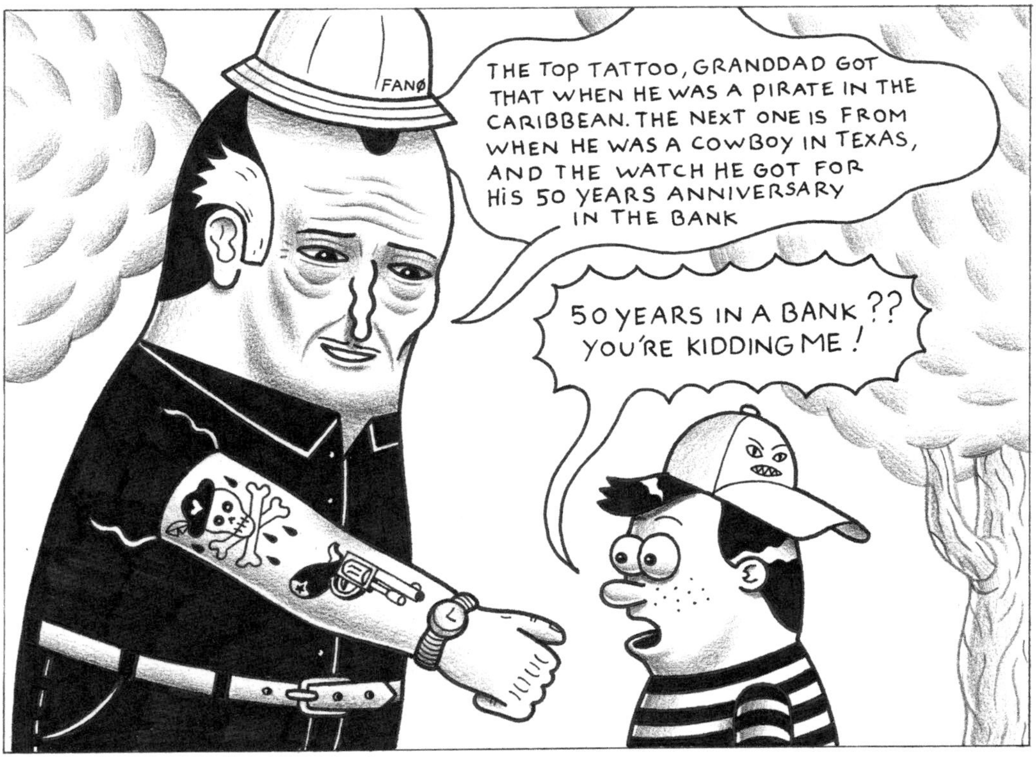
FANØ
THE TOP TATTOO, GRANDDAD GOT THAT WHEN HE WAS A PIRATE IN THE CARIBBEAN. THE NEXT ONE IS FROM WHEN HE WAS A COWBOY IN TEXAS, AND THE WATCH HE GOT FOR HIS 50 YEARS ANNIVERSARY IN THE BANK
50 YEARS IN A BANK?? YOU'RE KIDDING ME!

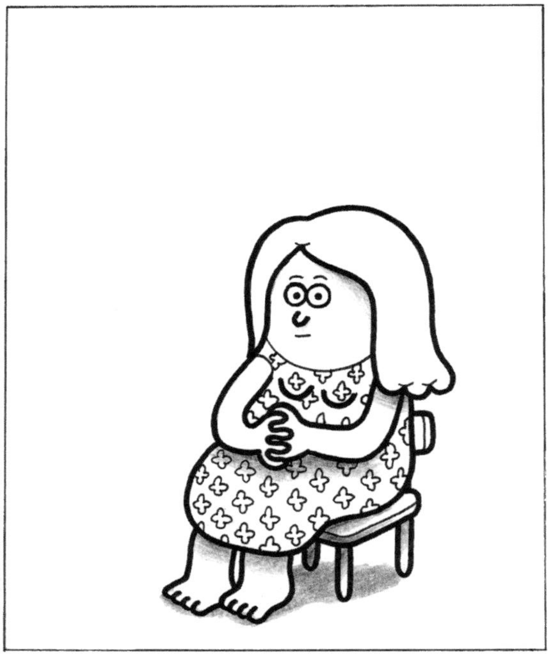

All good things come to those who wait. Just give it five more minutes.

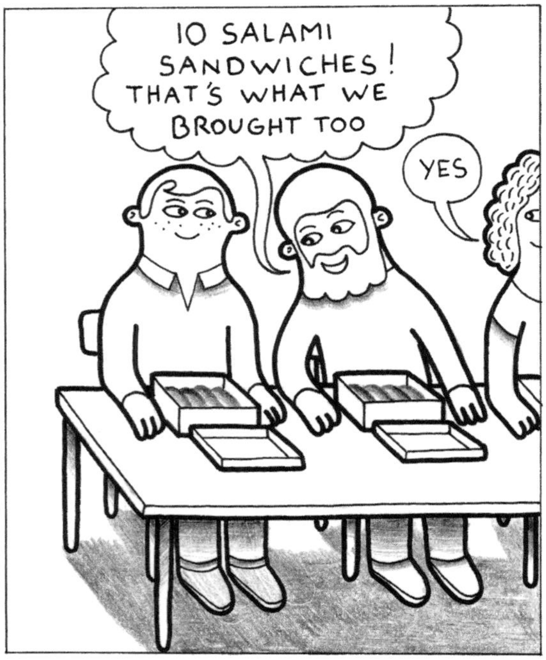

IO SALAMI SANDWICHES! THAT'S WHAT WE BROUGHT TOO
YES

Although Arne was new in the company, his colleagues thought that he fit right in.

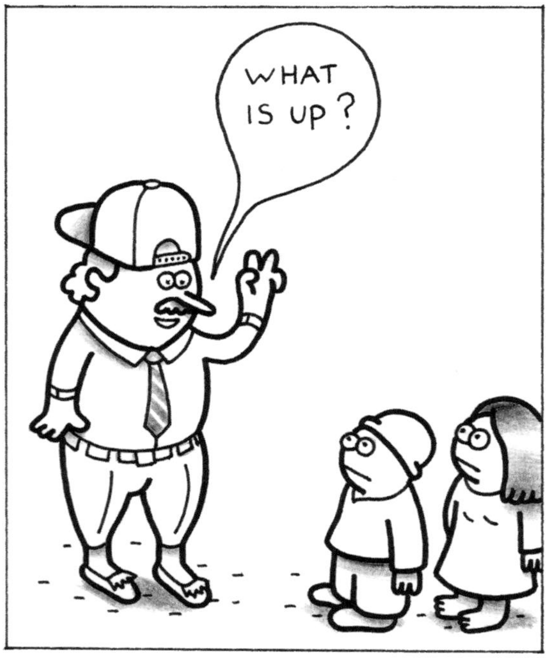

WHAT IS UP?

When Poul Erik wanted to be "down with the kids", he put on his reversed cap.

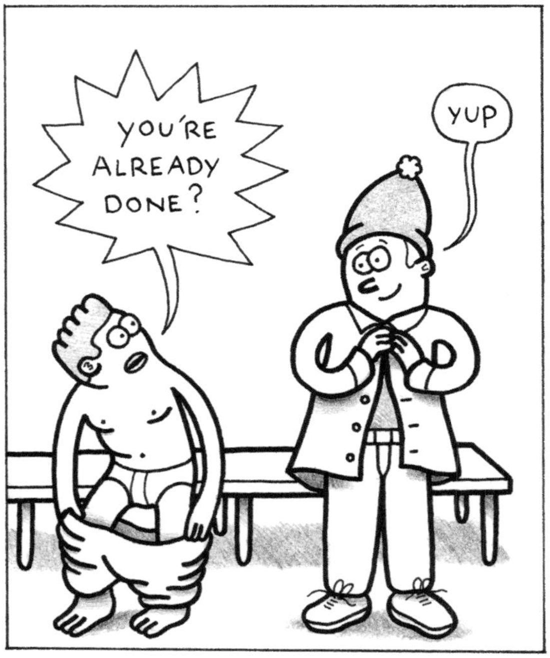

YOU'RE ALREADY DONE?
YUP

Jens was the worst on the soccer pitch, but he was the best at getting dressed afterwards.

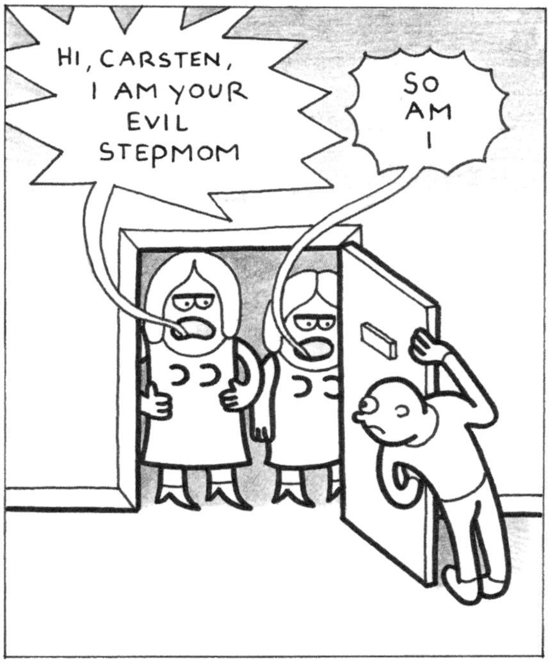
HI, CARSTEN, I AM YOUR EVIL STEPMOM
SO AM I

Misfortunes never come singly.

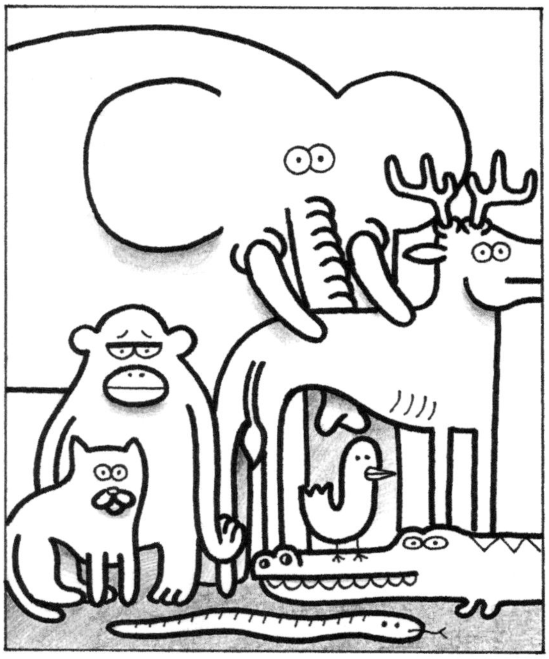

Animals have no ambitions.

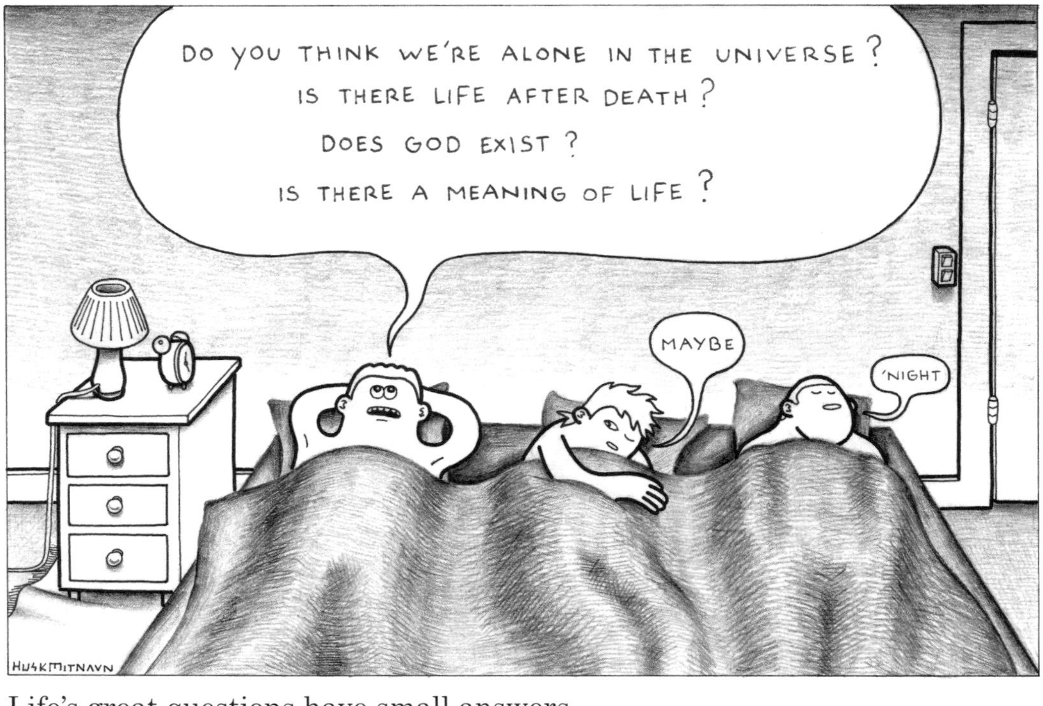
DO YOU THINK WE'RE ALONE IN THE UNIVERSE? IS THERE LIFE AFTER DEATH? DOES GOD EXIST? IS THERE A MEANING OF LIFE?
MAYBE
'NIGHT
HUSKMITNAVN

Life's great questions have small answers.

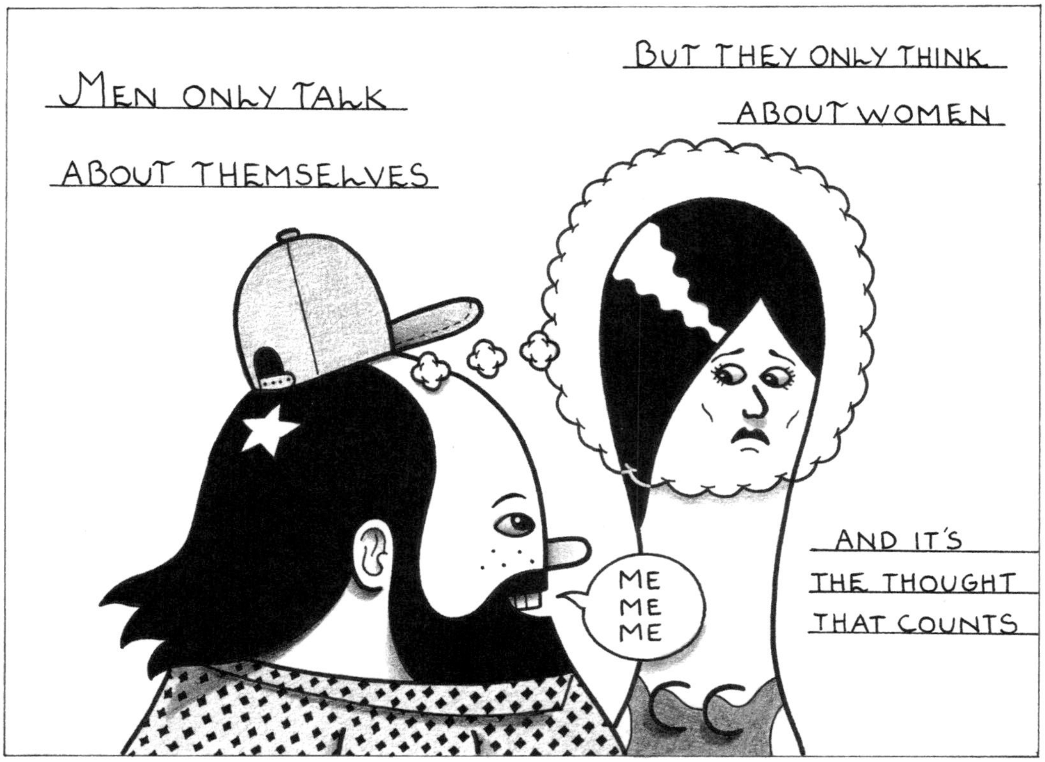
MEN ONLY TALK
ABOUT THEMSELVES
BUT THEY ONLY THINK
ABOUT WOMEN
ME
ME
ME
AND IT'S
THE THOUGHT
THAT COUNTS

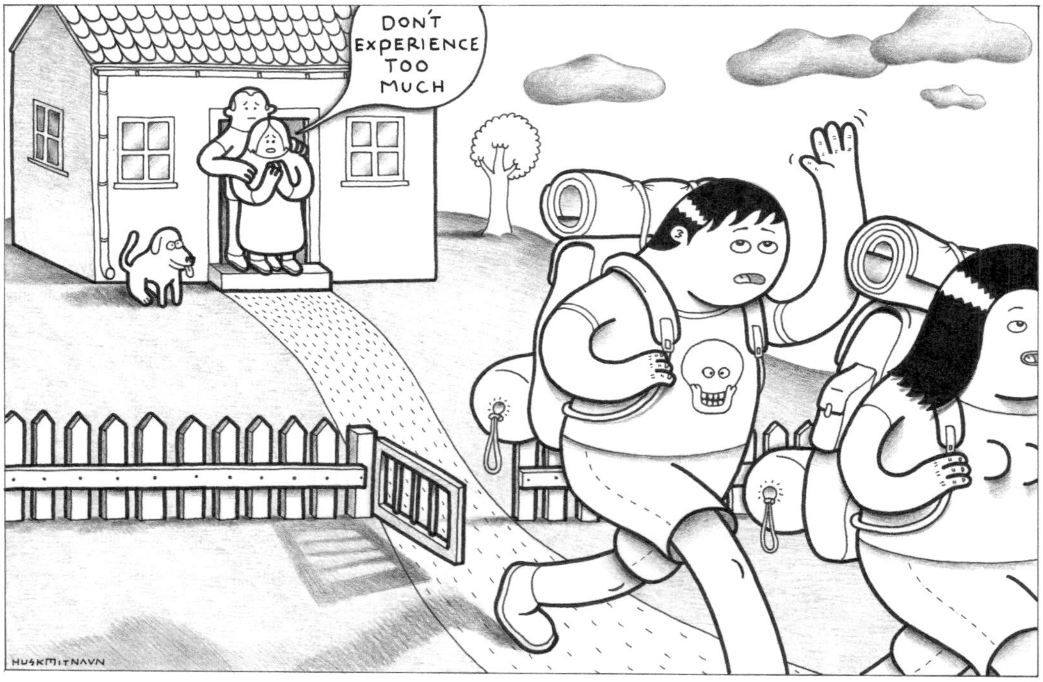
DON'T
EXPERIENCE
TOO
MUCH
HUSKMITNAVN

BIRTE

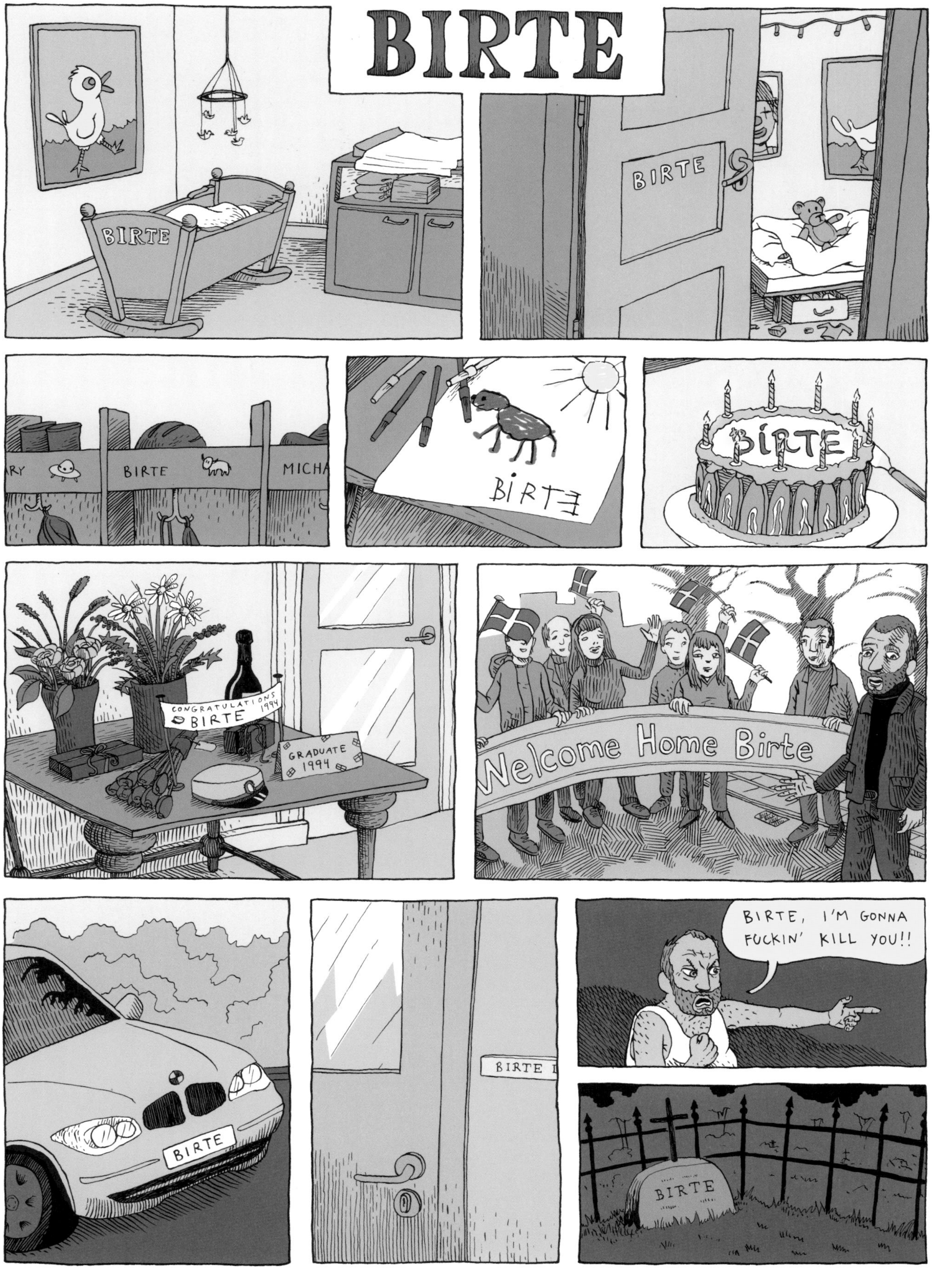
BIRTE
BIRTE
BIRTE
BIRTE
MICHA
BIRTE
BIRTE
CONGRATULATIONS
BIRTE 1994
GRADUATE
1994
Welcome Home Birte
BIRTE
BIRTE
BIRTE, I'M GONNA FUCKIN' KILL YOU!!
BIRTE

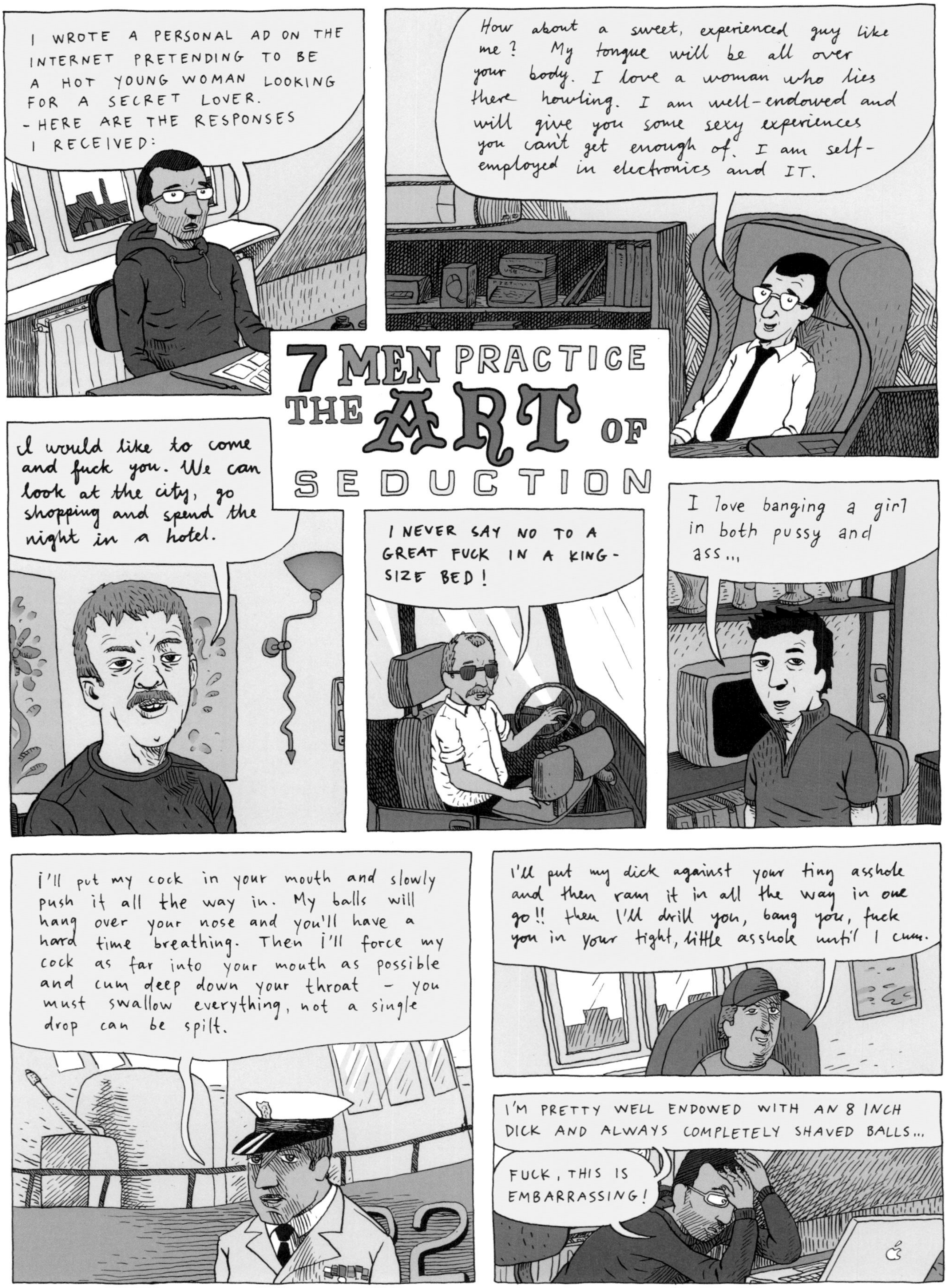

I WROTE A PERSONAL AD ON THE INTERNET PRETENDING TO BE A HOT YOUNG WOMAN LOOKING FOR A SECRET LOVER. - HERE ARE THE RESPONSES I RECEIVED:
How about a sweet, experienced guy like me? My tongue will be all over your body. I love a woman who lies there howling. I am well-endowed and will give you some sexy experiences you can't get enough of. I am self-employed in electronics and IT.
7 MEN PRACTICE THE ART OF SEDUCTION
I would like to come and fuck you. We can look at the city, go shopping and spend the night in a hotel.
I NEVER SAY NO TO A GREAT FUCK IN A KING-SIZE BED!
I love banging a girl in both pussy and ass...
i'll put my cock in your mouth and slowly push it all the way in. My balls will hang over your nose and you'll have a hard time breathing. Then i'll force my cock as far into your mouth as possible and cum deep down your throat - you must swallow everything, not a single drop can be spilt.
I'll put my dick against your tiny asshole and then ram it in all the way in one go!! then I'll drill you, bang you, fuck you in your tight, little asshole until I cum.
I'M PRETTY WELL ENDOWED WITH AN 8 INCH DICK AND ALWAYS COMPLETELY SHAVED BALLS...
FUCK, THIS IS EMBARRASSING!

Because I Love You So Much

Nikoline Werdelin

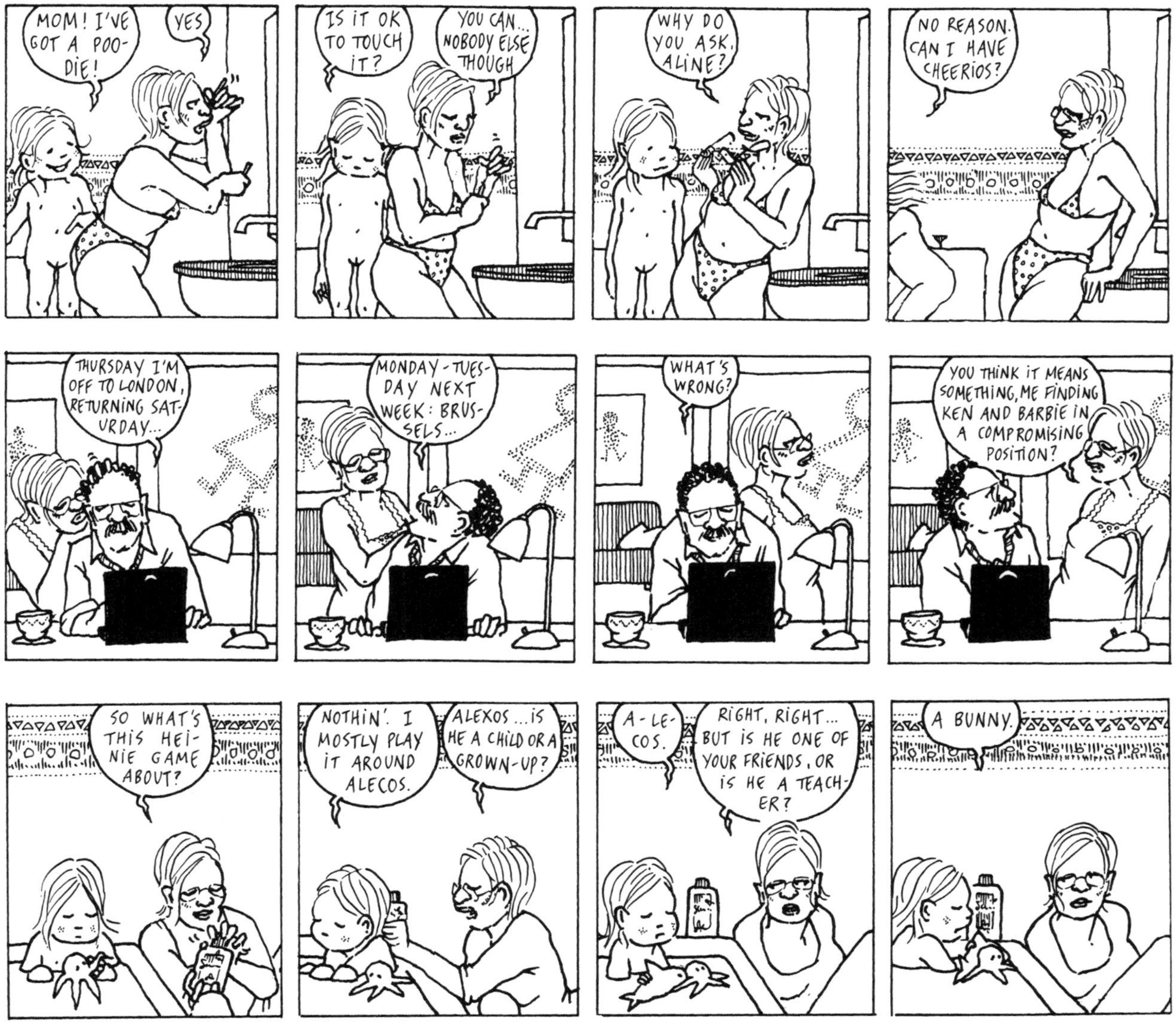
MOM! I'VE GOT A POO-DIE!
YES
IS IT OK TO TOUCH IT?
YOU CAN... NOBODY ELSE THOUGH
WHY DO YOU ASK, ALINE?
NO REASON. CAN I HAVE CHEERIOS?
THURSDAY I'M OFF TO LONDON, RETURNING SAT-URDAY...
MONDAY-TUES-DAY NEXT WEEK: BRUS-SELS...
WHAT'S WRONG?
YOU THINK IT MEANS SOMETHING, ME FINDING KEN AND BARBIE IN A COMPROMISING POSITION?
SO WHAT'S THIS HEI-NIE GAME ABOUT?
NOTHIN'. I MOSTLY PLAY IT AROUND ALECOS.
ALEXOS...IS HE A CHILD OR A GROWN-UP?
A-LE-COS.
RIGHT, RIGHT... BUT IS HE ONE OF YOUR FRIENDS, OR IS HE A TEACH-ER?
A BUNNY.

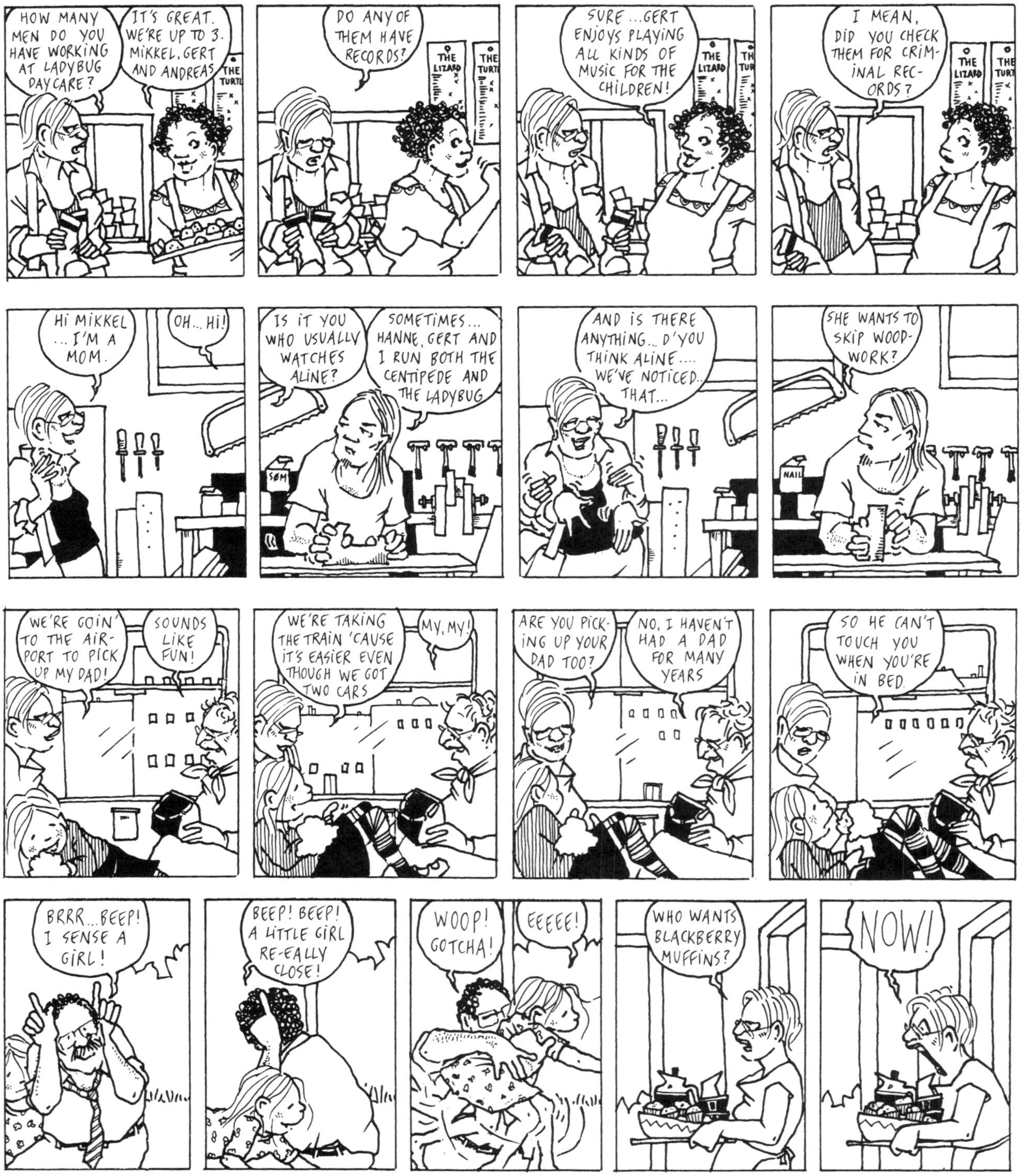
HOW MANY MEN DO YOU HAVE WORKING AT LADYBUG DAYCARE?
IT'S GREAT. WE'RE UP TO 3. MIKKEL, GERT AND ANDREAS
THE TURTLE
DO ANY OF THEM HAVE RECORDS?
THE LIZARD
THE TURTLE
SURE ...GERT ENJOYS PLAYING ALL KINDS OF MUSIC FOR THE CHILDREN!
THE LIZARD
I MEAN, DID YOU CHECK THEM FOR CRIMINAL RECORDS?
THE LIZARD
Hi MIKKEL ... I'M A MOM.
OH... Hi!
IS IT YOU WHO USUALLY WATCHES ALINE?
SOMETIMES... HANNE, GERT AND I RUN BOTH THE CENTIPEDE AND THE LADYBUG
SØM
AND IS THERE ANYTHING... D'YOU THINK ALINE.... WE'VE NOTICED.. THAT...
SHE WANTS TO SKIP WOODWORK?
NAIL
WE'RE GOIN' TO THE AIRPORT TO PICK UP MY DAD!
SOUNDS LIKE FUN!
WE'RE TAKING THE TRAIN 'CAUSE IT'S EASIER EVEN THOUGH WE GOT TWO CARS
MY, MY!
ARE YOU PICKING UP YOUR DAD TOO?
NO, I HAVEN'T HAD A DAD FOR MANY YEARS
SO HE CAN'T TOUCH YOU WHEN YOU'RE IN BED.
BRRR... BEEP! I SENSE A GIRL!
BEEP! BEEP! A LITTLE GIRL RE-EALLY CLOSE!
WOOP! GOTCHA!
EEEEE!
WHO WANTS BLACKBERRY MUFFINS?
NOW!

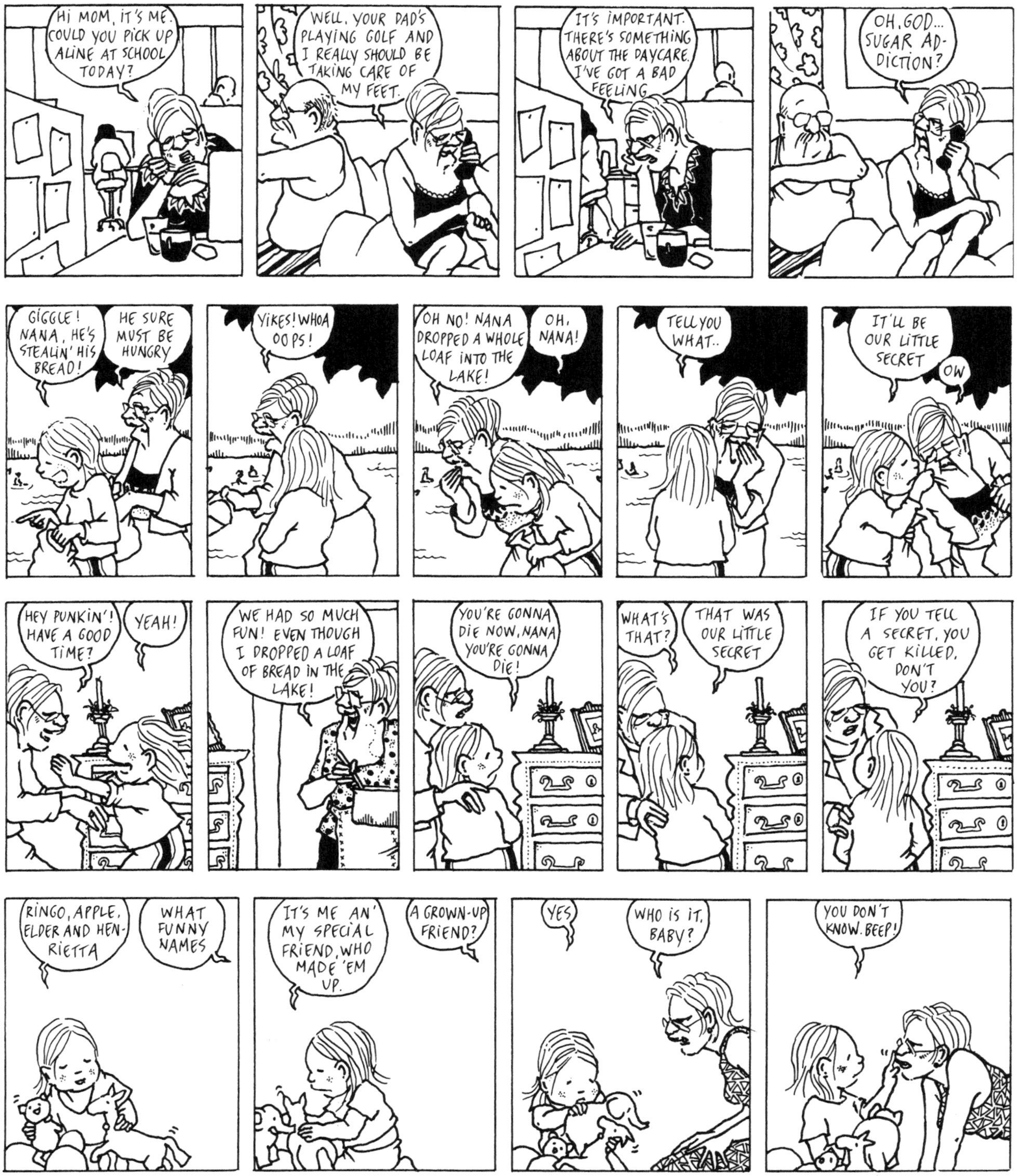
HI MOM, IT'S ME. COULD YOU PICK UP ALINE AT SCHOOL TODAY?
WELL, YOUR DAD'S PLAYING GOLF AND I REALLY SHOULD BE TAKING CARE OF MY FEET.
IT'S IMPORTANT. THERE'S SOMETHING ABOUT THE DAYCARE. I'VE GOT A BAD FEELING
OH, GOD... SUGAR ADDICTION?
GIGGLE! NANA, HE'S STEALIN' HIS BREAD!
HE SURE MUST BE HUNGRY
YIKES! WHOA OOPS!
OH NO! NANA DROPPED A WHOLE LOAF INTO THE LAKE!
OH, NANA!
TELL YOU WHAT..
IT'LL BE OUR LITTLE SECRET
OW
HEY PUNKIN'! HAVE A GOOD TIME?
YEAH!
WE HAD SO MUCH FUN! EVEN THOUGH I DROPPED A LOAF OF BREAD IN THE LAKE!
YOU'RE GONNA DIE NOW, NANA YOU'RE GONNA DIE!
WHAT'S THAT?
THAT WAS OUR LITTLE SECRET
IF YOU TELL A SECRET, YOU GET KILLED, DON'T YOU?
RINGO, APPLE, ELDER AND HENRIETTA
WHAT FUNNY NAMES
IT'S ME AN' MY SPECIAL FRIEND, WHO MADE 'EM UP.
A GROWN-UP FRIEND?
YES
WHO IS IT, BABY?
YOU DON'T KNOW. BEEP!

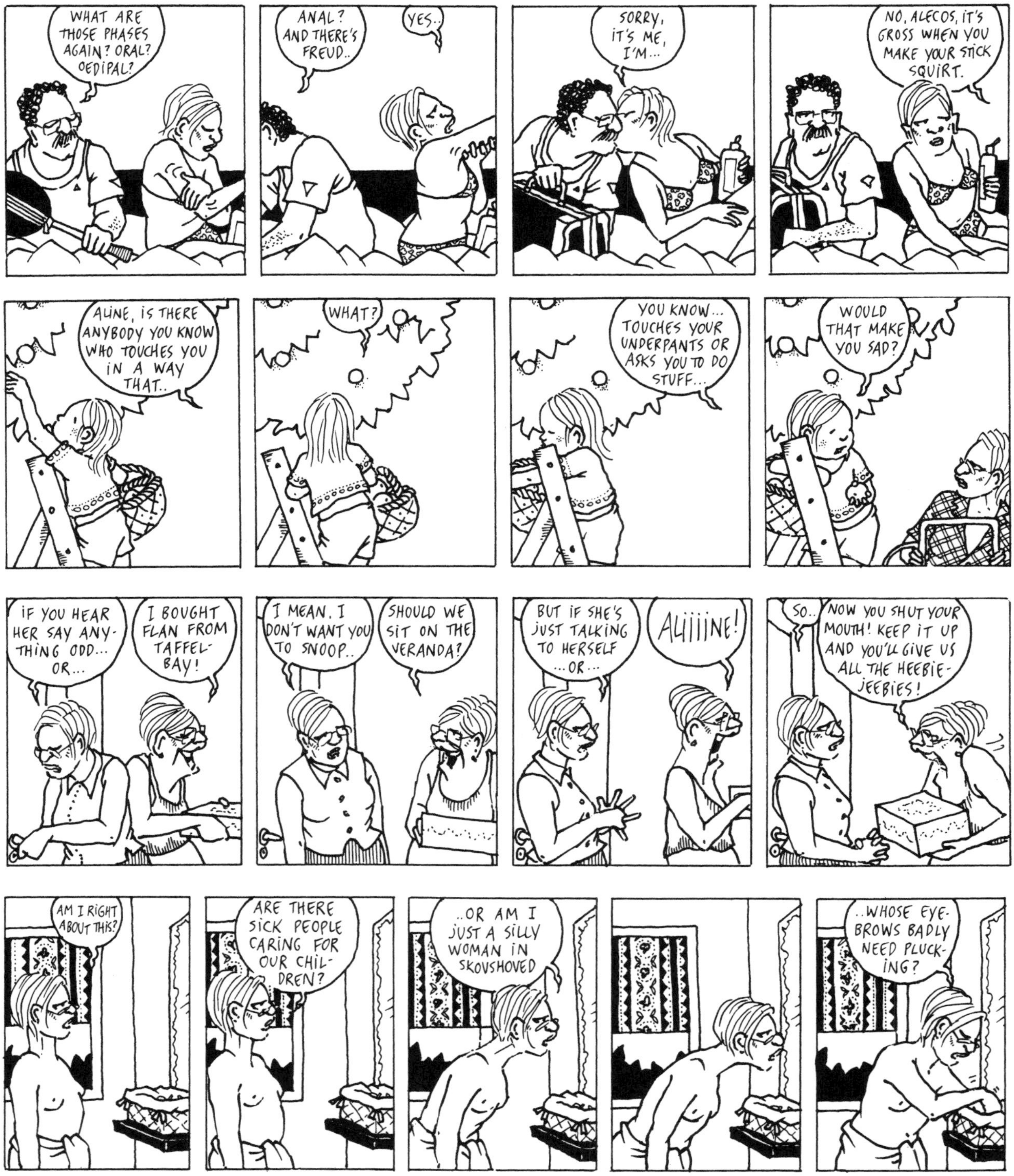
WHAT ARE THOSE PHASES AGAIN? ORAL? OEDIPAL?
ANAL? AND THERE'S FREUD..
YES..
SORRY, IT'S ME, I'M...
NO, ALECOS, IT'S GROSS WHEN YOU MAKE YOUR STICK SQUIRT.
ALINE, IS THERE ANYBODY YOU KNOW WHO TOUCHES YOU IN A WAY THAT..
WHAT?
YOU KNOW... TOUCHES YOUR UNDERPANTS OR ASKS YOU TO DO STUFF...
WOULD THAT MAKE YOU SAD?
IF YOU HEAR HER SAY ANYTHING ODD... OR...
I BOUGHT FLAN FROM TAFFELBAY!
I MEAN, I DON'T WANT YOU TO SNOOP..
SHOULD WE SIT ON THE VERANDA?
BUT IF SHE'S JUST TALKING TO HERSELF ...OR...
ALIIIINE!
SO..
NOW YOU SHUT YOUR MOUTH! KEEP IT UP AND YOU'LL GIVE US ALL THE HEEBIE-JEEBIES!
AM I RIGHT ABOUT THIS?
ARE THERE SICK PEOPLE CARING FOR OUR CHILDREN?
..OR AM I JUST A SILLY WOMAN IN SKOVSHOVED
..WHOSE EYEBROWS BADLY NEED PLUCKING?

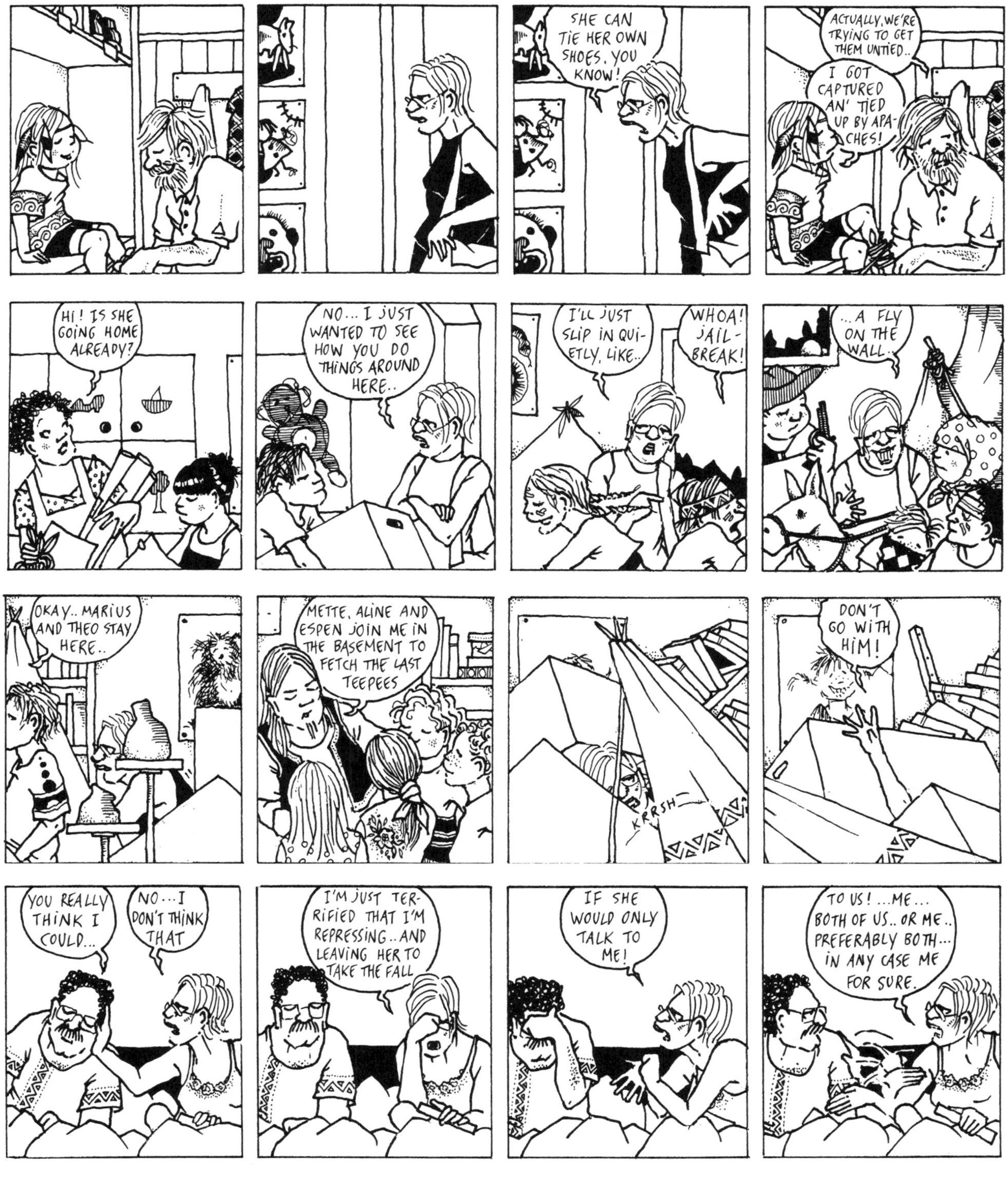
SHE CAN TIE HER OWN SHOES, YOU KNOW!
ACTUALLY, WE'RE TRYING TO GET THEM UNTIED..
I GOT CAPTURED AN' TIED UP BY APACHES!
HI! IS SHE GOING HOME ALREADY?
NO... I JUST WANTED TO SEE HOW YOU DO THINGS AROUND HERE..
I'LL JUST SLIP IN QUIETLY, LIKE..
WHOA! JAILBREAK!
...A FLY ON THE WALL..
OKAY.. MARIUS AND THEO STAY HERE..
METTE, ALINE AND ESPEN JOIN ME IN THE BASEMENT TO FETCH THE LAST TEEPEES
KRRSH
DON'T GO WITH HIM!
YOU REALLY THINK I COULD...
NO...I DON'T THINK THAT
I'M JUST TERRIFIED THAT I'M REPRESSING.. AND LEAVING HER TO TAKE THE FALL
IF SHE WOULD ONLY TALK TO ME!
TO US! ...ME... BOTH OF US.. OR ME.. PREFERABLY BOTH... IN ANY CASE ME FOR SURE.

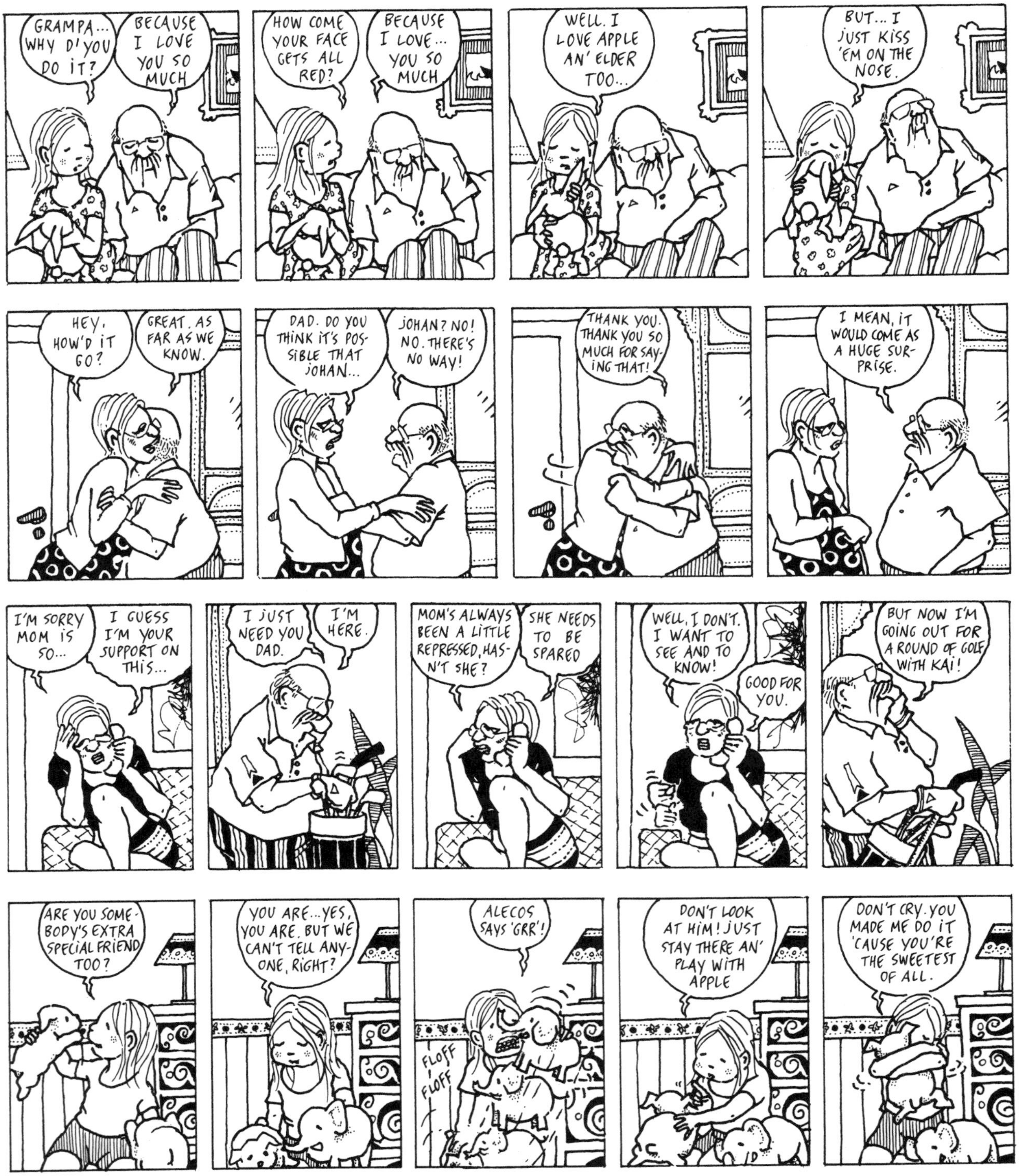

GRAMPA... WHY D'YOU DO IT?
BECAUSE I LOVE YOU SO MUCH
HOW COME YOUR FACE GETS ALL RED?
BECAUSE I LOVE... YOU SO MUCH
WELL. I LOVE APPLE AN' ELDER TOO...
BUT... I JUST KISS 'EM ON THE NOSE.
HEY. HOW'D IT GO?
GREAT. AS FAR AS WE KNOW.
DAD. DO YOU THINK IT'S POSSIBLE THAT JOHAN...
JOHAN? NO! NO. THERE'S NO WAY!
THANK YOU. THANK YOU SO MUCH FOR SAYING THAT!
I MEAN, IT WOULD COME AS A HUGE SURPRISE.
I'M SORRY MOM IS SO...
I GUESS I'M YOUR SUPPORT ON THIS...
I JUST NEED YOU DAD.
I'M HERE.
MOM'S ALWAYS BEEN A LITTLE REPRESSED, HASN'T SHE?
SHE NEEDS TO BE SPARED
WELL, I DON'T. I WANT TO SEE AND TO KNOW!
GOOD FOR YOU.
BUT NOW I'M GOING OUT FOR A ROUND OF GOLF WITH KAI!
ARE YOU SOMEBODY'S EXTRA SPECIAL FRIEND TOO?
YOU ARE... YES, YOU ARE. BUT WE CAN'T TELL ANYONE, RIGHT?
ALECOS SAYS 'GRR'!
FLOFF FLOFF
DON'T LOOK AT HIM! JUST STAY THERE AN' PLAY WITH APPLE
DON'T CRY. YOU MADE ME DO IT 'CAUSE YOU'RE THE SWEETEST OF ALL.

20

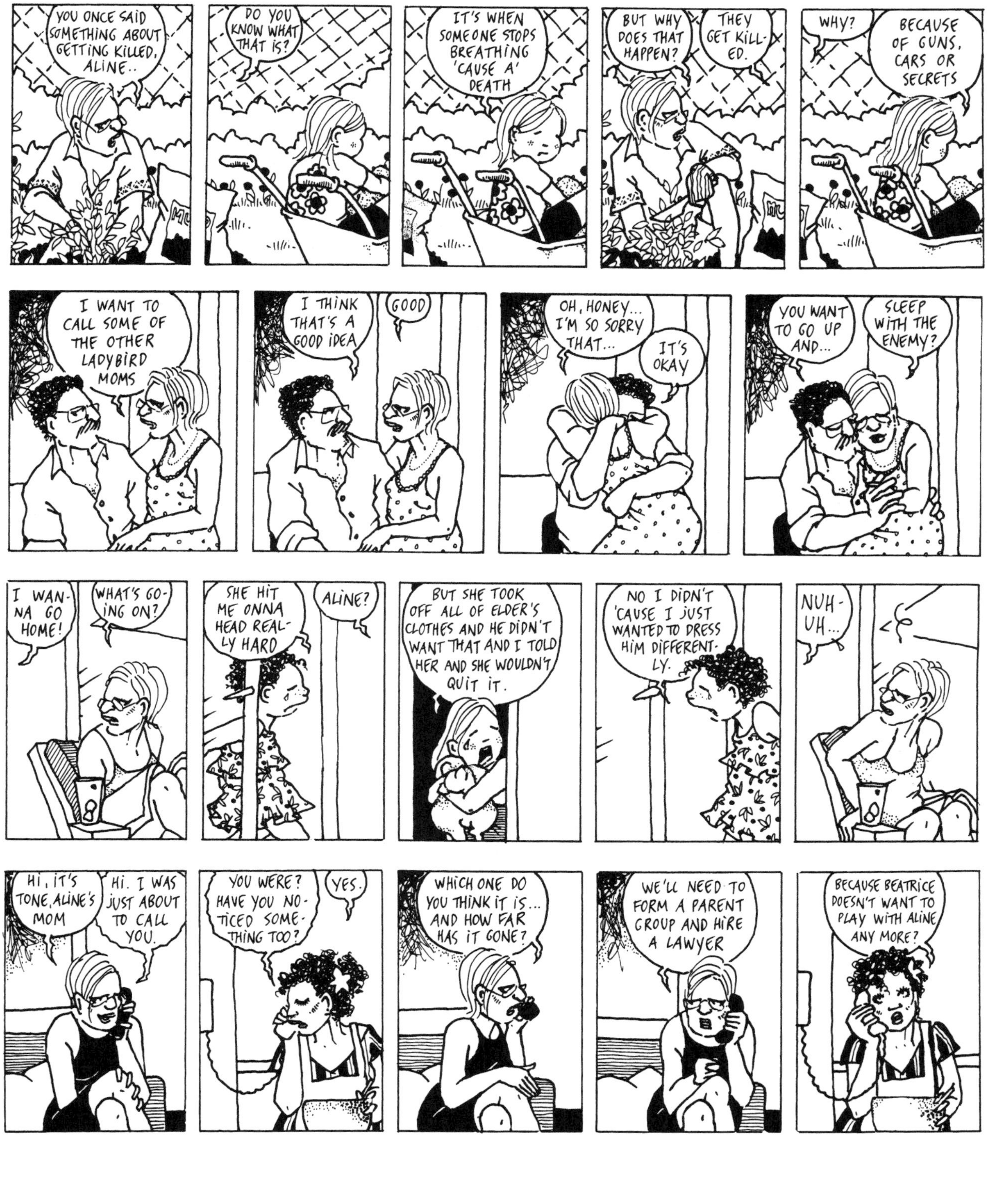
YOU ONCE SAID SOMETHING ABOUT GETTING KILLED, ALINE..
DO YOU KNOW WHAT THAT IS?
IT'S WHEN SOMEONE STOPS BREATHING 'CAUSE A' DEATH
BUT WHY DOES THAT HAPPEN?
THEY GET KILL-ED.
WHY?
BECAUSE OF GUNS, CARS OR SECRETS
I WANT TO CALL SOME OF THE OTHER LADYBIRD MOMS
I THINK THAT'S A GOOD IDEA
GOOD
OH, HONEY... I'M SO SORRY THAT...
IT'S OKAY
YOU WANT TO GO UP AND...
SLEEP WITH THE ENEMY?
I WAN-NA GO HOME!
WHAT'S GO-ING ON?
SHE HIT ME ONNA HEAD REAL-LY HARD
ALINE?
BUT SHE TOOK OFF ALL OF ELDER'S CLOTHES AND HE DIDN'T WANT THAT AND I TOLD HER AND SHE WOULDN'T QUIT IT.
NO I DIDN'T 'CAUSE I JUST WANTED TO DRESS HIM DIFFERENT-LY.
NUH-UH...
HI, IT'S TONE, ALINE'S MOM
HI. I WAS JUST ABOUT TO CALL YOU.
YOU WERE? HAVE YOU NO-TICED SOME-THING TOO?
YES.
WHICH ONE DO YOU THINK IT IS... AND HOW FAR HAS IT GONE?
WE'LL NEED TO FORM A PARENT GROUP AND HIRE A LAWYER
BECAUSE BEATRICE DOESN'T WANT TO PLAY WITH ALINE ANY MORE?

21

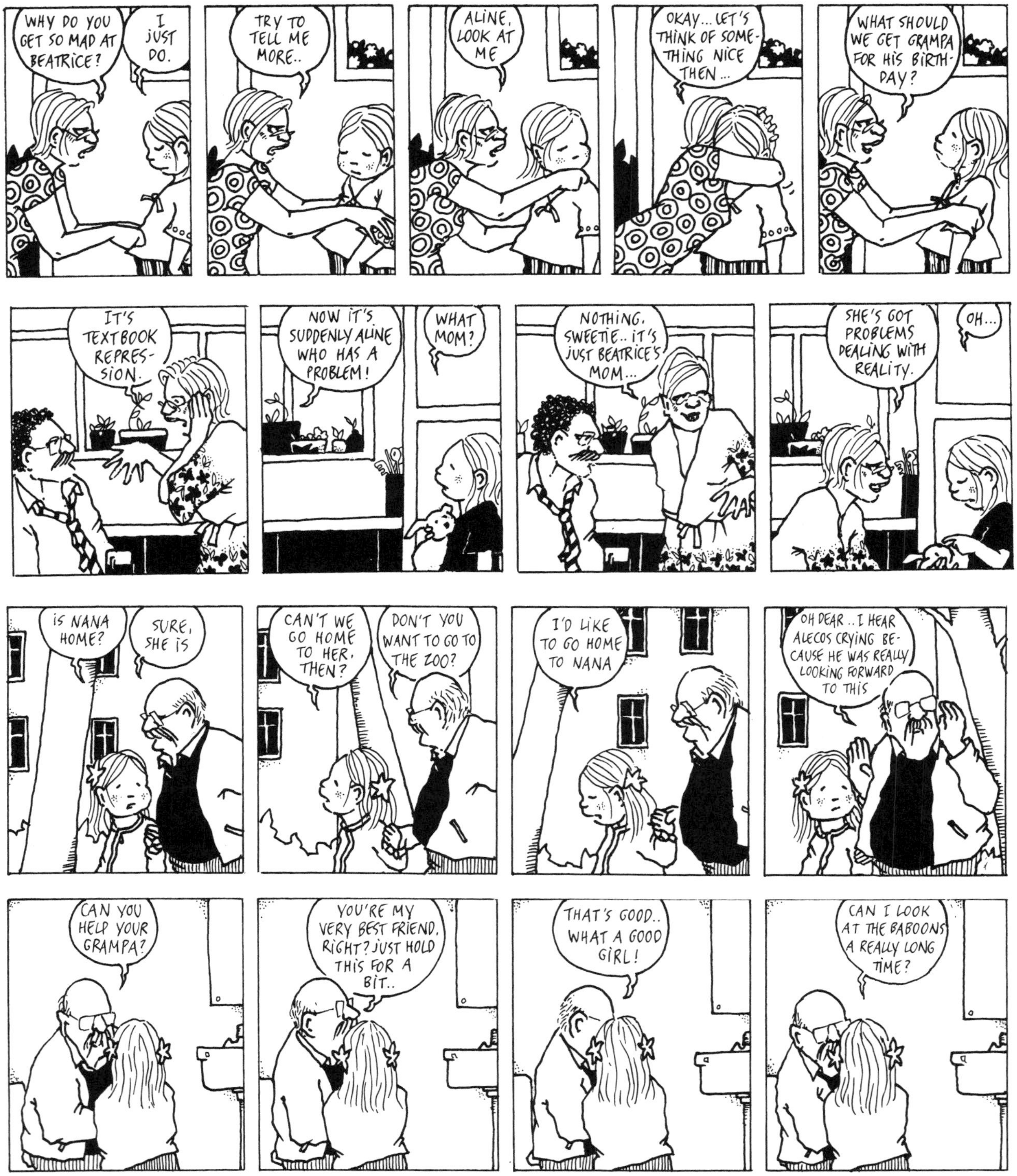
WHY DO YOU GET SO MAD AT BEATRICE?
I JUST DO.
TRY TO TELL ME MORE..
ALINE, LOOK AT ME
OKAY... LET'S THINK OF SOMETHING NICE THEN...
WHAT SHOULD WE GET GRAMPA FOR HIS BIRTHDAY?
IT'S TEXTBOOK REPRESSION.
NOW IT'S SUDDENLY ALINE WHO HAS A PROBLEM!
WHAT MOM?
NOTHING, SWEETIE.. IT'S JUST BEATRICE'S MOM...
SHE'S GOT PROBLEMS DEALING WITH REALITY.
OH...
IS NANA HOME?
SURE, SHE IS
CAN'T WE GO HOME TO HER, THEN?
DON'T YOU WANT TO GO TO THE ZOO?
I'D LIKE TO GO HOME TO NANA
OH DEAR.. I HEAR ALECOS CRYING BECAUSE HE WAS REALLY LOOKING FORWARD TO THIS
CAN YOU HELP YOUR GRAMPA?
YOU'RE MY VERY BEST FRIEND, RIGHT? JUST HOLD THIS FOR A BIT..
THAT'S GOOD.. WHAT A GOOD GIRL!
CAN I LOOK AT THE BABOONS A REALLY LONG TIME?

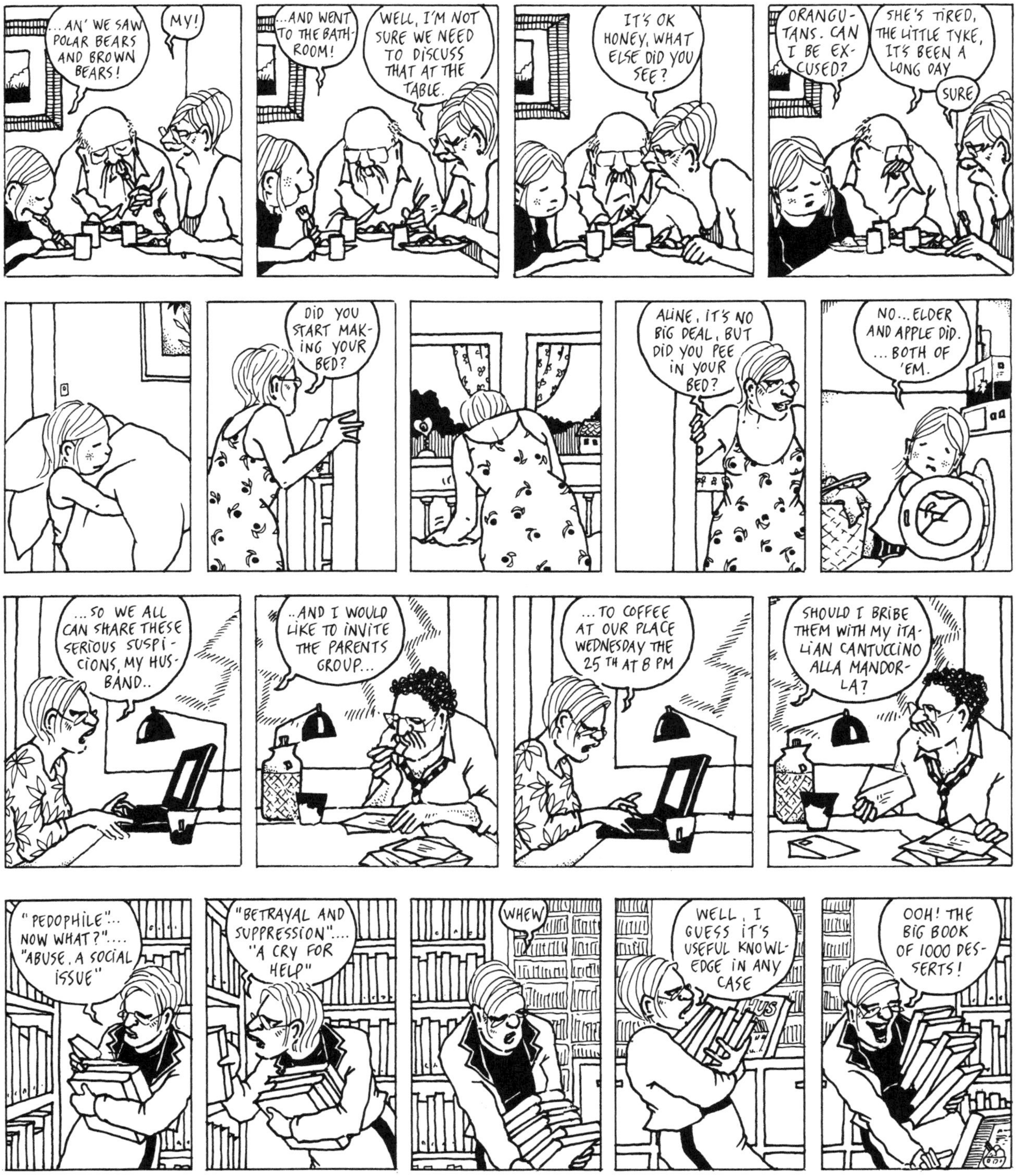
...AN' WE SAW POLAR BEARS AND BROWN BEARS!
MY!
...AND WENT TO THE BATH-ROOM!
WELL, I'M NOT SURE WE NEED TO DISCUSS THAT AT THE TABLE.
IT'S OK HONEY, WHAT ELSE DID YOU SEE?
ORANGU-TANS. CAN I BE EX-CUSED?
SHE'S TIRED, THE LITTLE TYKE, IT'S BEEN A LONG DAY
SURE
DID YOU START MAK-ING YOUR BED?
ALINE, IT'S NO BIG DEAL, BUT DID YOU PEE IN YOUR BED?
NO... ELDER AND APPLE DID. ... BOTH OF 'EM.
...SO WE ALL CAN SHARE THESE SERIOUS SUSPI-CIONS, MY HUS-BAND..
..AND I WOULD LIKE TO INVITE THE PARENTS GROUP...
...TO COFFEE AT OUR PLACE WEDNESDAY THE 25 TH AT 8 PM
SHOULD I BRIBE THEM WITH MY ITA-LIAN CANTUCCINO ALLA MANDOR-LA?
"PEDOPHILE"... NOW WHAT?".... "ABUSE, A SOCIAL ISSUE"
"BETRAYAL AND SUPPRESSION".... "A CRY FOR HELP"
WHEW
WELL, I GUESS IT'S USEFUL KNOWL-EDGE IN ANY CASE
HUS
OOH! THE BIG BOOK OF 1000 DES-SERTS!

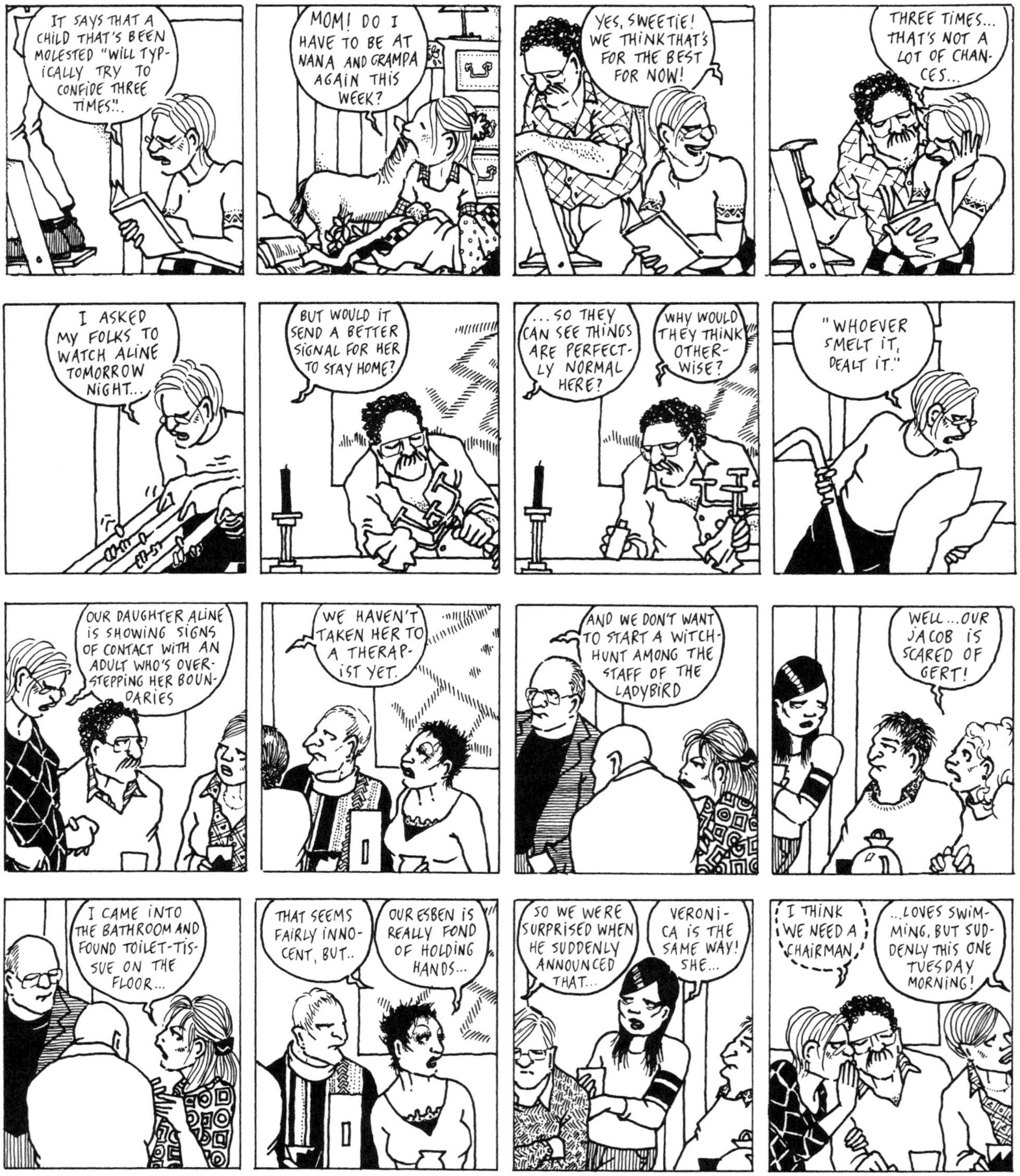
IT SAYS THAT A CHILD THAT'S BEEN MOLESTED "WILL TYPICALLY TRY TO CONFIDE THREE TIMES"...
MOM! DO I HAVE TO BE AT NANA AND GRAMPA AGAIN THIS WEEK?
YES, SWEETIE! WE THINK THAT'S FOR THE BEST FOR NOW!
THREE TIMES... THAT'S NOT A LOT OF CHANCES...
I ASKED MY FOLKS TO WATCH ALINE TOMORROW NIGHT...
BUT WOULD IT SEND A BETTER SIGNAL FOR HER TO STAY HOME?
...SO THEY CAN SEE THINGS ARE PERFECTLY NORMAL HERE?
WHY WOULD THEY THINK OTHERWISE?
"WHOEVER SMELT IT, DEALT IT."
OUR DAUGHTER ALINE IS SHOWING SIGNS OF CONTACT WITH AN ADULT WHO'S OVERSTEPPING HER BOUNDARIES
WE HAVEN'T TAKEN HER TO A THERAPIST YET.
AND WE DON'T WANT TO START A WITCH-HUNT AMONG THE STAFF OF THE LADYBIRD
WELL...OUR JACOB IS SCARED OF GERT!
I CAME INTO THE BATHROOM AND FOUND TOILET-TISSUE ON THE FLOOR...
THAT SEEMS FAIRLY INNOCENT, BUT..
OUR ESBEN IS REALLY FOND OF HOLDING HANDS...
SO WE WERE SURPRISED WHEN HE SUDDENLY ANNOUNCED THAT...
VERONICA IS THE SAME WAY! SHE...
I THINK WE NEED A CHAIRMAN.
...LOVES SWIMMING, BUT SUDDENLY THIS ONE TUESDAY MORNING!

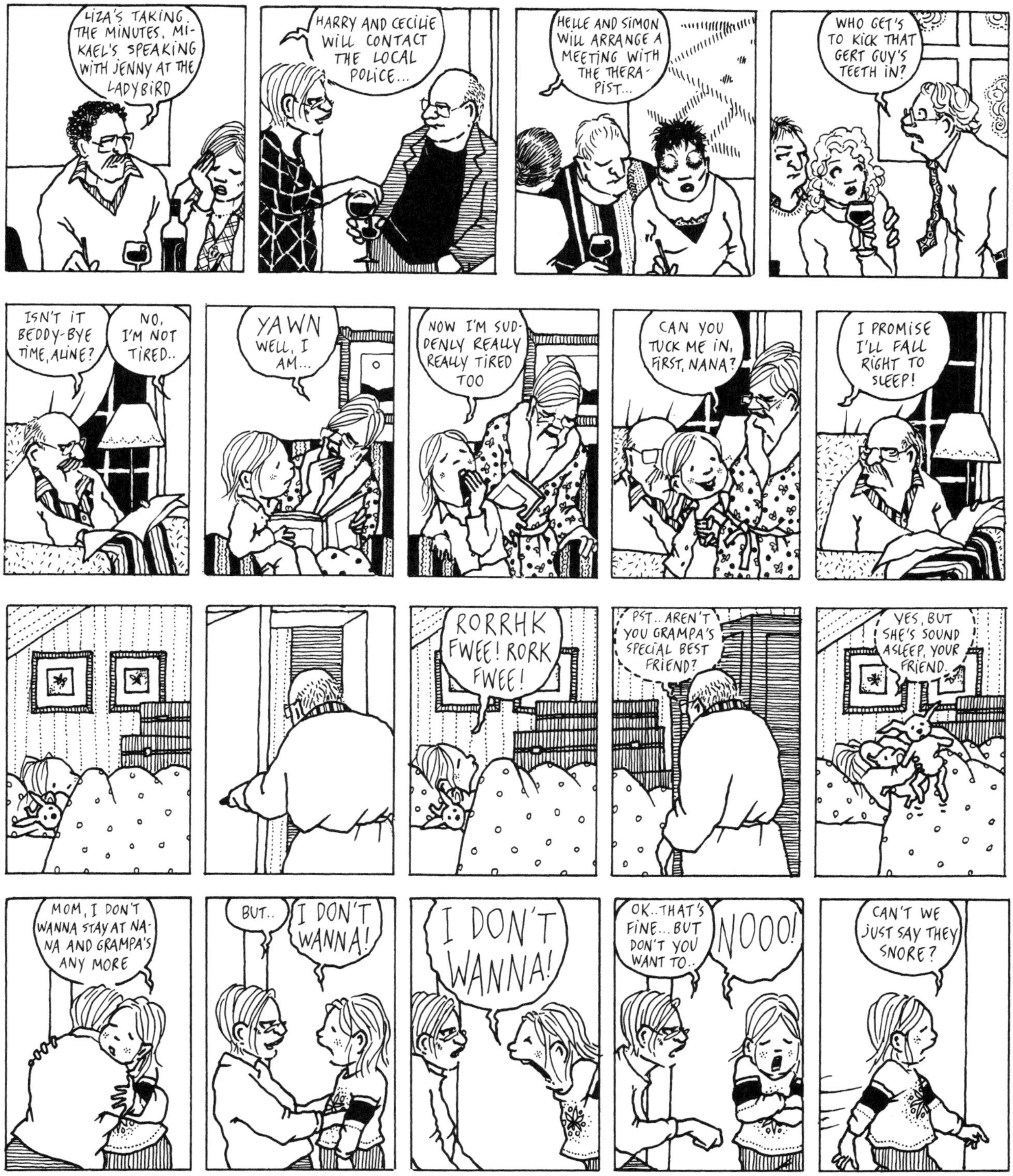
LIZA'S TAKING THE MINUTES, MI-KAEL'S SPEAKING WITH JENNY AT THE LADYBIRD
HARRY AND CECILIE WILL CONTACT THE LOCAL POLICE...
HELLE AND SIMON WILL ARRANGE A MEETING WITH THE THERA-PIST...
WHO GET'S TO KICK THAT GERT GUY'S TEETH IN?
ISN'T IT BEDDY-BYE TIME, ALINE?
NO, I'M NOT TIRED..
YAWN
WELL, I AM...
NOW I'M SUD-DENLY REALLY REALLY TIRED TOO
CAN YOU TUCK ME IN, FIRST, NANA?
I PROMISE I'LL FALL RIGHT TO SLEEP!
RORRHK FWEE! RORK FWEE!
PST... AREN'T YOU GRAMPA'S SPECIAL BEST FRIEND?
YES, BUT SHE'S SOUND ASLEEP, YOUR FRIEND.
MOM, I DON'T WANNA STAY AT NA-NA AND GRAMPA'S ANY MORE
BUT..
I DON'T WANNA!
I DON'T WANNA!
OK.. THAT'S FINE... BUT DON'T YOU WANT TO..
NOOO!
CAN'T WE JUST SAY THEY SNORE?

CAN YOU STAY AND MAKE SURE NOBODY COMES IN?
LIKE WHO?
SOMEONE, WHO CAN'T SLEEP AND NEEDS HIS... BEST FRIEND'S HELP
WHAT'RE YOU SAYING?
JUST SOMETHING I MADE UP!
HOW'D IT GO AT THE LADYBIRD TODAY?
OKAY. FIELD TRIP.
SO I SEE. YOUR CLOTHES ARE FILTHY DIRTY!
NOT YOU! YOU'RE NOT TOO DIRTY!
YES, I'M A FILTHY FILTHY DIRTY LITTLE GIRL
SHE'S BEEN WITH MY PARENTS FOR WEEKS!
THE BEE
THE BEETLE
BUT ONE TRIP WITH YOU AND THAT PIG AND SHE FEELS DIRTY!
I OUGHTA CUT-
RHK
GERT DIDN'T GO!
THE OTHER TEACHERS ARE COVERING FOR HIM SO WE THINK IT'S ORGANIZED
A WHOLE RING OF PEDOPHILES?
THE TWO SHRINKS FROM "SILENT AGONY" HAVE GOT TO TALK TO ALL THE KIDS!
WE'VE GOT TO CALL THE POLICE, TOO, NO?
NO, WAIT! MAYBE THEY'RE IN ON IT!

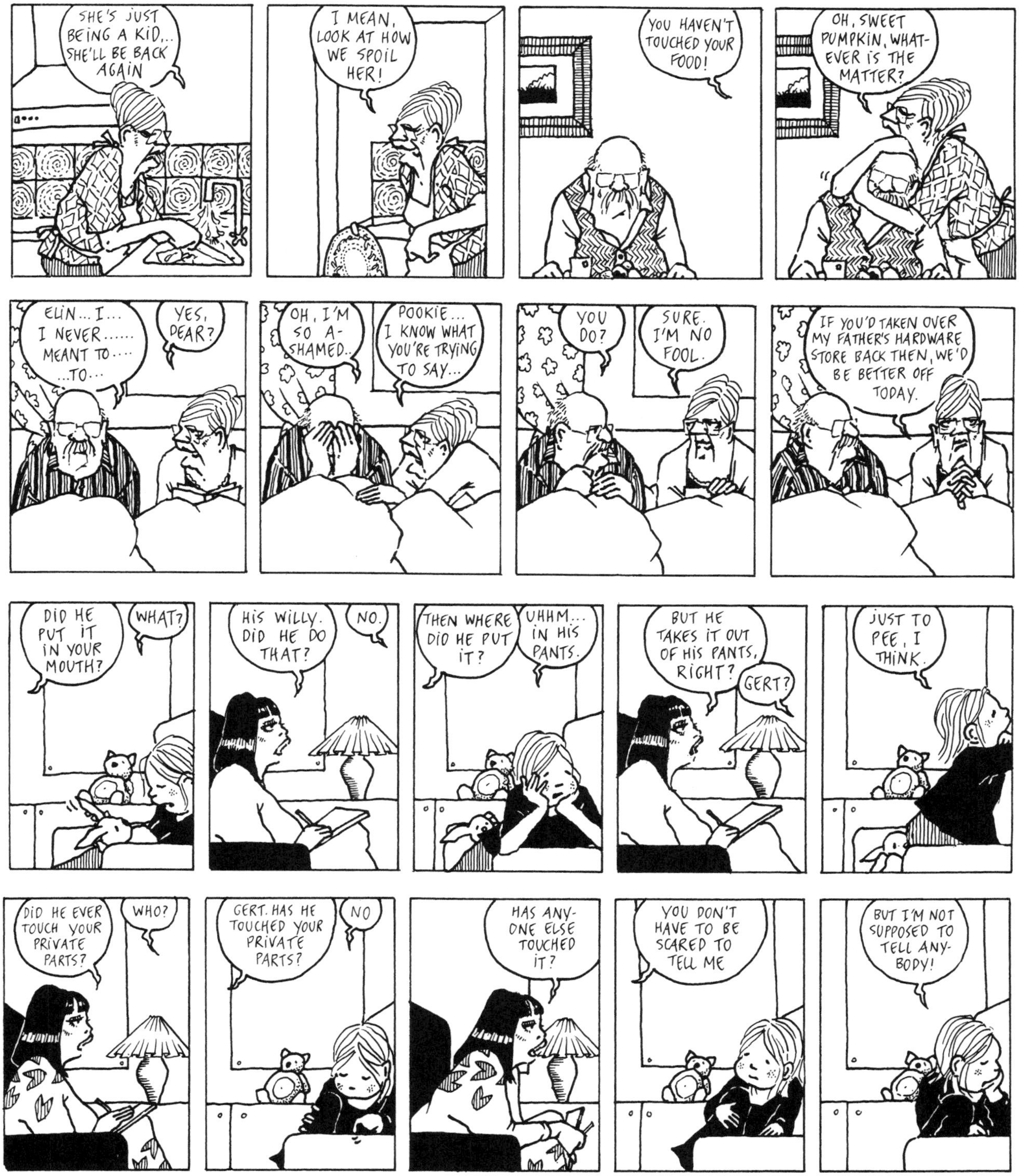
SHE'S JUST BEING A KID... SHE'LL BE BACK AGAIN
I MEAN, LOOK AT HOW WE SPOIL HER!
YOU HAVEN'T TOUCHED YOUR FOOD!
OH, SWEET PUMPKIN, WHATEVER IS THE MATTER?
ELIN... I... I NEVER...... MEANT TO.... ...TO...
YES, DEAR?
OH, I'M SO ASHAMED..
POOKIE... I KNOW WHAT YOU'RE TRYING TO SAY...
YOU DO?
SURE. I'M NO FOOL.
IF YOU'D TAKEN OVER MY FATHER'S HARDWARE STORE BACK THEN, WE'D BE BETTER OFF TODAY.
DID HE PUT IT IN YOUR MOUTH?
WHAT?
HIS WILLY. DID HE DO THAT?
NO.
THEN WHERE DID HE PUT IT?
UHHM... IN HIS PANTS.
BUT HE TAKES IT OUT OF HIS PANTS, RIGHT?
GERT?
JUST TO PEE, I THINK.
DID HE EVER TOUCH YOUR PRIVATE PARTS?
WHO?
GERT. HAS HE TOUCHED YOUR PRIVATE PARTS?
NO
HAS ANYONE ELSE TOUCHED IT?
YOU DON'T HAVE TO BE SCARED TO TELL ME
BUT I'M NOT SUPPOSED TO TELL ANYBODY!

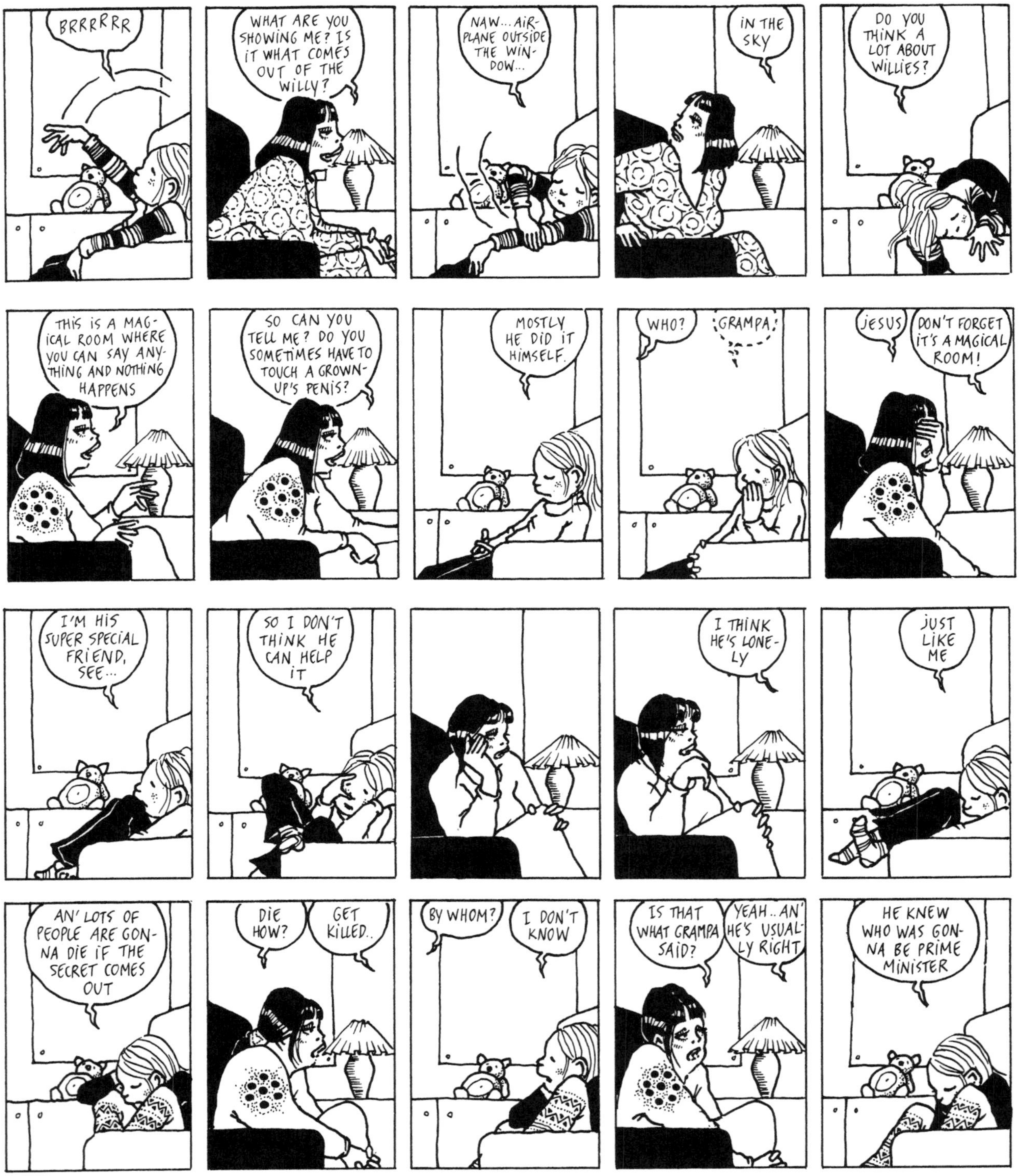
BRRRRRR
WHAT ARE YOU SHOWING ME? IS IT WHAT COMES OUT OF THE WILLY?
NAW... AIR-PLANE OUTSIDE THE WIN-DOW...
IN THE SKY
DO YOU THINK A LOT ABOUT WILLIES?
THIS IS A MAG-ICAL ROOM WHERE YOU CAN SAY ANY-THING AND NOTHING HAPPENS
SO CAN YOU TELL ME? DO YOU SOMETIMES HAVE TO TOUCH A GROWN-UP'S PENIS?
MOSTLY HE DID IT HIMSELF.
WHO?
GRAMPA
JESUS
DON'T FORGET IT'S A MAGICAL ROOM!
I'M HIS SUPER SPECIAL FRIEND, SEE...
SO I DON'T THINK HE CAN HELP IT
I THINK HE'S LONE-LY
JUST LIKE ME
AN' LOTS OF PEOPLE ARE GON-NA DIE IF THE SECRET COMES OUT
DIE HOW?
GET KILLED..
BY WHOM?
I DON'T KNOW
IS THAT WHAT GRAMPA SAID?
YEAH.. AN' HE'S USUAL-LY RIGHT
HE KNEW WHO WAS GON-NA BE PRIME MINISTER

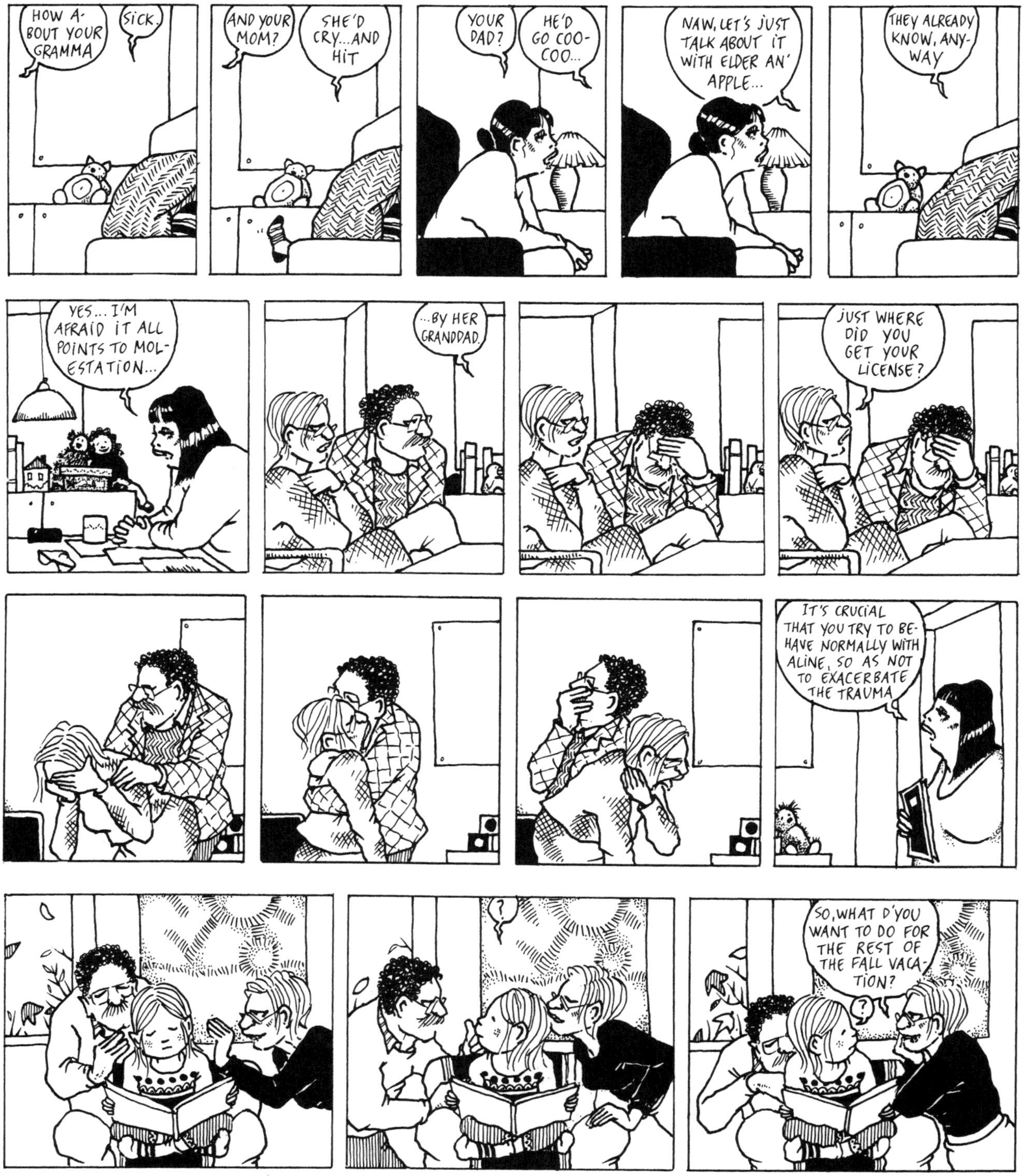
HOW ABOUT YOUR GRAMMA
SICK.
AND YOUR MOM?
SHE'D CRY... AND HIT
YOUR DAD?
HE'D GO COO-COO...
NAW, LET'S JUST TALK ABOUT IT WITH ELDER AN' APPLE...
THEY ALREADY KNOW, ANYWAY
YES... I'M AFRAID IT ALL POINTS TO MOLESTATION...
...BY HER GRANDDAD.
JUST WHERE DID YOU GET YOUR LICENSE?
IT'S CRUCIAL THAT YOU TRY TO BEHAVE NORMALLY WITH ALINE, SO AS NOT TO EXACERBATE THE TRAUMA
?
SO, WHAT D'YOU WANT TO DO FOR THE REST OF THE FALL VACATION?
?

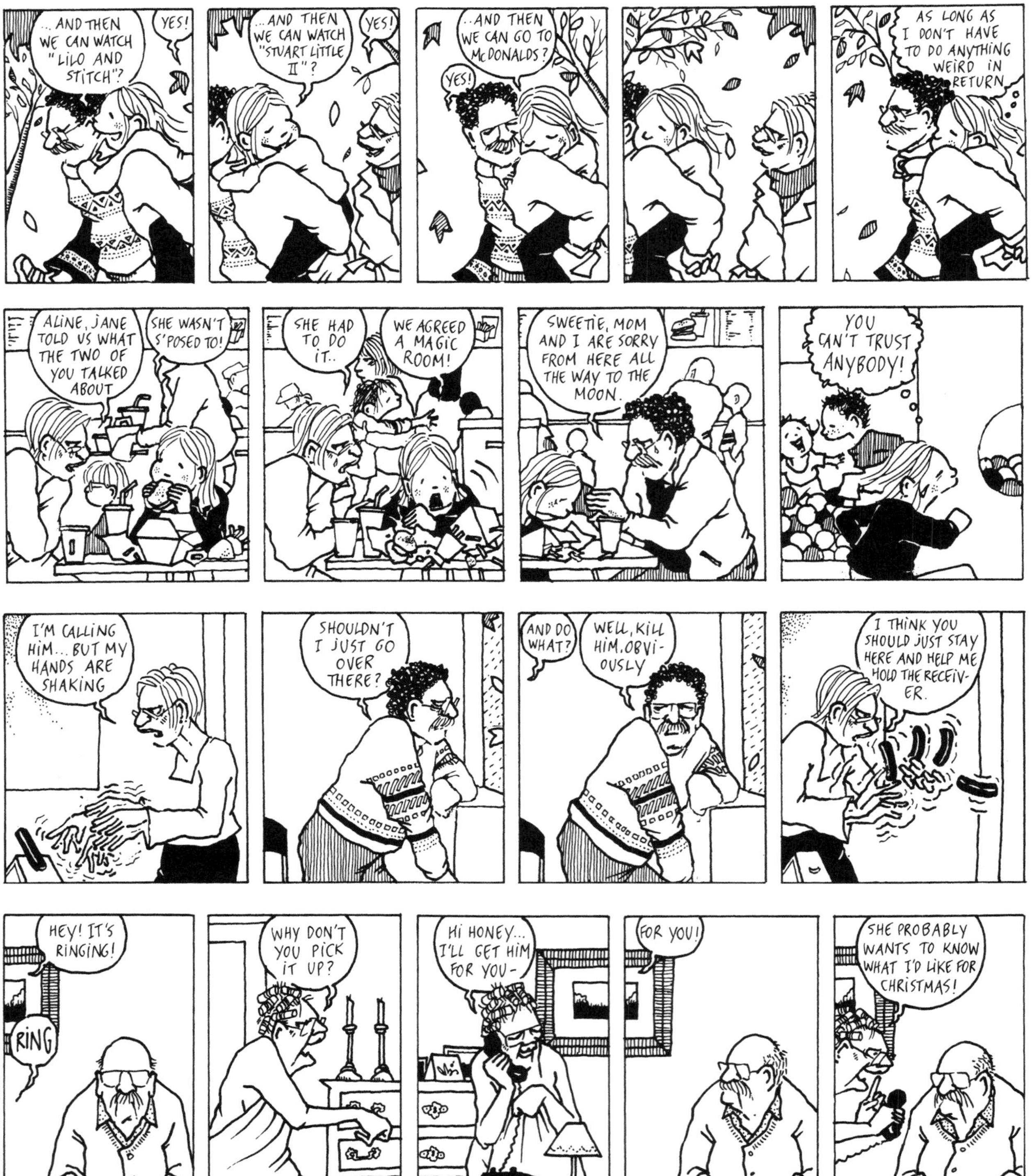
...AND THEN WE CAN WATCH "LILO AND STITCH"?
YES!
...AND THEN WE CAN WATCH "STUART LITTLE II"?
YES!
..AND THEN WE CAN GO TO McDONALDS?
YES!
AS LONG AS I DON'T HAVE TO DO ANYTHING WEIRD IN RETURN
ALINE, JANE TOLD US WHAT THE TWO OF YOU TALKED ABOUT
SHE WASN'T S'POSED TO!
SHE HAD TO DO IT..
WE AGREED A MAGIC ROOM!
SWEETIE, MOM AND I ARE SORRY FROM HERE ALL THE WAY TO THE MOON.
YOU CAN'T TRUST ANYBODY!
I'M CALLING HIM...BUT MY HANDS ARE SHAKING
SHOULDN'T I JUST GO OVER THERE?
AND DO WHAT?
WELL, KILL HIM, OBVIOUSLY
I THINK YOU SHOULD JUST STAY HERE AND HELP ME HOLD THE RECEIVER.
HEY! IT'S RINGING!
RING
WHY DON'T YOU PICK IT UP?
HI HONEY... I'LL GET HIM FOR YOU-
FOR YOU!
SHE PROBABLY WANTS TO KNOW WHAT I'D LIKE FOR CHRISTMAS!

30

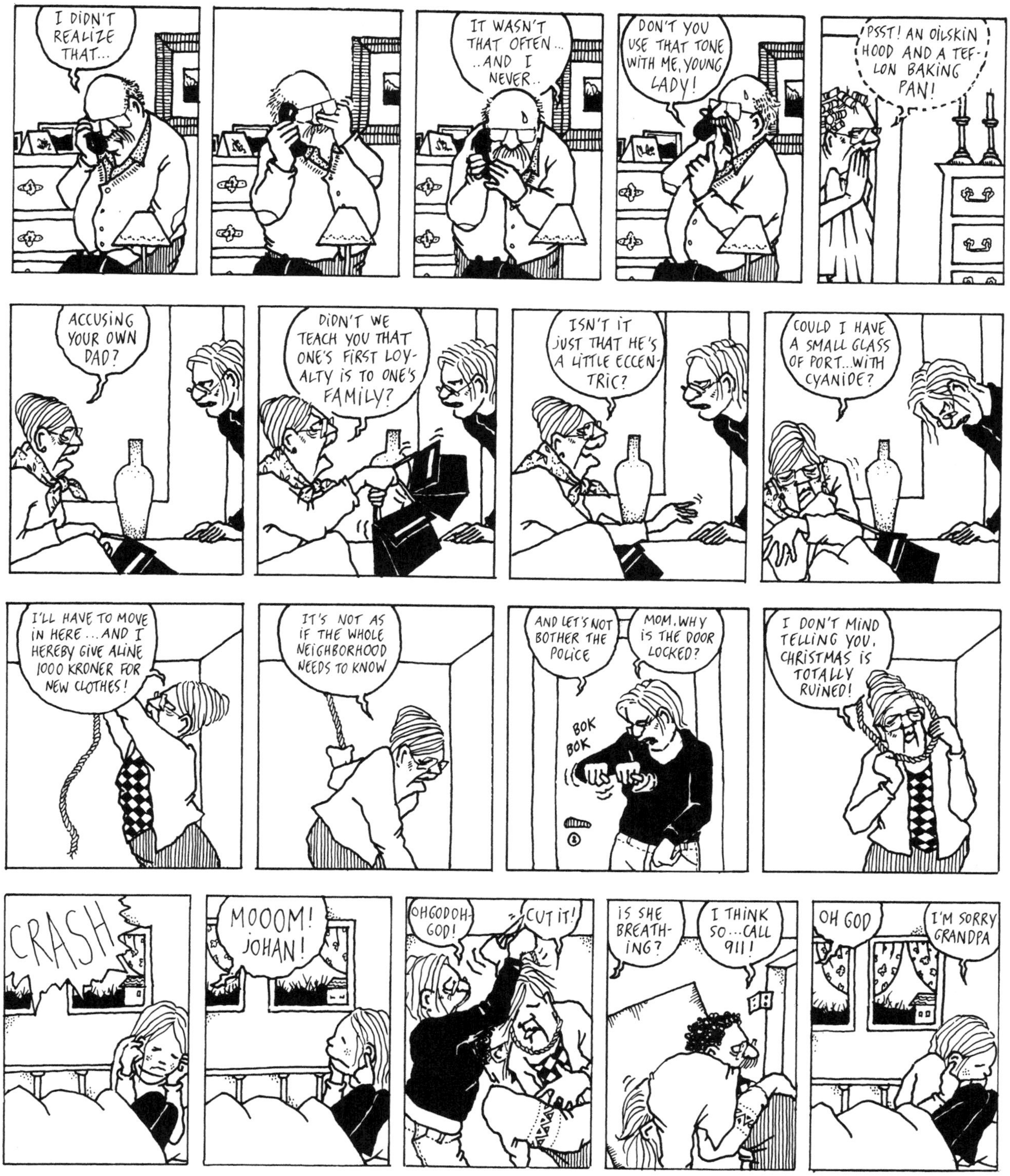
I DIDN'T REALIZE THAT...
IT WASN'T THAT OFTEN... ..AND I NEVER..
DON'T YOU USE THAT TONE WITH ME, YOUNG LADY!
PSST! AN OILSKIN HOOD AND A TEFLON BAKING PAN!
ACCUSING YOUR OWN DAD?
DIDN'T WE TEACH YOU THAT ONE'S FIRST LOYALTY IS TO ONE'S FAMILY?
ISN'T IT JUST THAT HE'S A LITTLE ECCENTRIC?
COULD I HAVE A SMALL GLASS OF PORT...WITH CYANIDE?
I'LL HAVE TO MOVE IN HERE...AND I HEREBY GIVE ALINE 1000 KRONER FOR NEW CLOTHES!
IT'S NOT AS IF THE WHOLE NEIGHBORHOOD NEEDS TO KNOW
AND LET'S NOT BOTHER THE POLICE
MOM, WHY IS THE DOOR LOCKED?
BOK BOK
I DON'T MIND TELLING YOU, CHRISTMAS IS TOTALLY RUINED!
CRASH
MOOOM! JOHAN!
OHGODOH-GOD!
CUT IT!
IS SHE BREATHING?
I THINK SO...CALL 911!
OH GOD
I'M SORRY GRANDPA

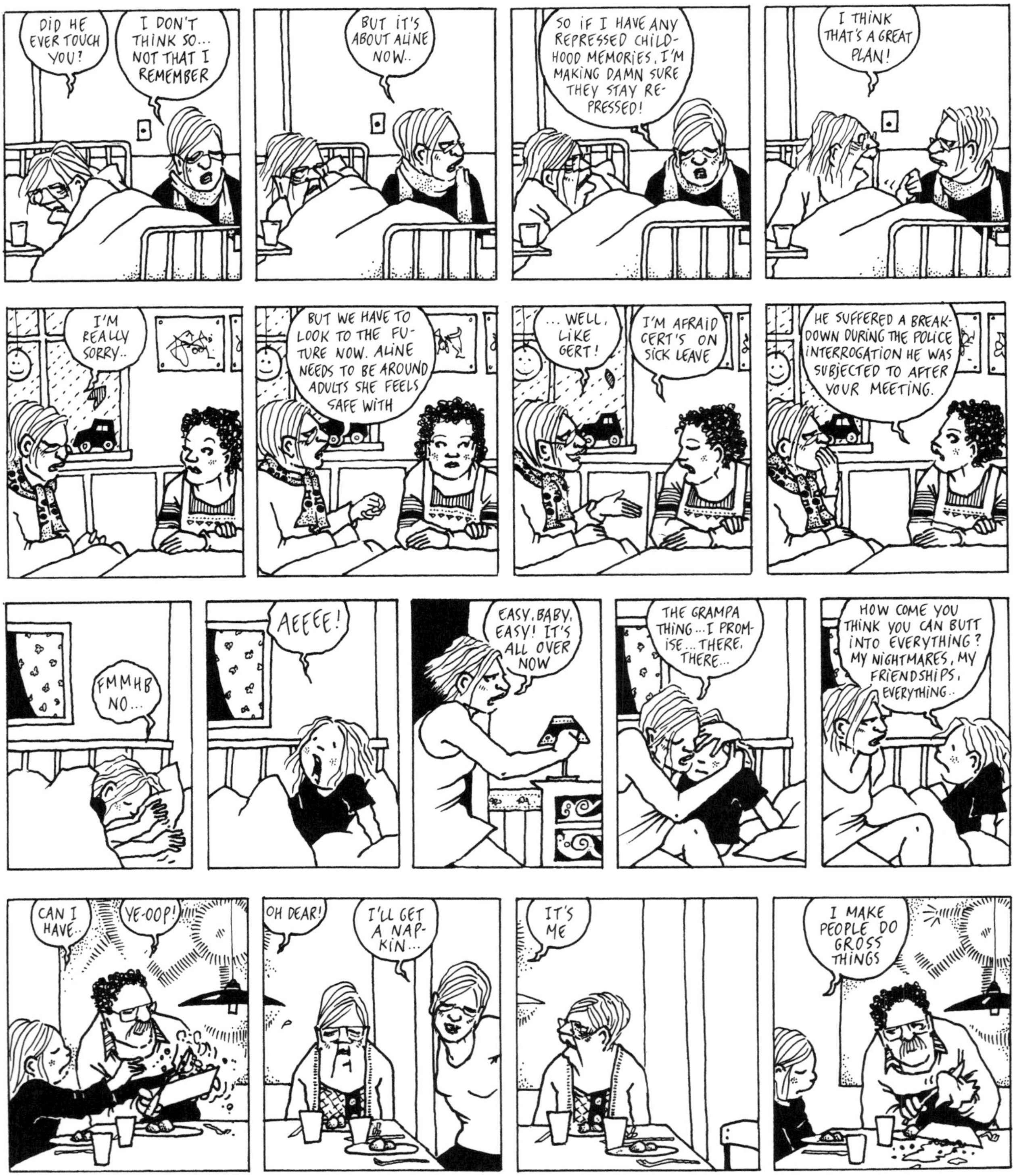
DID HE EVER TOUCH YOU?
I DON'T THINK SO... NOT THAT I REMEMBER
BUT IT'S ABOUT ALINE NOW..
SO IF I HAVE ANY REPRESSED CHILDHOOD MEMORIES, I'M MAKING DAMN SURE THEY STAY REPRESSED!
I THINK THAT'S A GREAT PLAN!
I'M REALLY SORRY..
BUT WE HAVE TO LOOK TO THE FUTURE NOW. ALINE NEEDS TO BE AROUND ADULTS SHE FEELS SAFE WITH
... WELL, LIKE GERT!
I'M AFRAID GERT'S ON SICK LEAVE
HE SUFFERED A BREAKDOWN DURING THE POLICE INTERROGATION HE WAS SUBJECTED TO AFTER YOUR MEETING.
FMMHB NO...
AEEEE!
EASY, BABY, EASY! IT'S ALL OVER NOW
THE GRAMPA THING... I PROMISE... THERE, THERE...
HOW COME YOU THINK YOU CAN BUTT INTO EVERYTHING? MY NIGHTMARES, MY FRIENDSHIPS, EVERYTHING..
CAN I HAVE..
YE-OOP!
OH DEAR!
I'LL GET A NAPKIN...
IT'S ME
I MAKE PEOPLE DO GROSS THINGS

BUT... I HAVE TO SEE HIM!
WHY?
I HAVE TO SEE WHAT KIND OF CREA-TURE..
CAN BREAK... DESTROY... THE FINEST... DEAR-EST, BEST THING I HAVE...
AND WHO GAVE ME MY FIRST RED BIKE!
WHO ARE YOU?
A MONSTER? A DIRTY OLD MAN? A PENSIONER?
LIAR? MANI-PULATOR? BELOVED HUSBAND, DAD AND GRAMPA?
I THINK OF MYSELF AS A GARDENING MAN...
..WHO JUST LOST HIS ENTIRE FAM-ILY AND IS WAIT-ING FOR THE POLICE.
WE'VE GOT TO MOVE ON...CAN'T WE DO THIS TOGETHER?
I'M GOING TO MY ROOM.

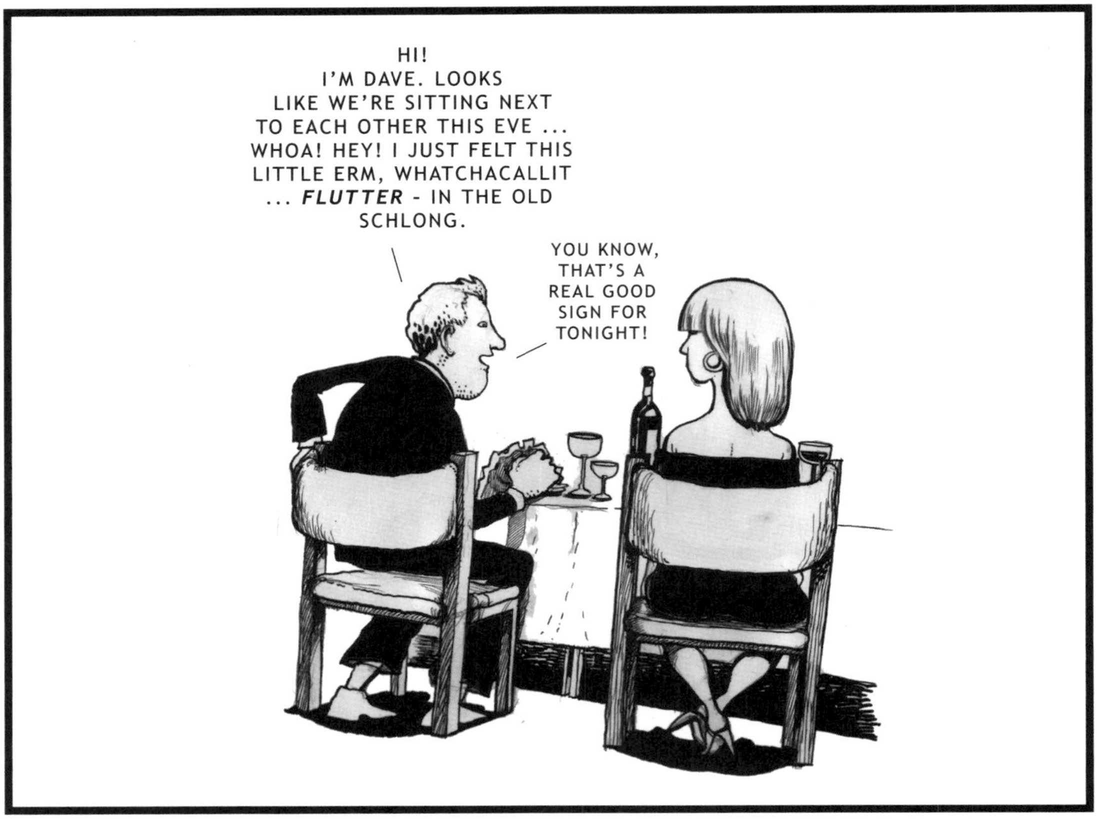
HI!
I'M DAVE. LOOKS LIKE WE'RE SITTING NEXT TO EACH OTHER THIS EVE ... WHOA! HEY! I JUST FELT THIS LITTLE ERM, WHATCHACALLIT ... *FLUTTER* - IN THE OLD SCHLONG.
YOU KNOW, THAT'S A REAL GOOD SIGN FOR TONIGHT!

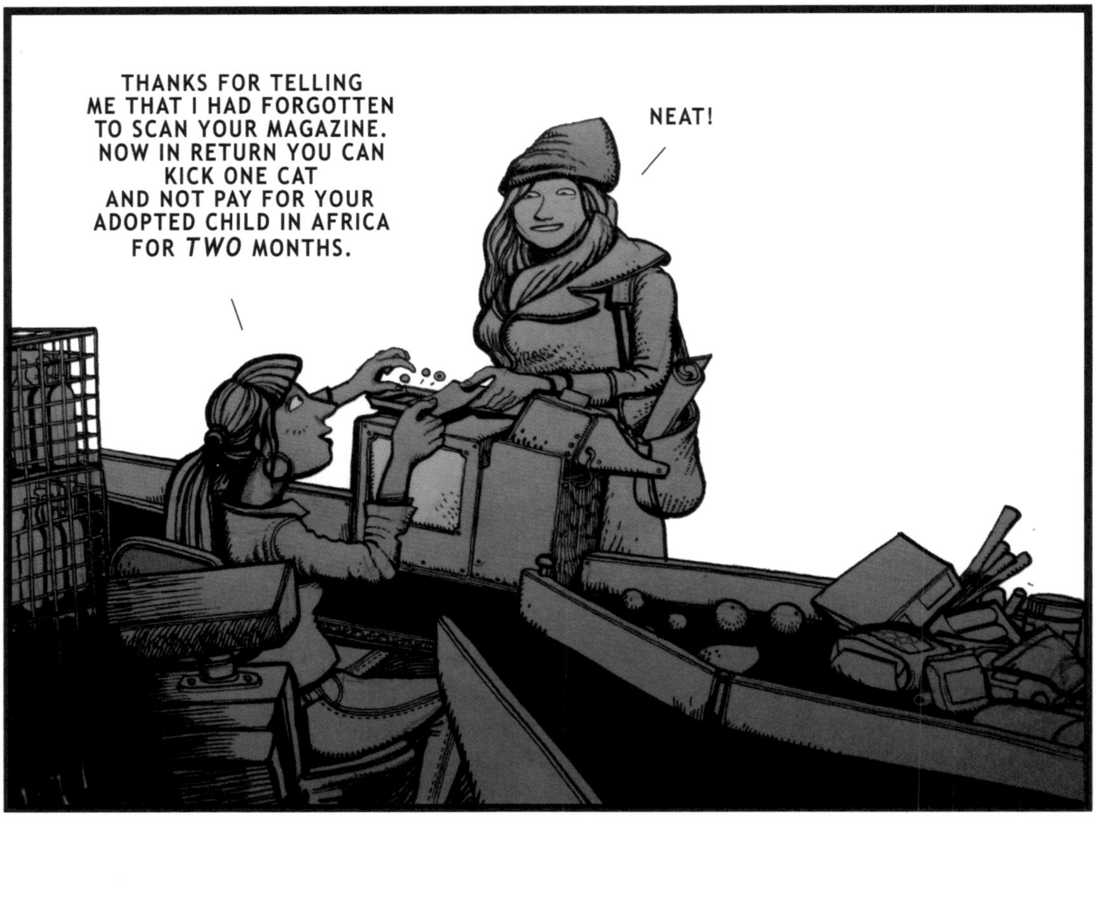
THANKS FOR TELLING ME THAT I HAD FORGOTTEN TO SCAN YOUR MAGAZINE. NOW IN RETURN YOU CAN KICK ONE CAT AND NOT PAY FOR YOUR ADOPTED CHILD IN AFRICA FOR *TWO* MONTHS.
NEAT!

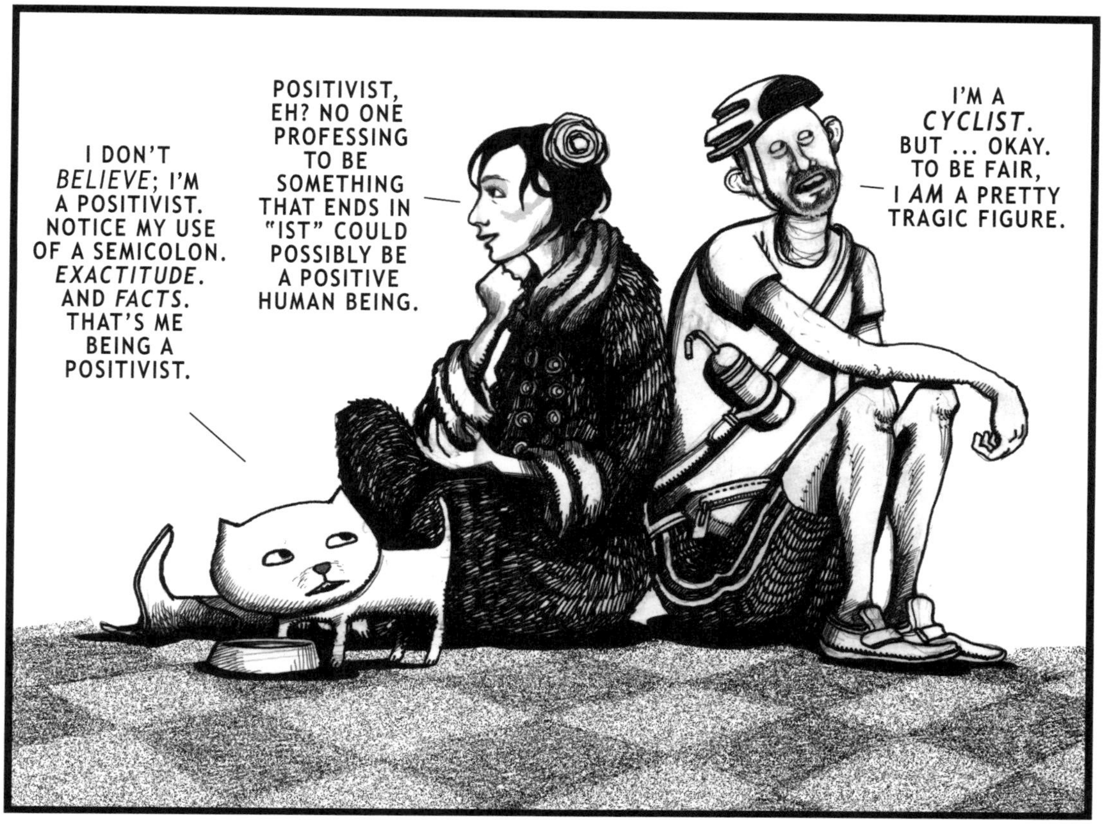
I DON'T *BELIEVE*; I'M A POSITIVIST. NOTICE MY USE OF A SEMICOLON. *EXACTITUDE*. AND *FACTS*. THAT'S ME BEING A POSITIVIST.
POSITIVIST, EH? NO ONE PROFESSING TO BE SOMETHING THAT ENDS IN "IST" COULD POSSIBLY BE A POSITIVE HUMAN BEING.
I'M A *CYCLIST*. BUT ... OKAY. TO BE FAIR, I *AM* A PRETTY TRAGIC FIGURE.

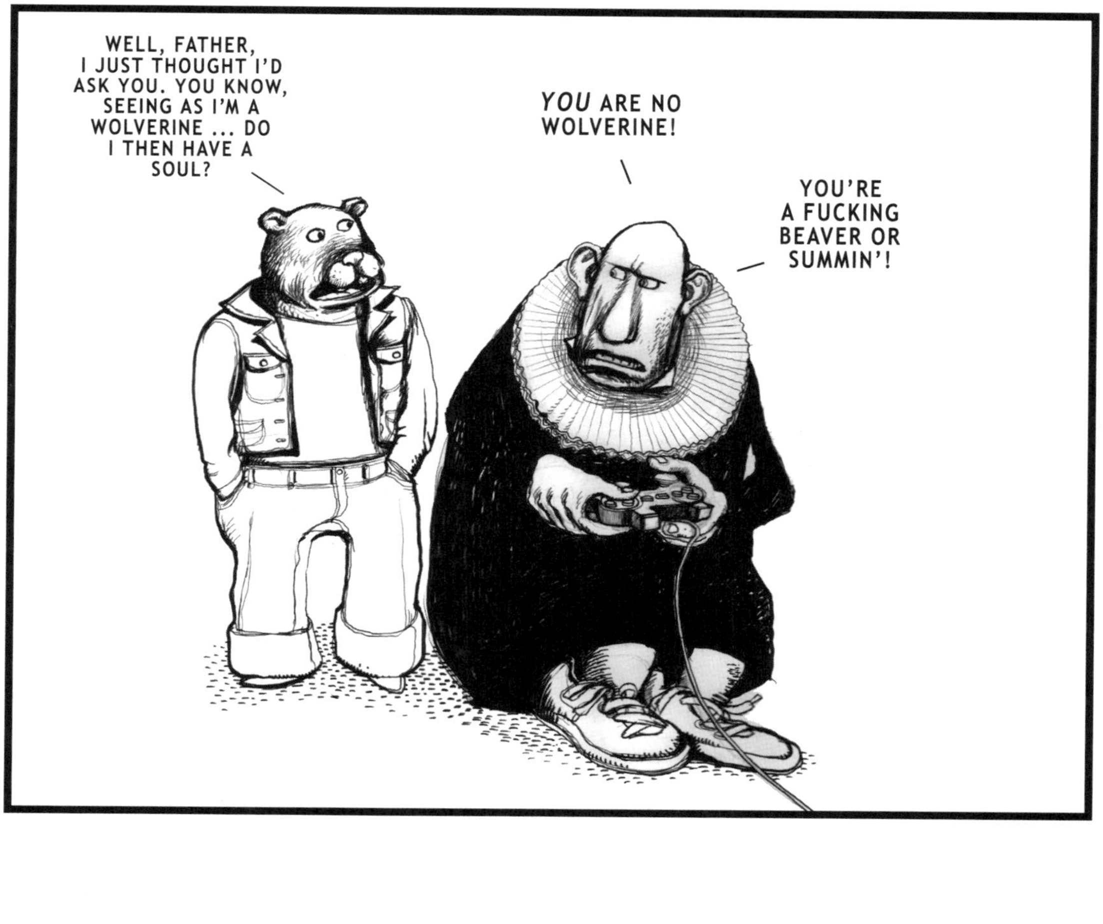
WELL, FATHER, I JUST THOUGHT I'D ASK YOU. YOU KNOW, SEEING AS I'M A WOLVERINE ... DO I THEN HAVE A SOUL?
YOU ARE NO WOLVERINE!
YOU'RE A FUCKING BEAVER OR SUMMIN'!

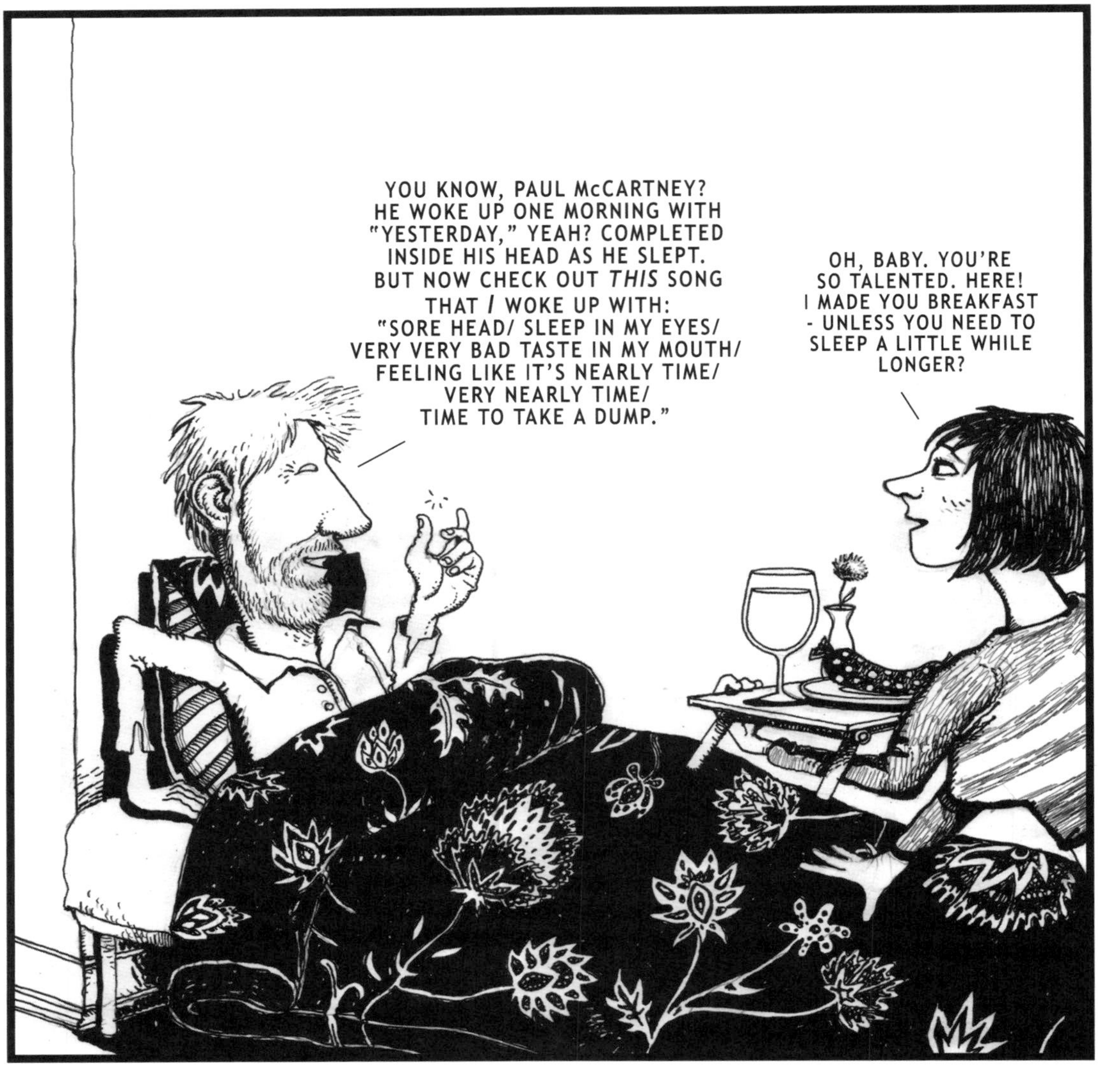
YOU KNOW, PAUL McCARTNEY? HE WOKE UP ONE MORNING WITH "YESTERDAY," YEAH? COMPLETED INSIDE HIS HEAD AS HE SLEPT. BUT NOW CHECK OUT *THIS* SONG THAT *I* WOKE UP WITH: "SORE HEAD/ SLEEP IN MY EYES/ VERY VERY BAD TASTE IN MY MOUTH/ FEELING LIKE IT'S NEARLY TIME/ VERY NEARLY TIME/ TIME TO TAKE A DUMP."
OH, BABY. YOU'RE SO TALENTED. HERE! I MADE YOU BREAKFAST - UNLESS YOU NEED TO SLEEP A LITTLE WHILE LONGER?

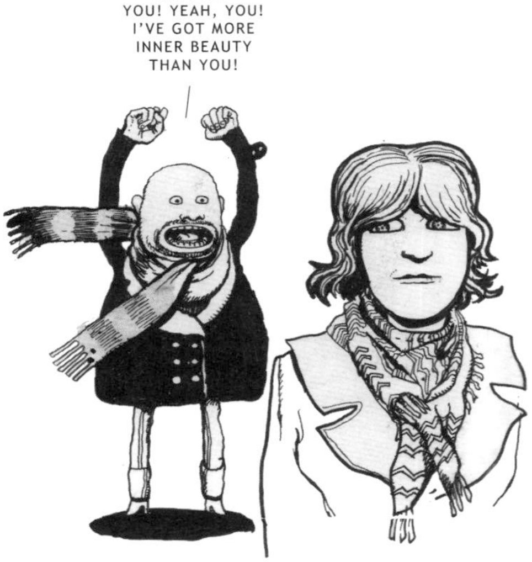
HEY! YO! YOU! YEAH, YOU! I'VE GOT MORE INNER BEAUTY THAN YOU!

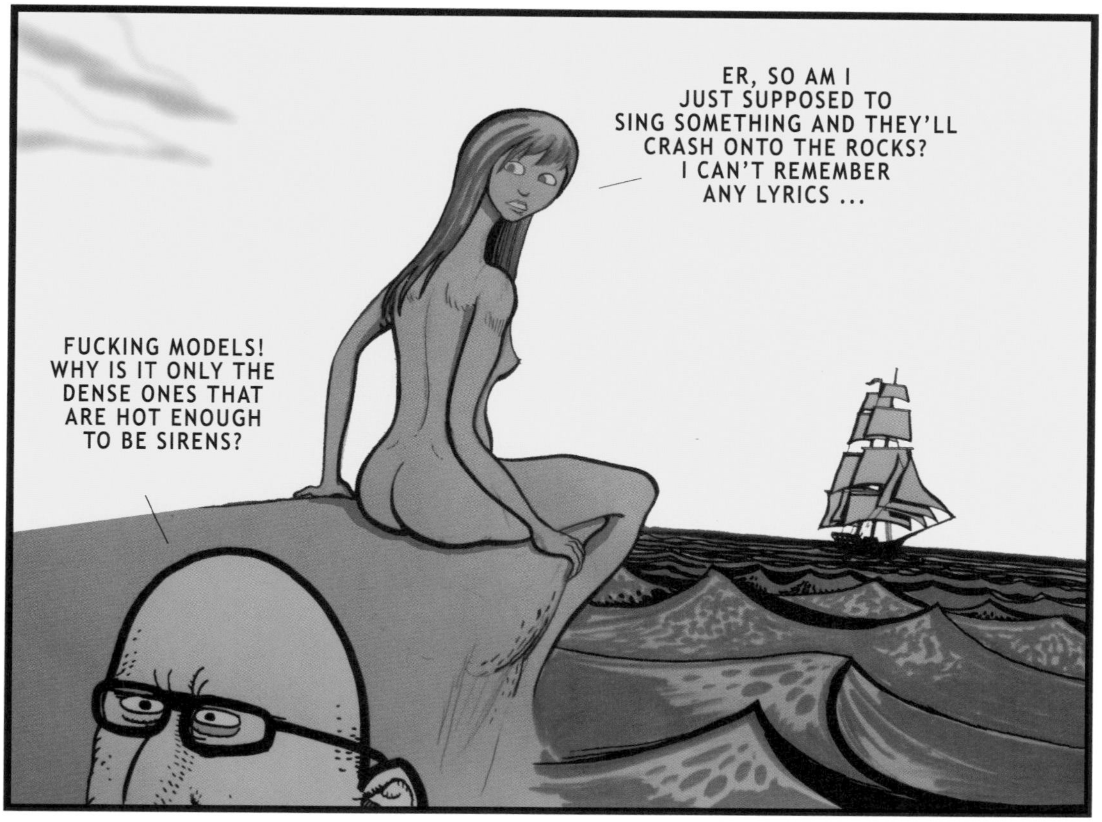
ER, SO AM I JUST SUPPOSED TO SING SOMETHING AND THEY'LL CRASH ONTO THE ROCKS? I CAN'T REMEMBER ANY LYRICS ...
FUCKING MODELS! WHY IS IT ONLY THE DENSE ONES THAT ARE HOT ENOUGH TO BE SIRENS?

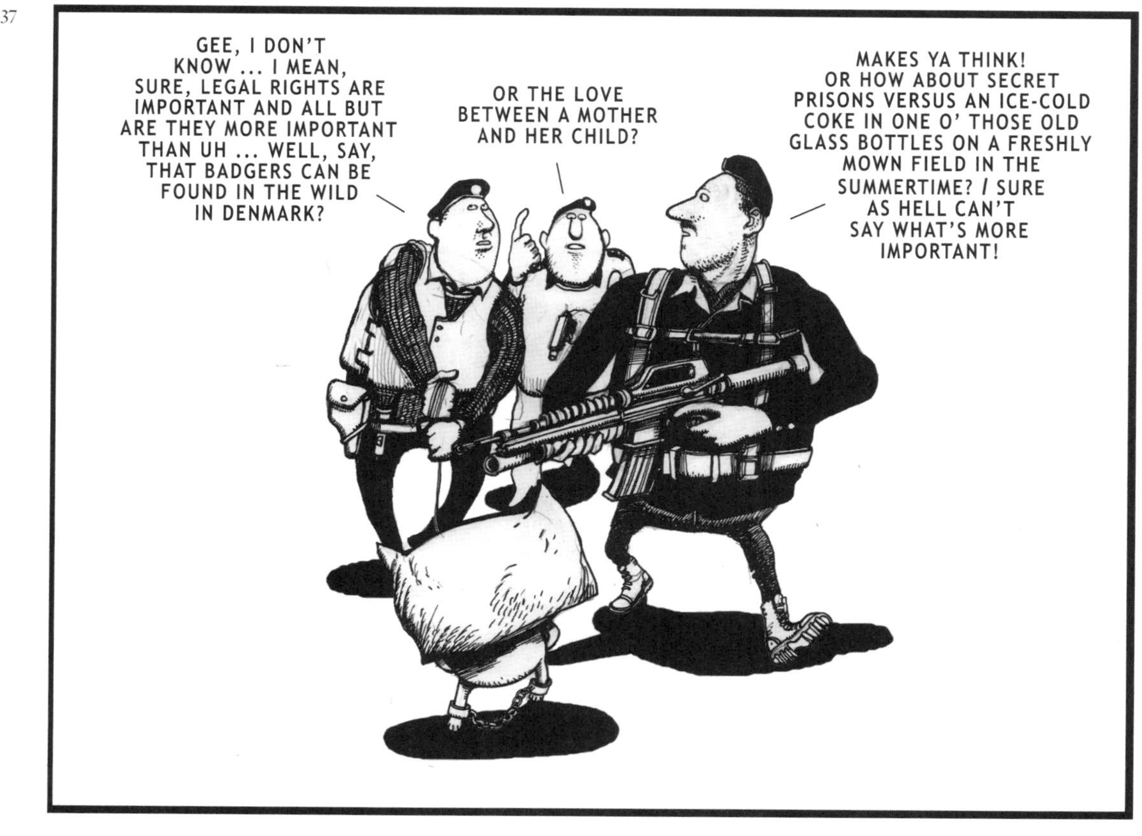
GEE, I DON'T KNOW ... I MEAN, SURE, LEGAL RIGHTS ARE IMPORTANT AND ALL BUT ARE THEY MORE IMPORTANT THAN UH ... WELL, SAY, THAT BADGERS CAN BE FOUND IN THE WILD IN DENMARK?
OR THE LOVE BETWEEN A MOTHER AND HER CHILD?
MAKES YA THINK! OR HOW ABOUT SECRET PRISONS VERSUS AN ICE-COLD COKE IN ONE O' THOSE OLD GLASS BOTTLES ON A FRESHLY MOWN FIELD IN THE SUMMERTIME? I SURE AS HELL CAN'T SAY WHAT'S MORE IMPORTANT!

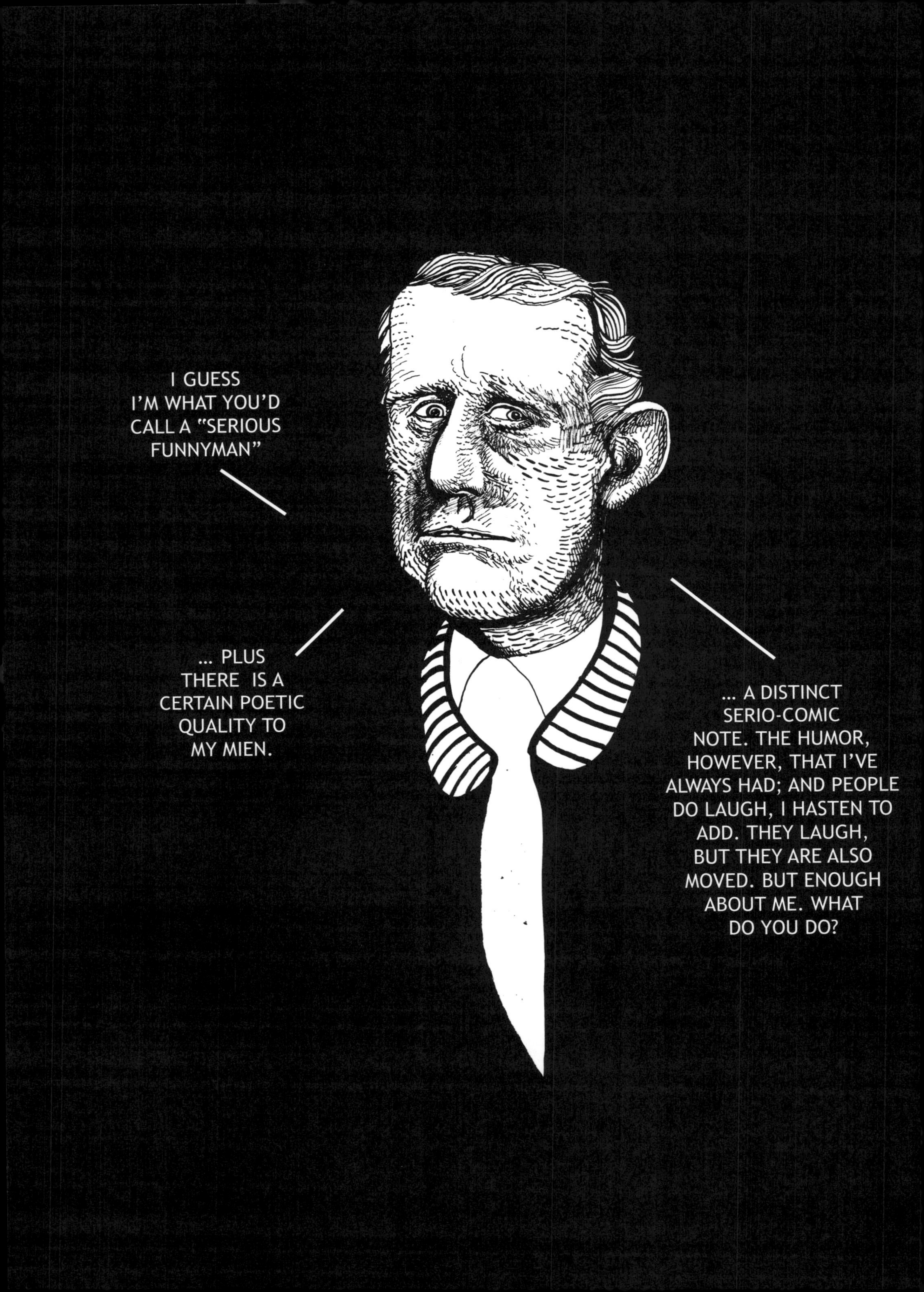
I GUESS I'M WHAT YOU'D CALL A "SERIOUS FUNNYMAN"
... PLUS THERE IS A CERTAIN POETIC QUALITY TO MY MIEN.
... A DISTINCT SERIO-COMIC NOTE. THE HUMOR, HOWEVER, THAT I'VE ALWAYS HAD; AND PEOPLE DO LAUGH, I HASTEN TO ADD. THEY LAUGH, BUT THEY ARE ALSO MOVED. BUT ENOUGH ABOUT ME. WHAT DO YOU DO?

... I REALLY NEED TO GO POOPIE.

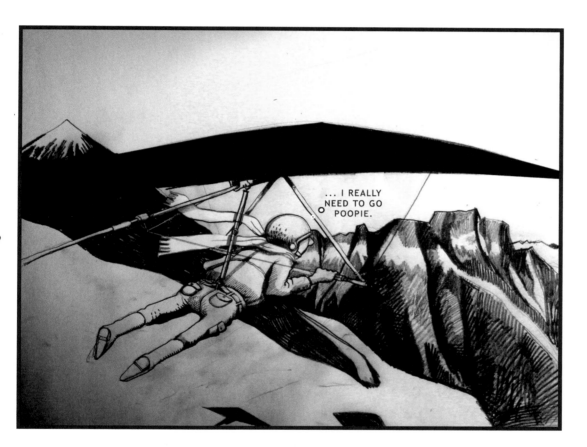

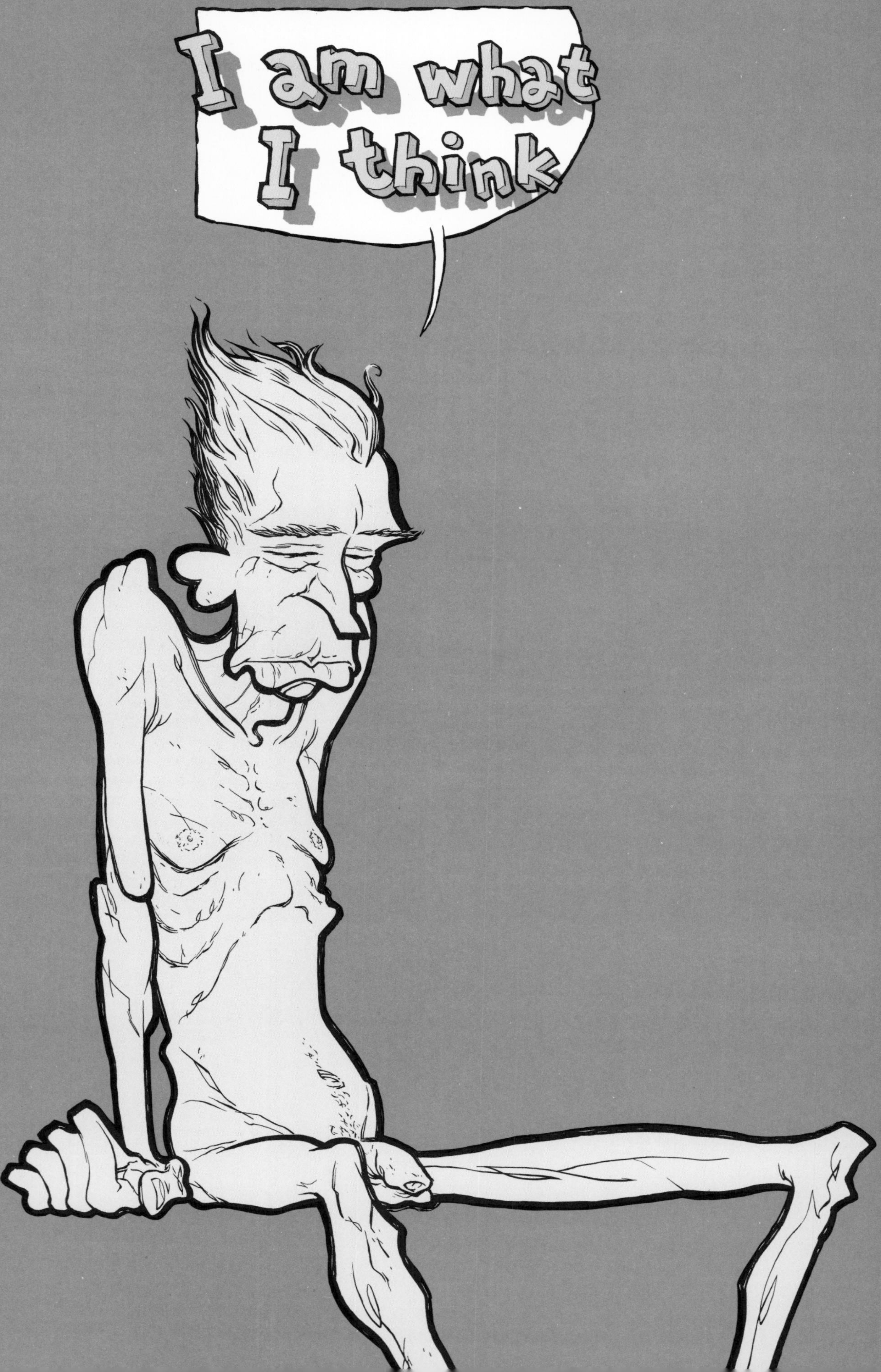
I am what I think

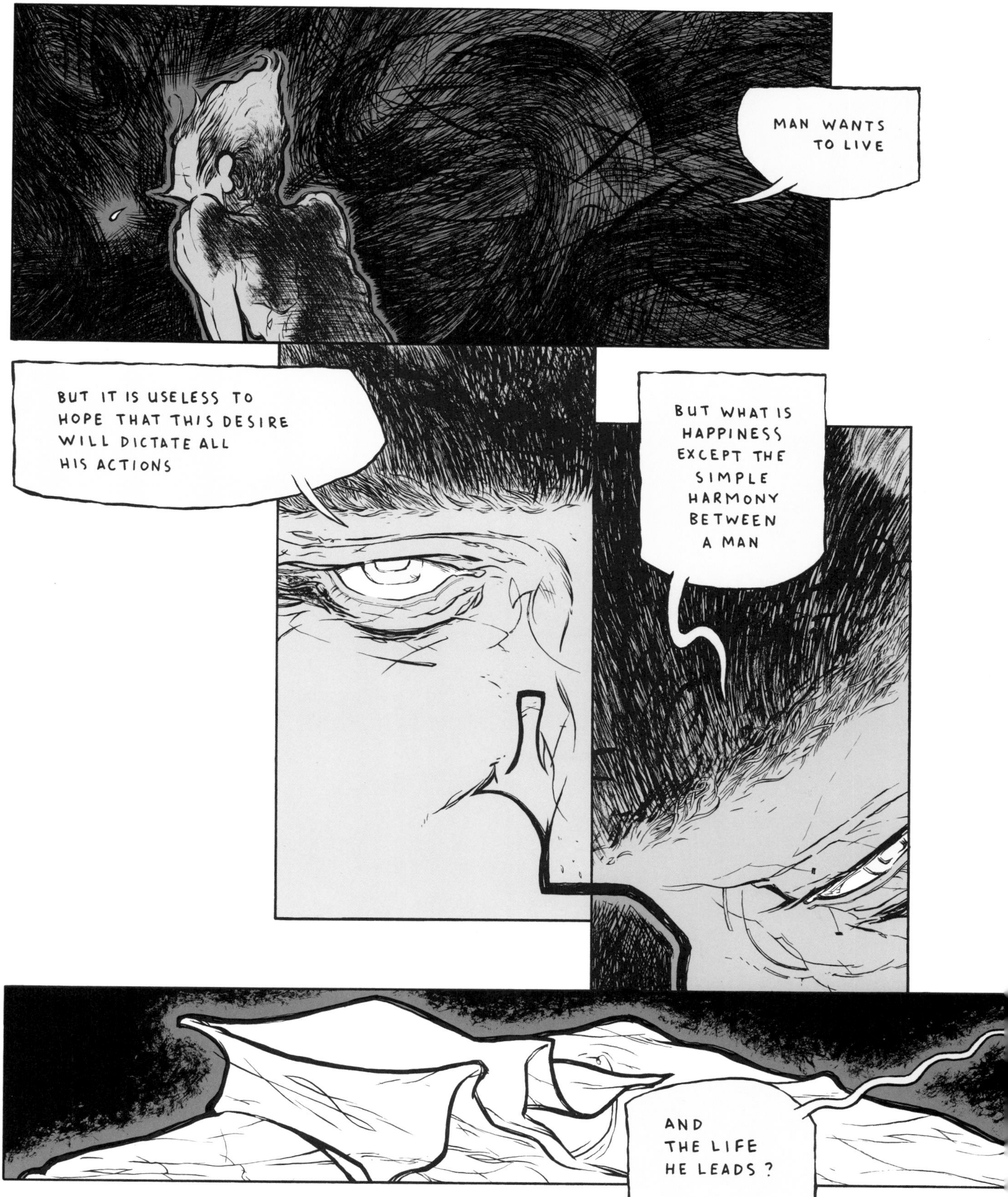
MAN WANTS TO LIVE
BUT IT IS USELESS TO HOPE THAT THIS DESIRE WILL DICTATE ALL HIS ACTIONS
BUT WHAT IS HAPPINESS EXCEPT THE SIMPLE HARMONY BETWEEN A MAN
AND THE LIFE HE LEADS ?

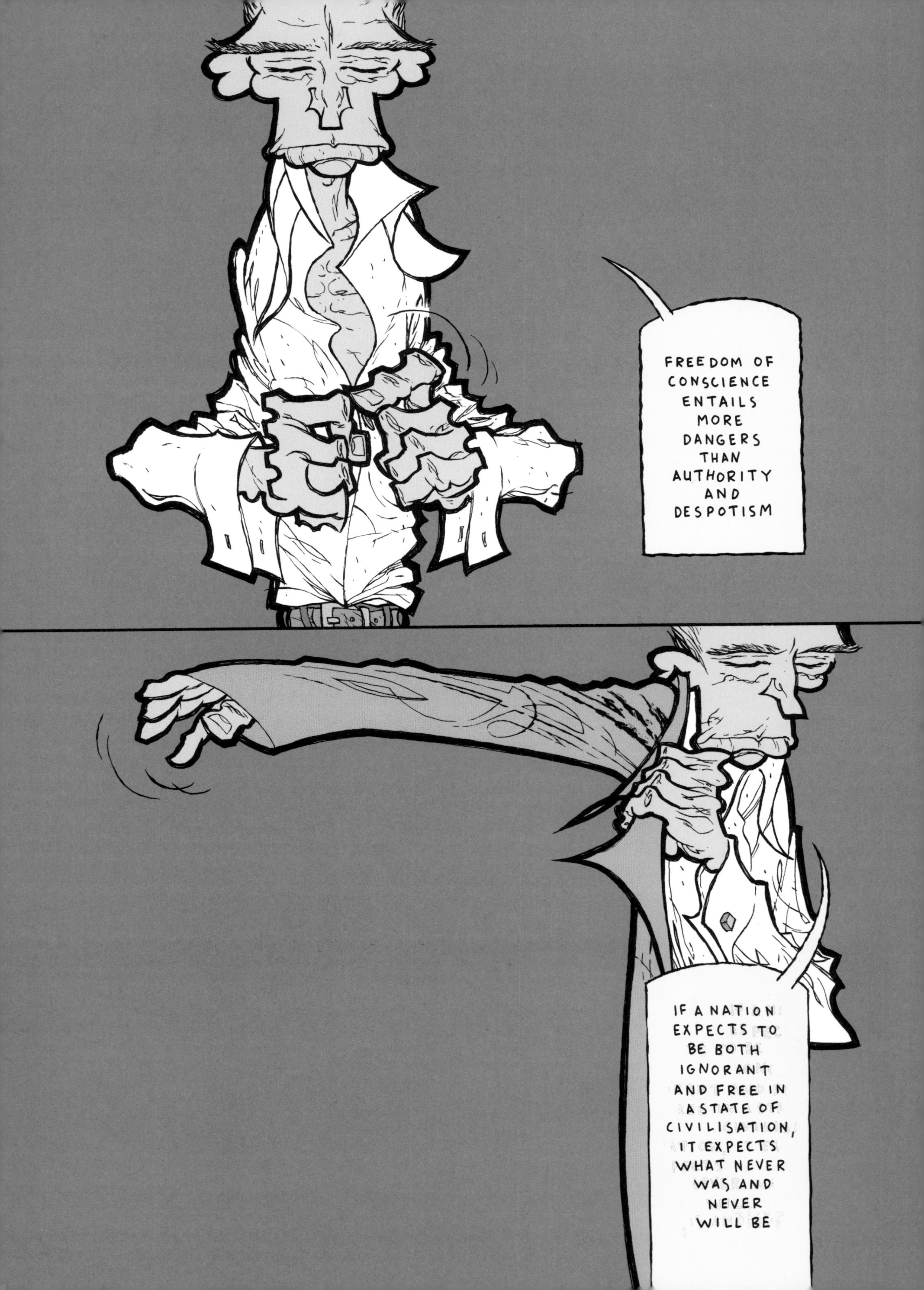
FREEDOM OF CONSCIENCE ENTAILS MORE DANGERS THAN AUTHORITY AND DESPOTISM
IF A NATION EXPECTS TO BE BOTH IGNORANT AND FREE IN A STATE OF CIVILISATION, IT EXPECTS WHAT NEVER WAS AND NEVER WILL BE

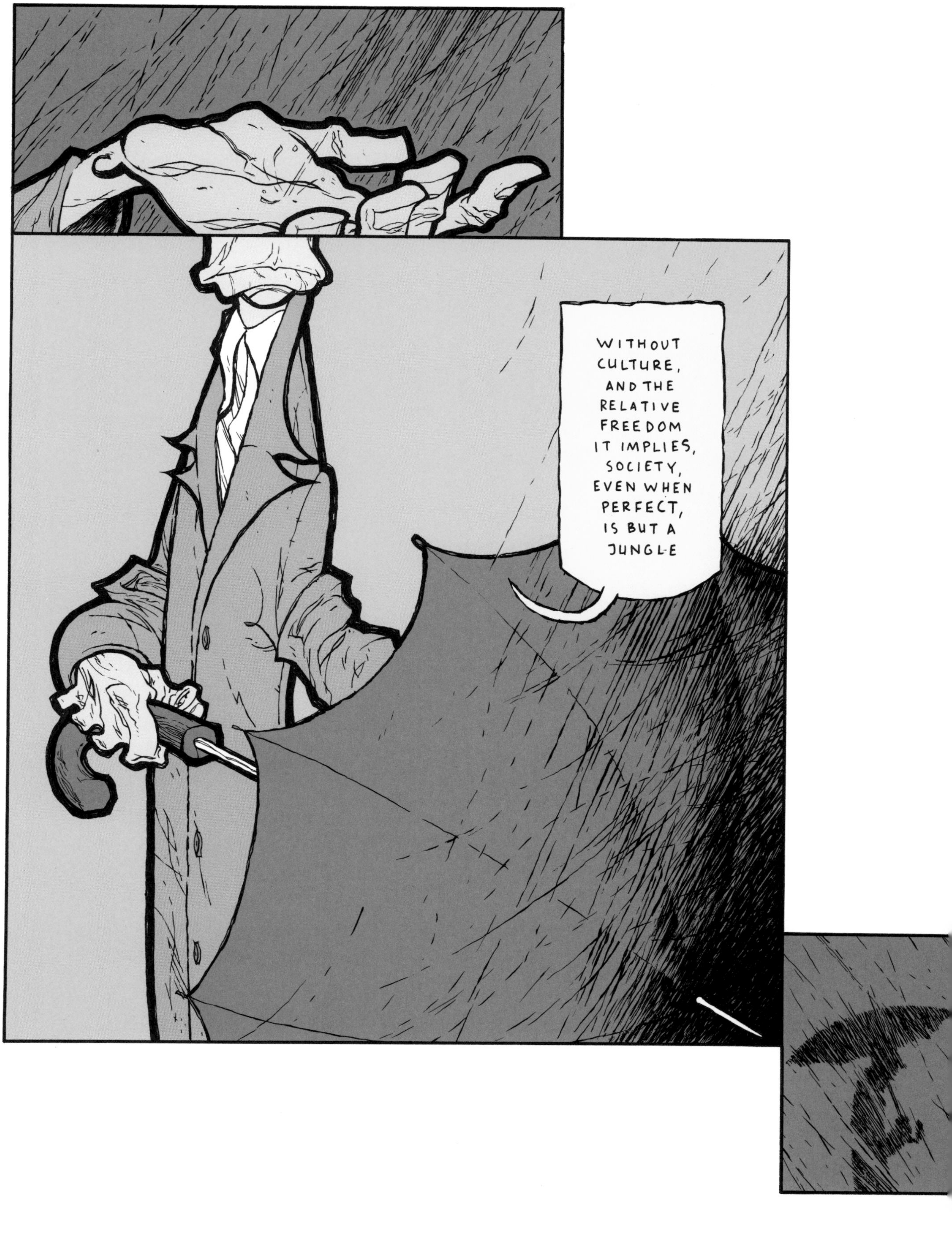
WITHOUT CULTURE, AND THE RELATIVE FREEDOM IT IMPLIES, SOCIETY, EVEN WHEN PERFECT, IS BUT A JUNGLE

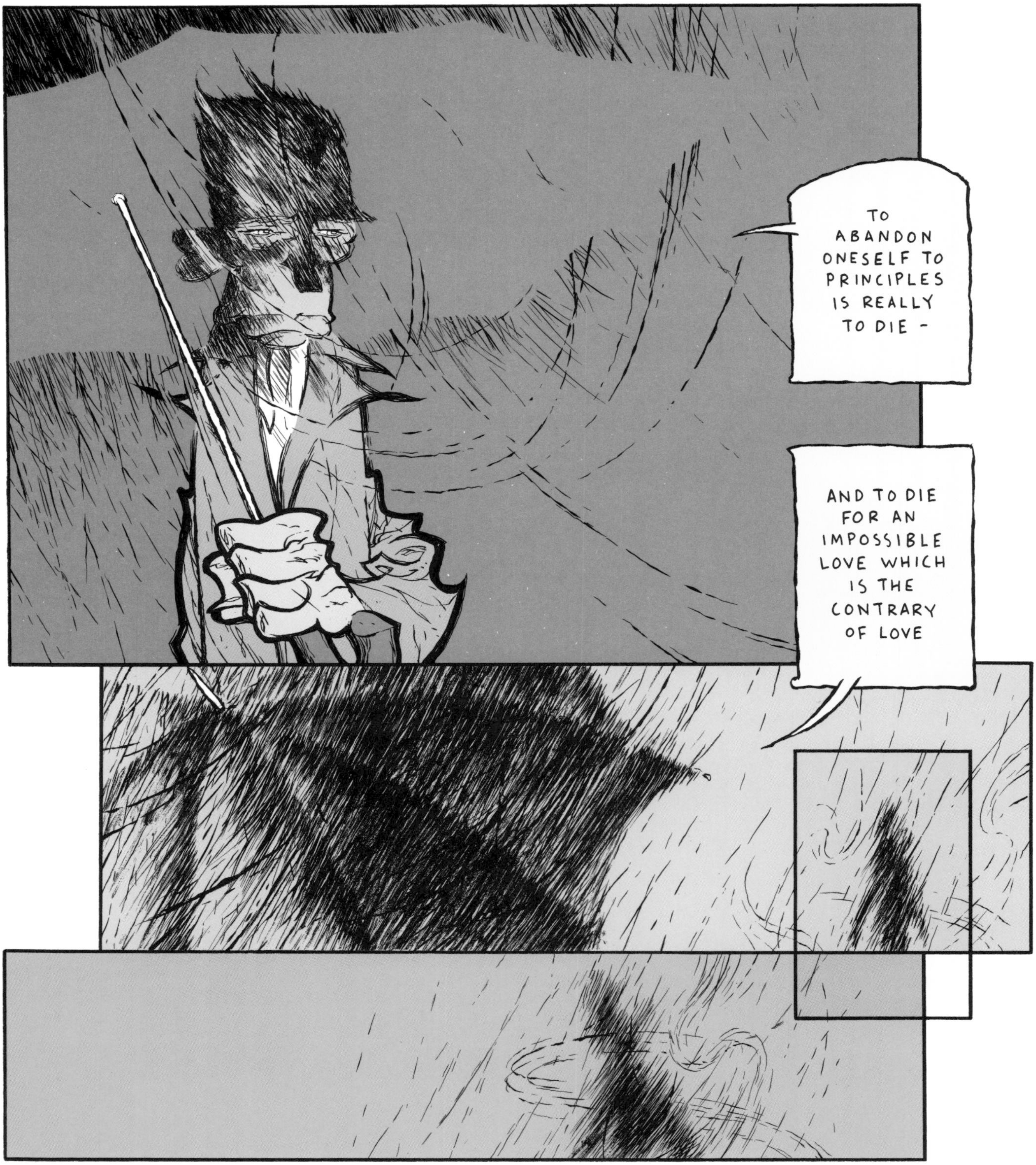
TO ABANDON ONESELF TO PRINCIPLES IS REALLY TO DIE -
AND TO DIE FOR AN IMPOSSIBLE LOVE WHICH IS THE CONTRARY OF LOVE

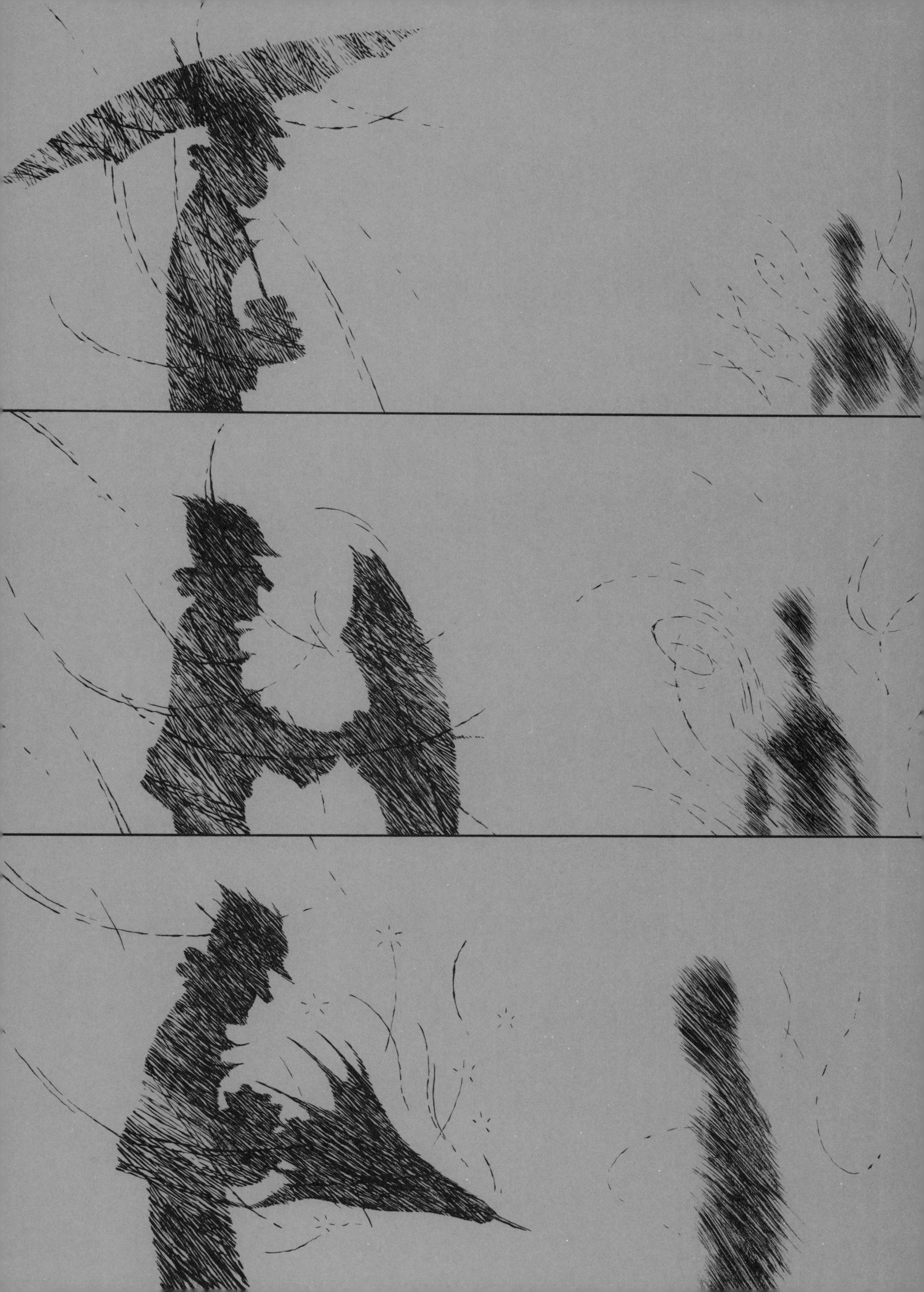

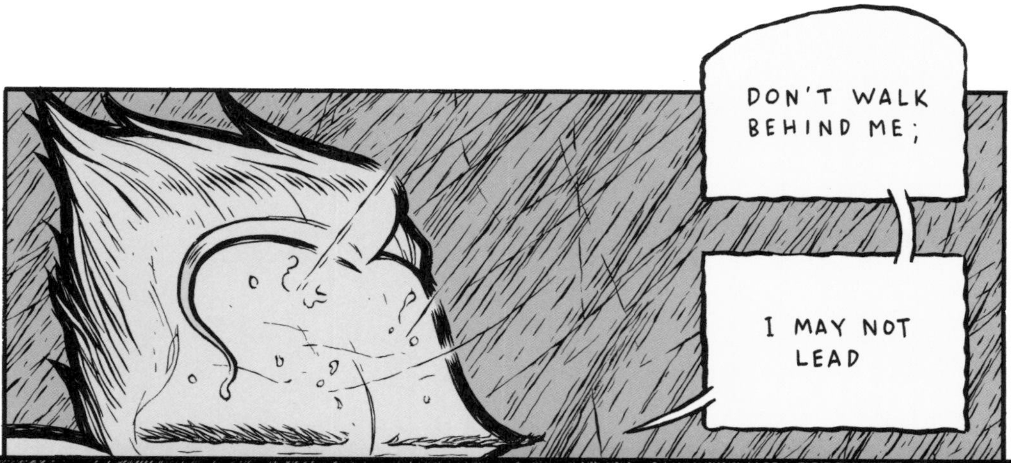
DON'T WALK BEHIND ME;
I MAY NOT LEAD

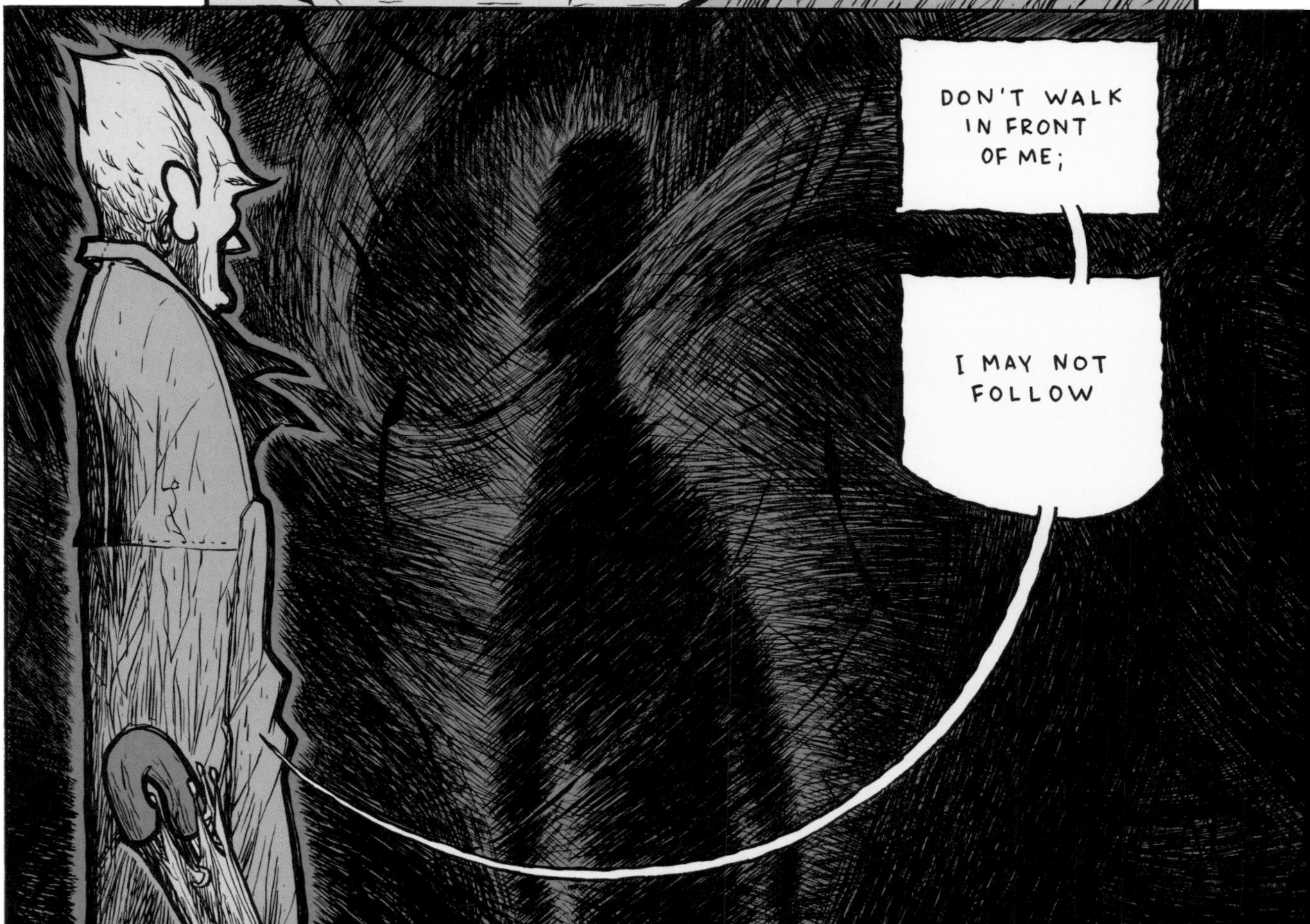
DON'T WALK IN FRONT OF ME;
I MAY NOT FOLLOW

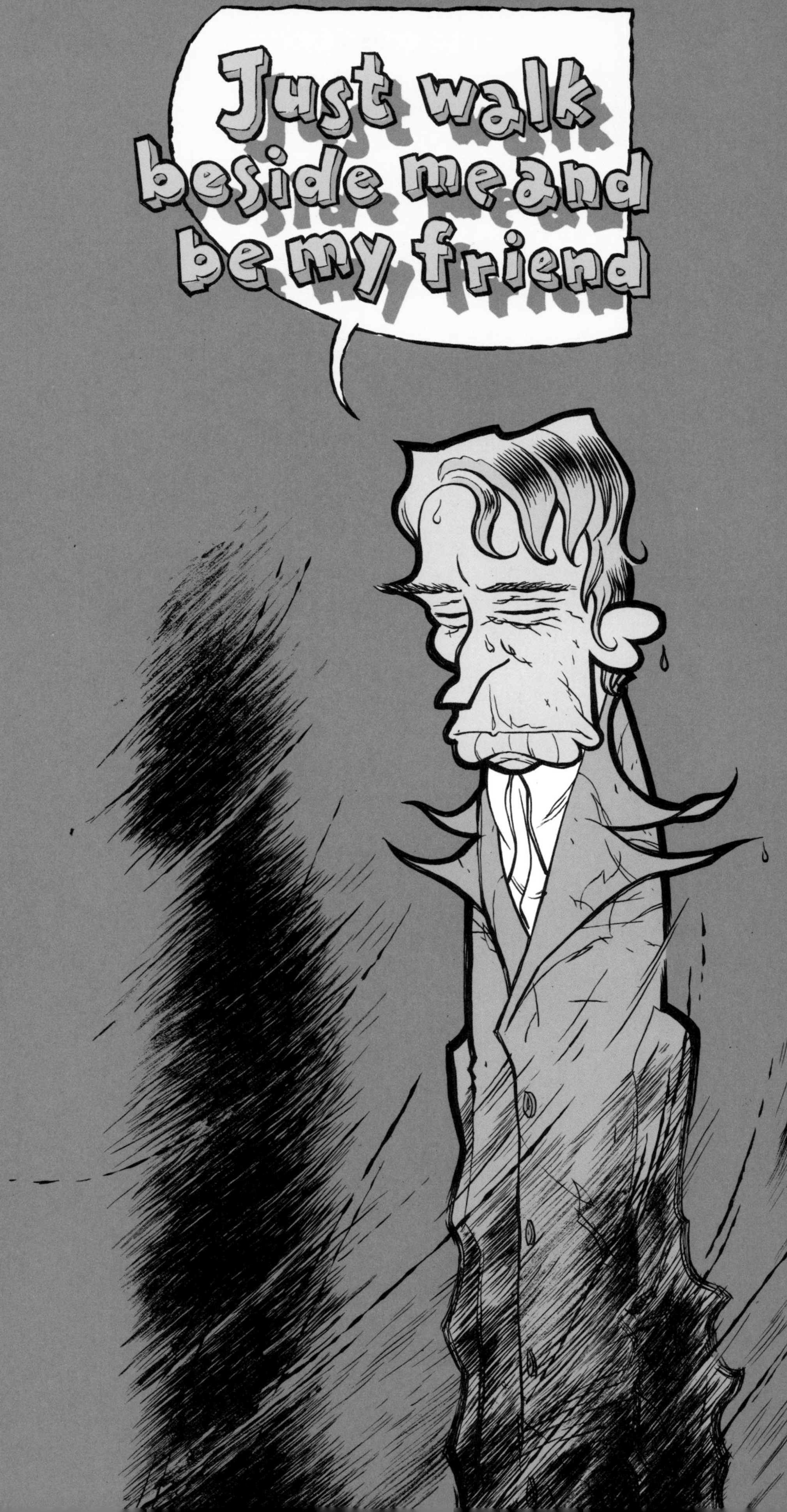
Just walk beside me and be my friend

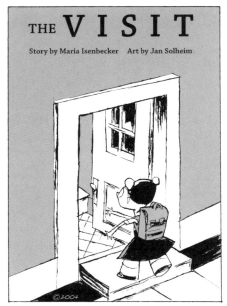

THE VISIT

Story by Maria Isenbecker   Art by Jan Solheim

©2004

48

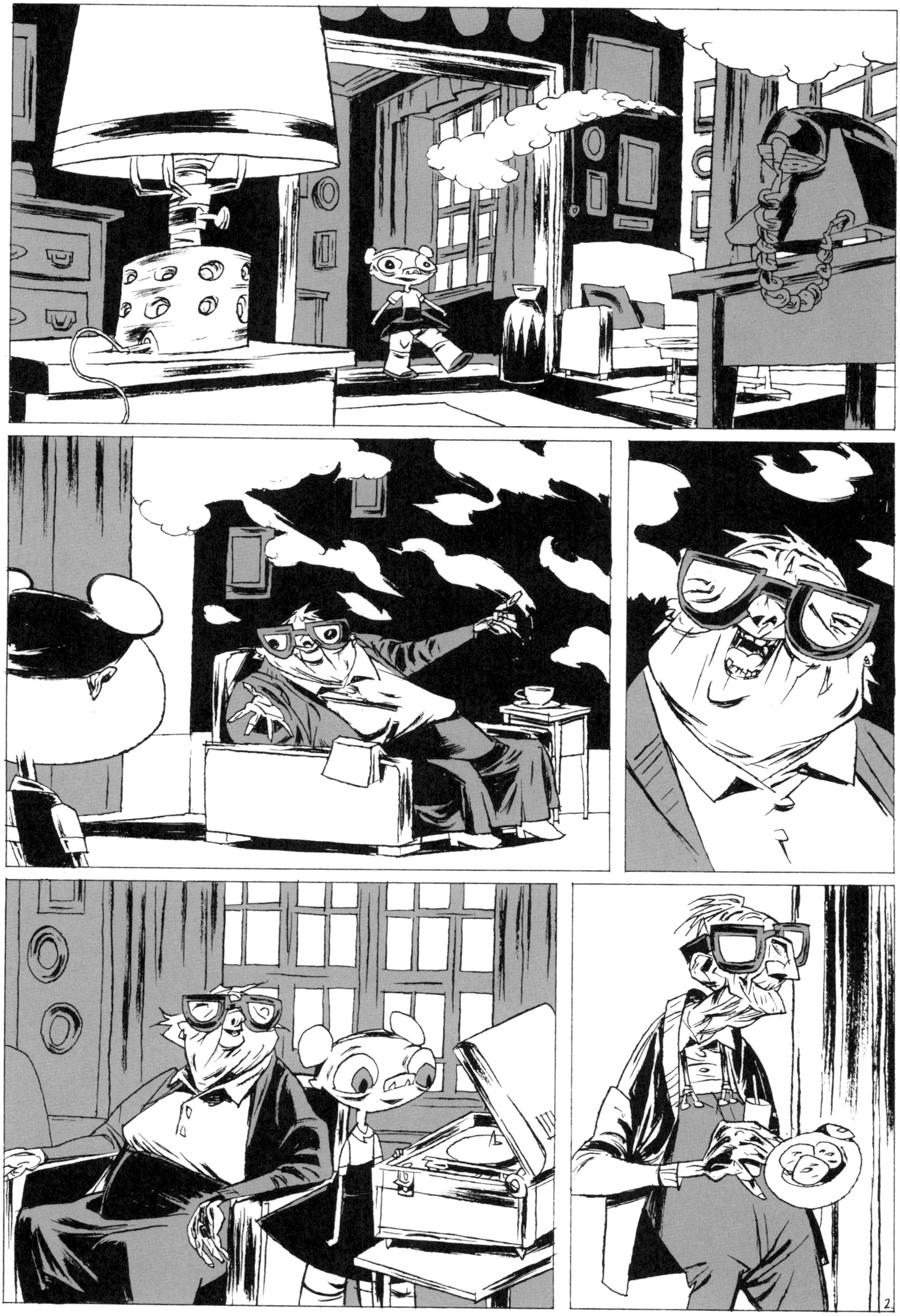
2.

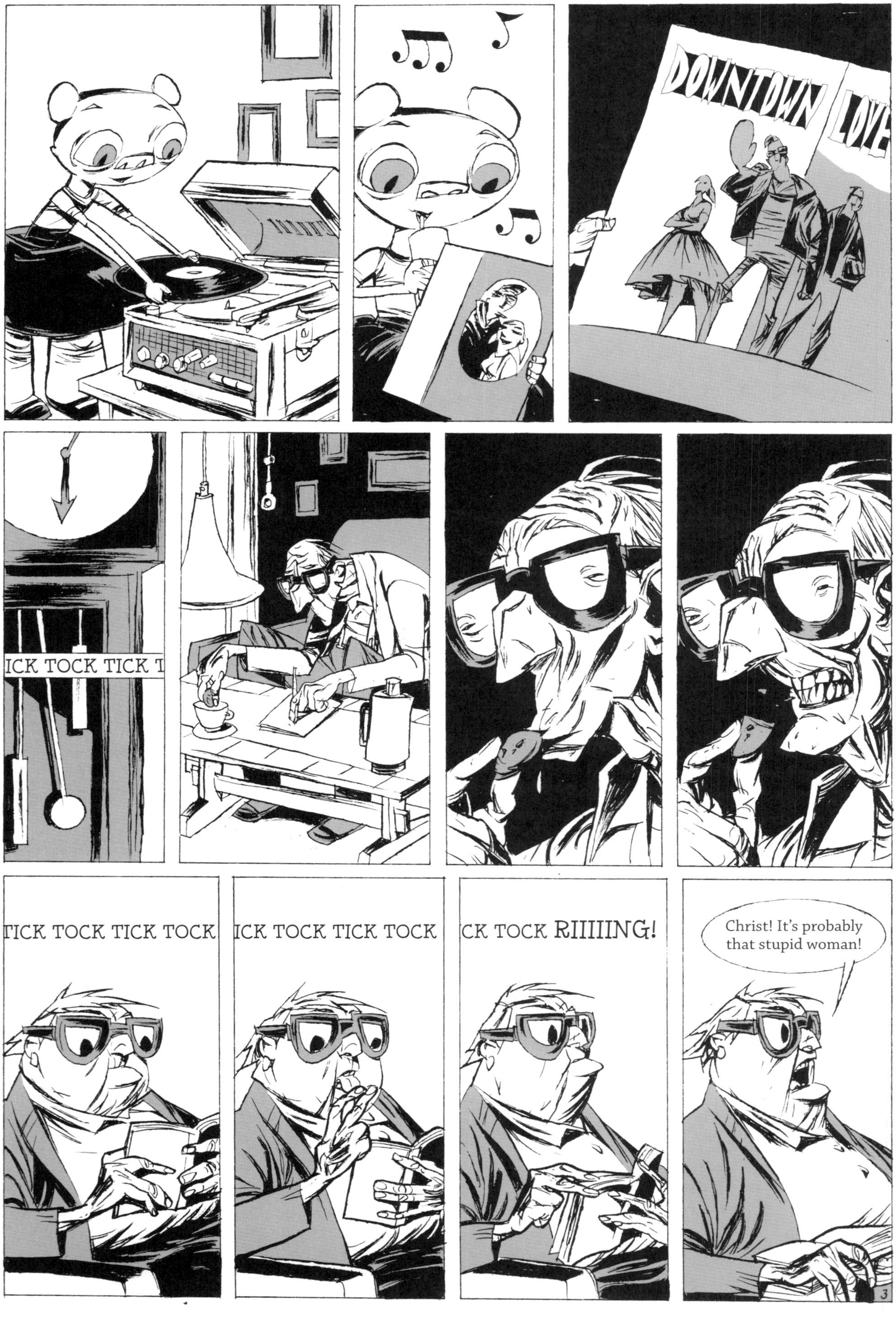
DOWNTOWN LOVE
TICK TOCK TICK T
TICK TOCK TICK TOCK
ICK TOCK TICK TOCK
CK TOCK RIIIIING!
Christ! It's probably that stupid woman!

50

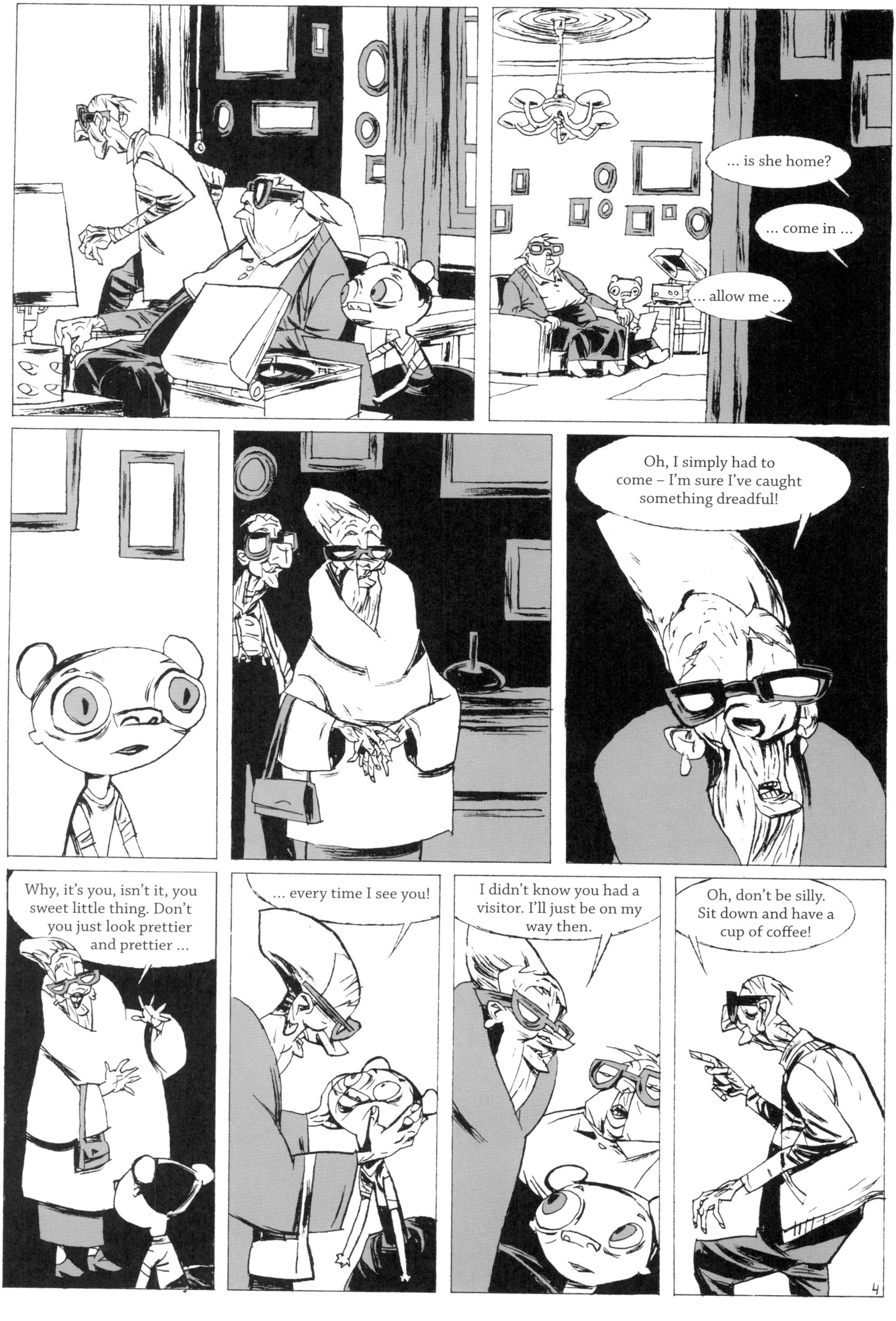
... is she home?
... come in ...
... allow me ...
Oh, I simply had to come – I'm sure I've caught something dreadful!
Why, it's you, isn't it, you sweet little thing. Don't you just look prettier and prettier ...
... every time I see you!
I didn't know you had a visitor. I'll just be on my way then.
Oh, don't be silly. Sit down and have a cup of coffee!
4

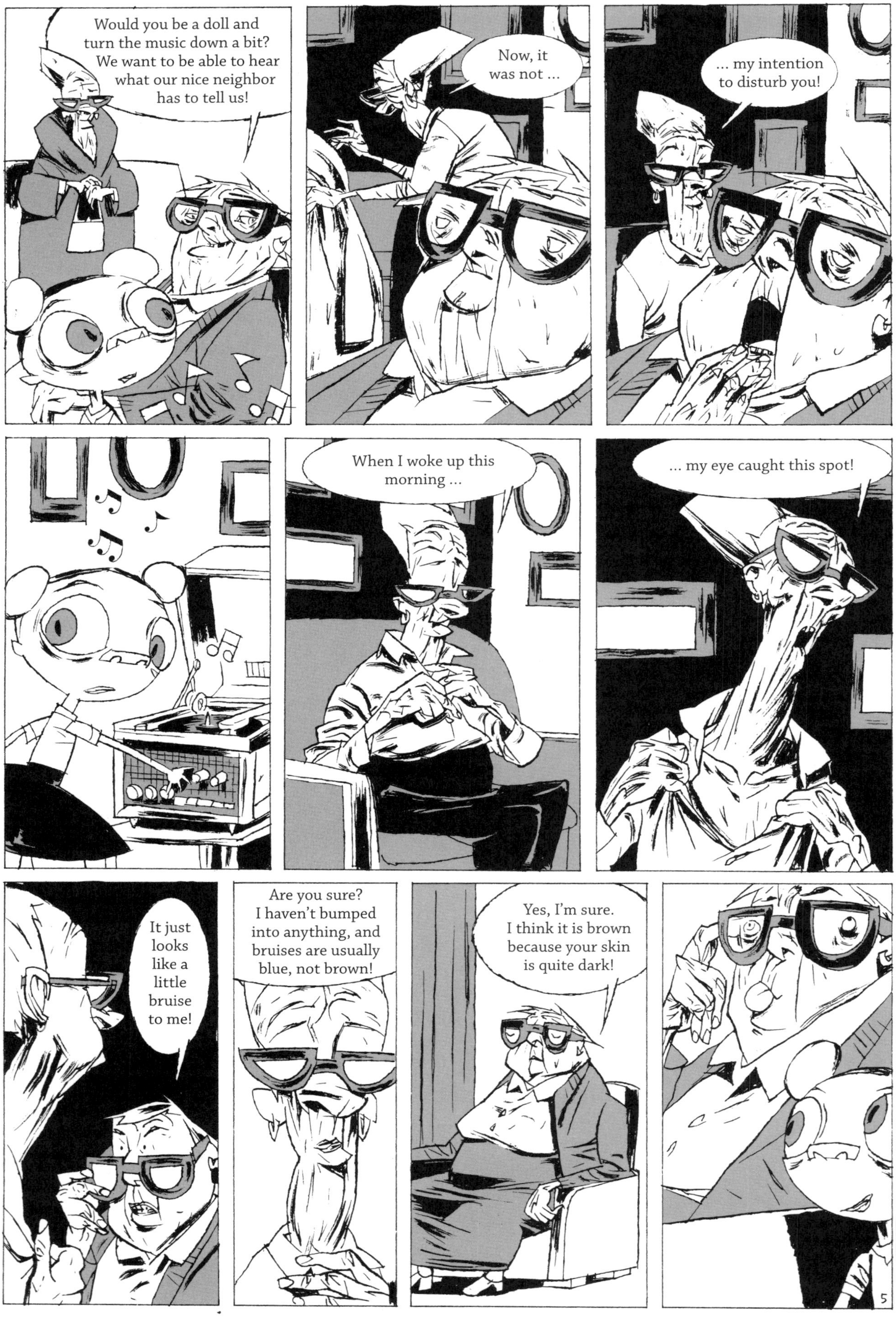
Would you be a doll and turn the music down a bit? We want to be able to hear what our nice neighbor has to tell us!
Now, it was not ...
... my intention to disturb you!
When I woke up this morning ...
... my eye caught this spot!
It just looks like a little bruise to me!
Are you sure? I haven't bumped into anything, and bruises are usually blue, not brown!
Yes, I'm sure. I think it is brown because your skin is quite dark!
5
52

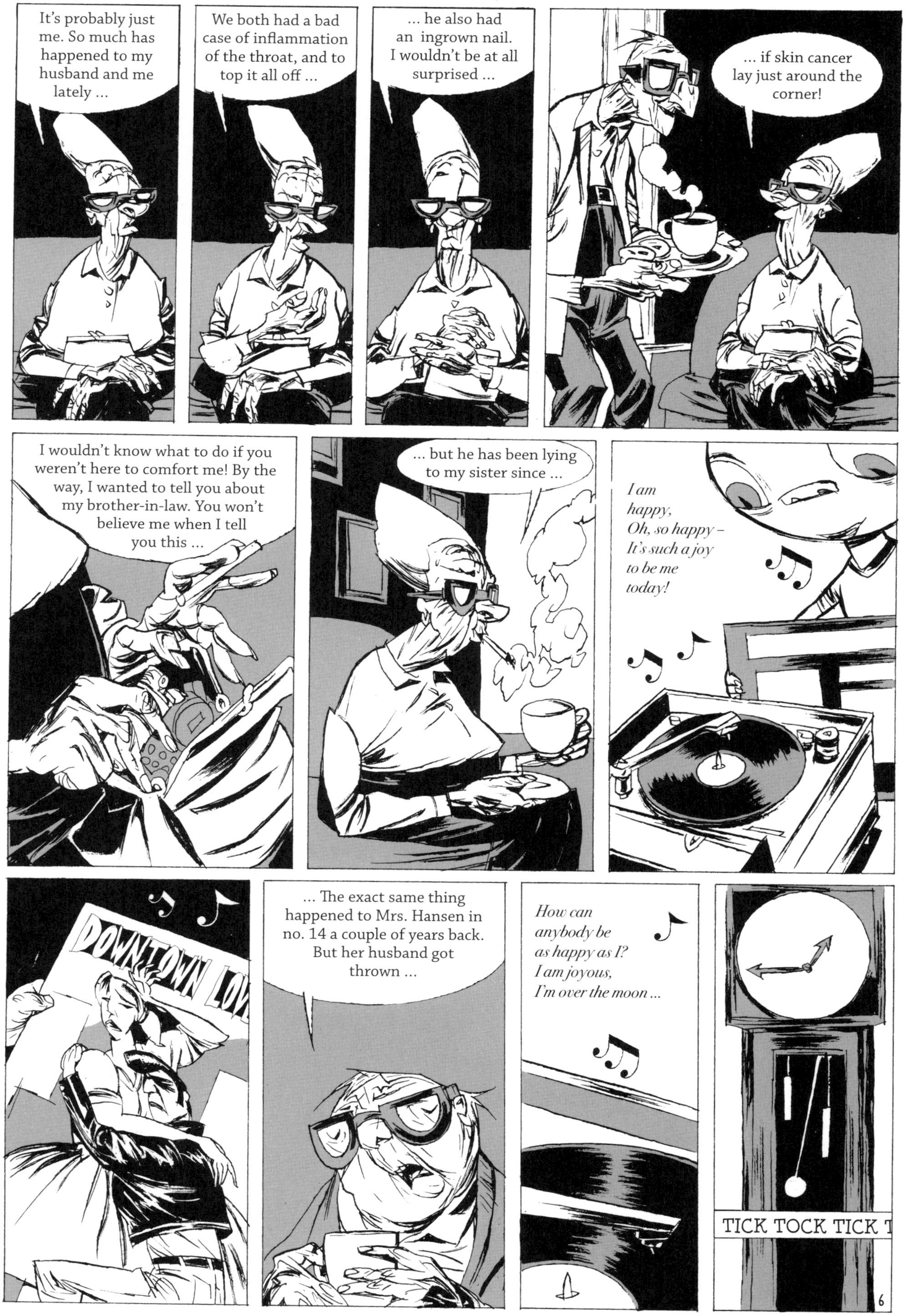

It's probably just me. So much has happened to my husband and me lately ...
We both had a bad case of inflammation of the throat, and to top it all off ...
... he also had an ingrown nail. I wouldn't be at all surprised ...
... if skin cancer lay just around the corner!
I wouldn't know what to do if you weren't here to comfort me! By the way, I wanted to tell you about my brother-in-law. You won't believe me when I tell you this ...
... but he has been lying to my sister since ...
I am happy, Oh, so happy – It's such a joy to be me today!
DOWNTOWN LOV
... The exact same thing happened to Mrs. Hansen in no. 14 a couple of years back. But her husband got thrown ...
How can anybody be as happy as I? I am joyous, I'm over the moon ...
TICK TOCK TICK T
6

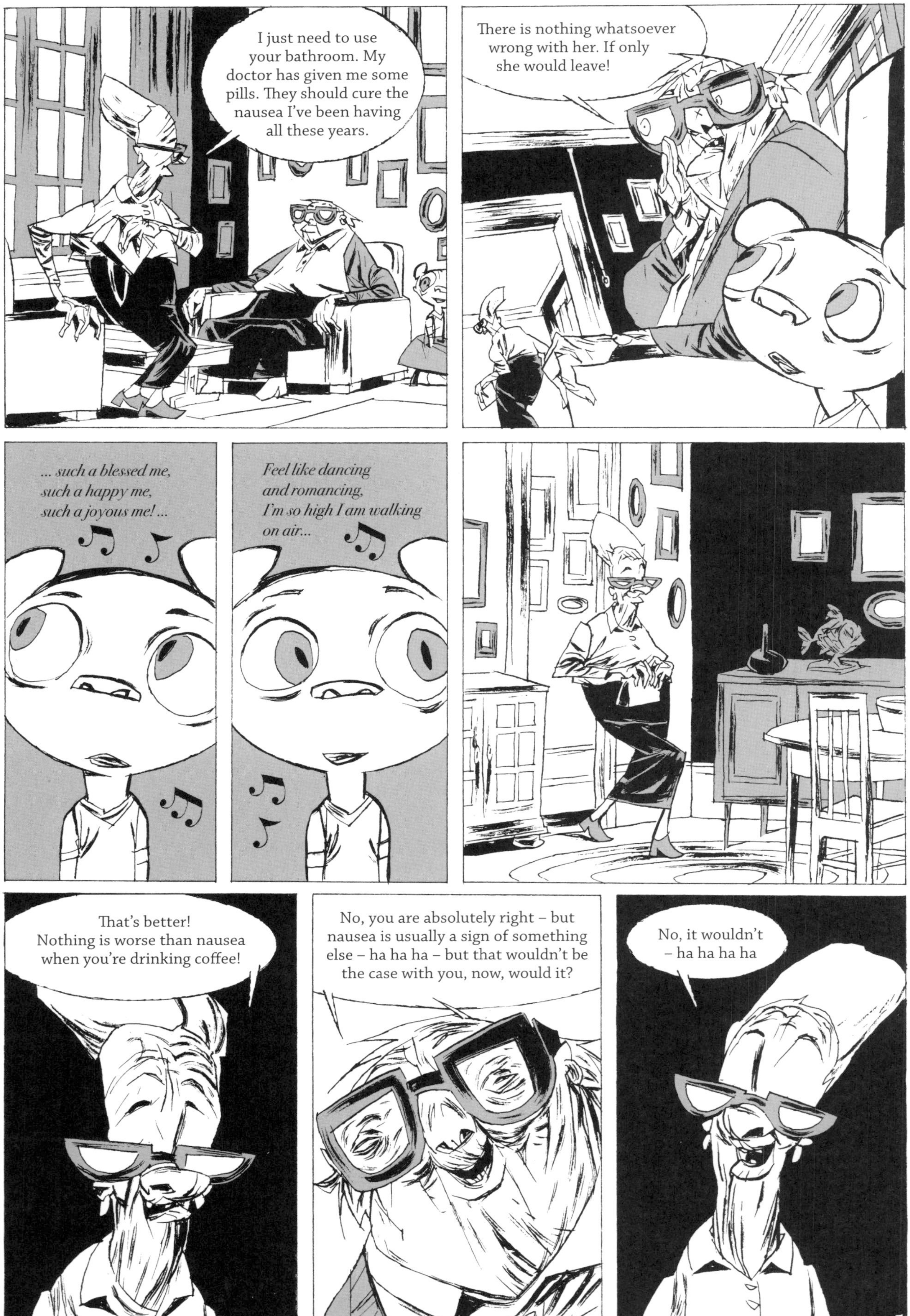

I just need to use your bathroom. My doctor has given me some pills. They should cure the nausea I've been having all these years.
There is nothing whatsoever wrong with her. If only she would leave!
... such a blessed me, such a happy me, such a joyous me! ...
Feel like dancing and romancing, I'm so high I am walking on air...
That's better! Nothing is worse than nausea when you're drinking coffee!
No, you are absolutely right – but nausea is usually a sign of something else – ha ha ha – but that wouldn't be the case with you, now, would it?
No, it wouldn't – ha ha ha ha
7

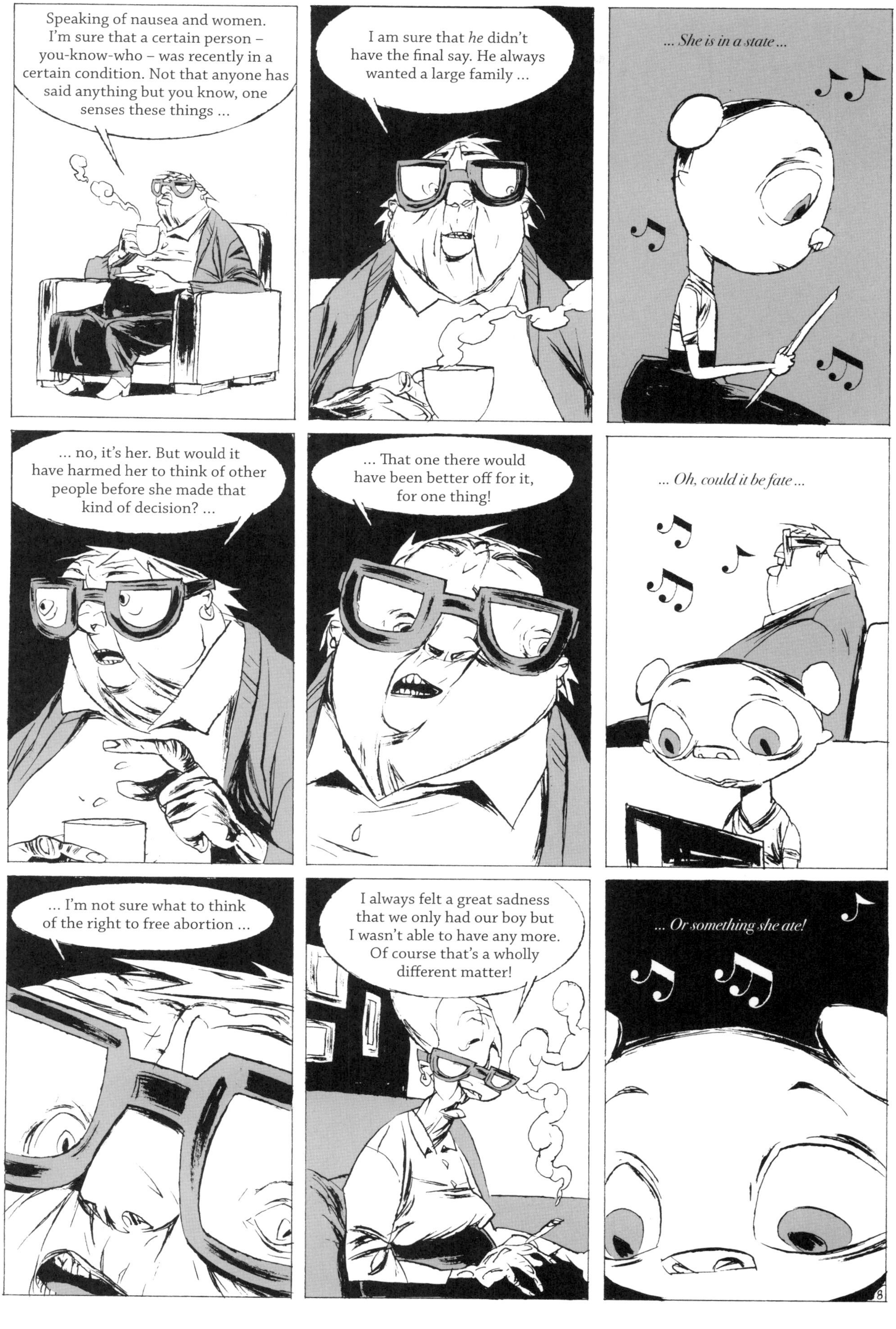
Speaking of nausea and women. I'm sure that a certain person – you-know-who – was recently in a certain condition. Not that anyone has said anything but you know, one senses these things ...
I am sure that *he* didn't have the final say. He always wanted a large family ...
... She is in a state ...
... no, it's her. But would it have harmed her to think of other people before she made that kind of decision? ...
... That one there would have been better off for it, for one thing!
... Oh, could it be fate ...
... I'm not sure what to think of the right to free abortion ...
I always felt a great sadness that we only had our boy but I wasn't able to have any more. Of course that's a wholly different matter!
... Or something she ate!
8

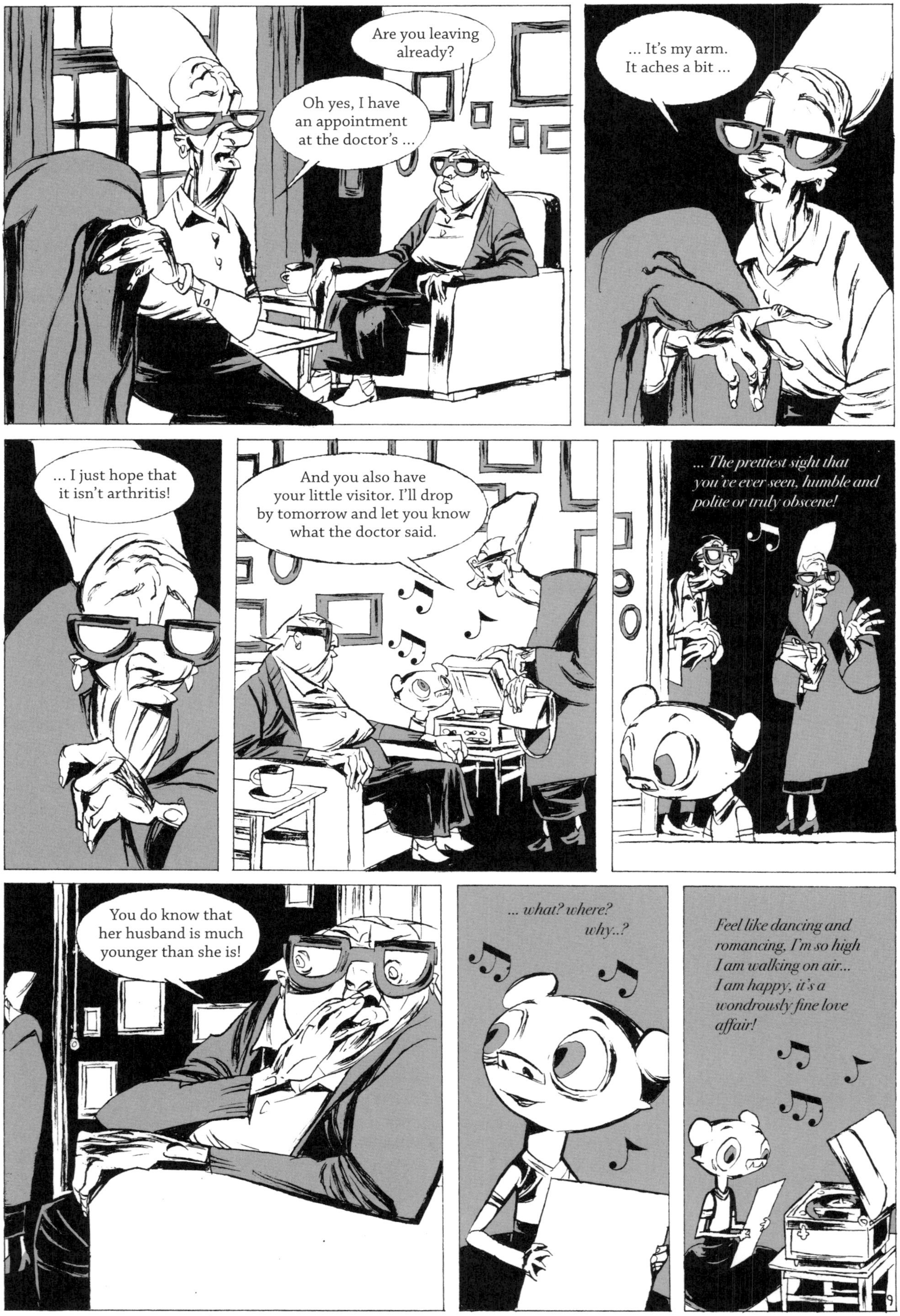
Are you leaving already?
Oh yes, I have an appointment at the doctor's ...
... It's my arm. It aches a bit ...
... I just hope that it isn't arthritis!
And you also have your little visitor. I'll drop by tomorrow and let you know what the doctor said.
... The prettiest sight that you've ever seen, humble and polite or truly obscene!
You do know that her husband is much younger than she is!
... what? where? why..?
Feel like dancing and romancing, I'm so high I am walking on air... I am happy, it's a wondrously fine love affair!
9

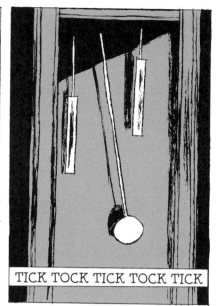

TICK TOCK TICK TOCK TICK

Will we see you tomorrow?

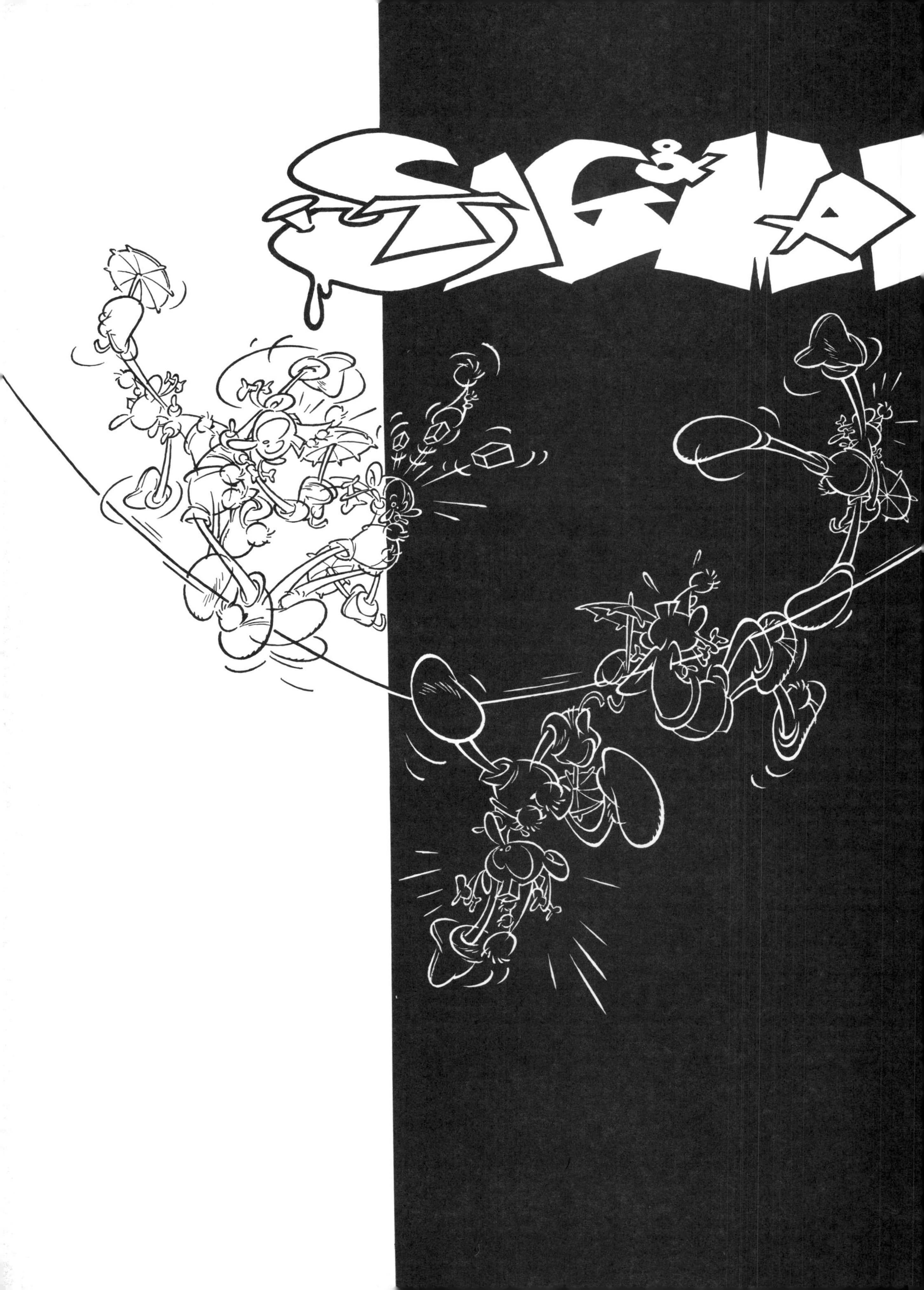

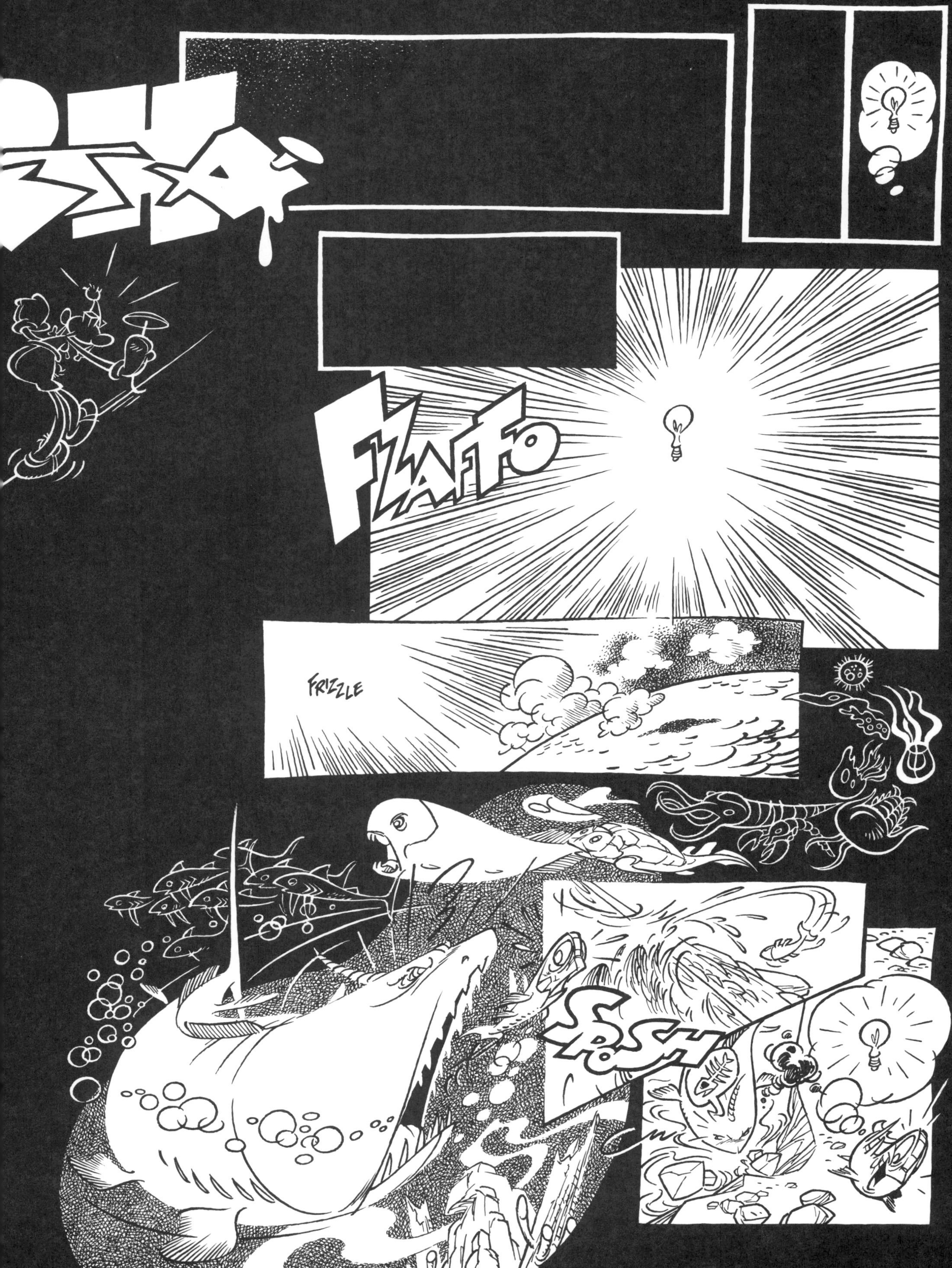
FZAFFO
FRIZZLE
SPOSH

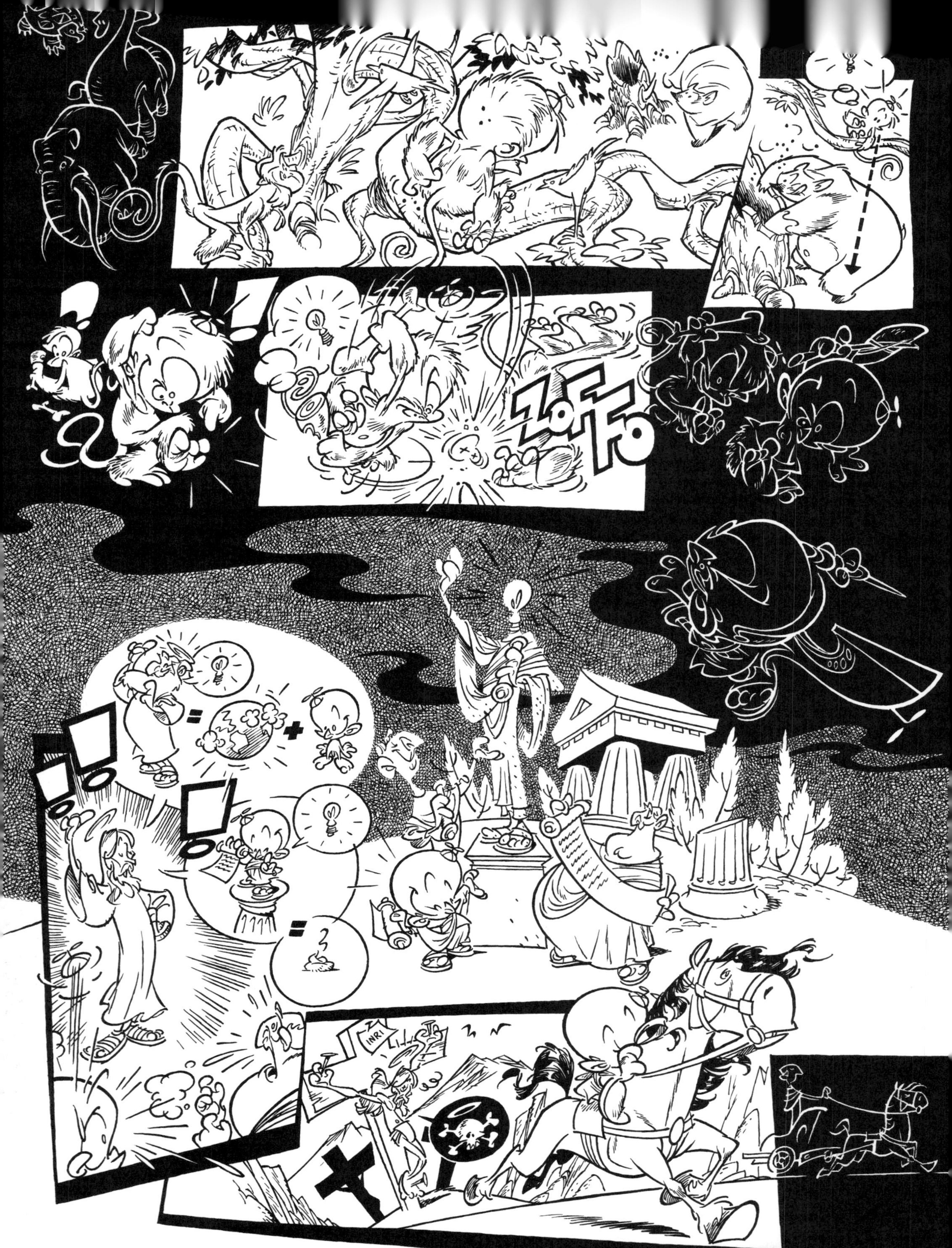
ZOFFO
INRI

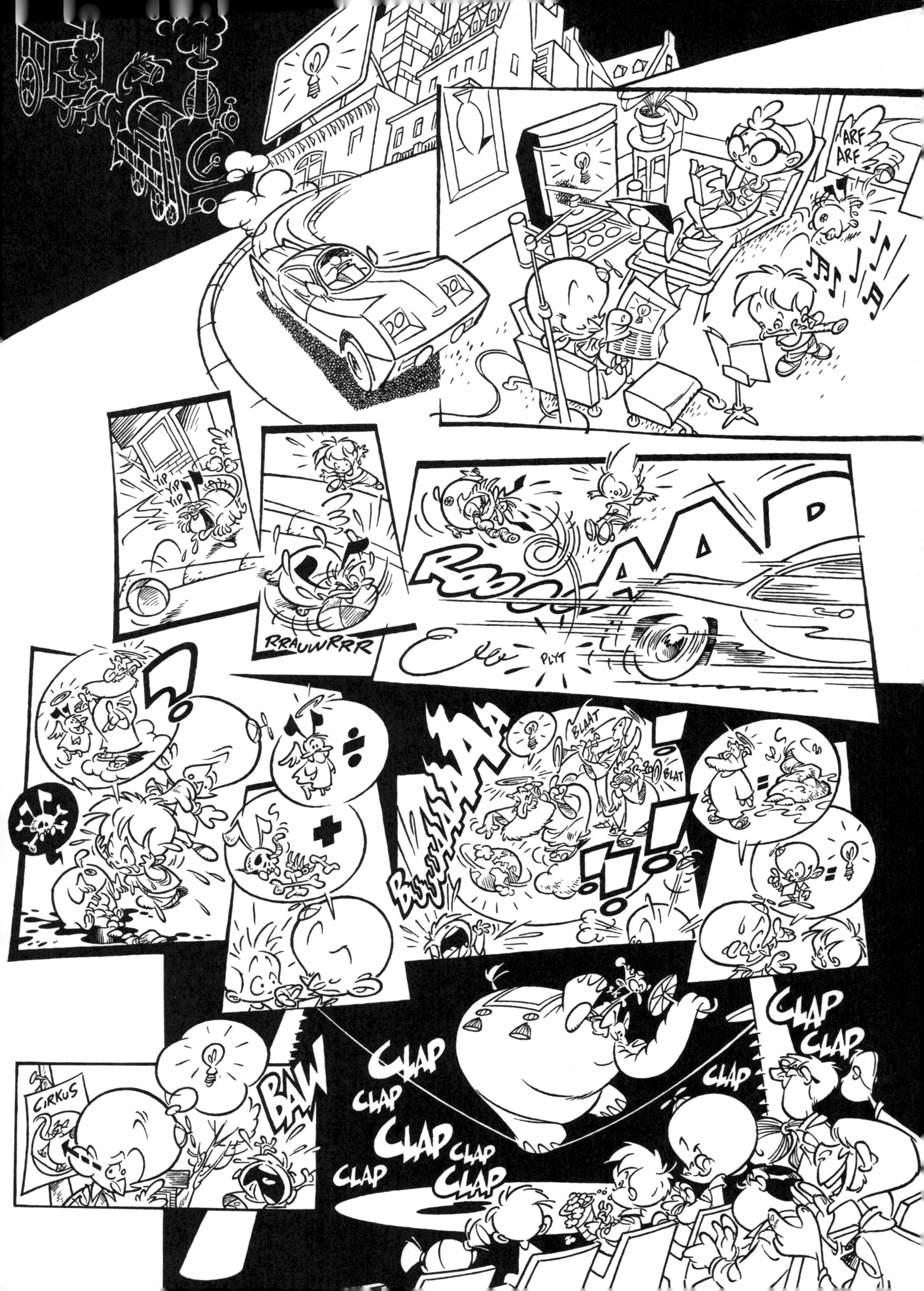
ARF ARF
YIP YIP YIP
RRAUWRRR
PLYT
BLAAT
BLAT
CIRKUS
BAW
CLAP CLAP CLAP
CLAP CLAP CLAP
CLAP CLAP CLAP CLAP

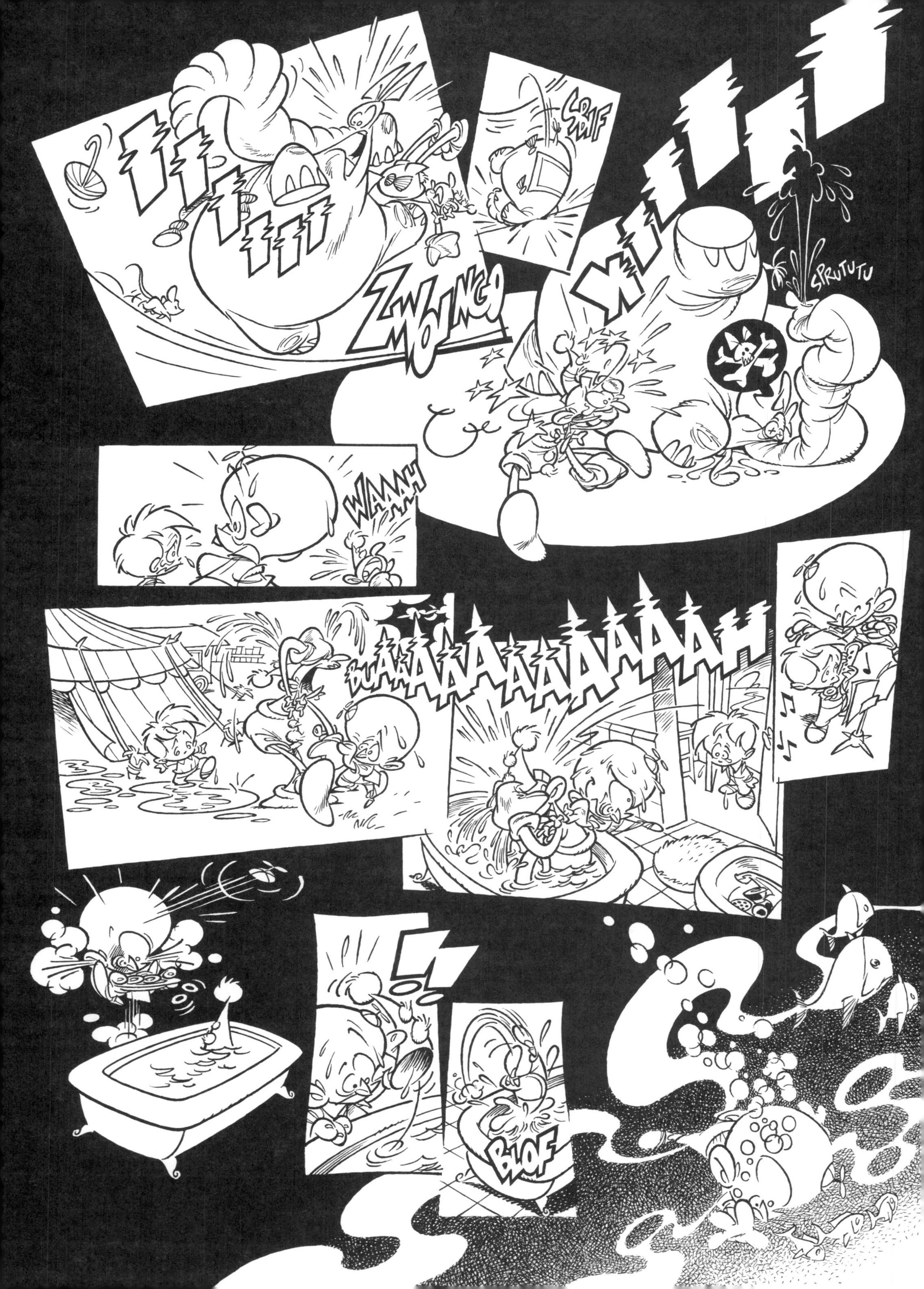
ZWOING!
SPRUTUTU
WAAAH
BUAAAAAAAAAAAAH
BLOF

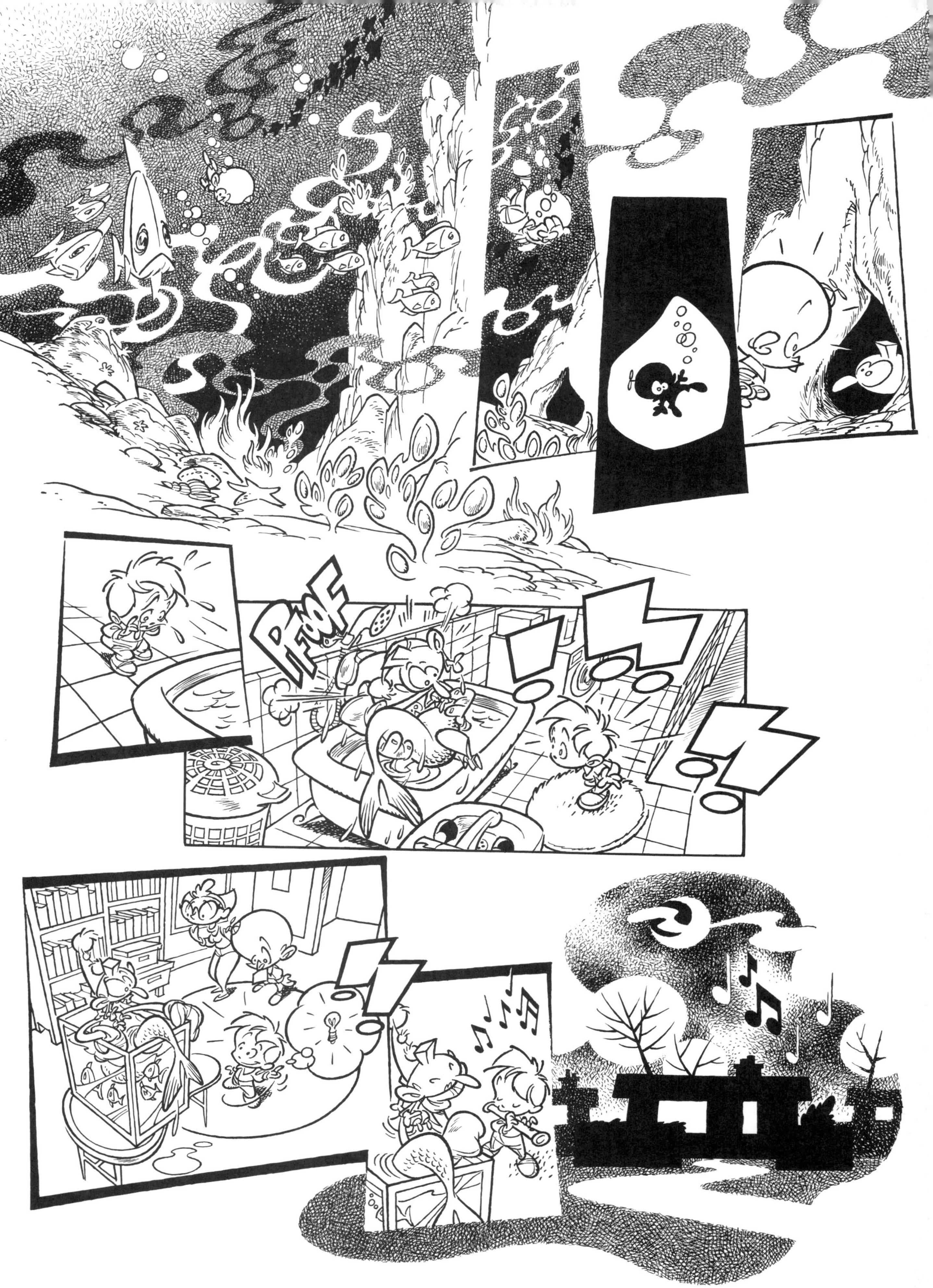
PFOOF

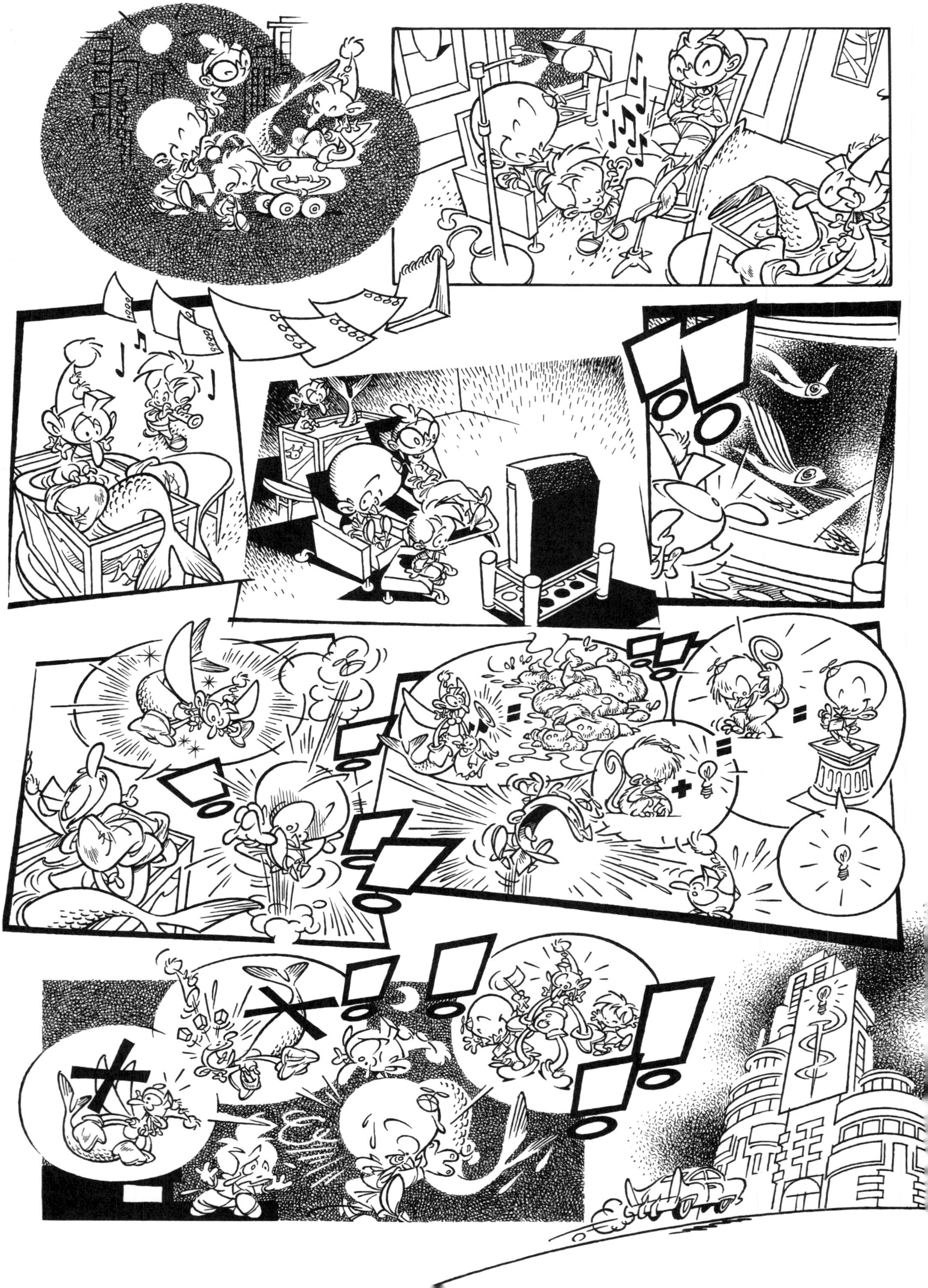

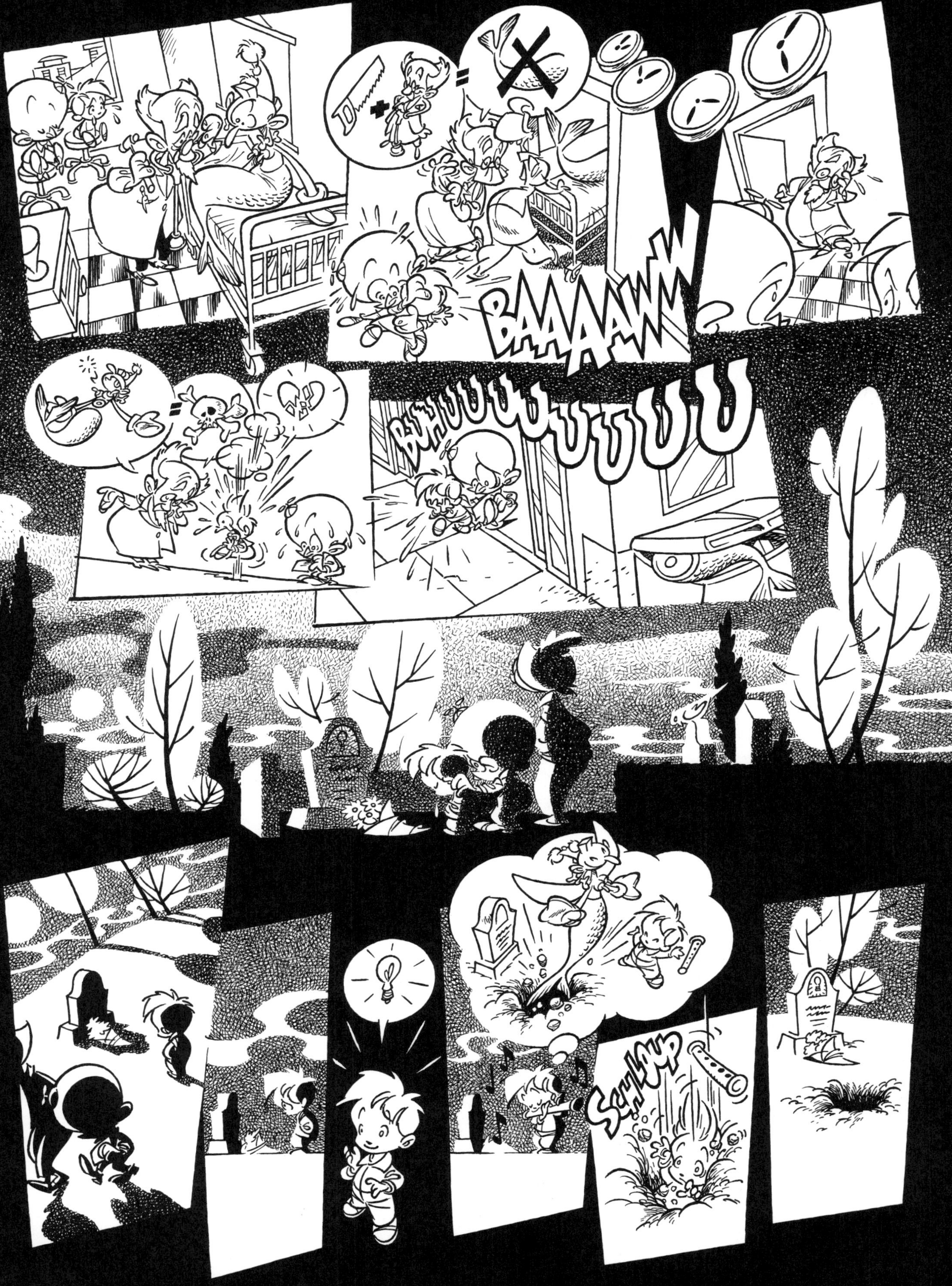
BAAAAWW
BUHUUUUUUUUU
SCHLUP

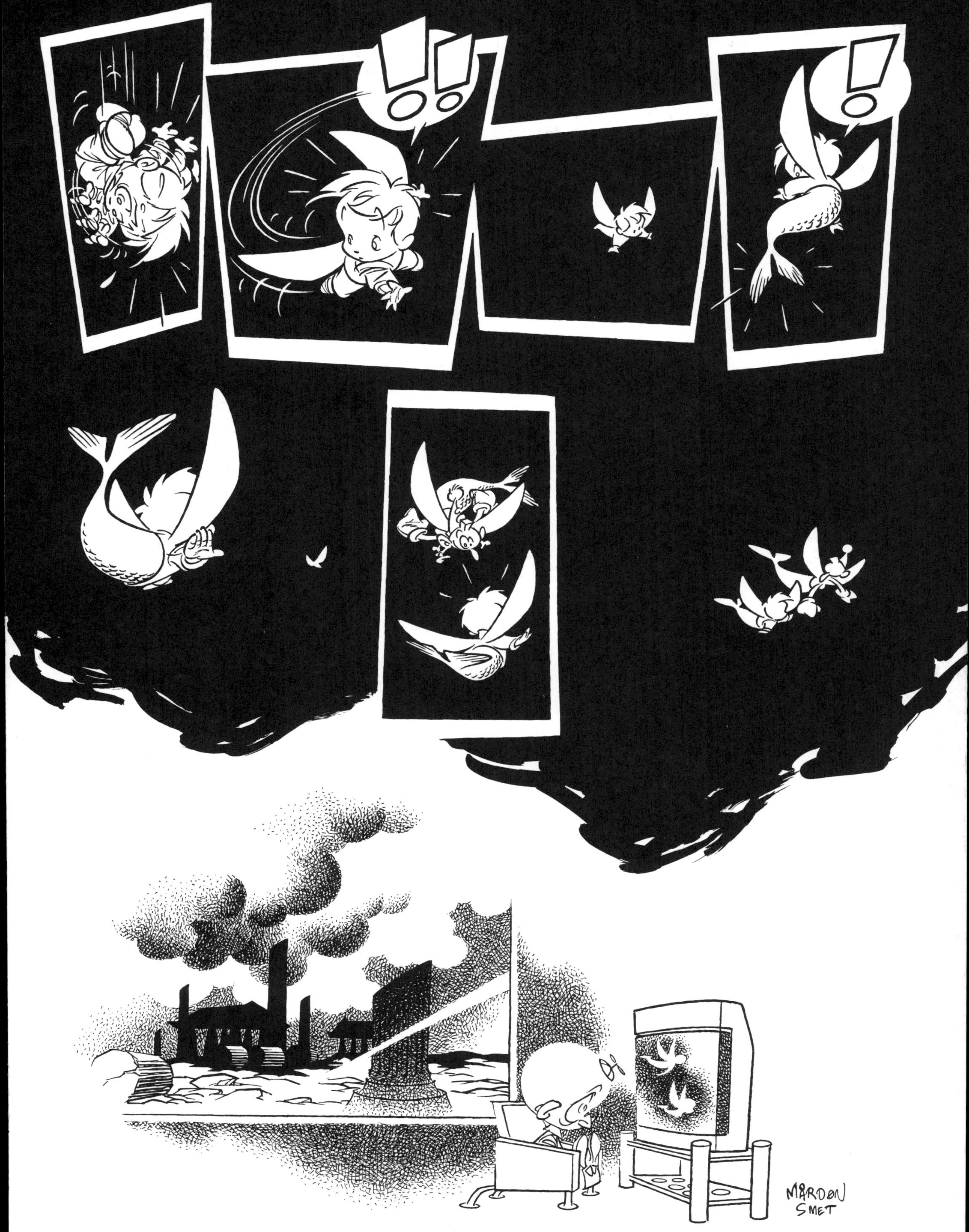
!!
!
MARDON
SMET

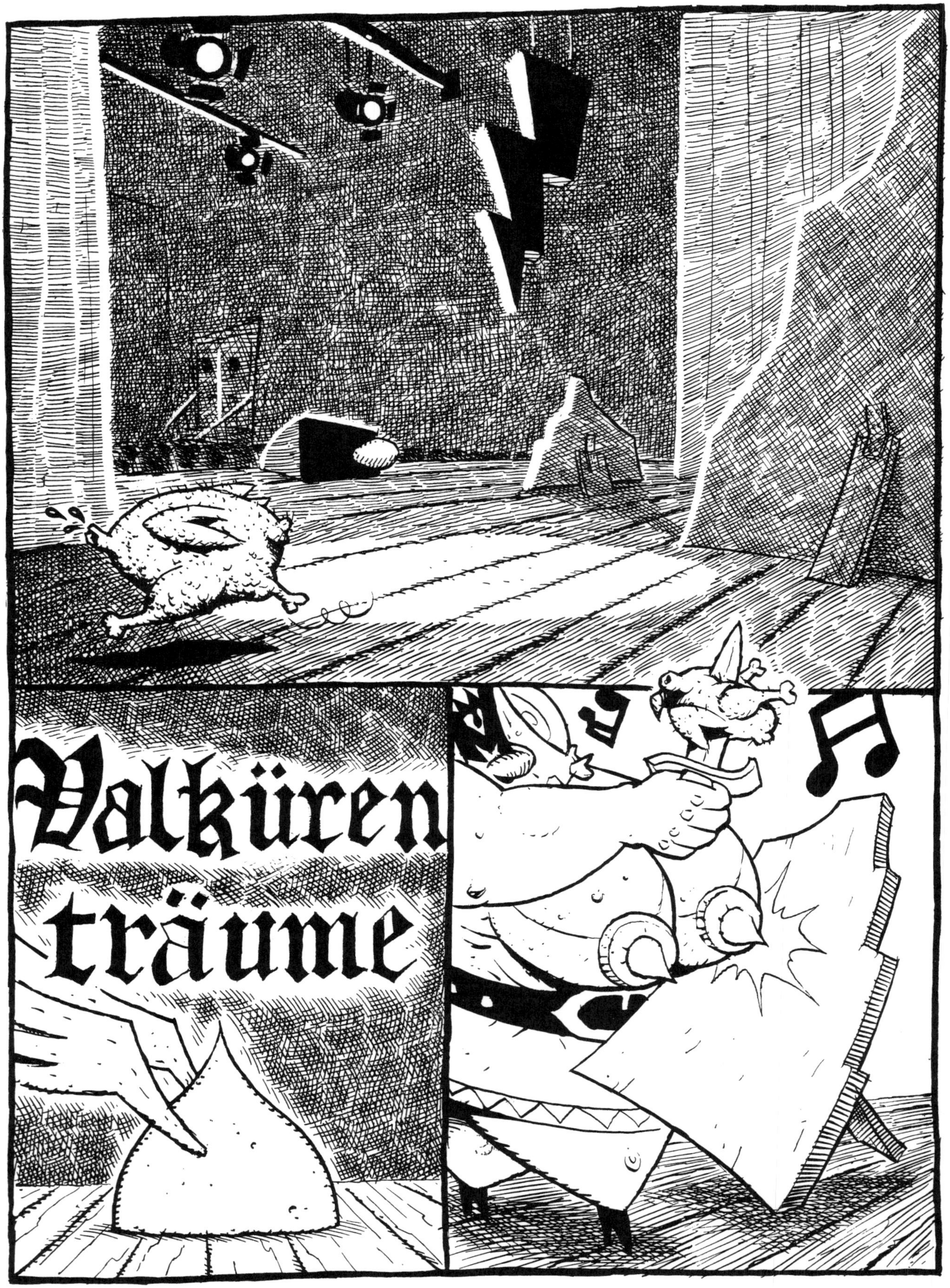
Valküren
träume

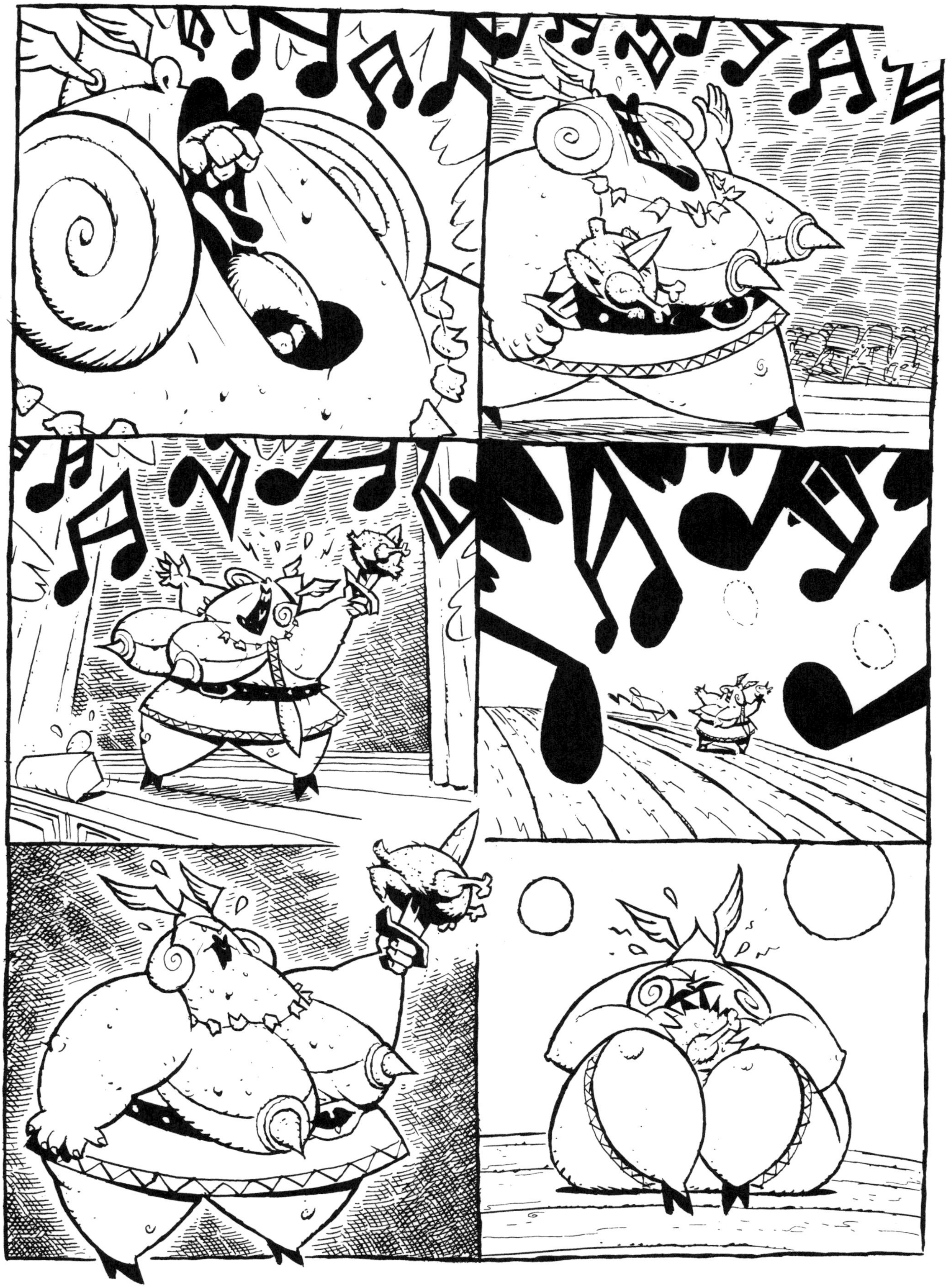

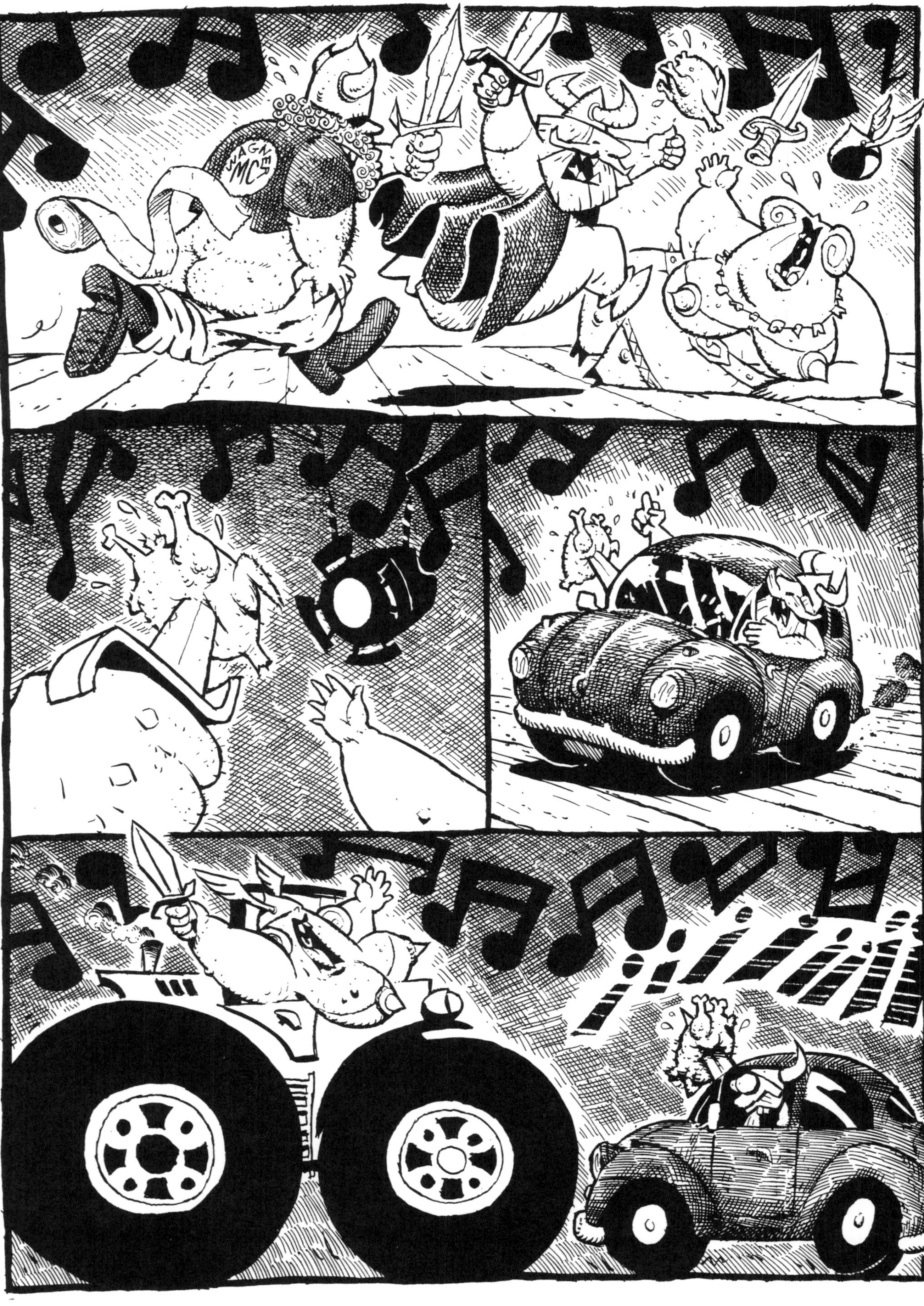

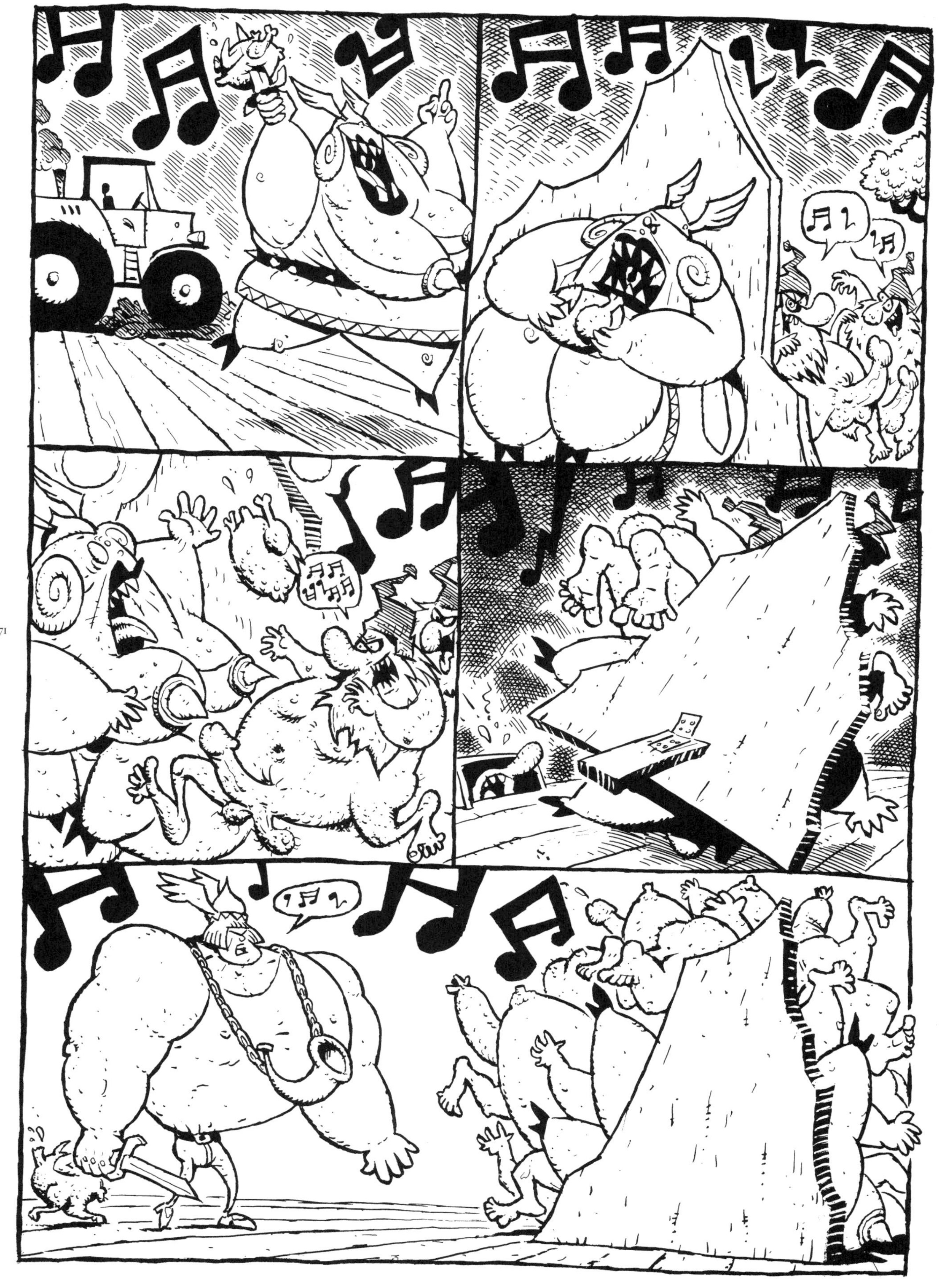

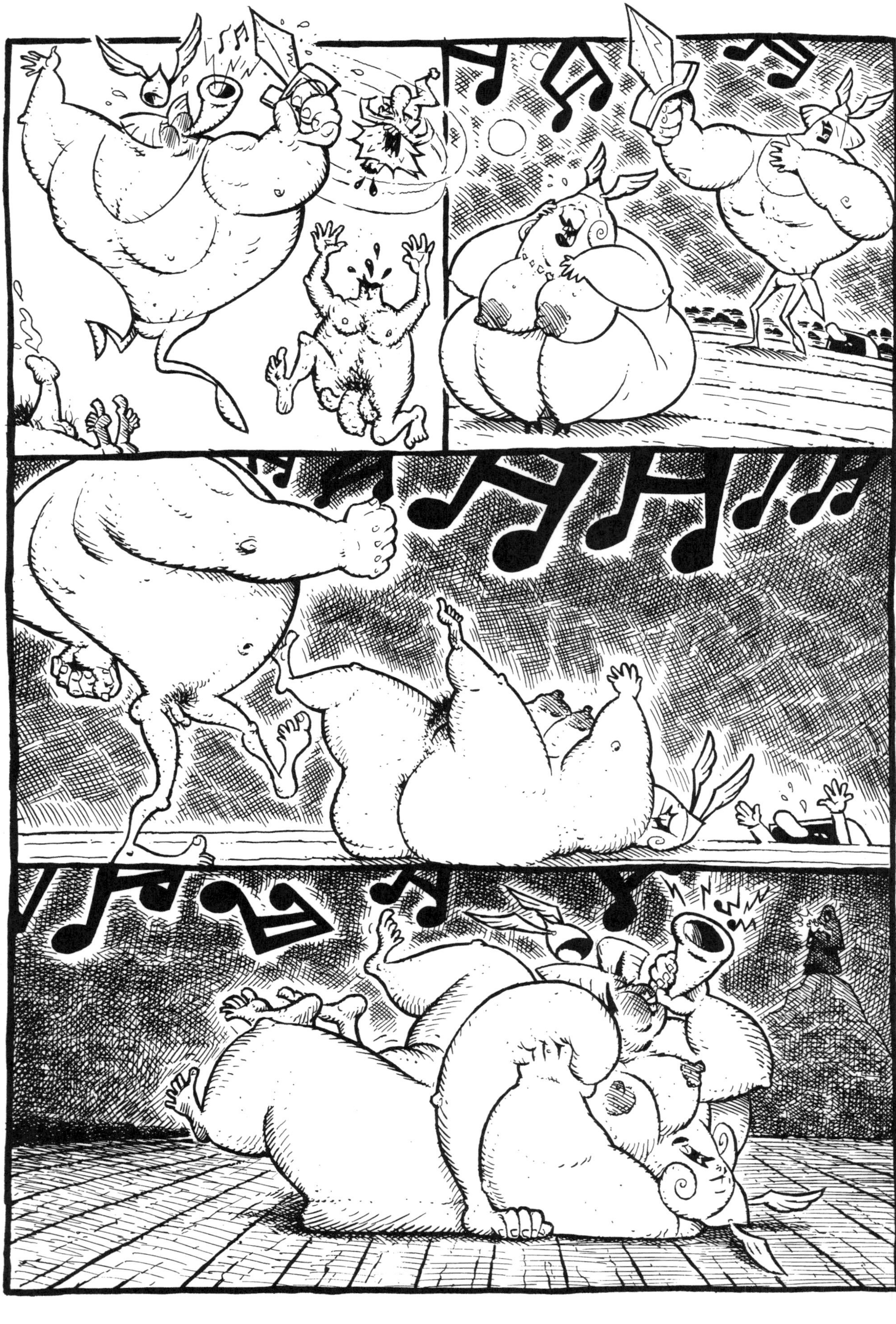

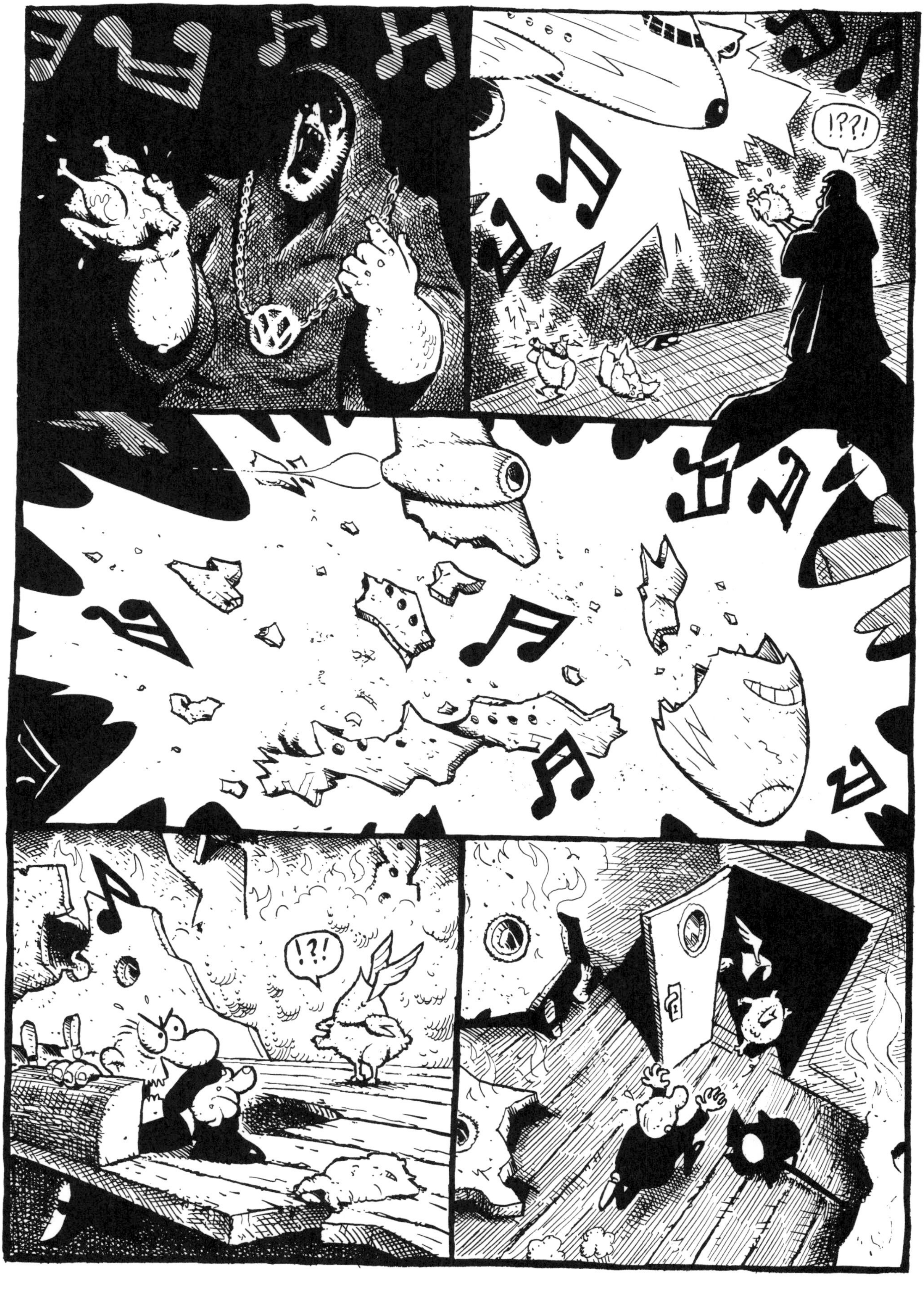
!??!
!?!

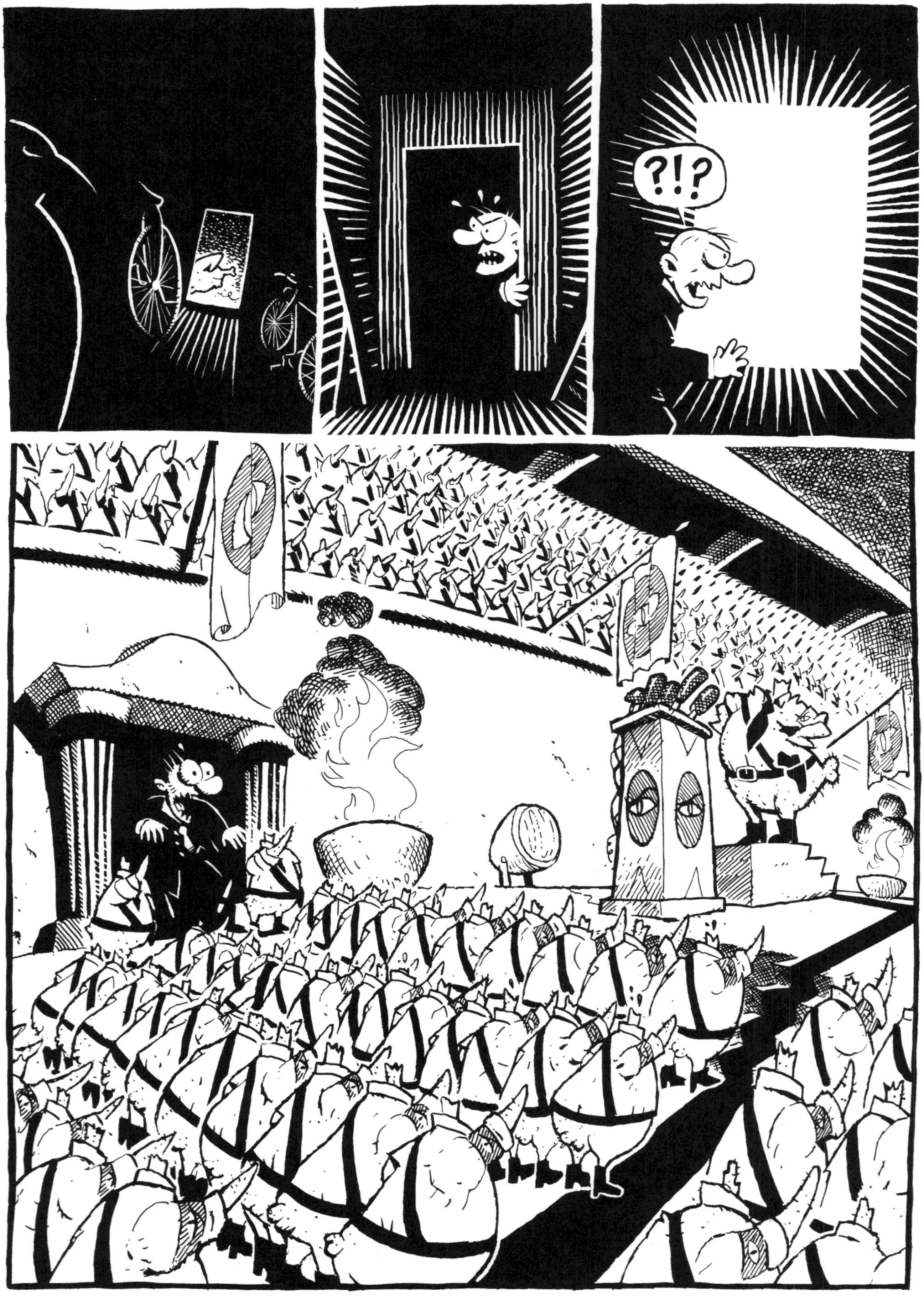
?!?

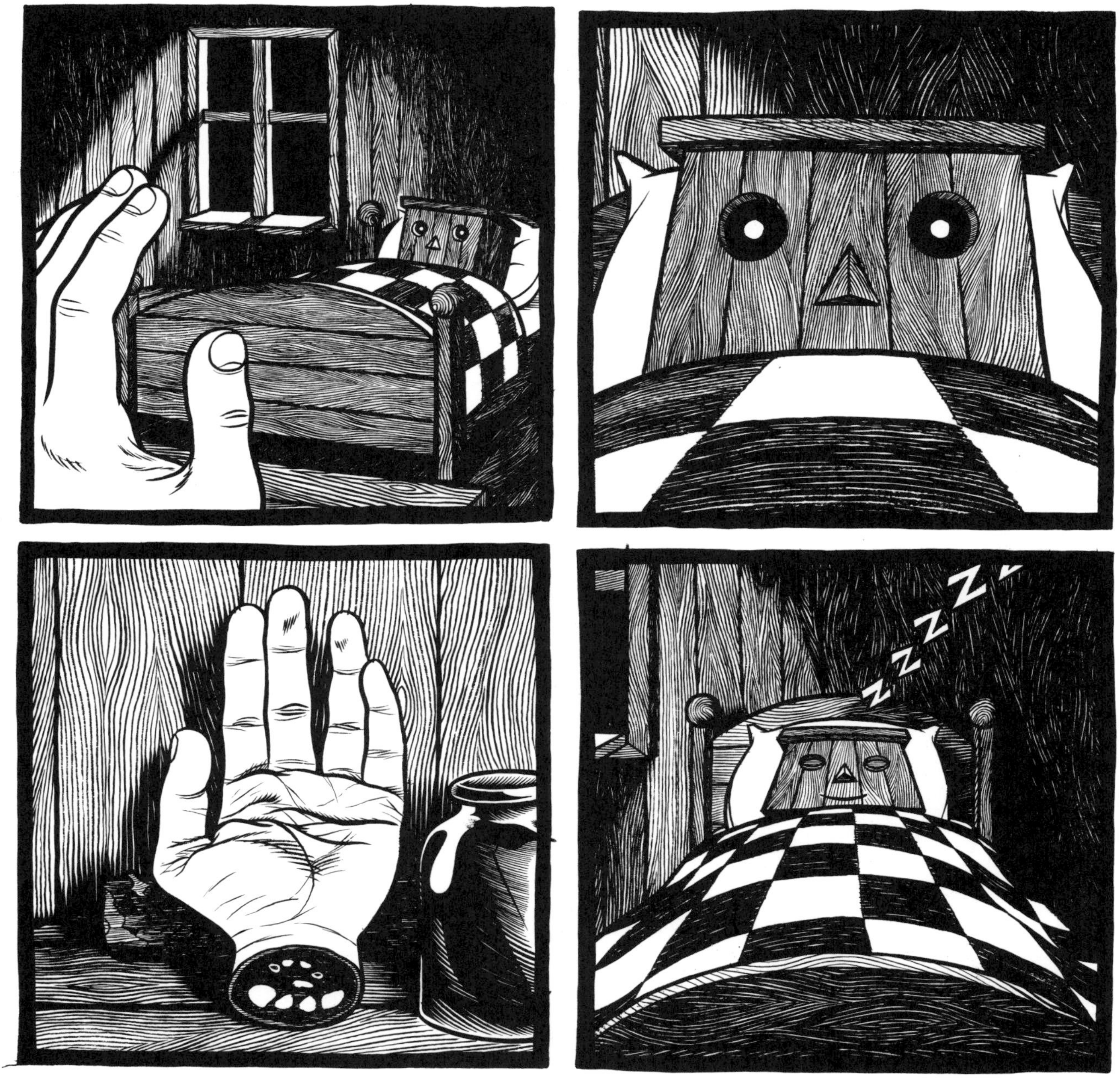
ZZZZ

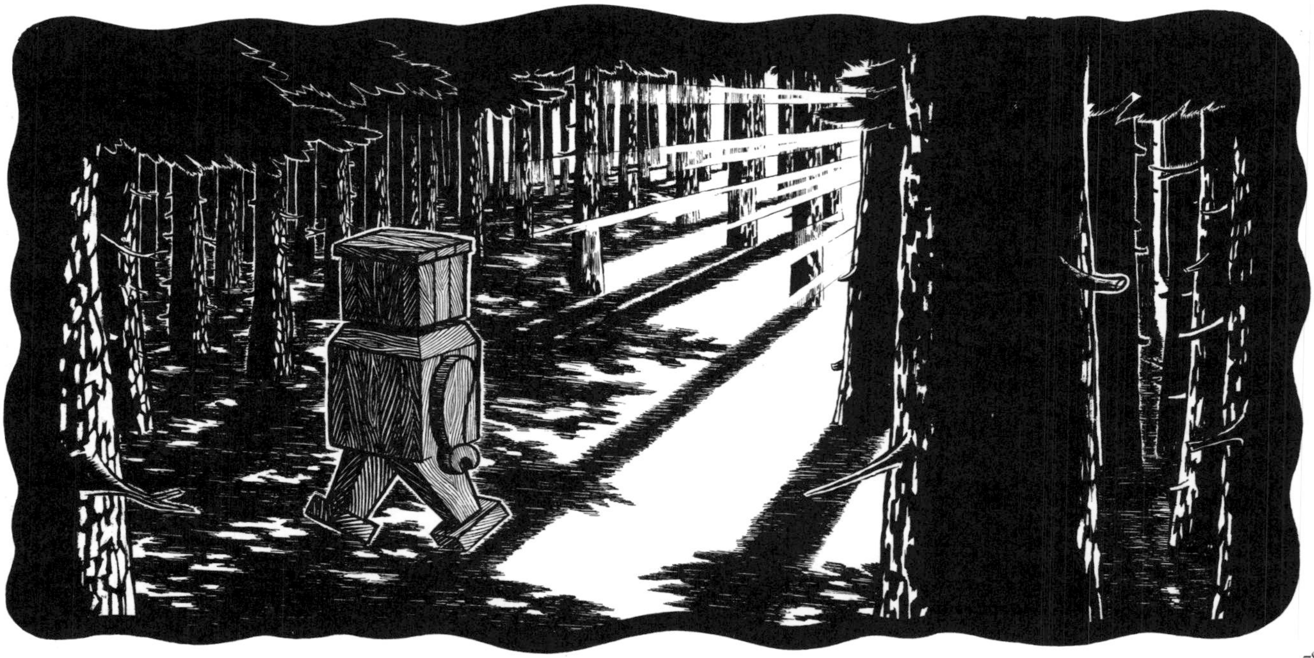

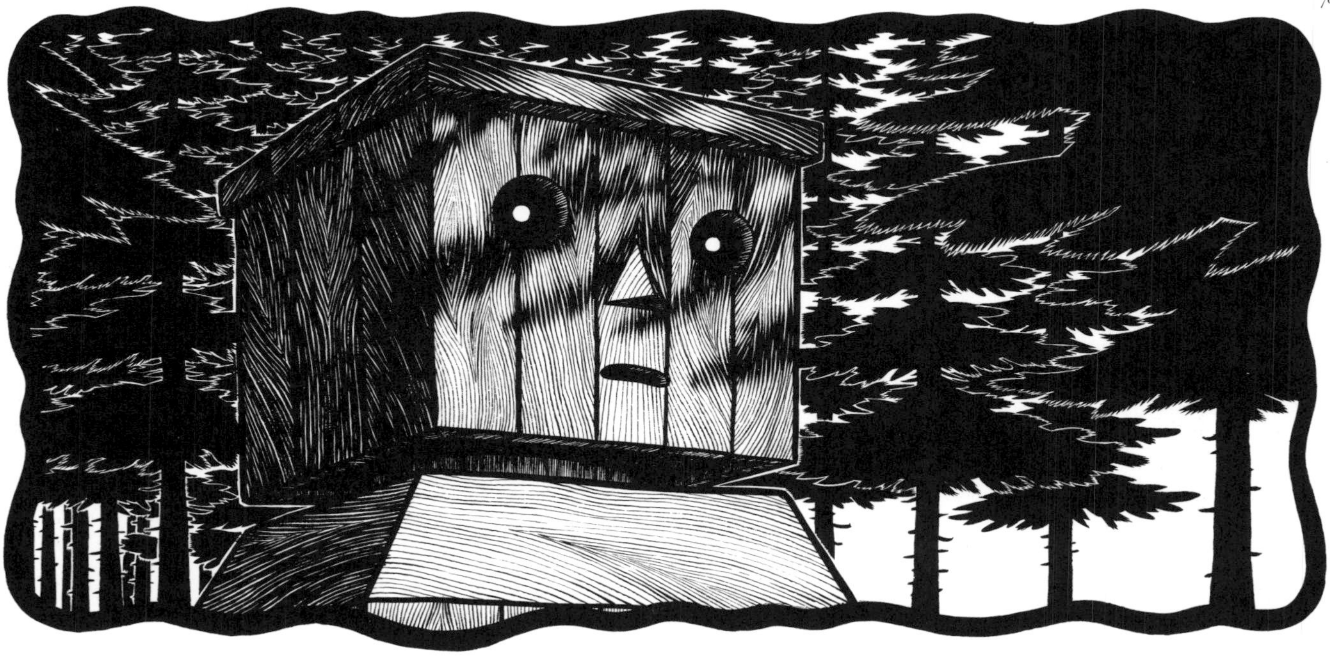

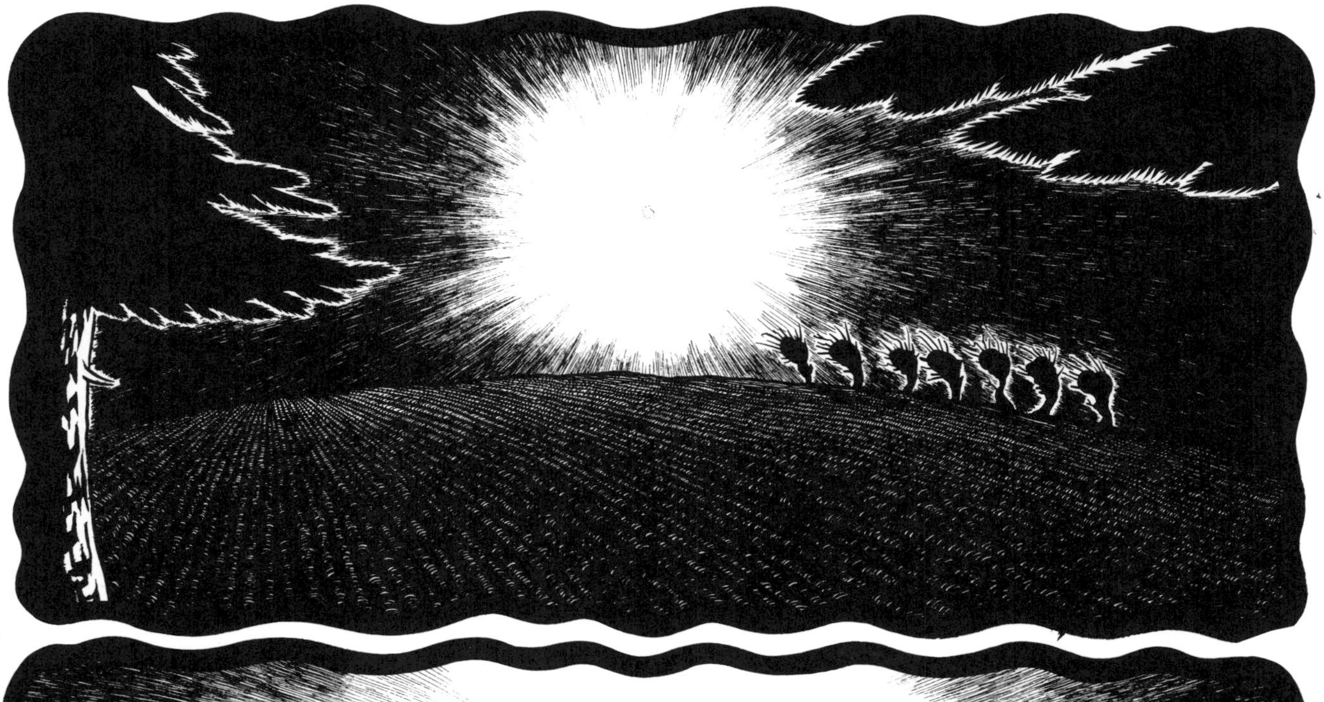

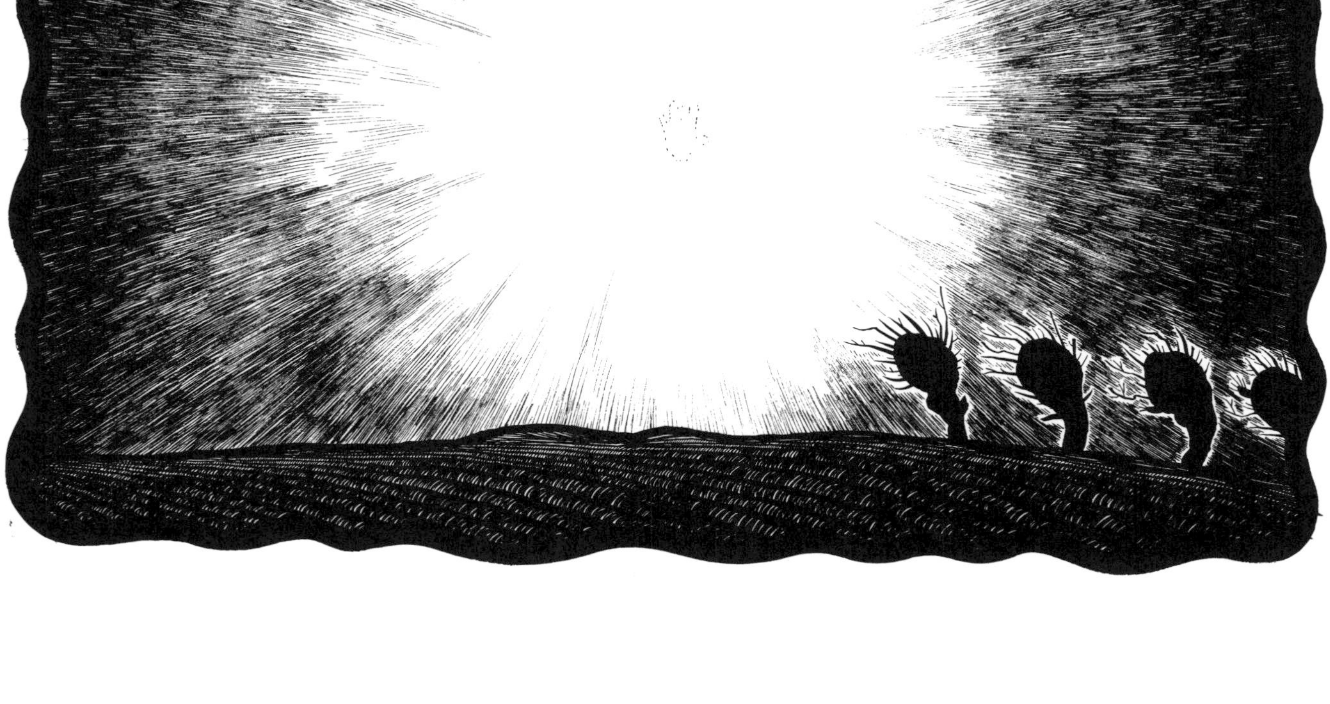

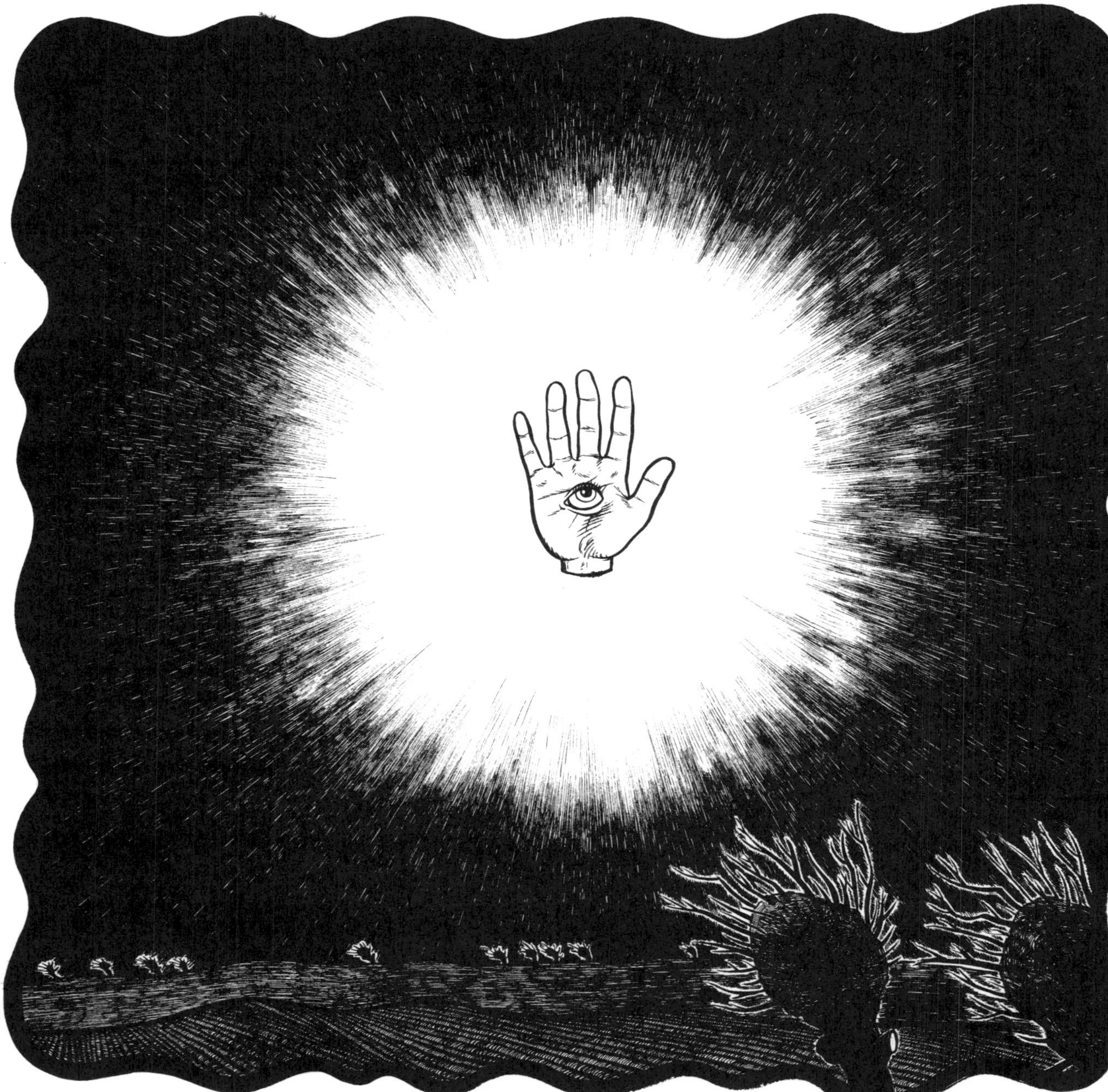

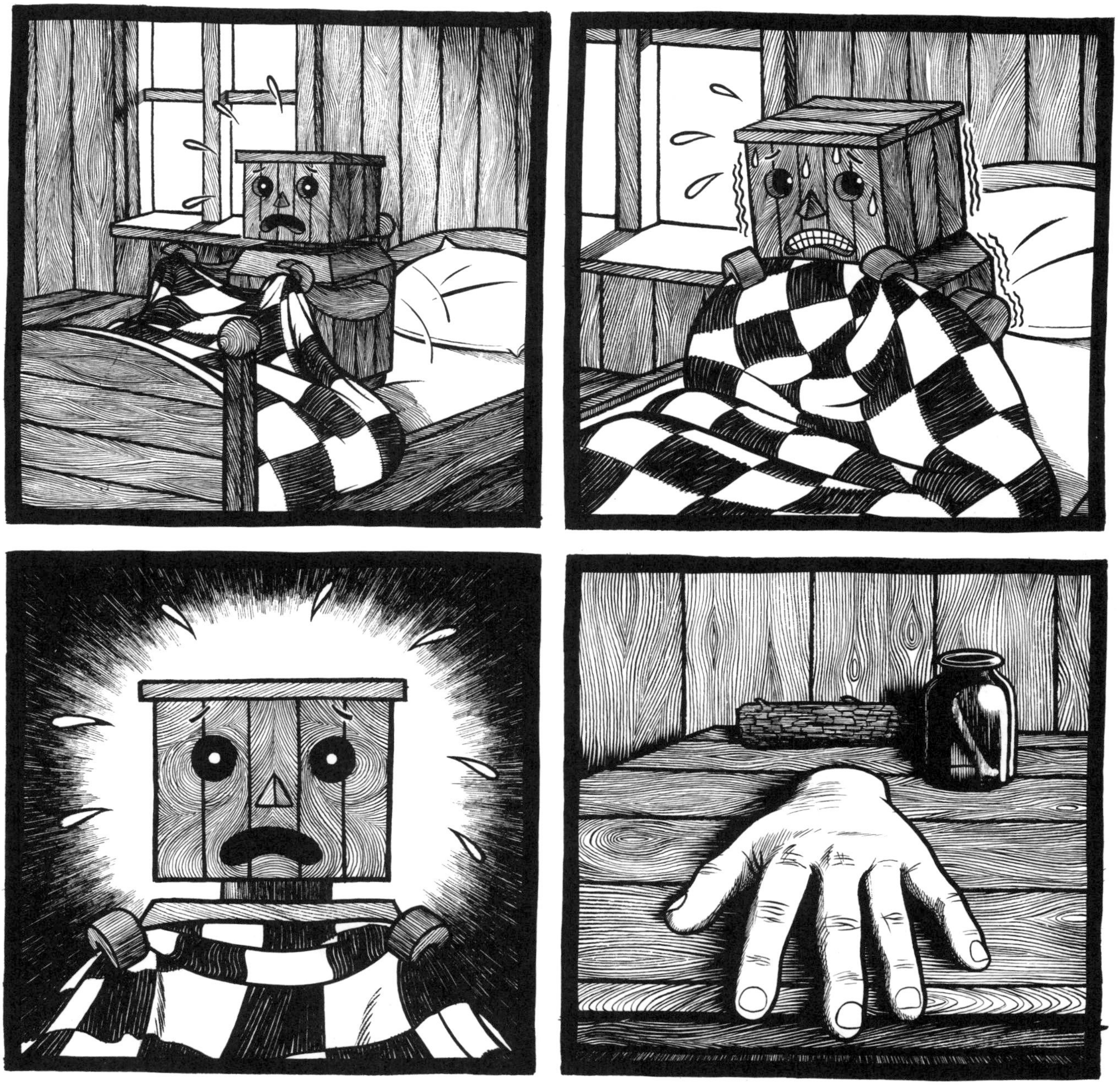

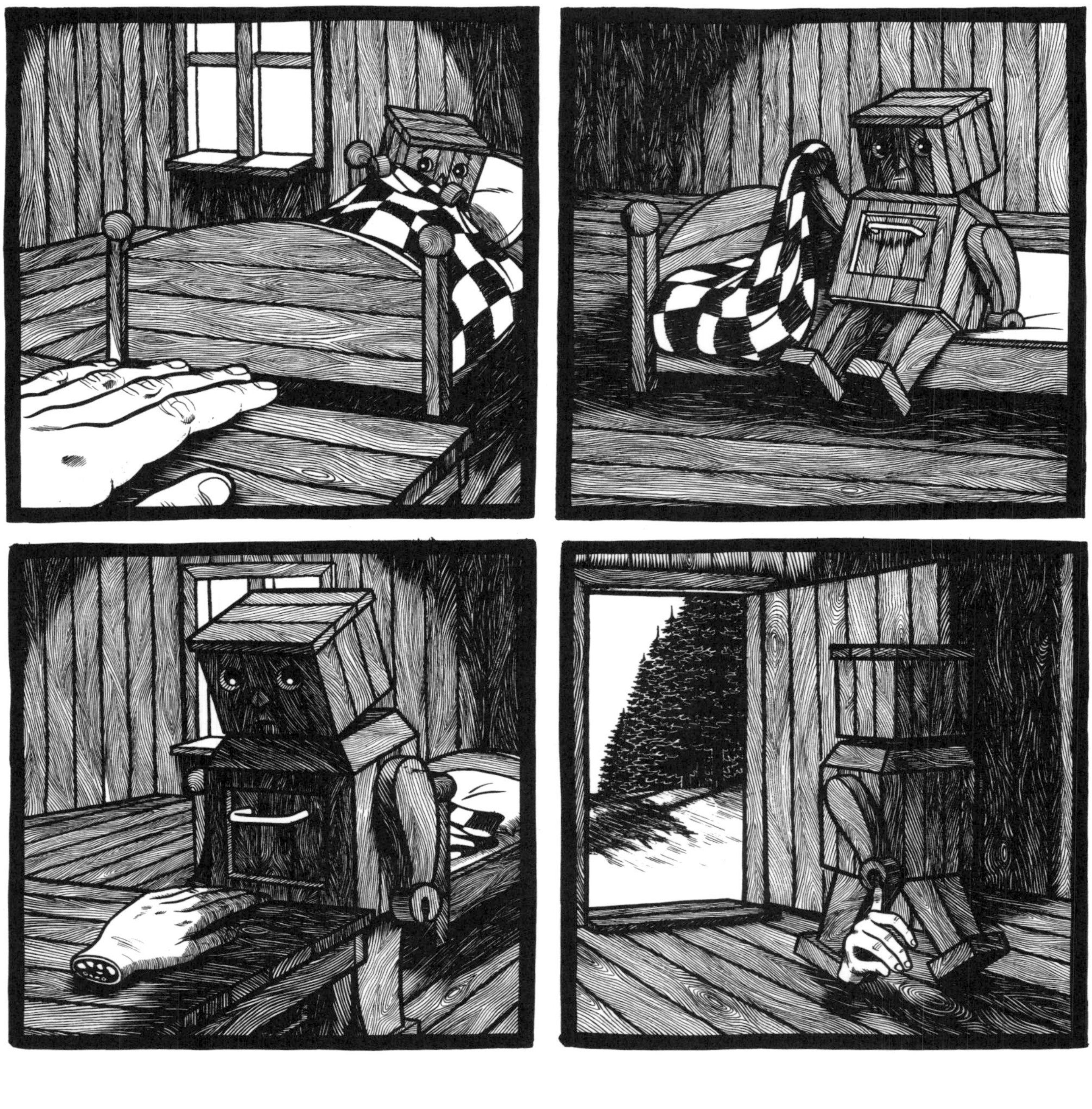

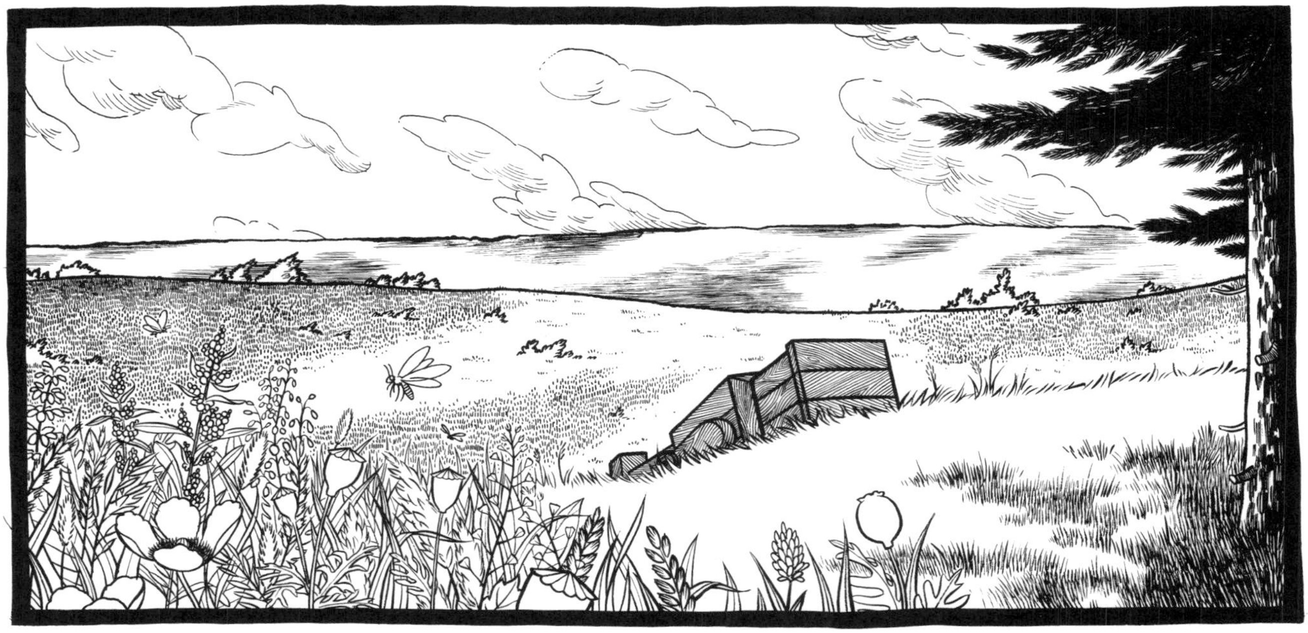

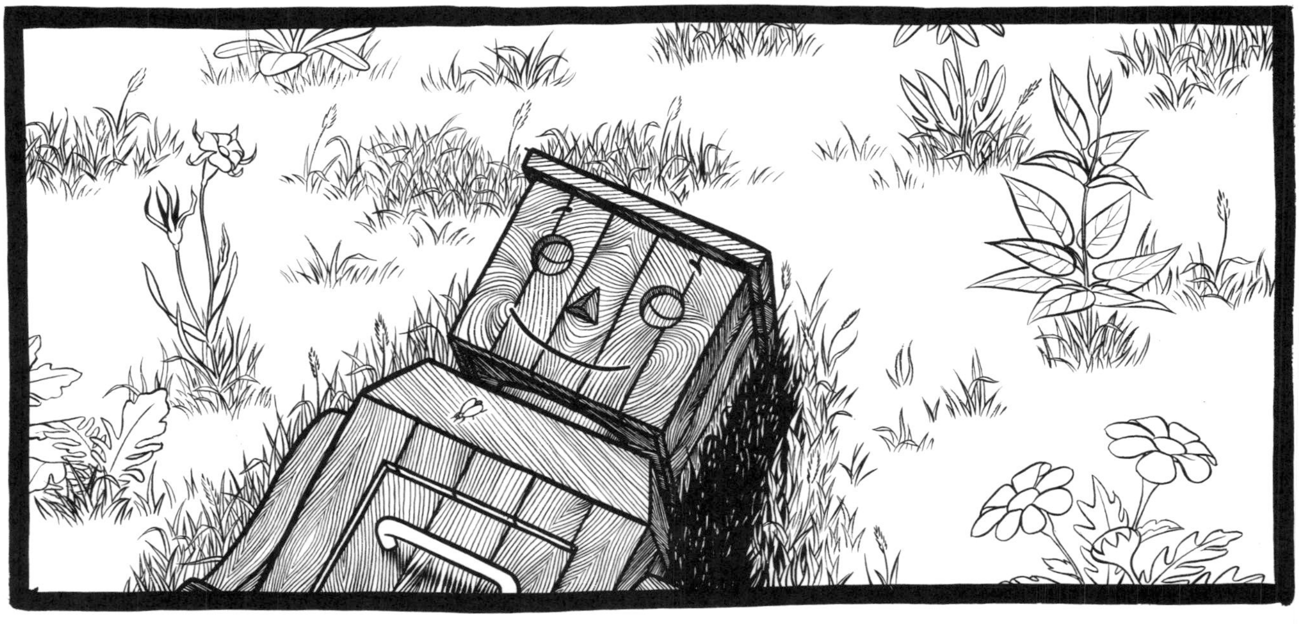

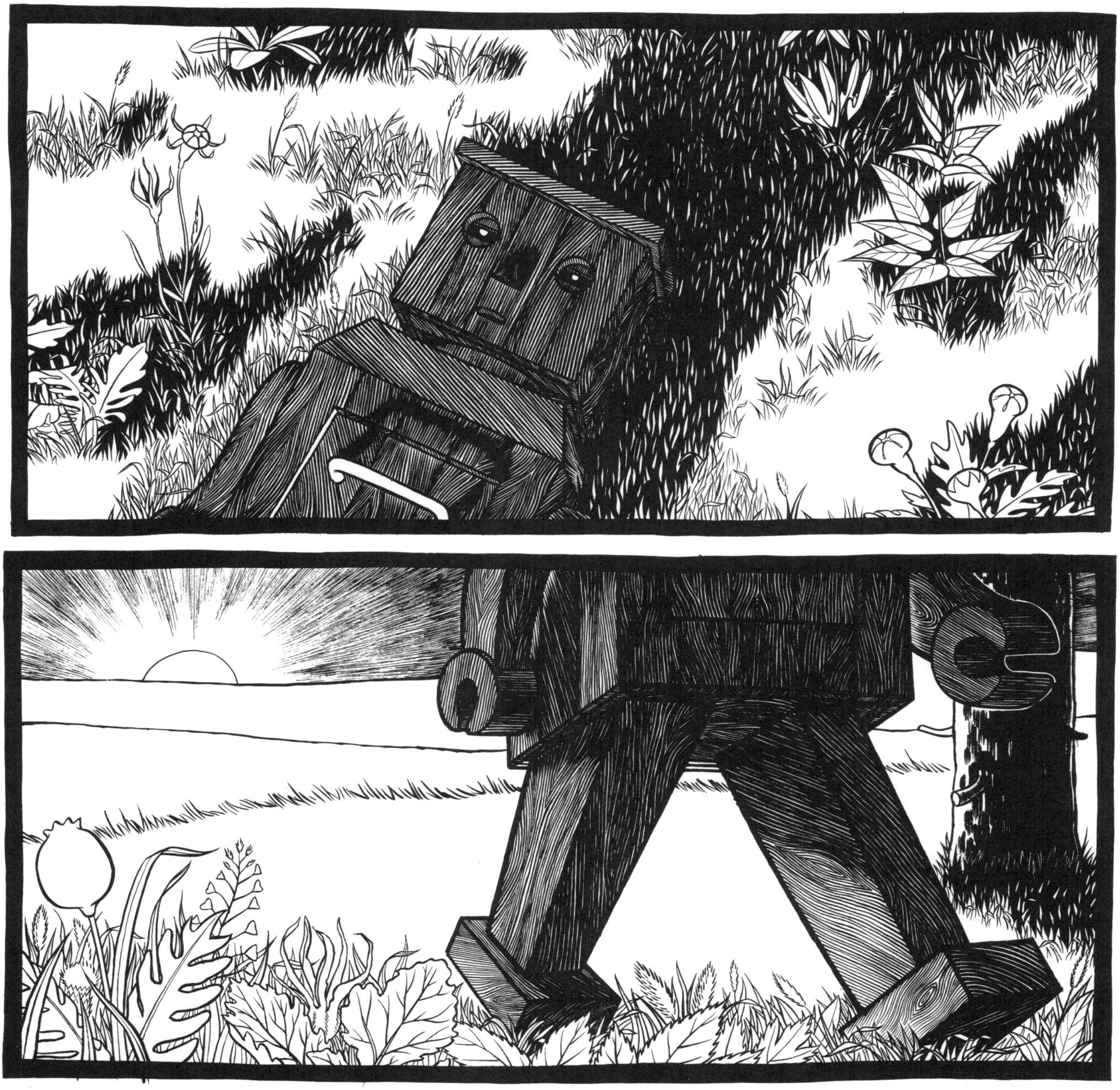

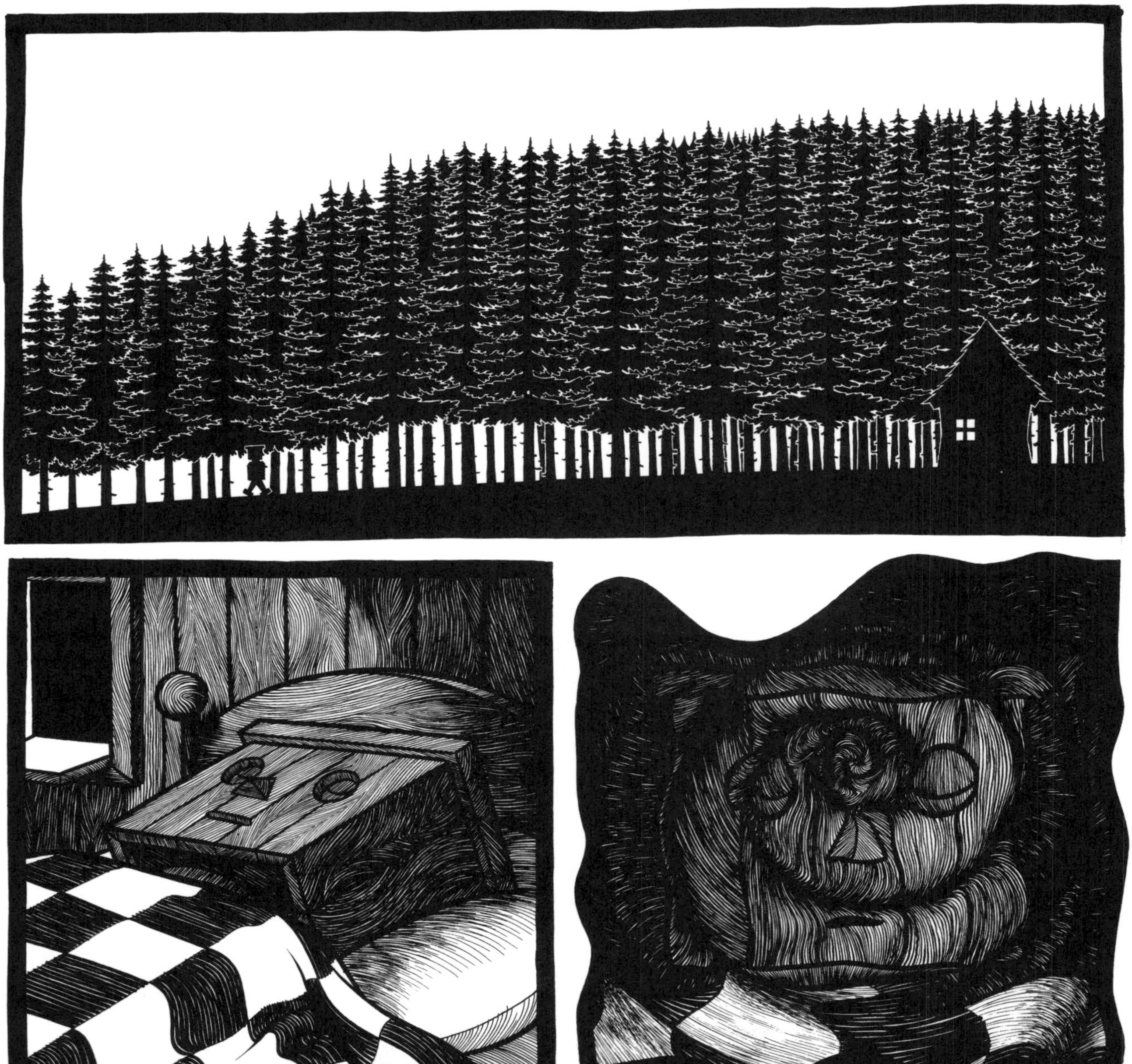

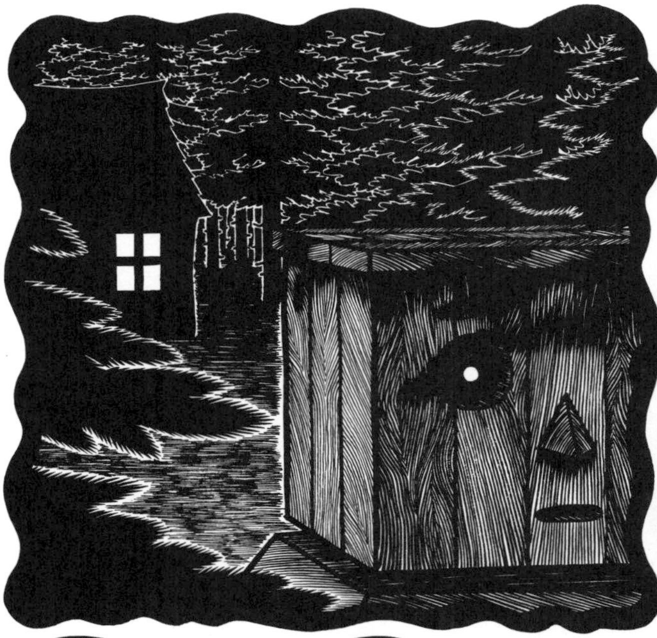

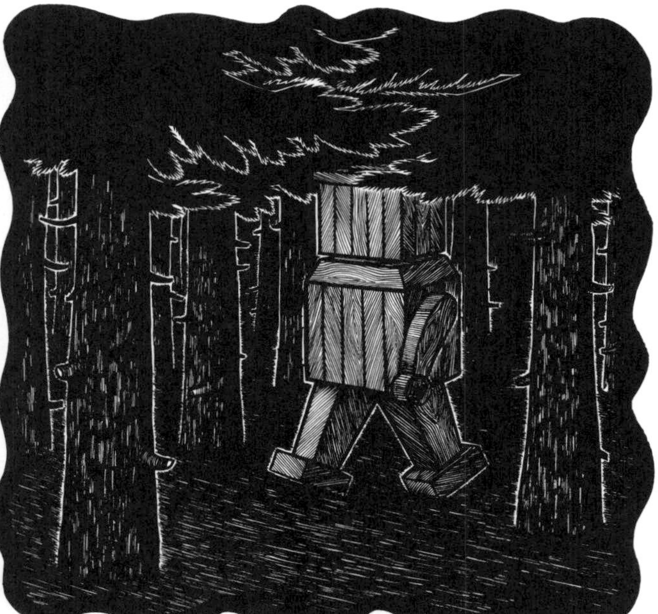

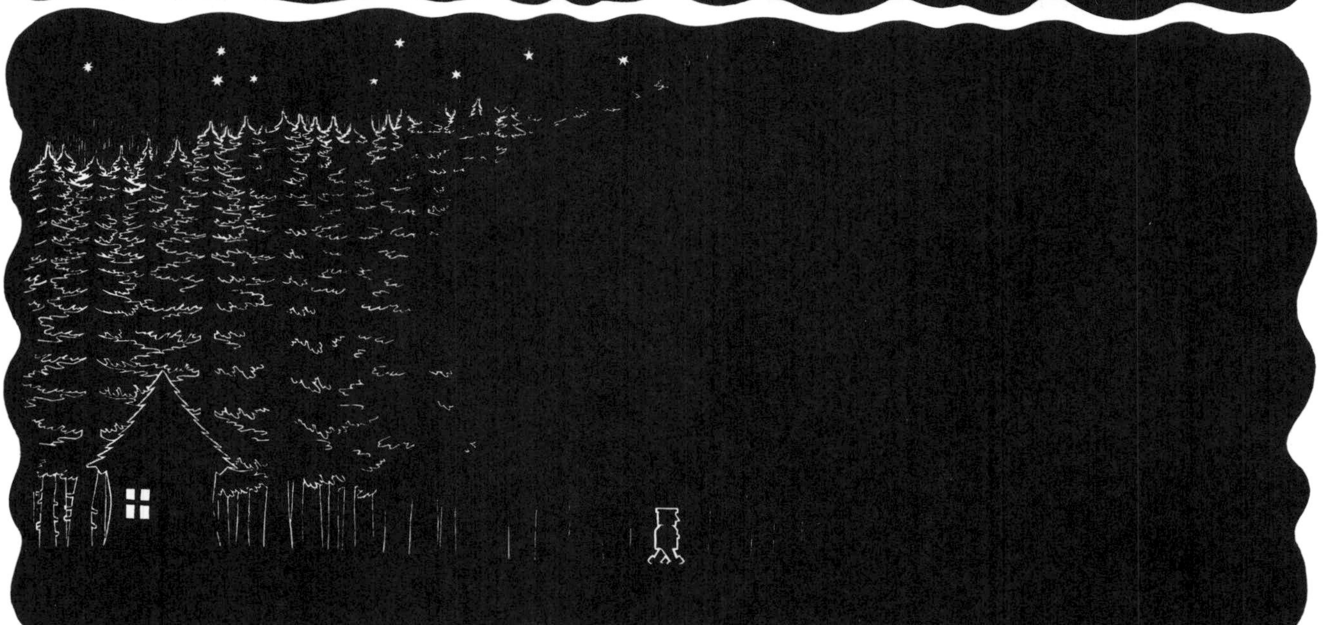

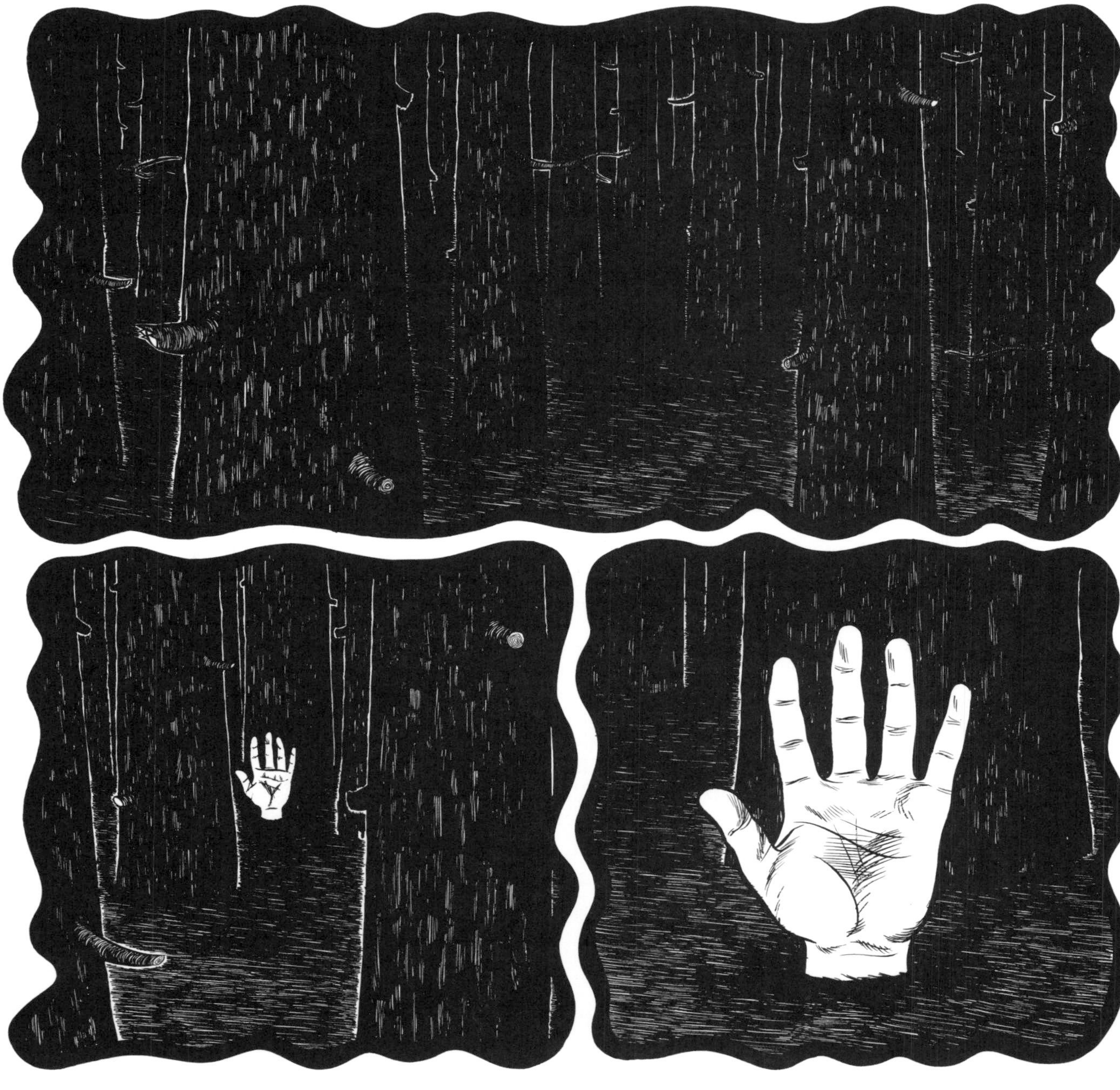

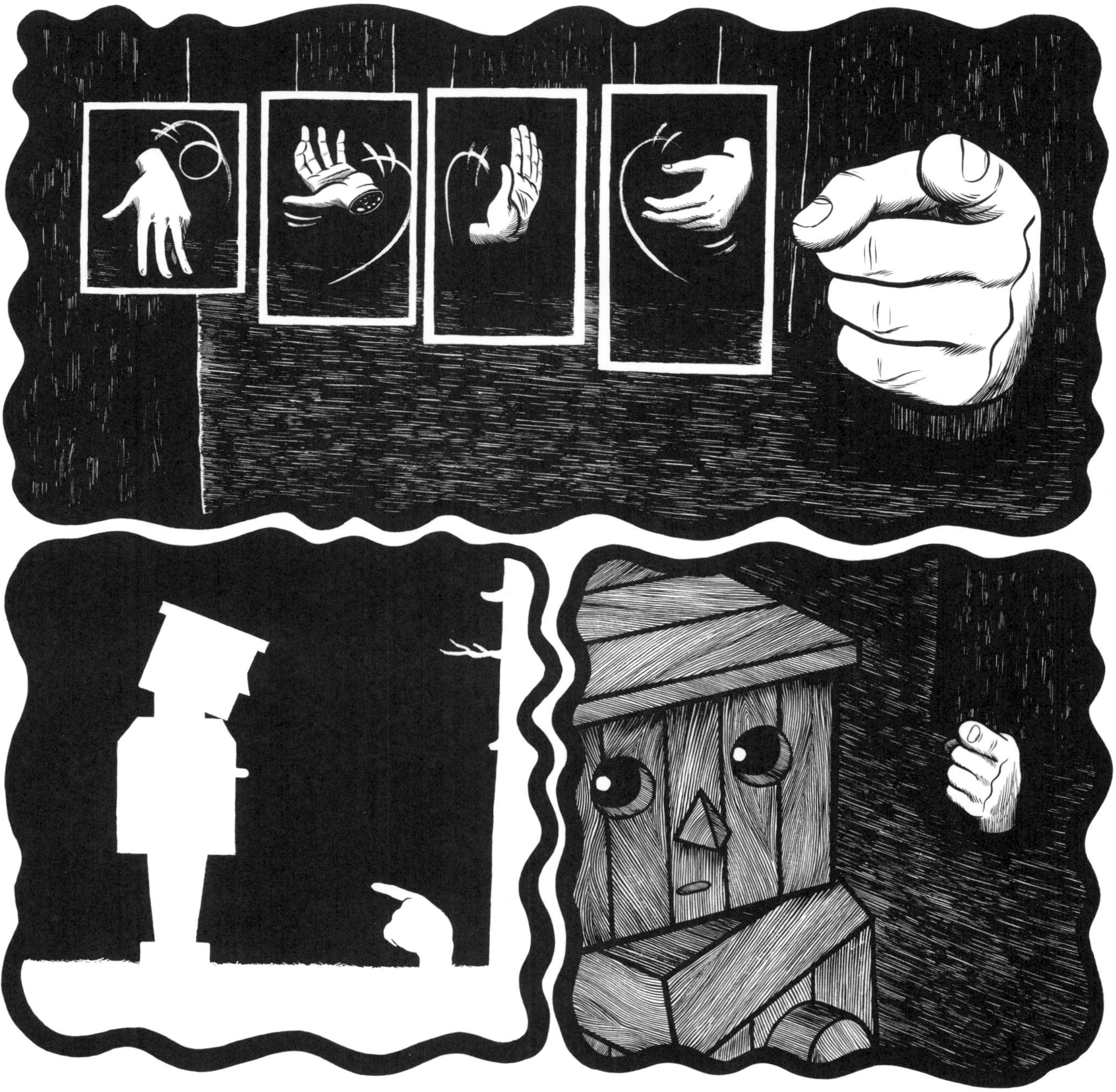

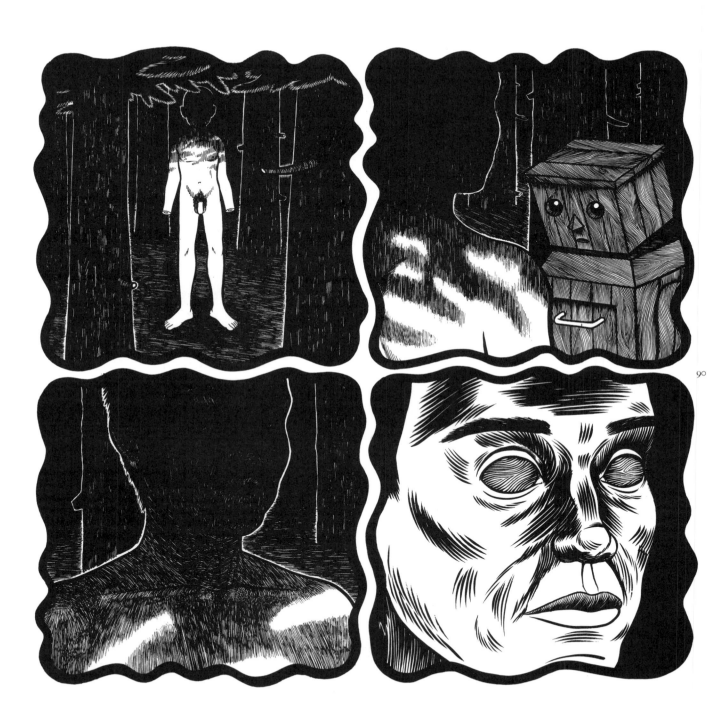

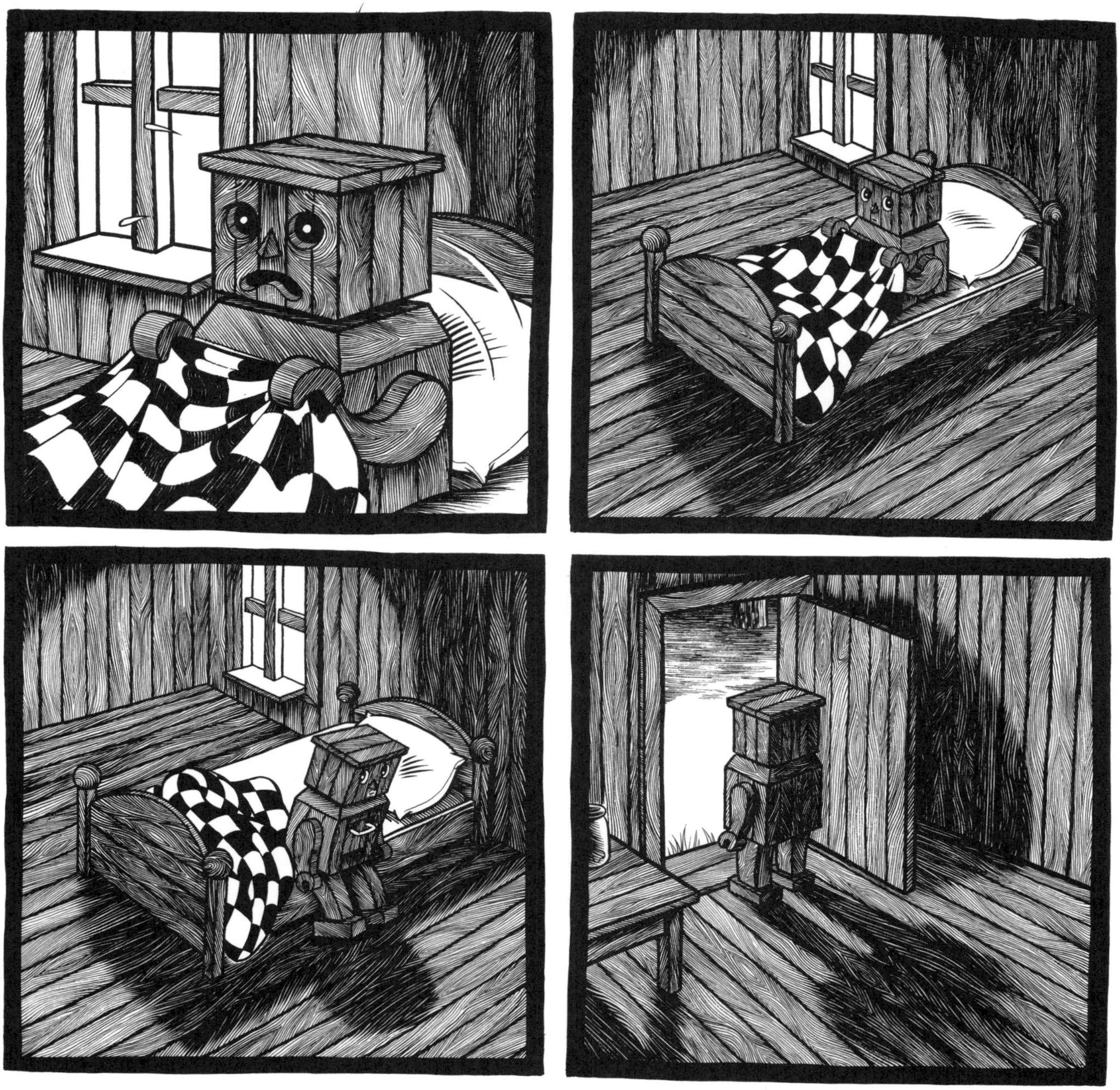

The morning sun had begun to penetrate the trees of the forest...

Now that I was sobering up, little by little I was becoming aware of my sore toe. I sat down at the foot of a tree...

...to take a closer look at it. I wondered why I had left the party without saying good-bye to the girl.

I vaguely recalled that I had blathered on about the fancy shoe store in Monaco that I had visited earlier in the week.

She had not been particularly impressed. My own conviction was that my shoes were among the finest to be found on the entire Riviera.

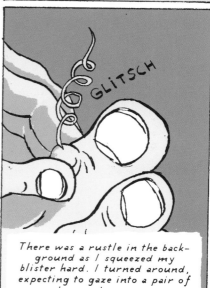

GLITSCH

There was a rustle in the background as I squeezed my blister hard. I turned around, expecting to gaze into a pair of brown doe eyes...

Instead it was an old man rummaging through a garbage can — one of those always asking for change. So I quickly asked him:

Excuse me, would you have two francs?

"Since when is it the job of old men to su-su-support young people?"

he remarked, surly, and grumbled: "If I had had t-t-two francs in my pockets..."

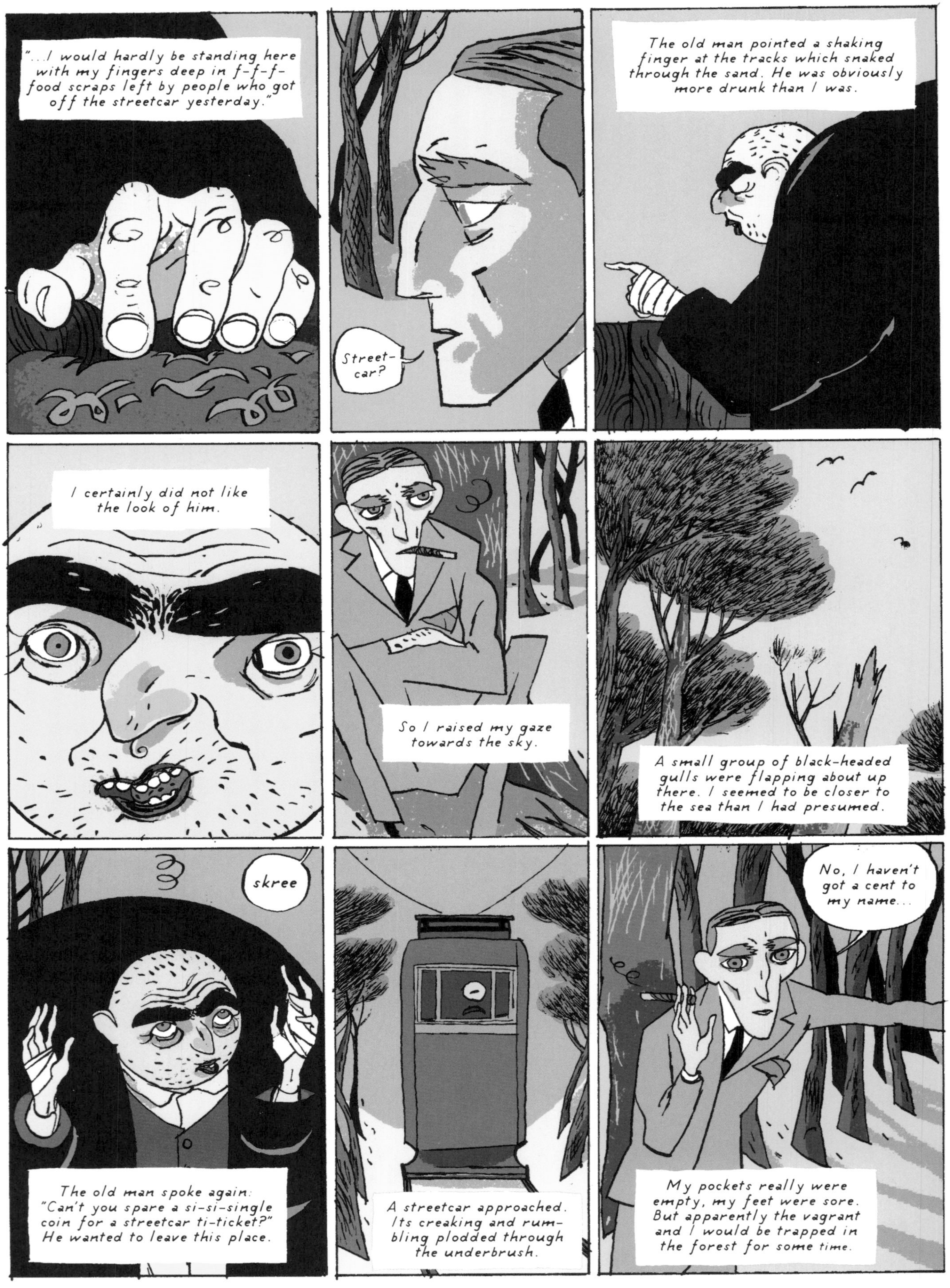
"...I would hardly be standing here with my fingers deep in f-f-f-food scraps left by people who got off the streetcar yesterday."
Street-car?
The old man pointed a shaking finger at the tracks which snaked through the sand. He was obviously more drunk than I was.
I certainly did not like the look of him.
So I raised my gaze towards the sky.
A small group of black-headed gulls were flapping about up there. I seemed to be closer to the sea than I had presumed.
skree
The old man spoke again: "Can't you spare a si-si-single coin for a streetcar ti-ticket?" He wanted to leave this place.
A streetcar approached. Its creaking and rum-bling plodded through the underbrush.
No, I haven't got a cent to my name...
My pockets really were empty, my feet were sore. But apparently the vagrant and I would be trapped in the forest for some time.

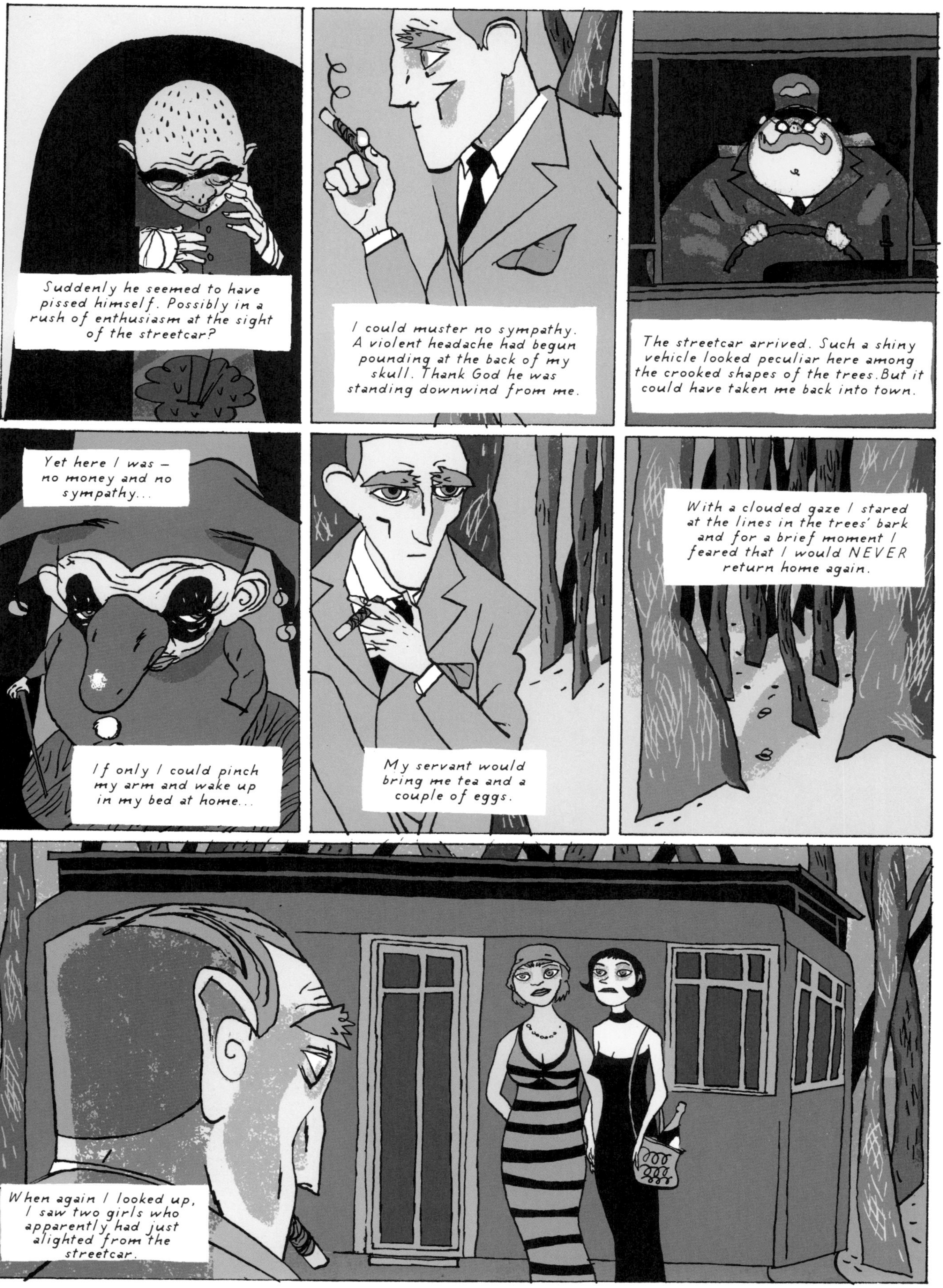
Suddenly he seemed to have pissed himself. Possibly in a rush of enthusiasm at the sight of the streetcar?
I could muster no sympathy. A violent headache had begun pounding at the back of my skull. Thank God he was standing downwind from me.
The streetcar arrived. Such a shiny vehicle looked peculiar here among the crooked shapes of the trees. But it could have taken me back into town.
Yet here I was — no money and no sympathy...
If only I could pinch my arm and wake up in my bed at home...
My servant would bring me tea and a couple of eggs.
With a clouded gaze I stared at the lines in the trees' bark and for a brief moment I feared that I would NEVER return home again.
When again I looked up, I saw two girls who apparently had just alighted from the streetcar.

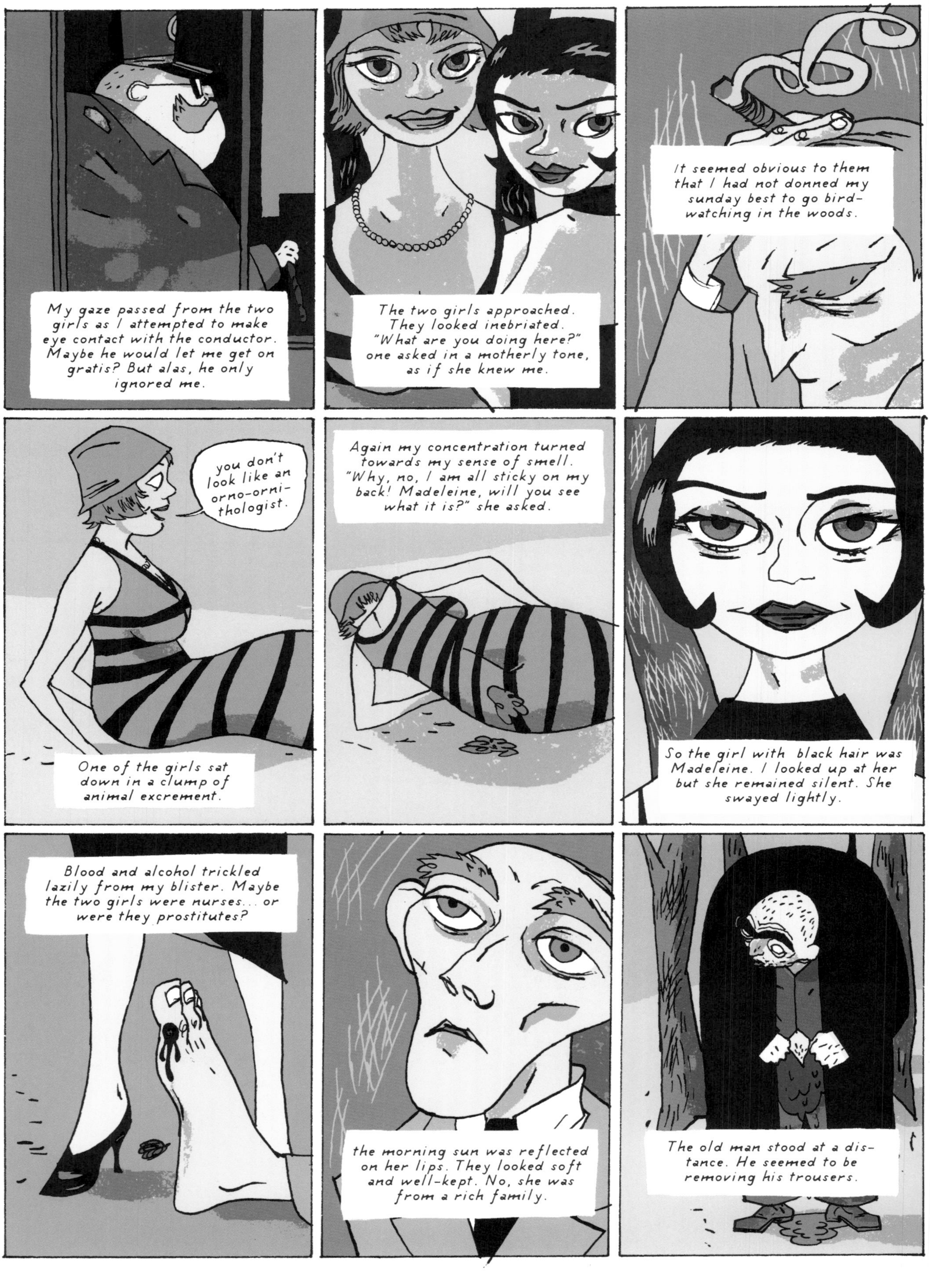
My gaze passed from the two girls as I attempted to make eye contact with the conductor. Maybe he would let me get on gratis? But alas, he only ignored me.
The two girls approached. They looked inebriated. "What are you doing here?" one asked in a motherly tone, as if she knew me.
It seemed obvious to them that I had not donned my sunday best to go bird-watching in the woods.
you don't look like an orno-orni-thologist.
One of the girls sat down in a clump of animal excrement.
Again my concentration turned towards my sense of smell. "Why, no, I am all sticky on my back! Madeleine, will you see what it is?" she asked.
So the girl with black hair was Madeleine. I looked up at her but she remained silent. She swayed lightly.
Blood and alcohol trickled lazily from my blister. Maybe the two girls were nurses... or were they prostitutes?
the morning sun was reflected on her lips. They looked soft and well-kept. No, she was from a rich family.
The old man stood at a distance. He seemed to be removing his trousers.

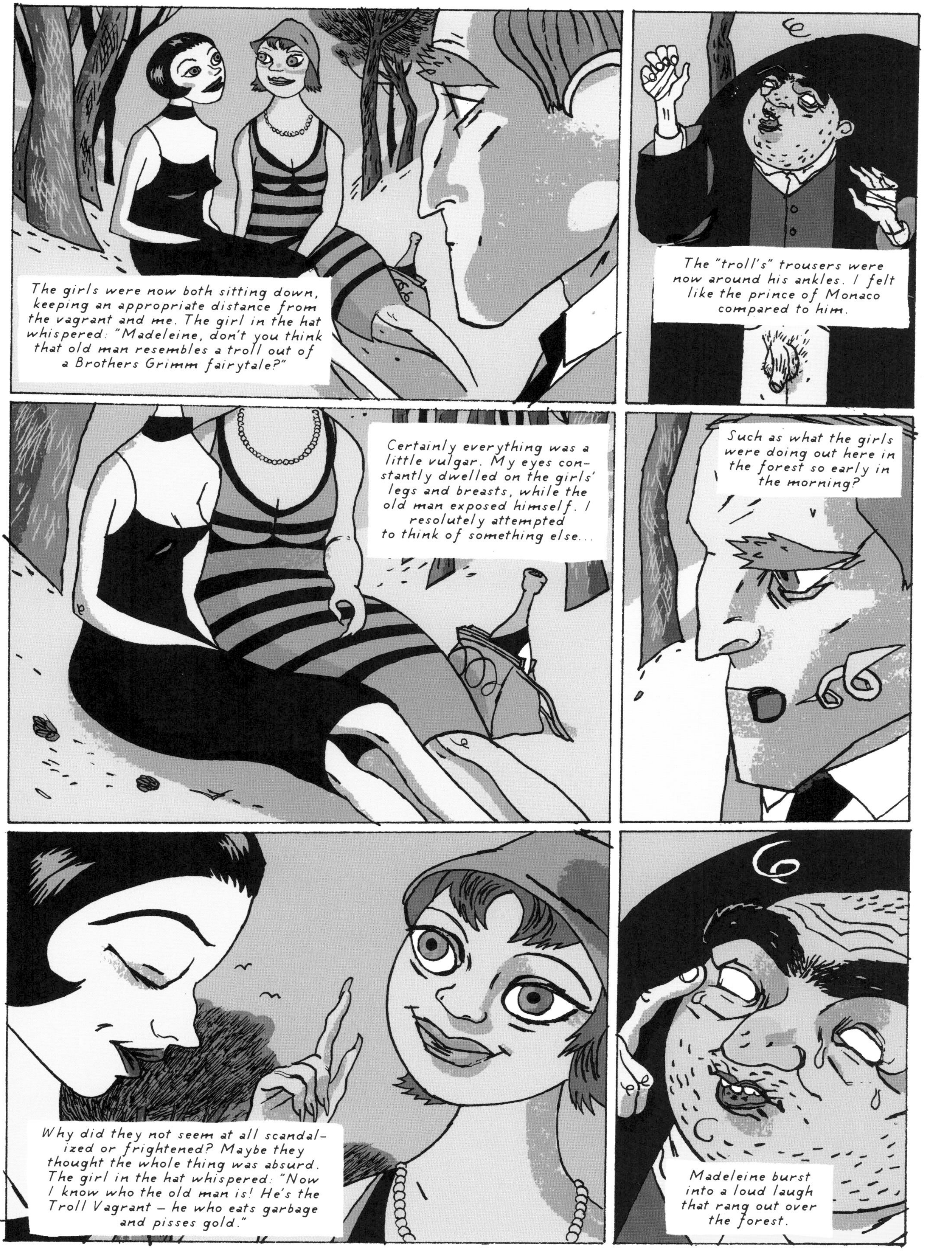
The girls were now both sitting down, keeping an appropriate distance from the vagrant and me. The girl in the hat whispered: "Madeleine, don't you think that old man resembles a troll out of a Brothers Grimm fairytale?"
The "troll's" trousers were now around his ankles. I felt like the prince of Monaco compared to him.
Certainly everything was a little vulgar. My eyes constantly dwelled on the girls' legs and breasts, while the old man exposed himself. I resolutely attempted to think of something else...
Such as what the girls were doing out here in the forest so early in the morning?
Why did they not seem at all scandalized or frightened? Maybe they thought the whole thing was absurd. The girl in the hat whispered: "Now I know who the old man is! He's the Troll Vagrant – he who eats garbage and pisses gold."
Madeleine burst into a loud laugh that rang out over the forest.

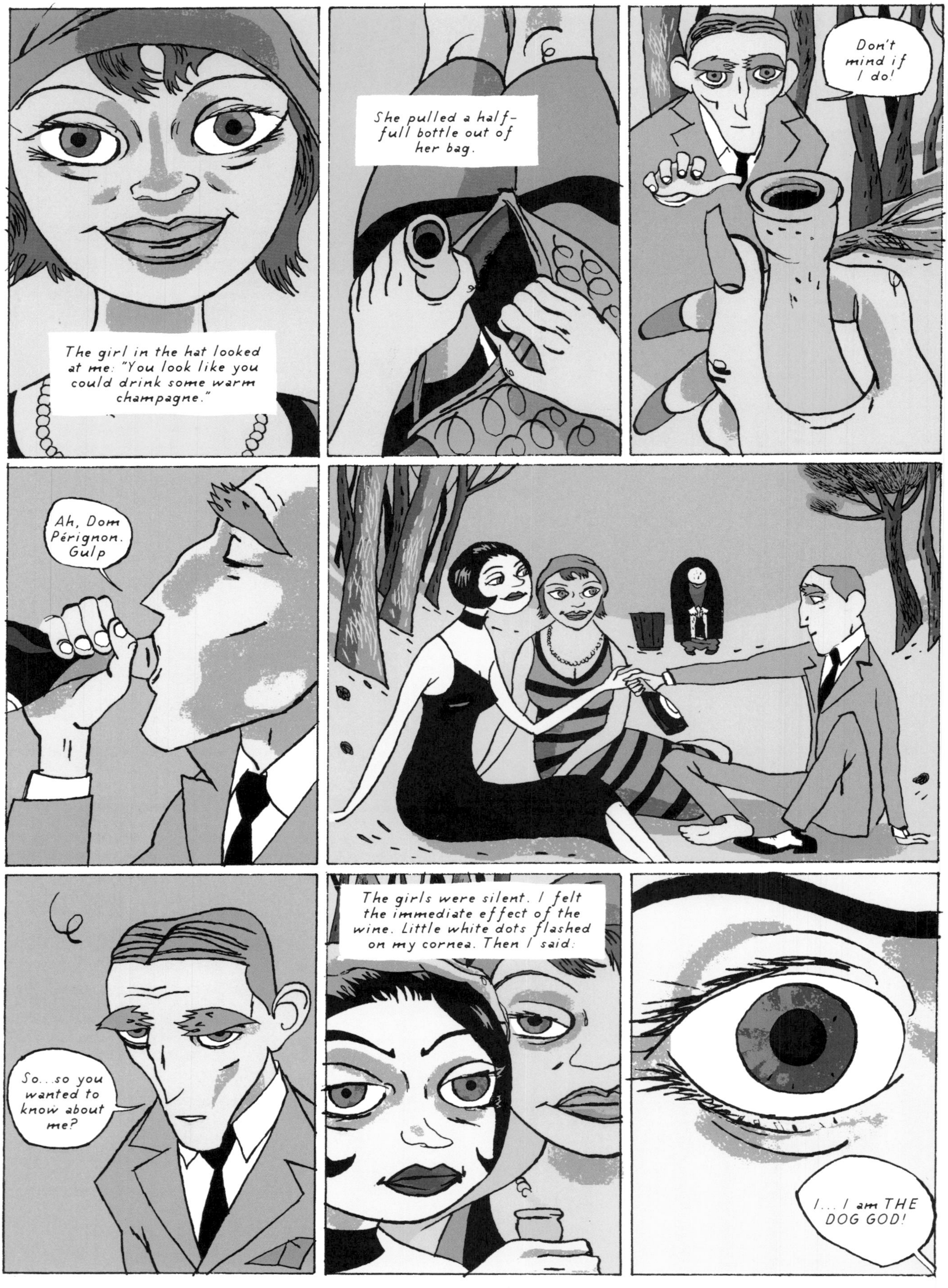

The girl in the hat looked at me: "You look like you could drink some warm champagne."
She pulled a half-full bottle out of her bag.
Don't mind if I do!
Ah, Dom Pérignon. Gulp
So...so you wanted to know about me?
The girls were silent. I felt the immediate effect of the wine. Little white dots flashed on my cornea. Then I said:
I... I am THE DOG GOD!

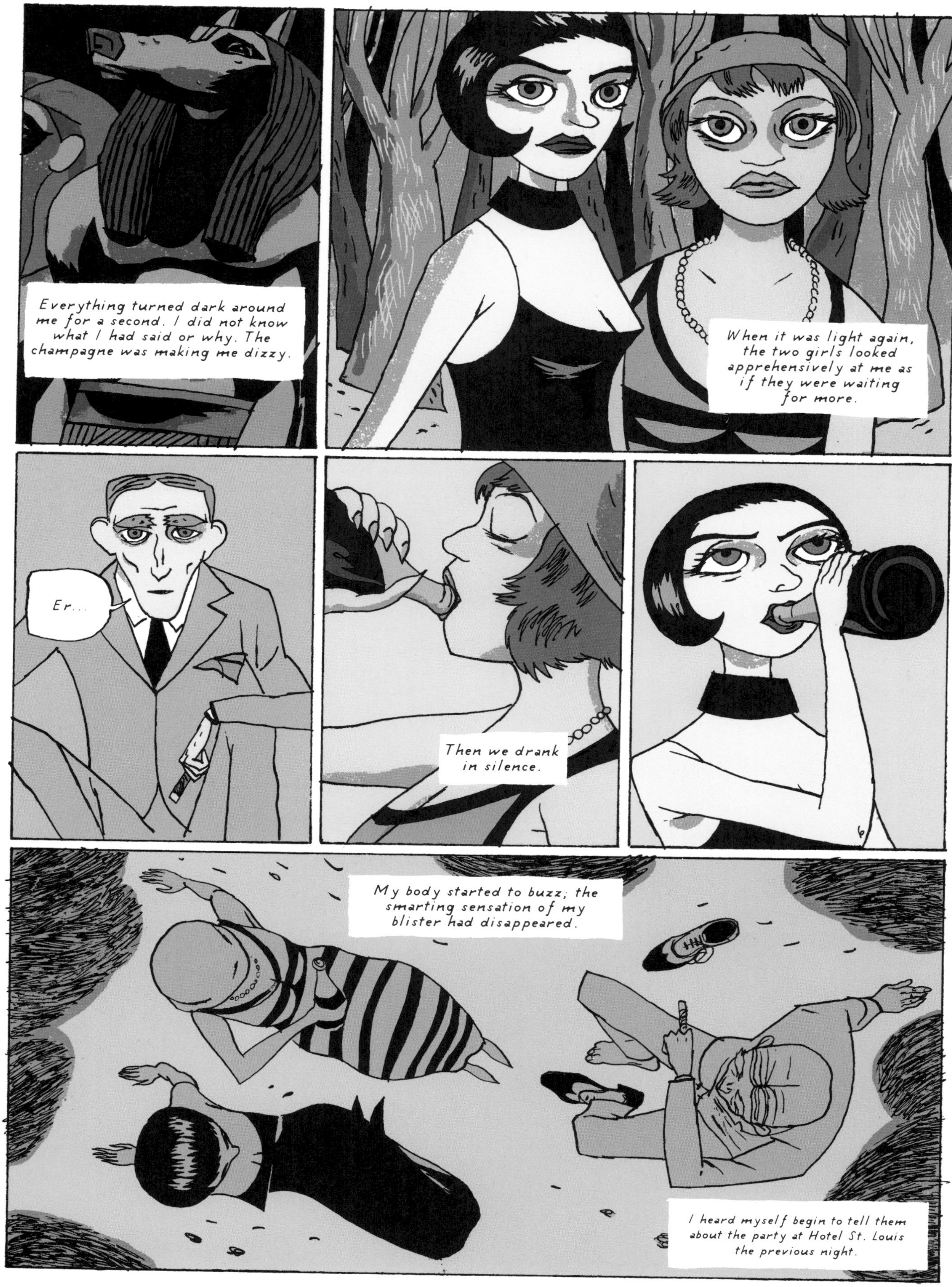

Everything turned dark around me for a second. I did not know what I had said or why. The champagne was making me dizzy.
When it was light again, the two girls looked apprehensively at me as if they were waiting for more.
Er...
Then we drank in silence.
My body started to buzz; the smarting sensation of my blister had disappeared.
I heard myself begin to tell them about the party at Hotel St. Louis the previous night.

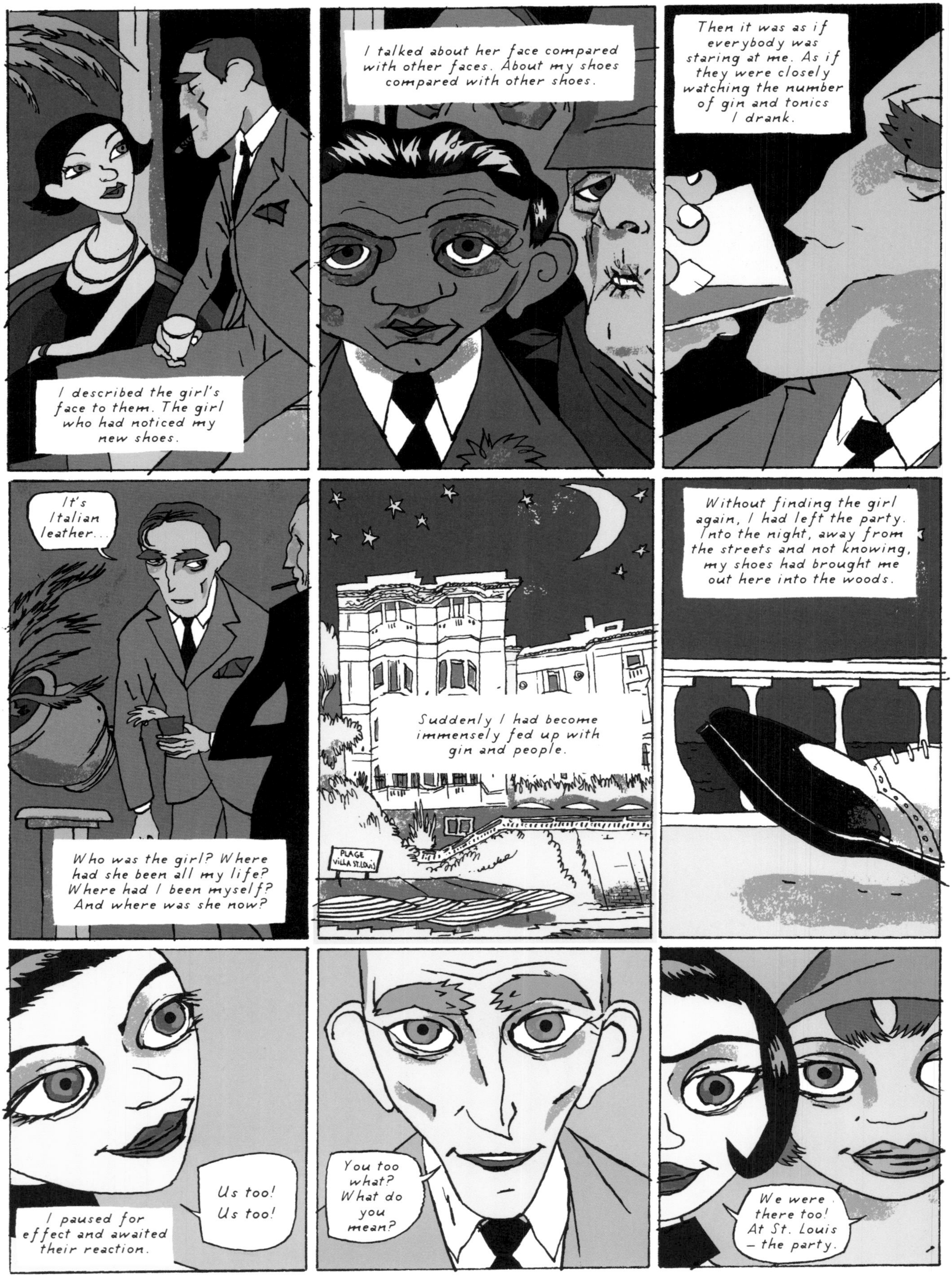
I described the girl's face to them. The girl who had noticed my new shoes.
I talked about her face compared with other faces. About my shoes compared with other shoes.
Then it was as if everybody was staring at me. As if they were closely watching the number of gin and tonics I drank.
It's Italian leather...
Who was the girl? Where had she been all my life? Where had I been myself? And where was she now?
PLAGE VILLA ST. LOUIS
Suddenly I had become immensely fed up with gin and people.
Without finding the girl again, I had left the party. Into the night, away from the streets and not knowing, my shoes had brought me out here into the woods.
I paused for effect and awaited their reaction.
Us too! Us too!
You too what? What do you mean?
We were there too! At St. Louis – the party.

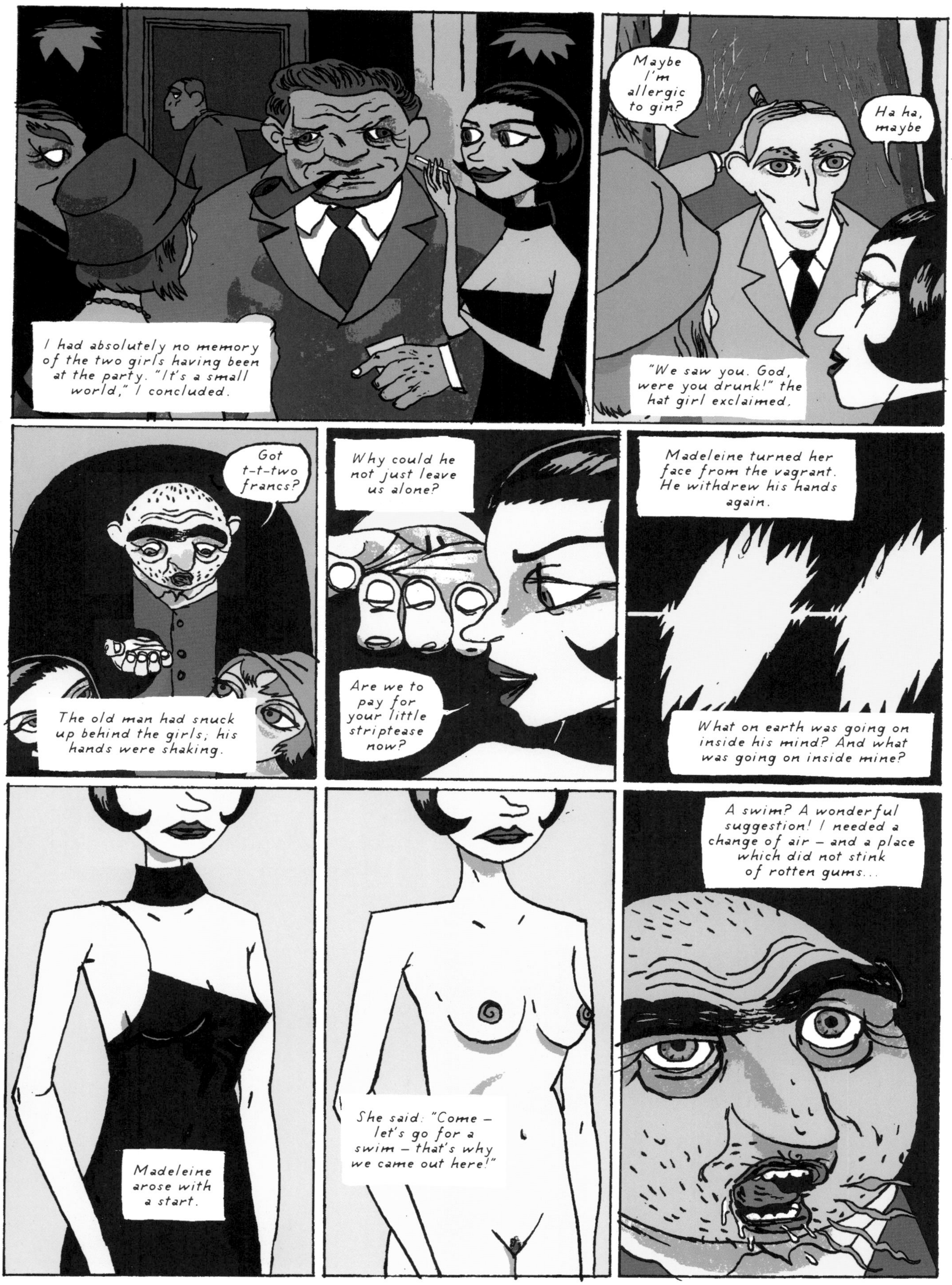
I had absolutely no memory of the two girls having been at the party. "It's a small world," I concluded.
Maybe I'm allergic to gin?
Ha ha, maybe
"We saw you. God, were you drunk!" the hat girl exclaimed.
Got t-t-two francs?
The old man had snuck up behind the girls; his hands were shaking.
Why could he not just leave us alone?
Are we to pay for your little striptease now?
Madeleine turned her face from the vagrant. He withdrew his hands again.
What on earth was going on inside his mind? And what was going on inside mine?
Madeleine arose with a start.
She said: "Come – let's go for a swim – that's why we came out here!"
A swim? A wonderful suggestion! I needed a change of air – and a place which did not stink of rotten gums...

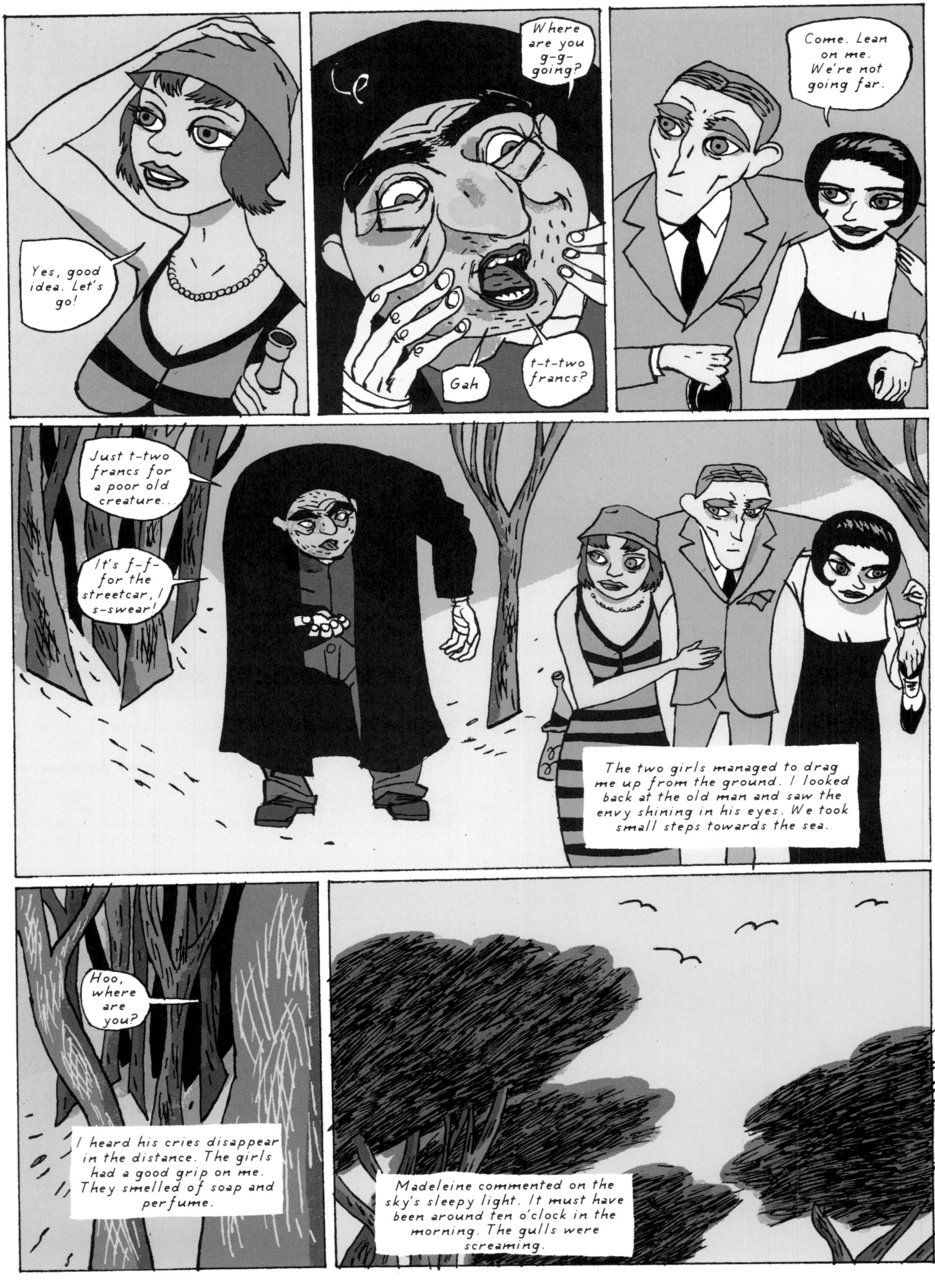
Yes, good idea. Let's go!
Where are you g-g-going?
Gah
t-t-two francs?
Come. Lean on me. We're not going far.
Just t-two francs for a poor old creature...
It's f-f-for the streetcar, I s-swear!
The two girls managed to drag me up from the ground. I looked back at the old man and saw the envy shining in his eyes. We took small steps towards the sea.
Hoo, where are you?
I heard his cries disappear in the distance. The girls had a good grip on me. They smelled of soap and perfume.
Madeleine commented on the sky's sleepy light. It must have been around ten o'clock in the morning. The gulls were screaming.

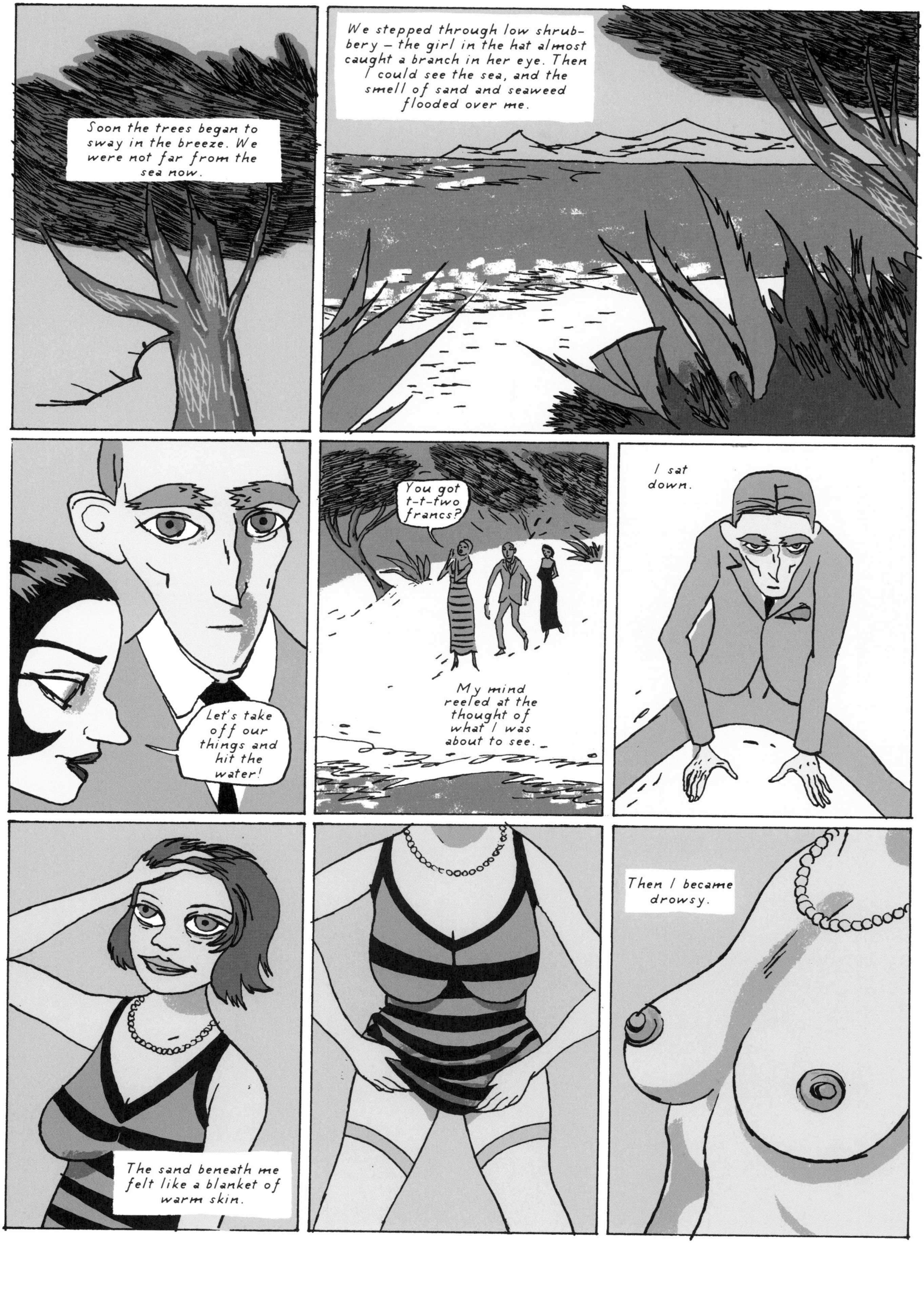

Soon the trees began to sway in the breeze. We were not far from the sea now.
We stepped through low shrubbery – the girl in the hat almost caught a branch in her eye. Then I could see the sea, and the smell of sand and seaweed flooded over me.
Let's take off our things and hit the water!
You got t-t-two francs?
My mind reeled at the thought of what I was about to see.
I sat down.
The sand beneath me felt like a blanket of warm skin.
Then I became drowsy.

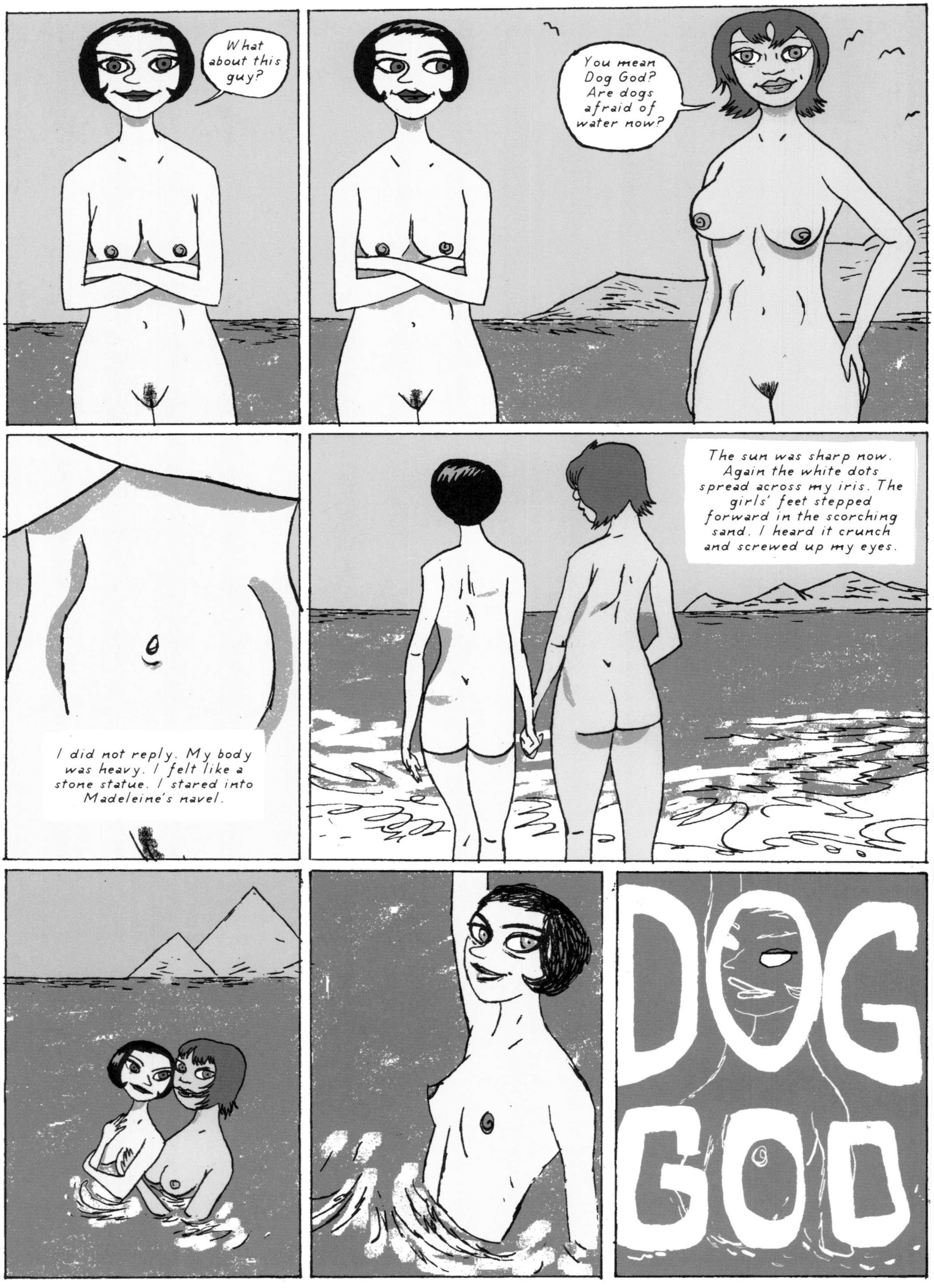
What about this guy?
You mean Dog God? Are dogs afraid of water now?
I did not reply. My body was heavy. I felt like a stone statue. I stared into Madeleine's navel.
The sun was sharp now. Again the white dots spread across my iris. The girls' feet stepped forward in the scorching sand. I heard it crunch and screwed up my eyes.
DOG GOD

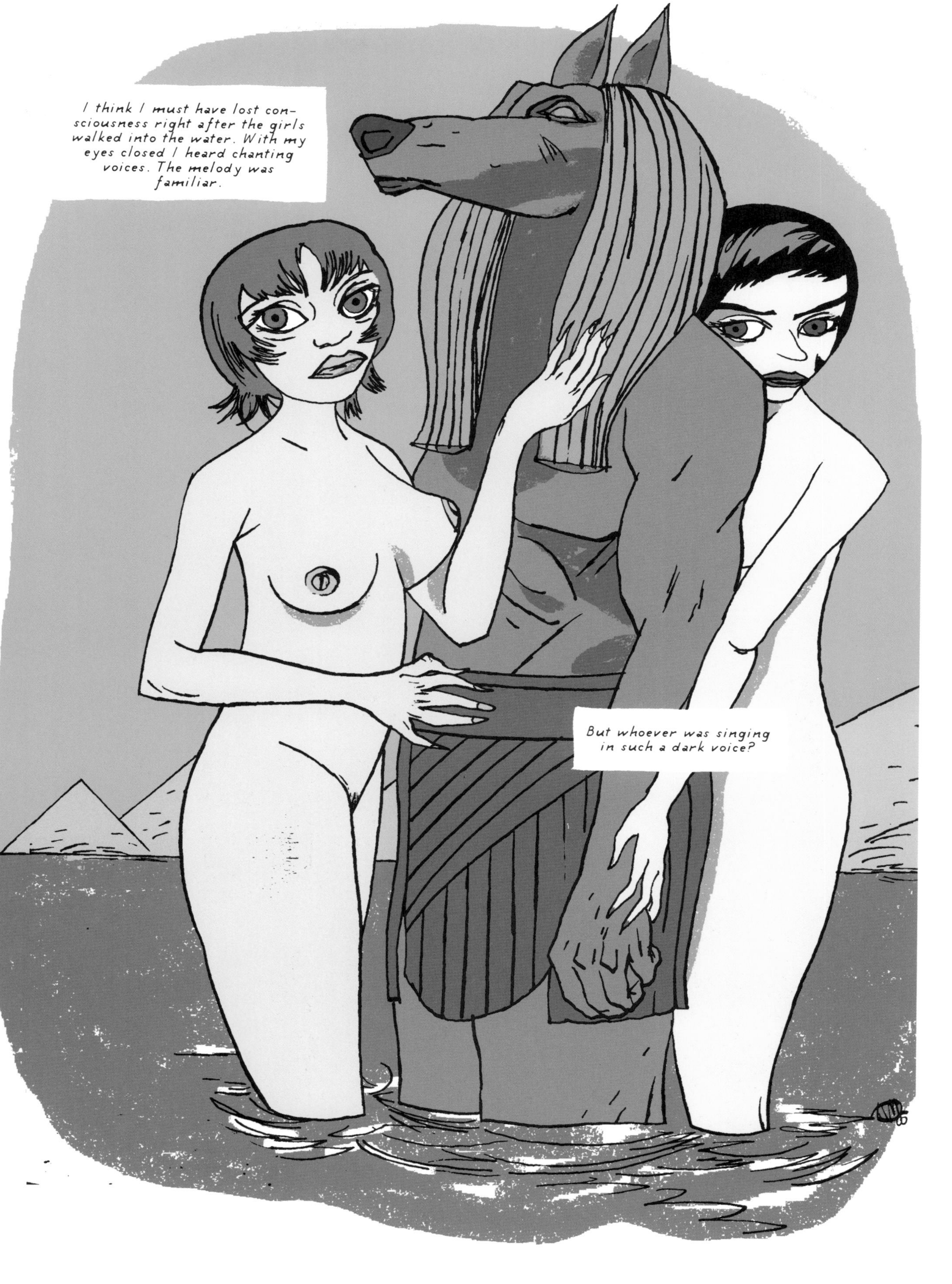
I think I must have lost consciousness right after the girls walked into the water. With my eyes closed I heard chanting voices. The melody was familiar.
But whoever was singing in such a dark voice?

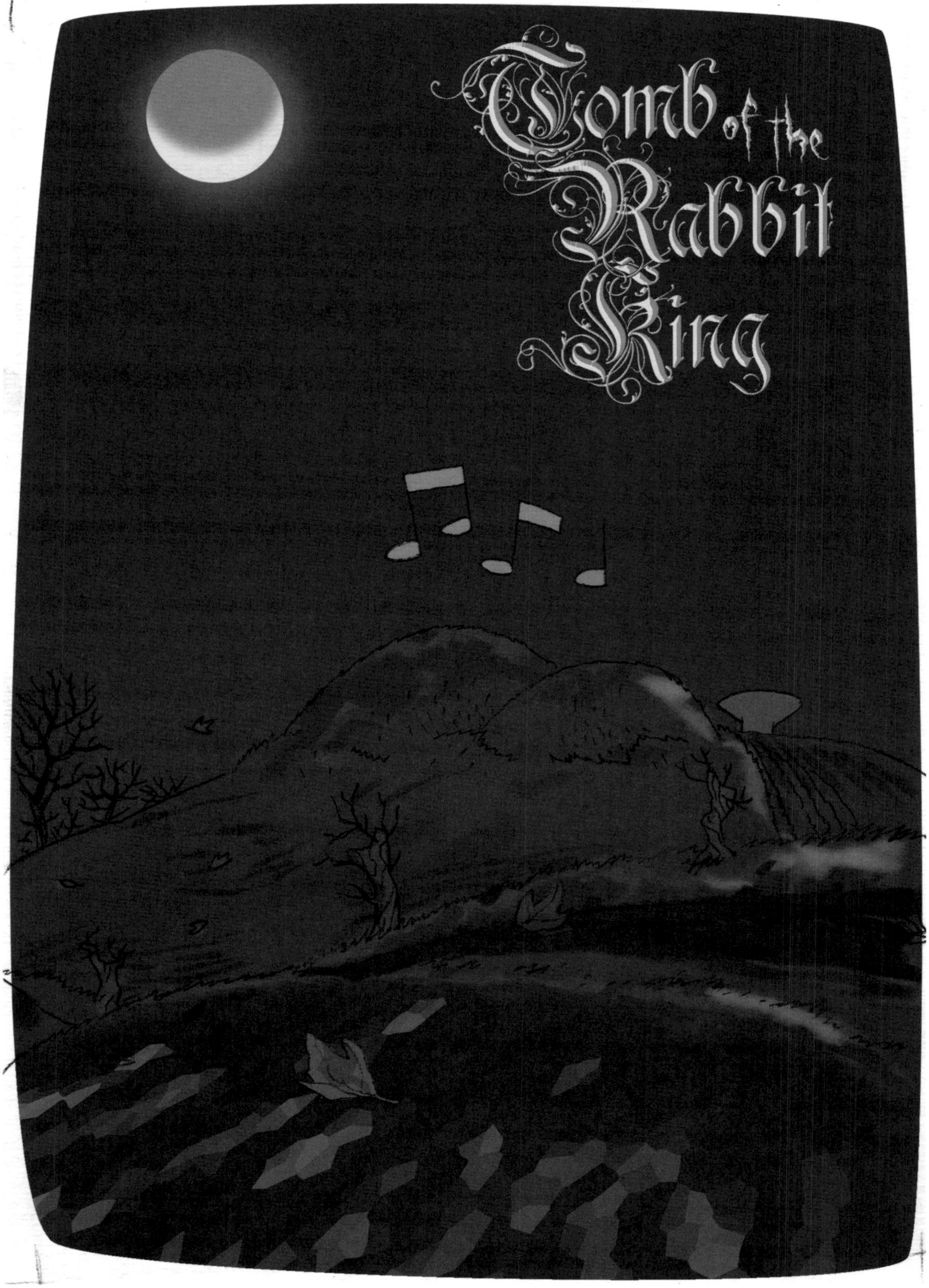
Tomb of the Rabbit King

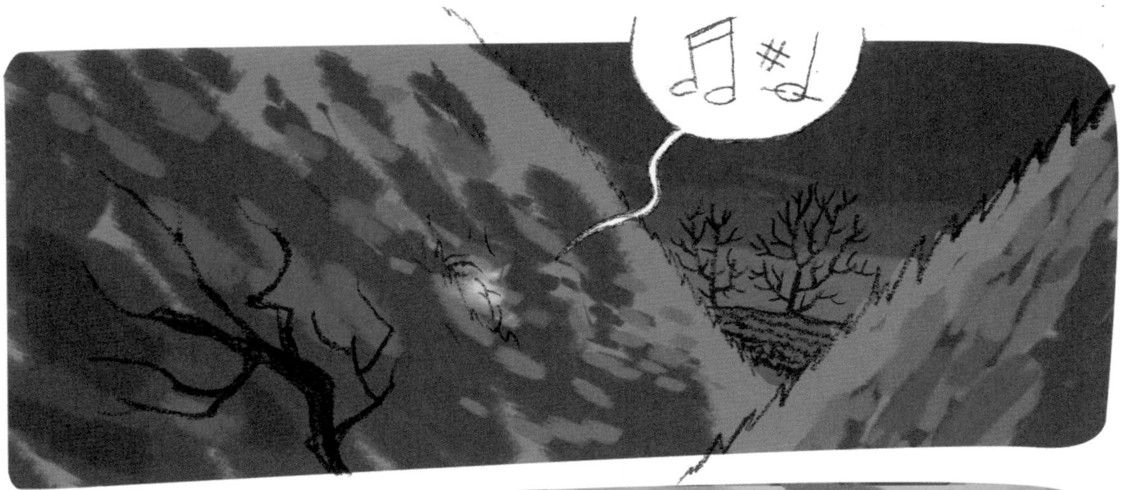

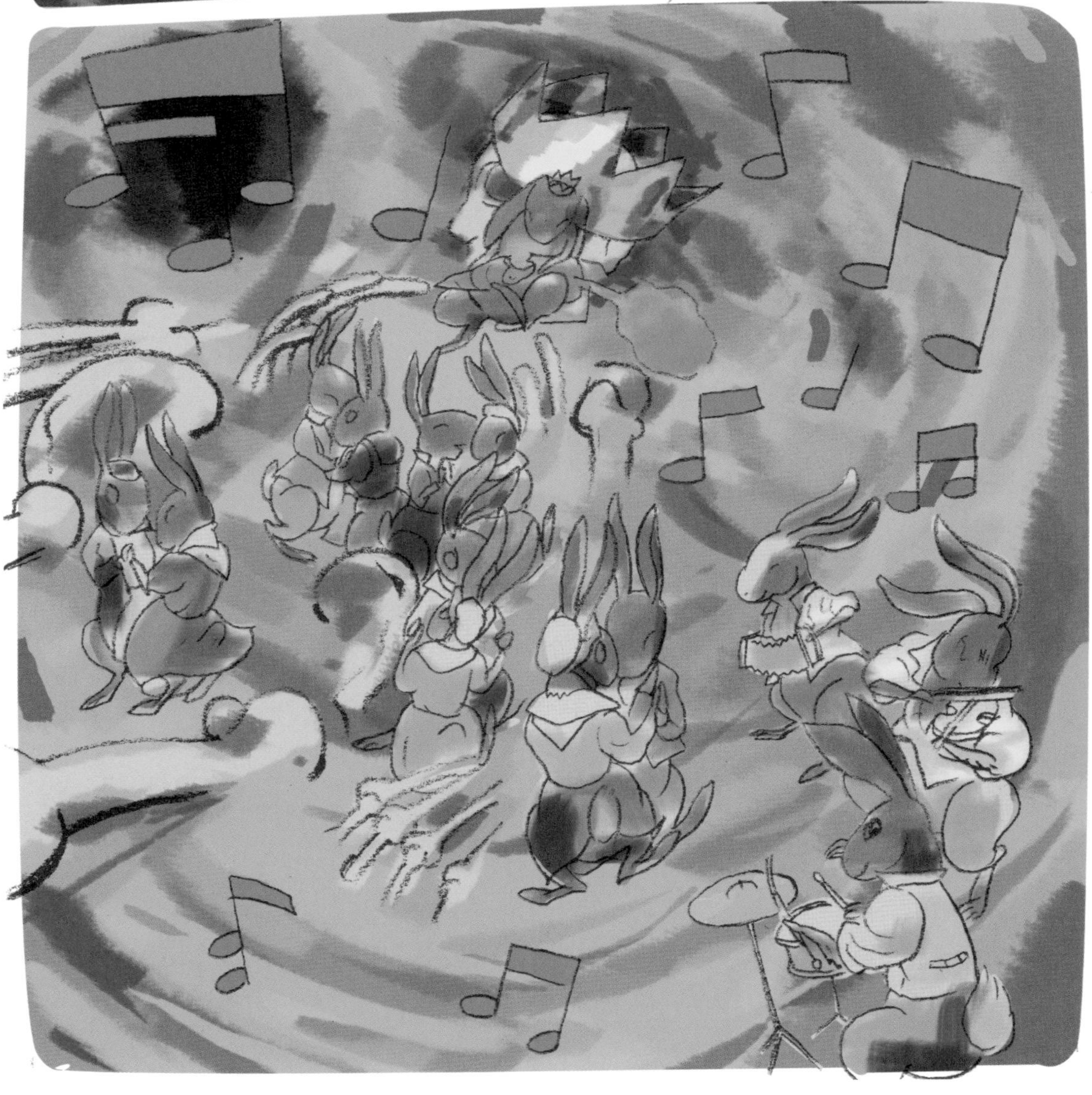

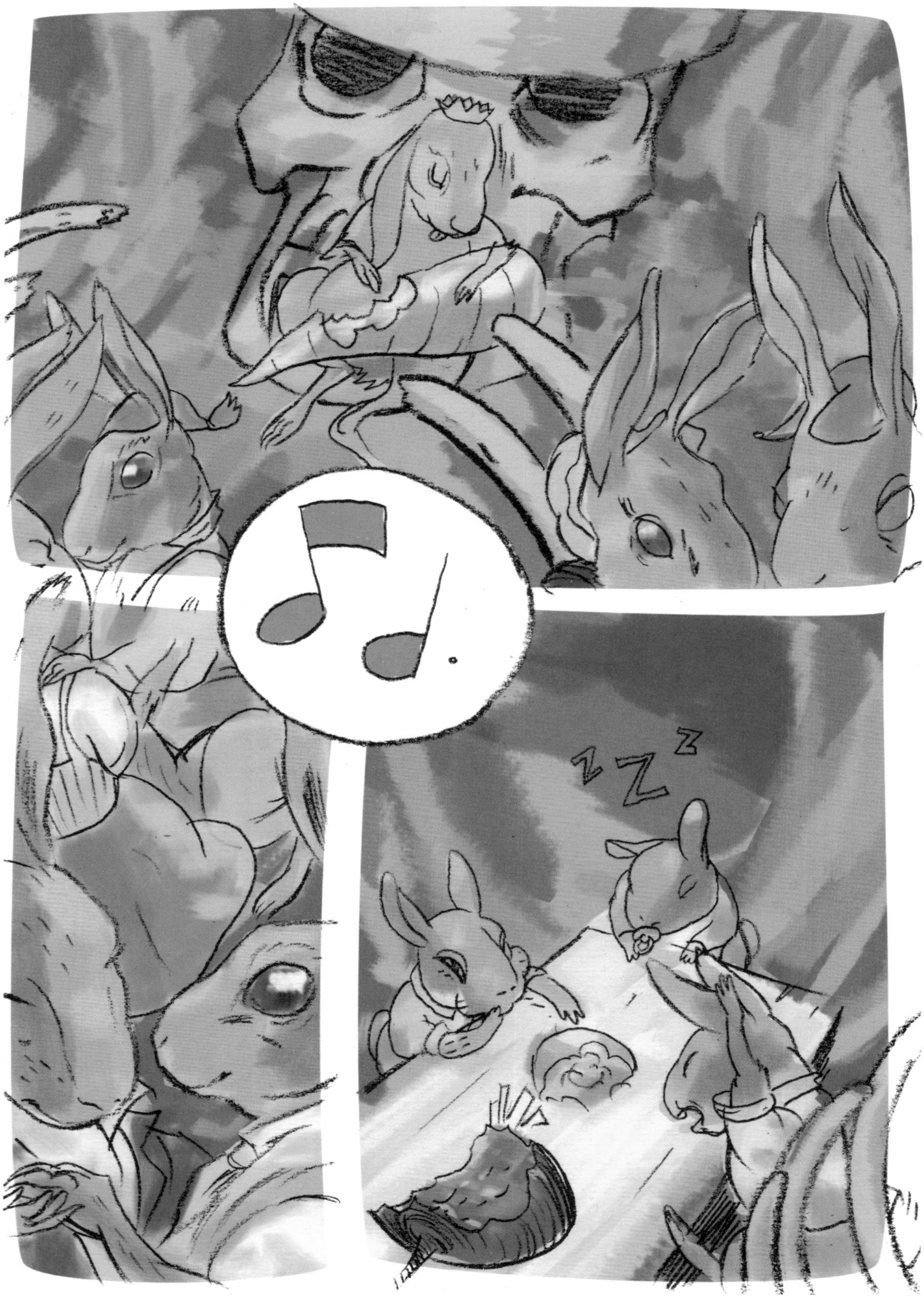
ZZZ

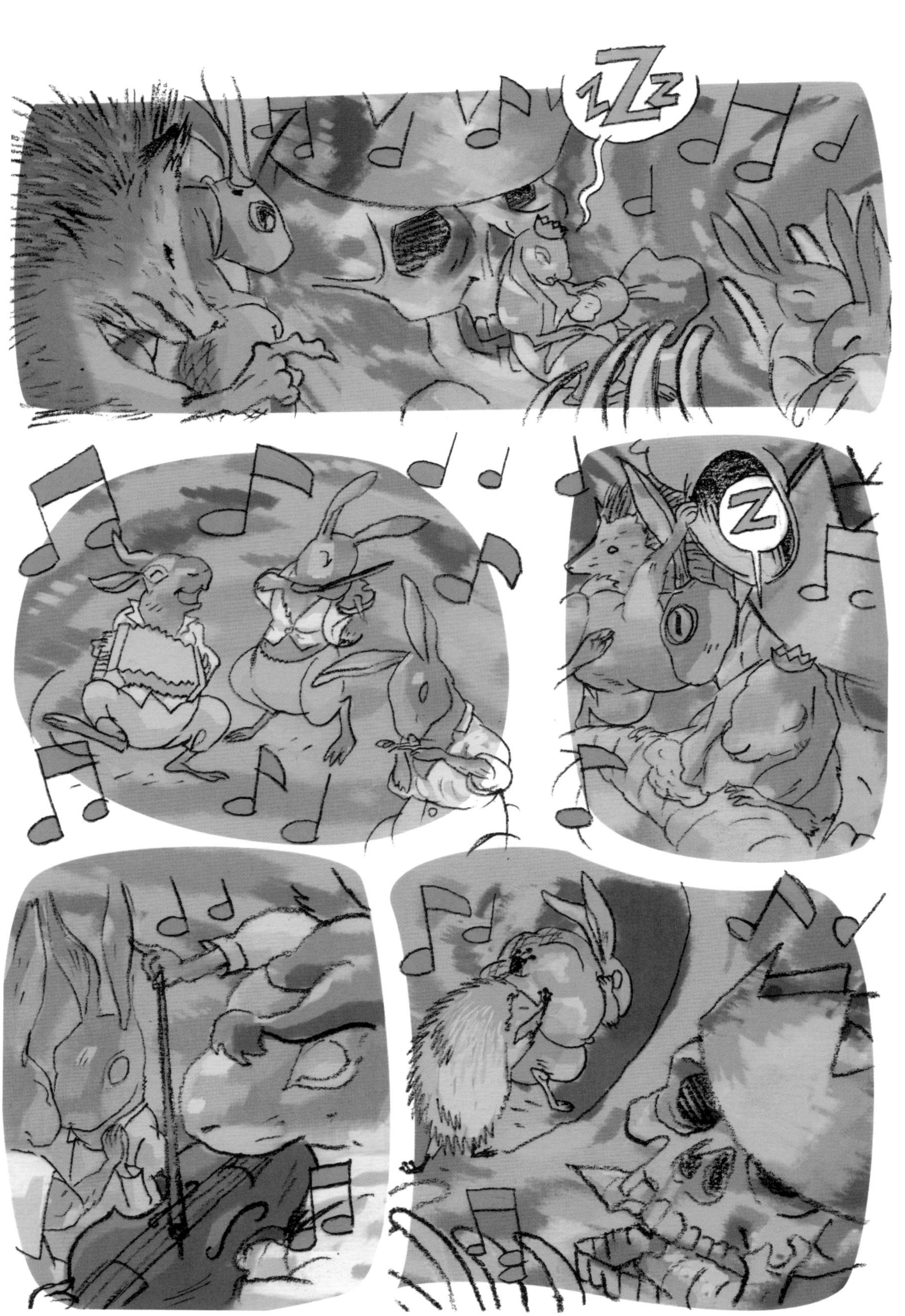
zZz
Z

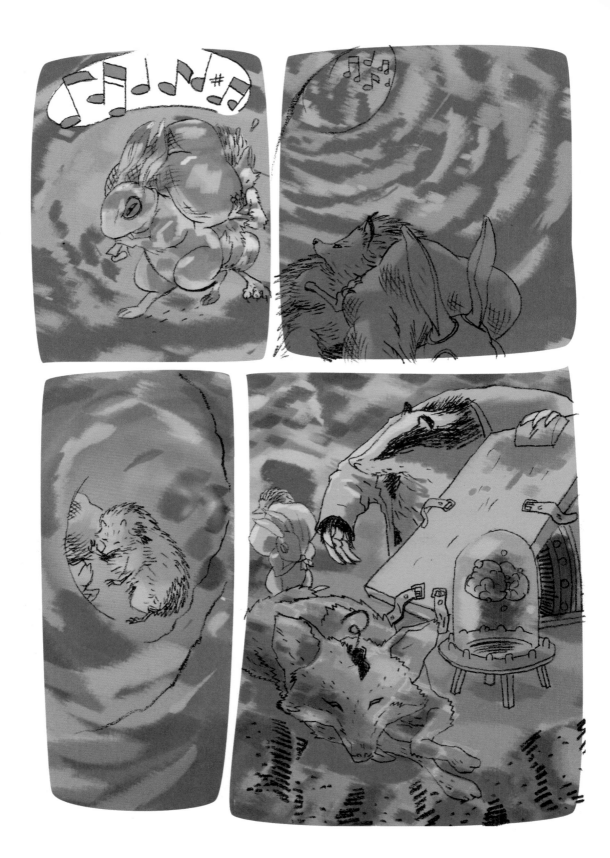

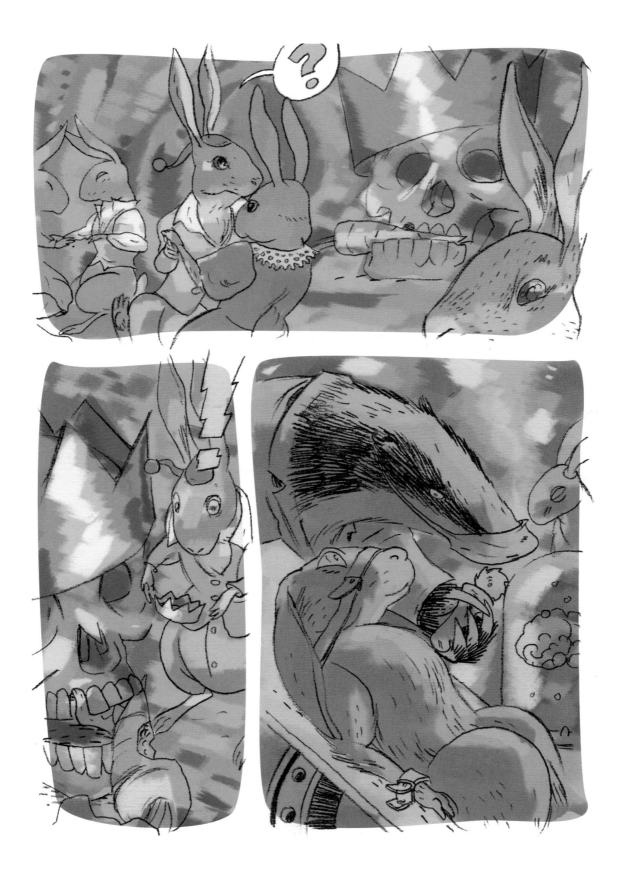

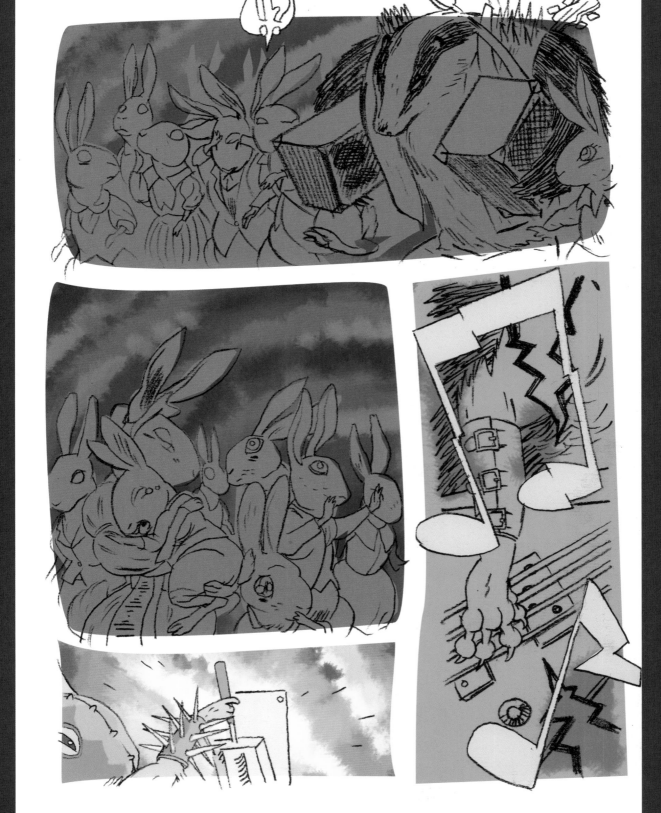

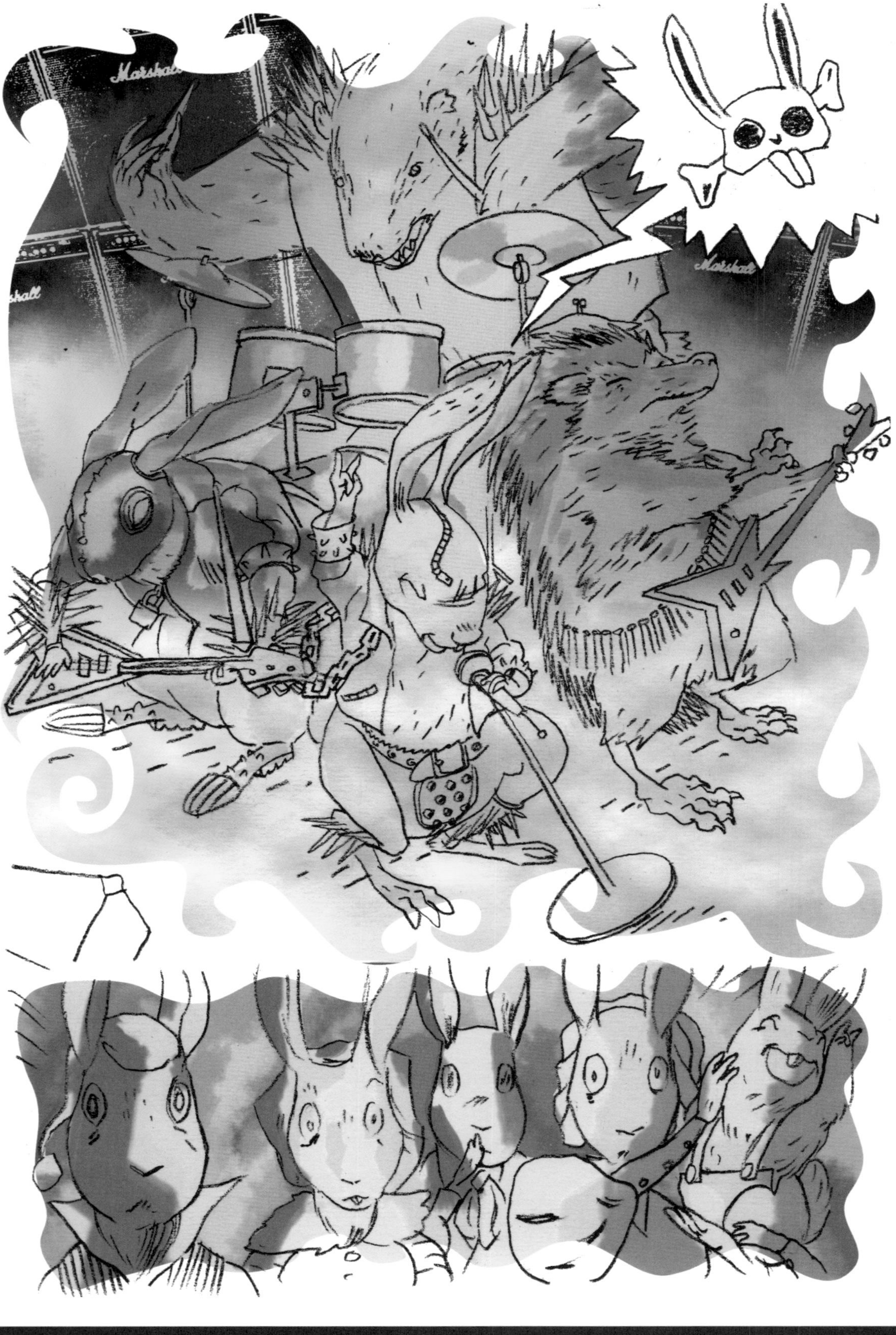
Marshall
Marshall
Marshall

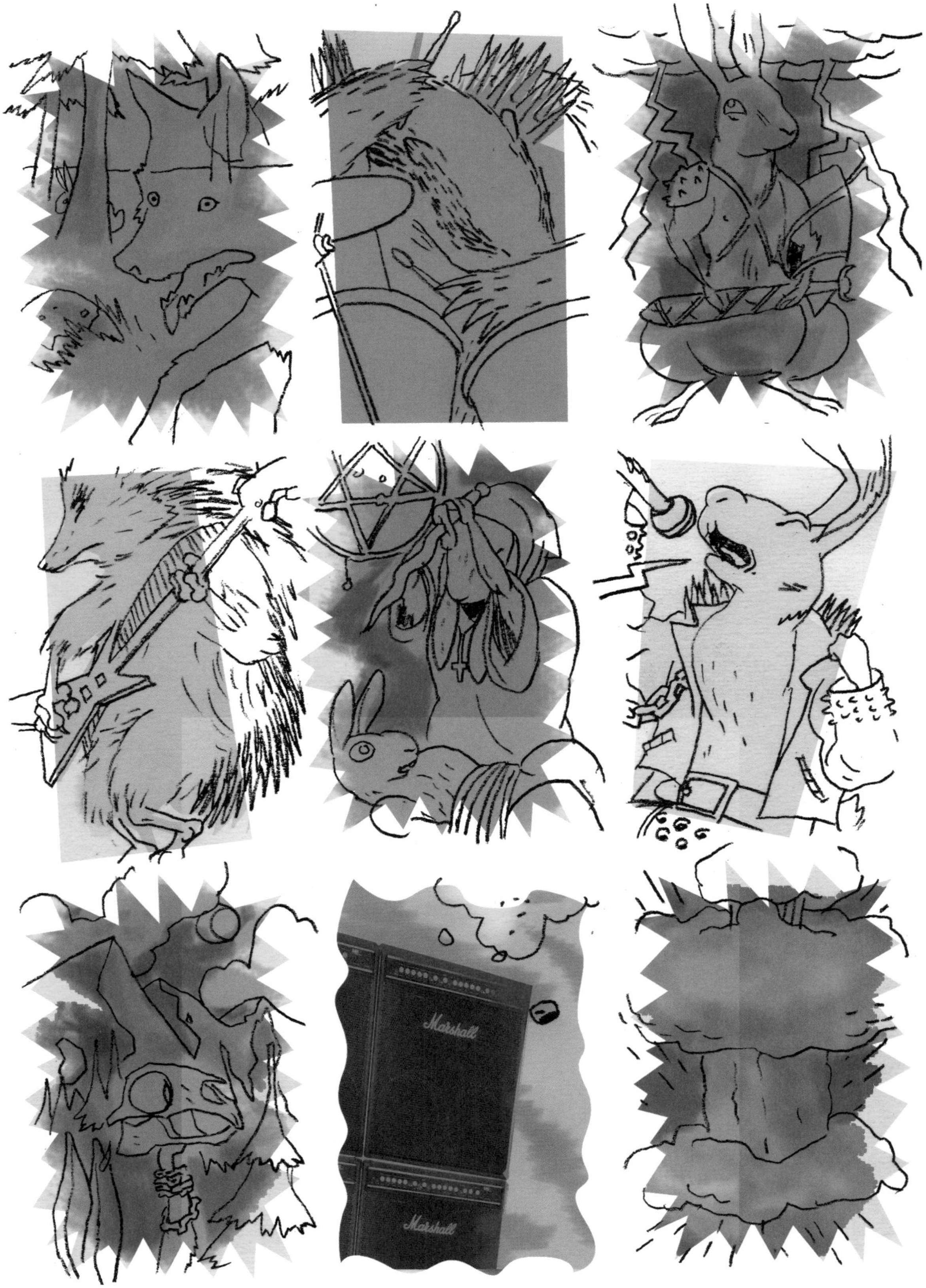
Marshall
Marshall

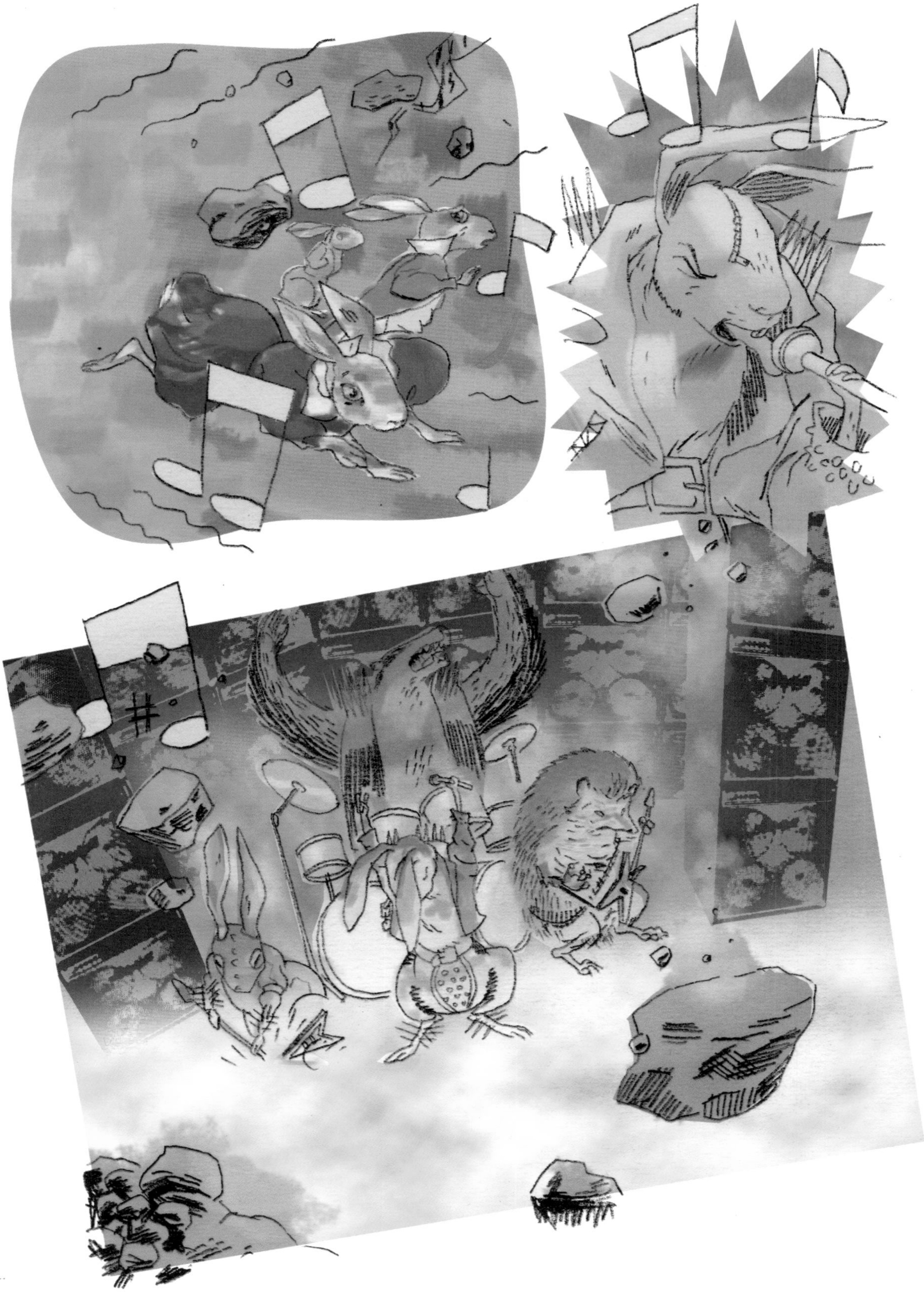

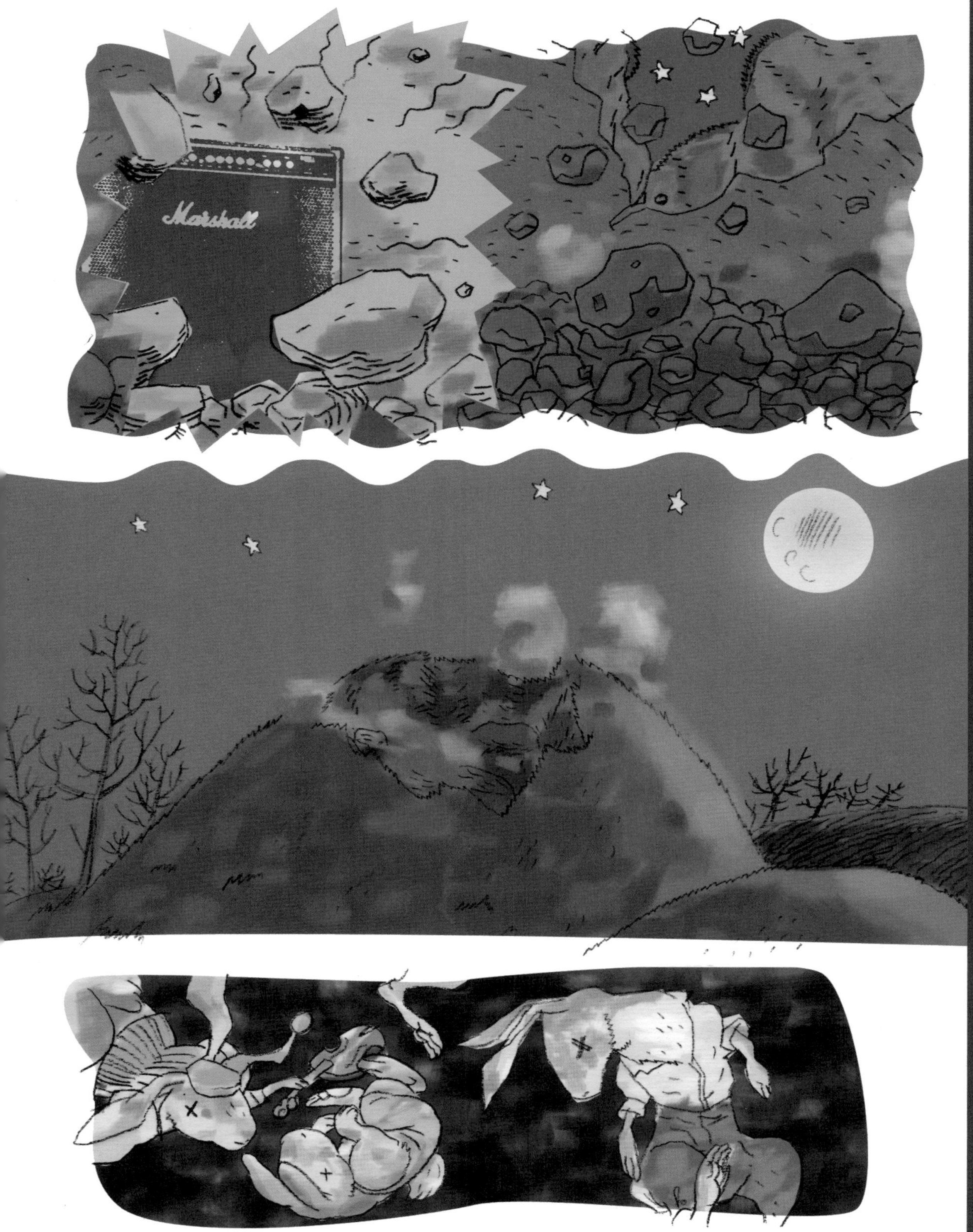
Marshall

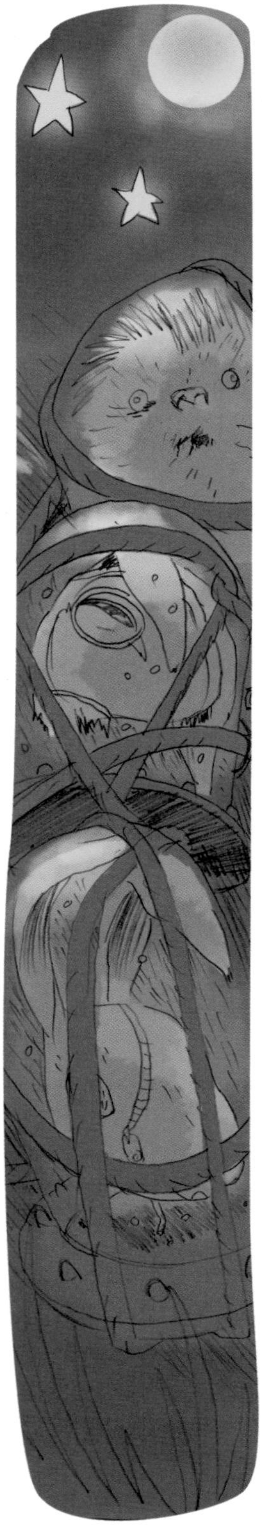
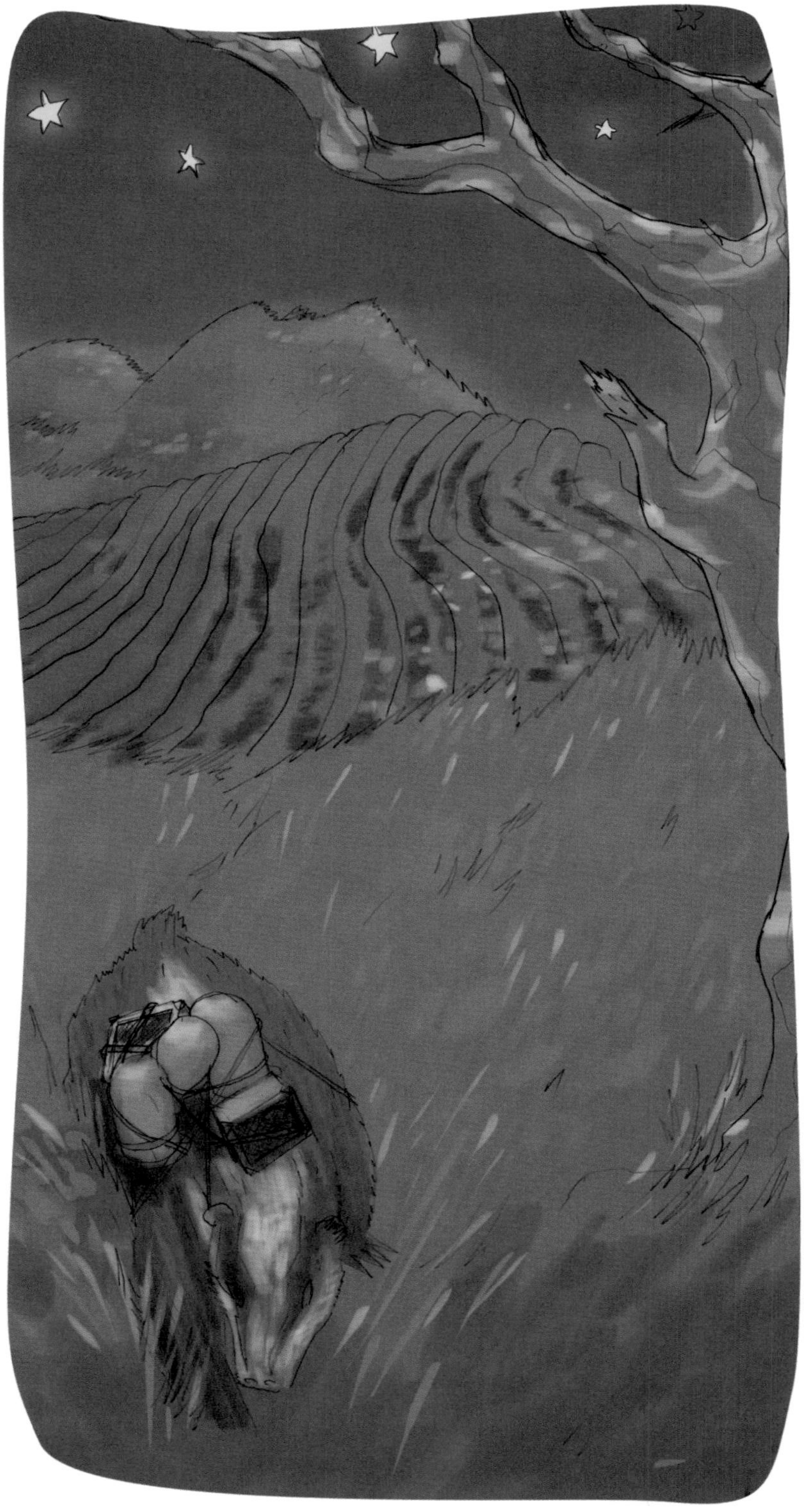

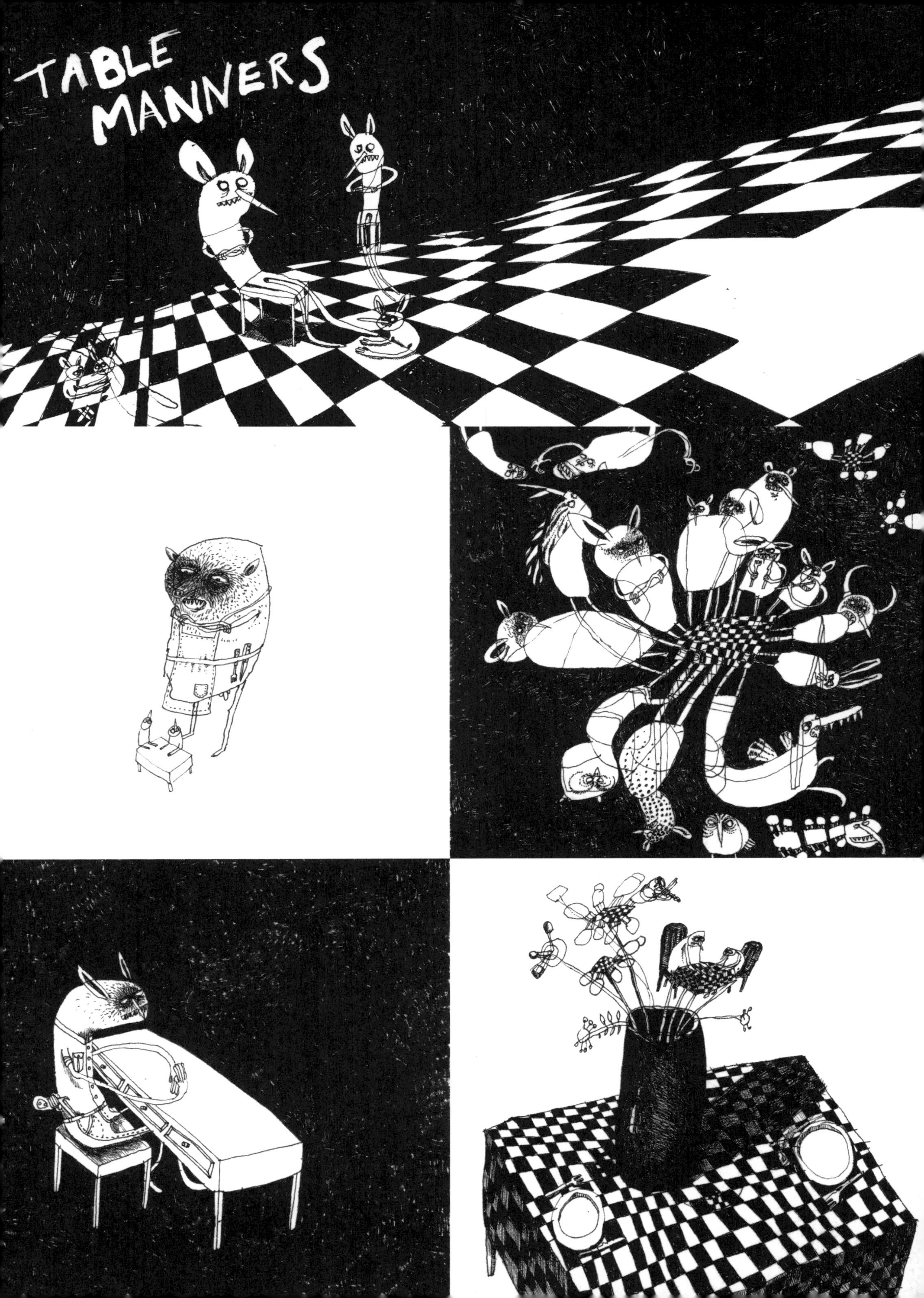
TABLE MANNERS

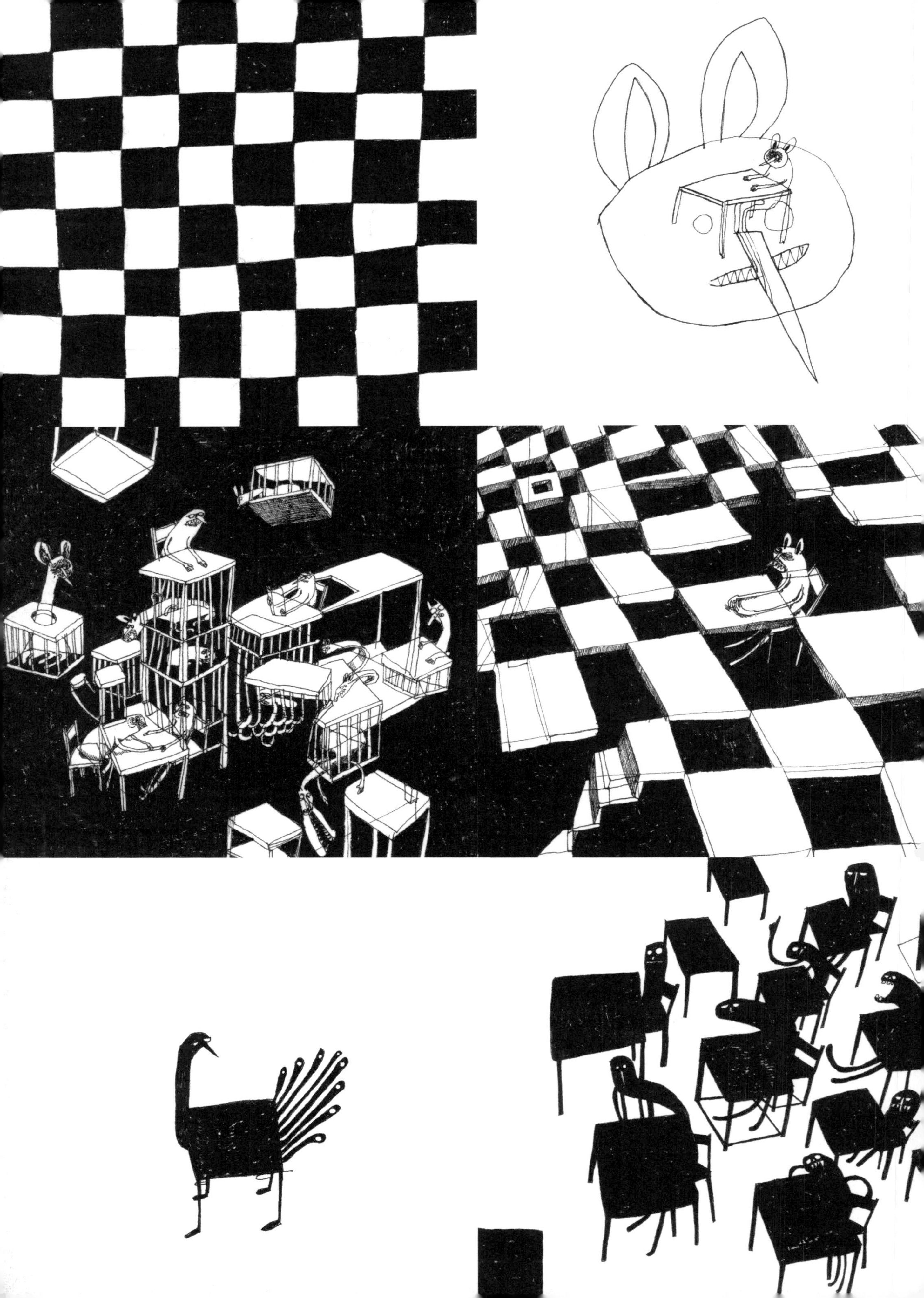

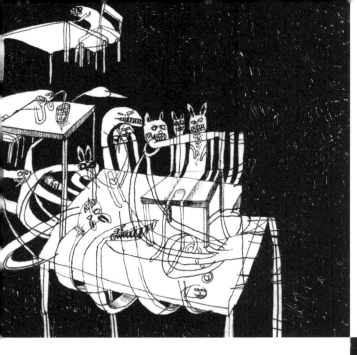

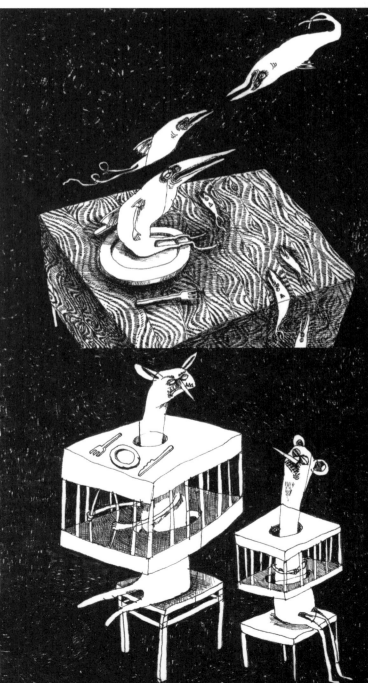

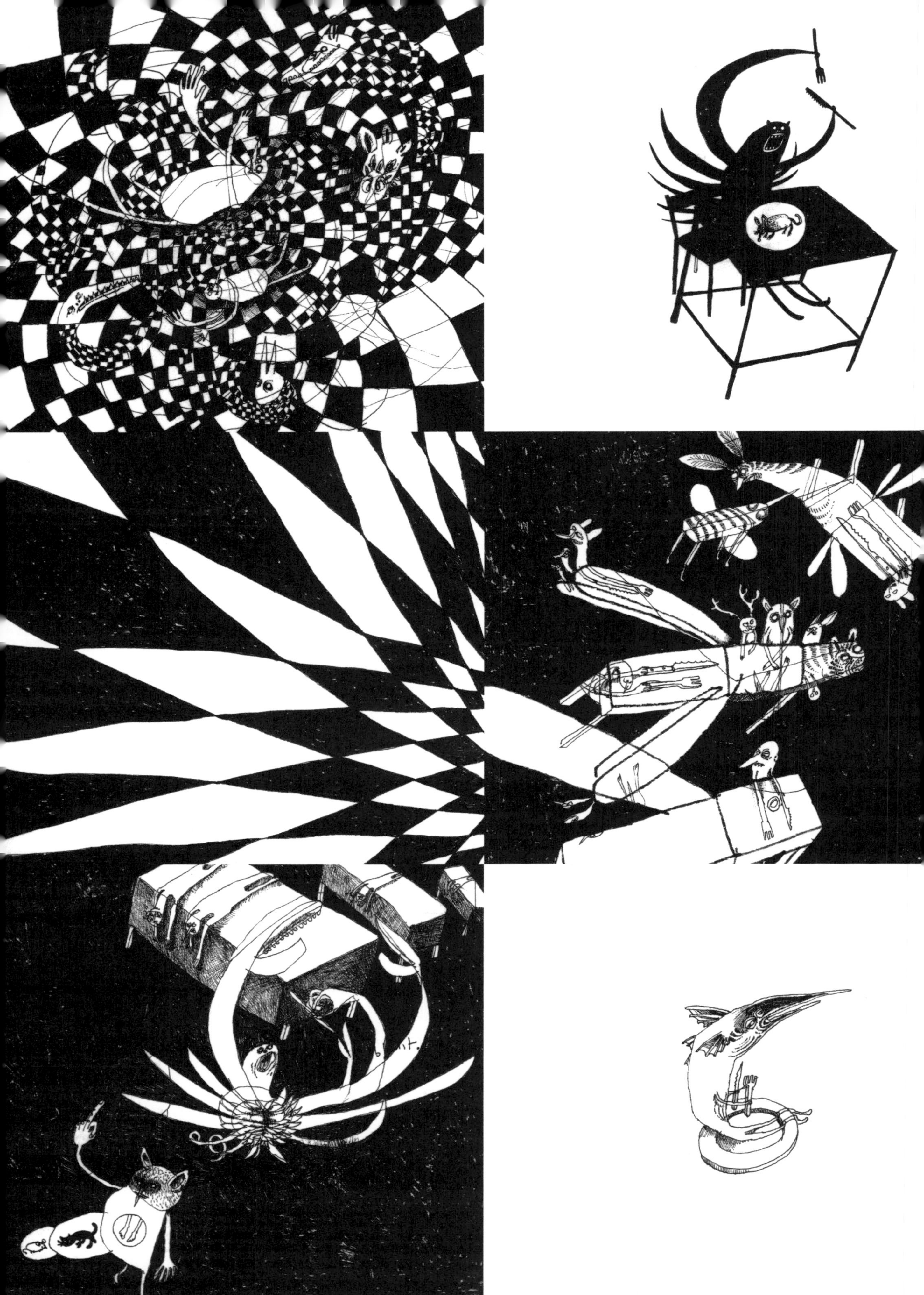

Sloth

Ib Kjeldsmark

yo!
yo!o!
TEN THOUSAND YEARS OF EGGY SLEEP ARE OVER... LET'S GO CRAZY!
feel like dancing
PAST, PISS OFF!

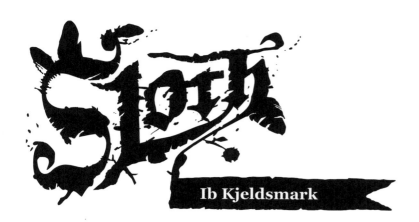

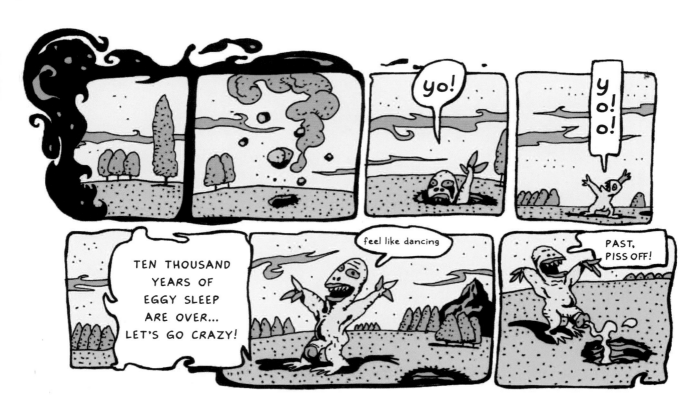

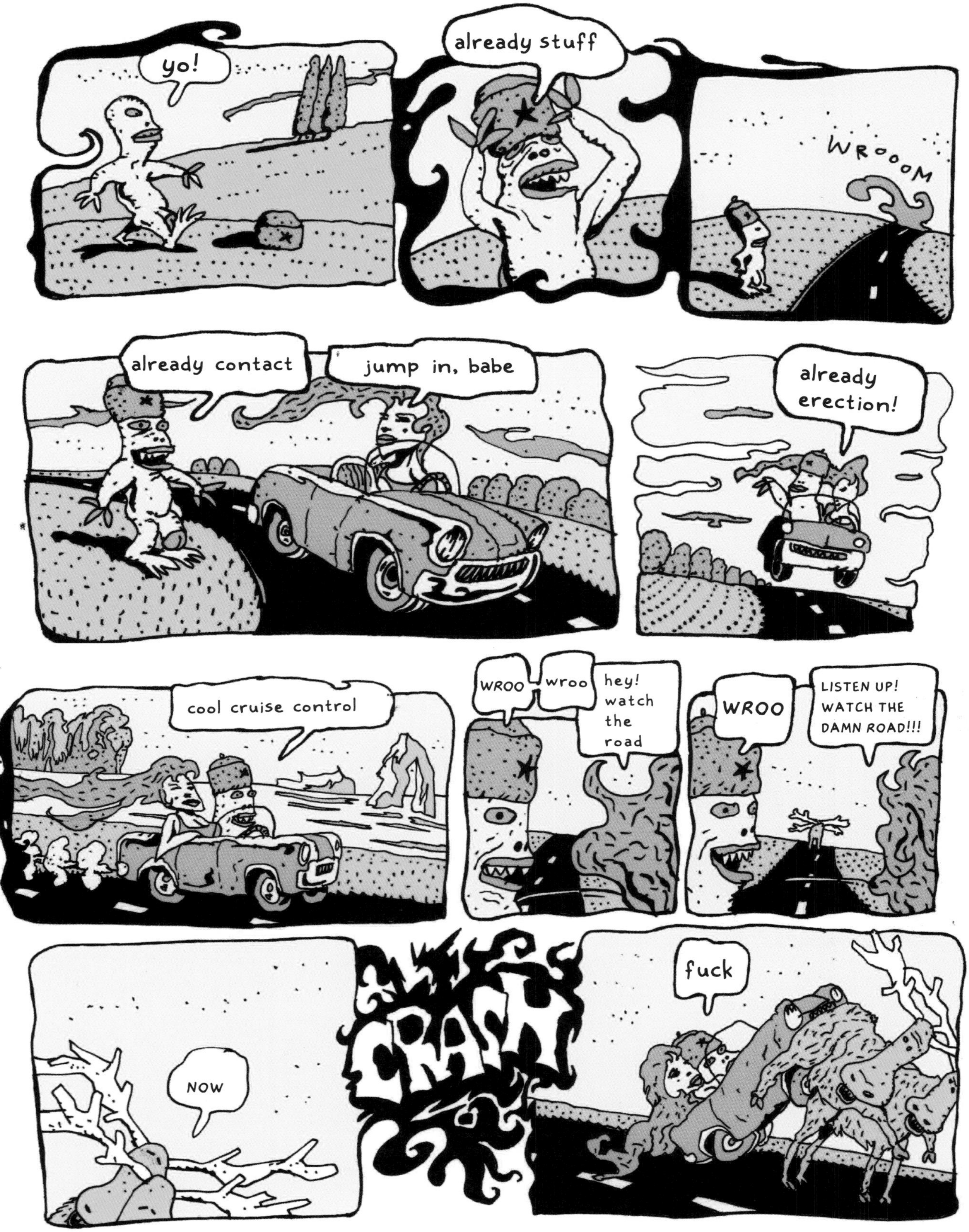
yo!
already stuff
WROOOOM
already contact
jump in, babe
already erection!
cool cruise control
WROO
wroo
hey! watch the road
WROO
LISTEN UP! WATCH THE DAMN ROAD!!!
NOW
CRASH
fuck

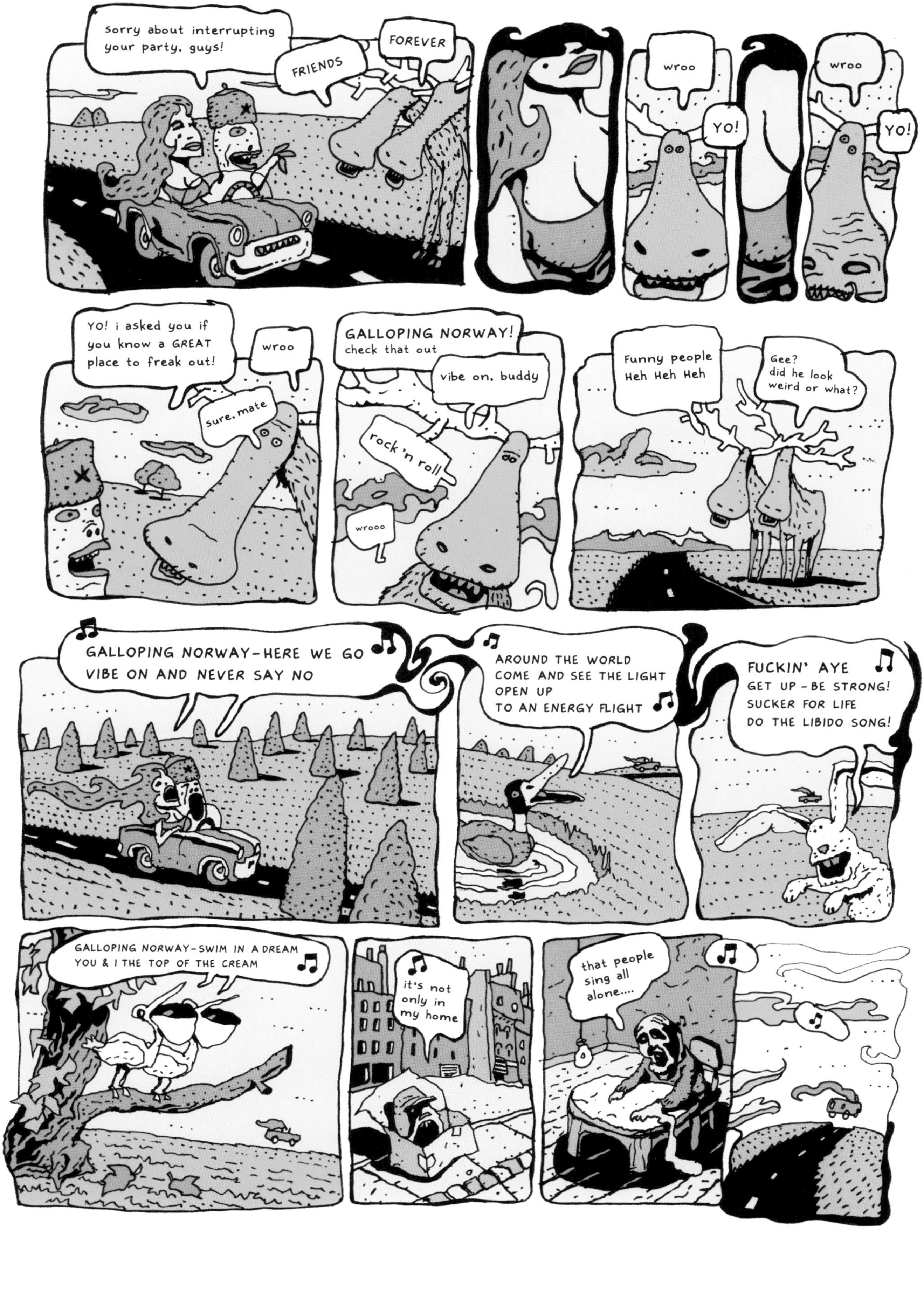

sorry about interrupting your party, guys!
FRIENDS
FOREVER
wroo
YO!
wroo
YO!
YO! i asked you if you know a GREAT place to freak out!
wroo
sure, mate
GALLOPING NORWAY! check that out
vibe on, buddy
rock 'n roll
wrooo
Funny people Heh Heh Heh
Gee? did he look weird or what?
GALLOPING NORWAY-HERE WE GO VIBE ON AND NEVER SAY NO
AROUND THE WORLD COME AND SEE THE LIGHT OPEN UP TO AN ENERGY FLIGHT
FUCKIN' AYE GET UP-BE STRONG! SUCKER FOR LIFE DO THE LIBIDO SONG!
GALLOPING NORWAY-SWIM IN A DREAM YOU & I THE TOP OF THE CREAM
it's not only in my home
that people sing all alone....

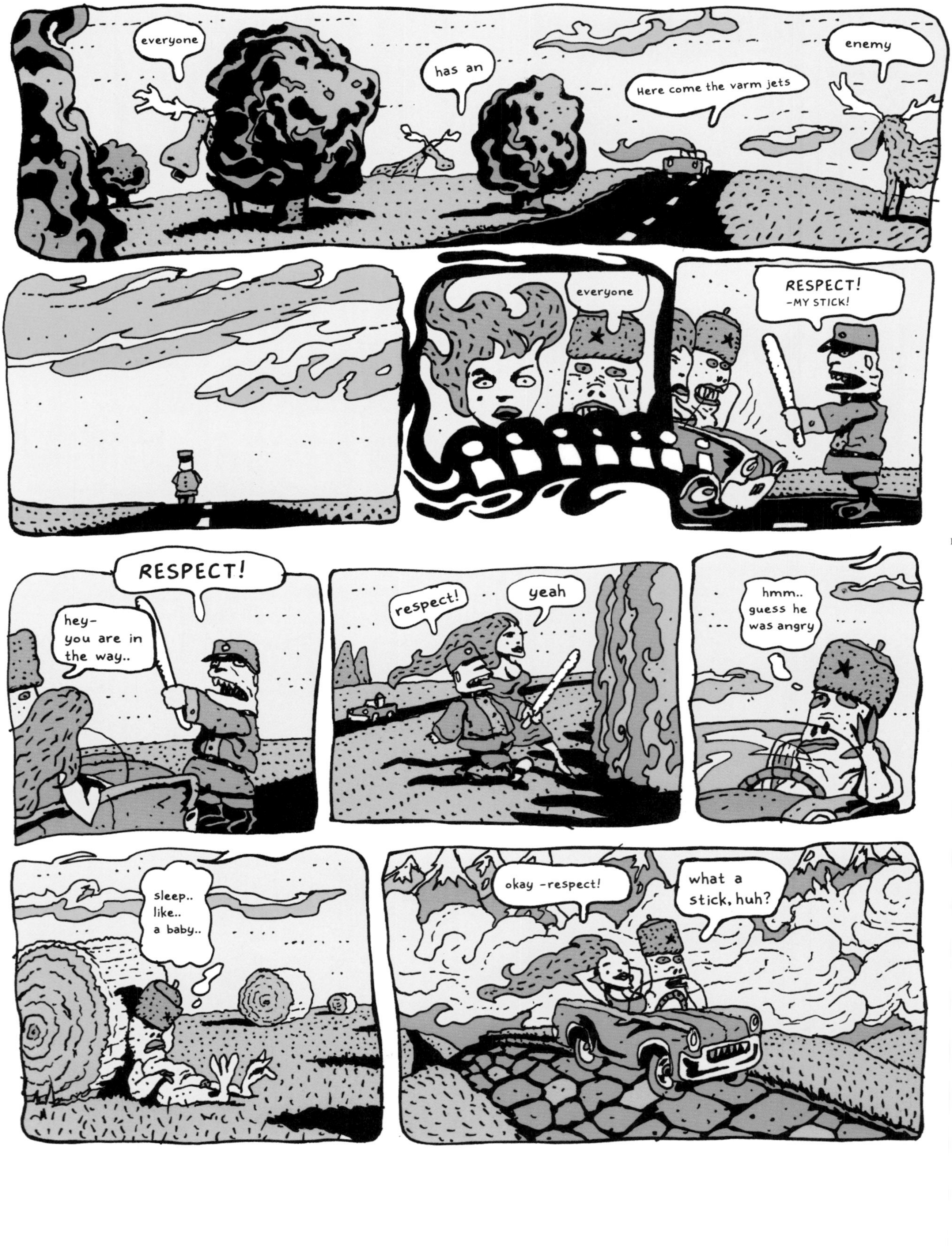
everyone
has an
Here come the varm jets
enemy
everyone
RESPECT!
-MY STICK!
RESPECT!
hey-
you are in
the way..
respect!
yeah
hmm..
guess he
was angry
sleep..
like..
a baby..
okay -respect!
what a
stick, huh?

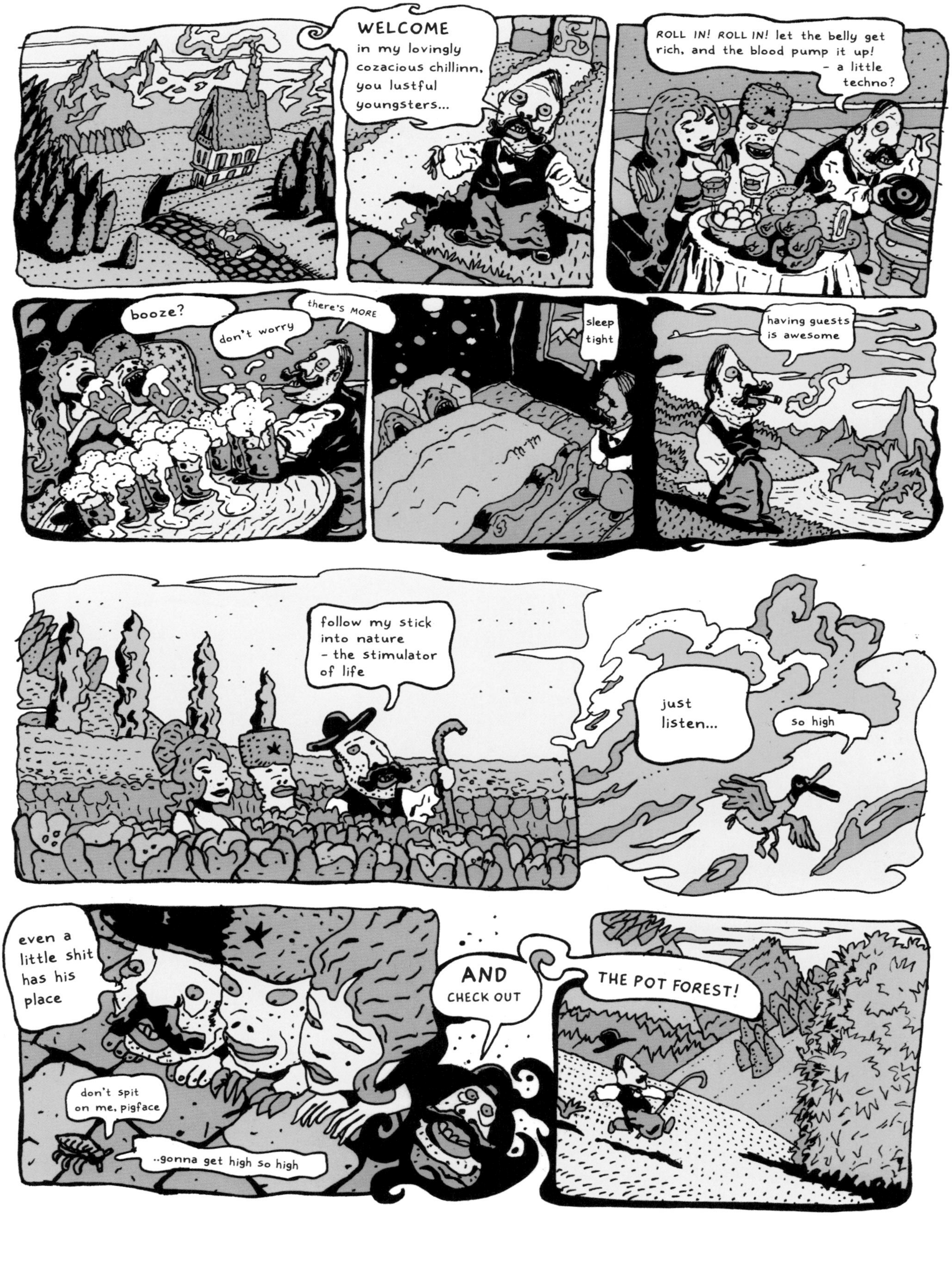
WELCOME
in my lovingly cozacious chillinn, you lustful youngsters...
ROLL IN! ROLL IN! let the belly get rich, and the blood pump it up!
- a little techno?
booze?
don't worry
there's MORE
sleep tight
having guests is awesome
follow my stick into nature - the stimulator of life
just listen...
so high
even a little shit has his place
don't spit on me, pigface
..gonna get high so high
AND CHECK OUT
THE POT FOREST!

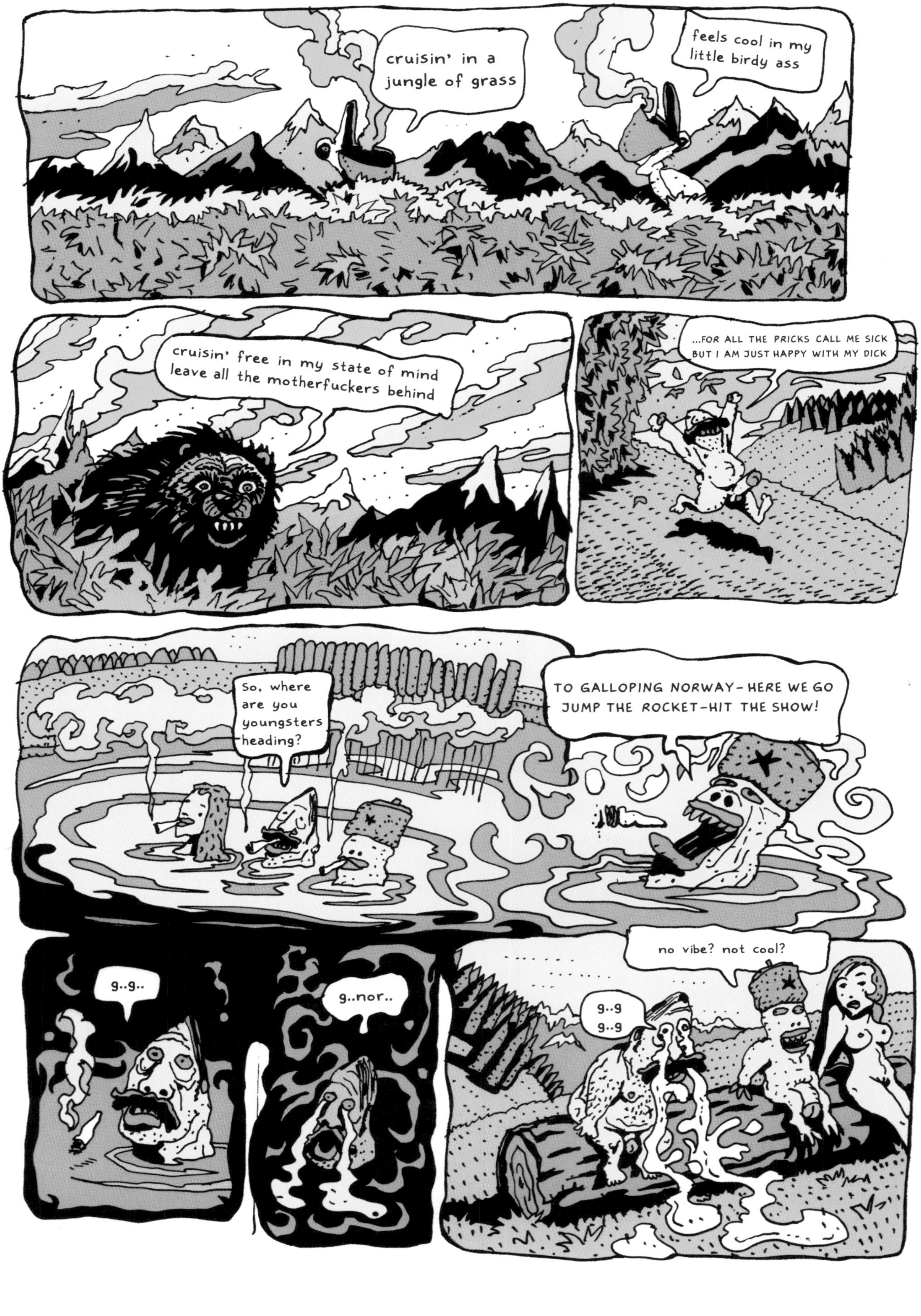
cruisin' in a jungle of grass
feels cool in my little birdy ass
cruisin' free in my state of mind leave all the motherfuckers behind
...FOR ALL THE PRICKS CALL ME SICK BUT I AM JUST HAPPY WITH MY DICK
So, where are you youngsters heading?
TO GALLOPING NORWAY - HERE WE GO JUMP THE ROCKET - HIT THE SHOW!
g..g..
g..nor..
no vibe? not cool?
g..g g..g

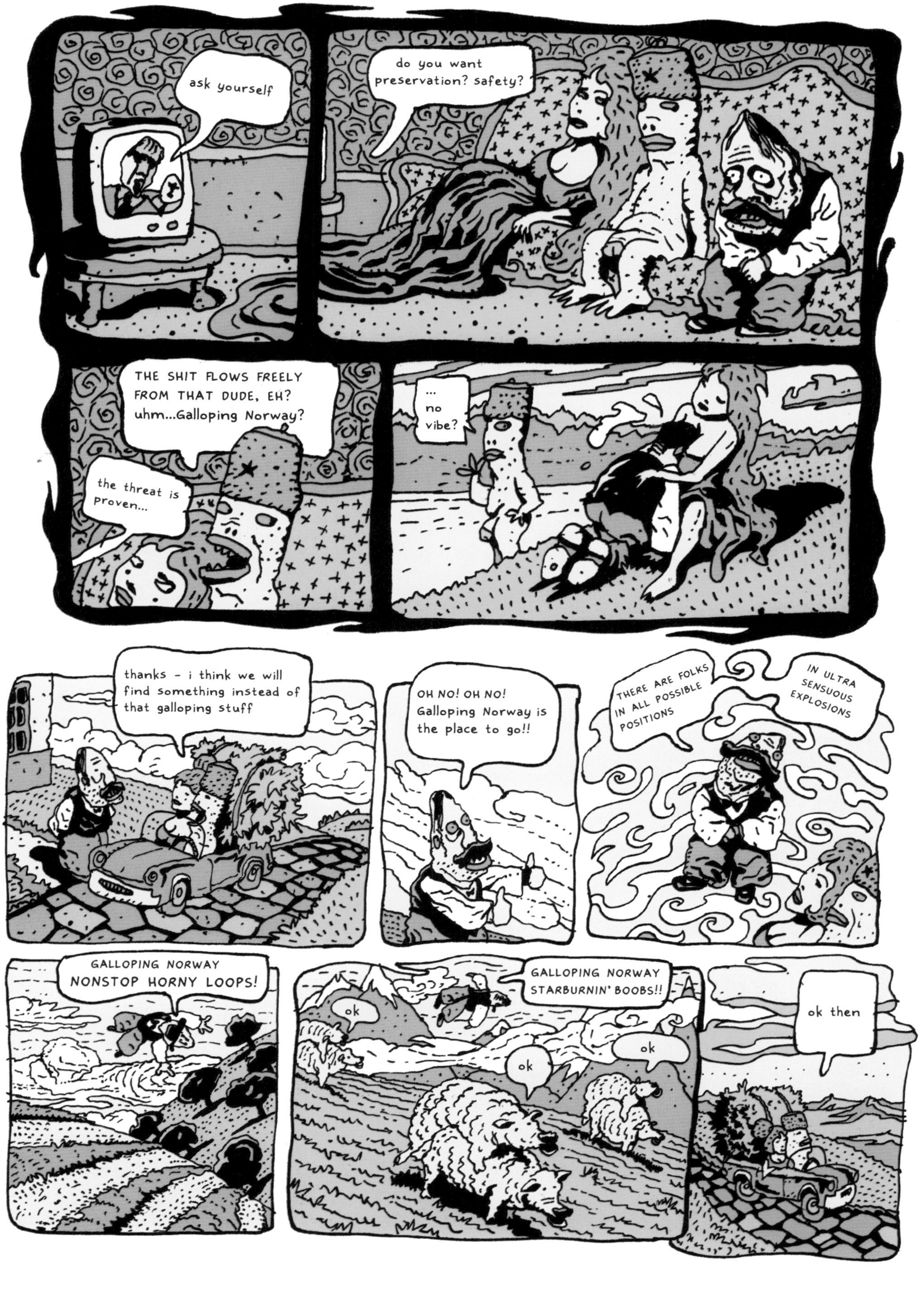
ask yourself
do you want preservation? safety?
THE SHIT FLOWS FREELY FROM THAT DUDE, EH? uhm...Galloping Norway?
the threat is proven...
... no vibe?
thanks - i think we will find something instead of that galloping stuff
OH NO! OH NO! Galloping Norway is the place to go!!
THERE ARE FOLKS IN ALL POSSIBLE POSITIONS
IN ULTRA SENSUOUS EXPLOSIONS
GALLOPING NORWAY NONSTOP HORNY LOOPS!
GALLOPING NORWAY STARBURNIN' BOOBS!!
ok
ok
ok
ok then

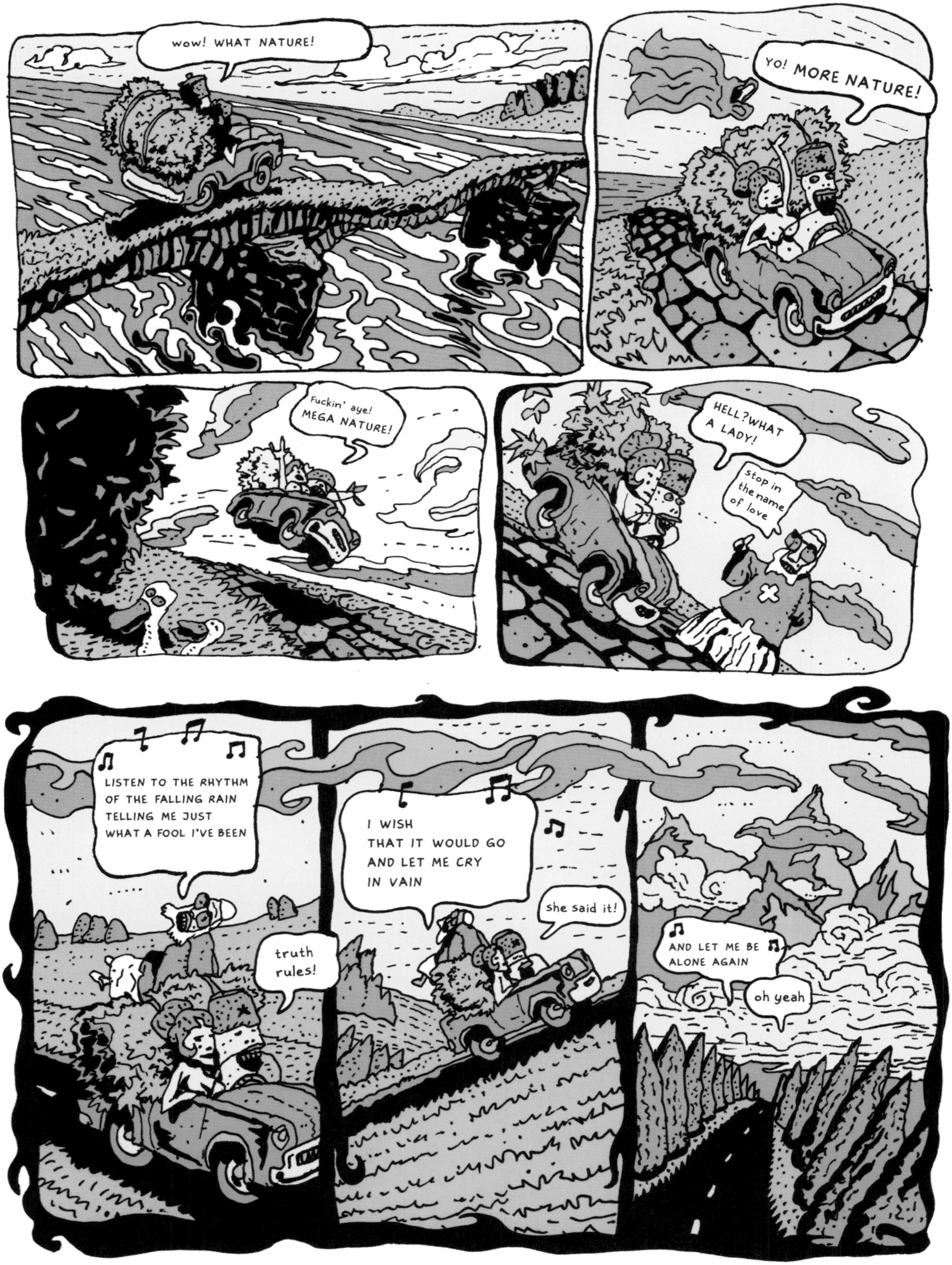
wow! WHAT NATURE!
YO! MORE NATURE!
Fuckin' aye! MEGA NATURE!
HELL? WHAT A LADY!
stop in the name of love
LISTEN TO THE RHYTHM OF THE FALLING RAIN TELLING ME JUST WHAT A FOOL I'VE BEEN
truth rules!
I WISH THAT IT WOULD GO AND LET ME CRY IN VAIN
she said it!
AND LET ME BE ALONE AGAIN
oh yeah

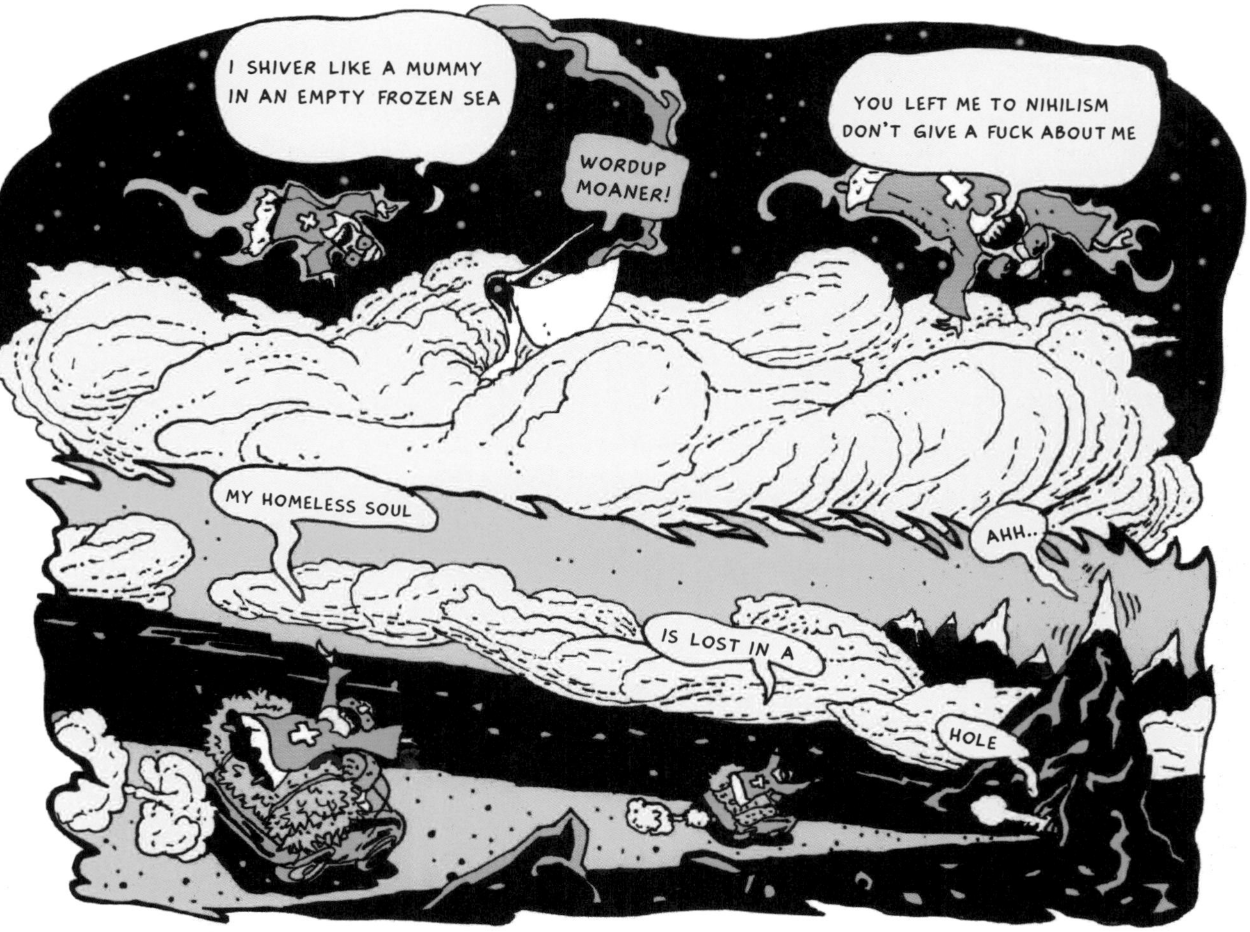
I SHIVER LIKE A MUMMY
IN AN EMPTY FROZEN SEA
WORDUP
MOANER!
YOU LEFT ME TO NIHILISM
DON'T GIVE A FUCK ABOUT ME
MY HOMELESS SOUL
AHH..
IS LOST IN A
HOLE

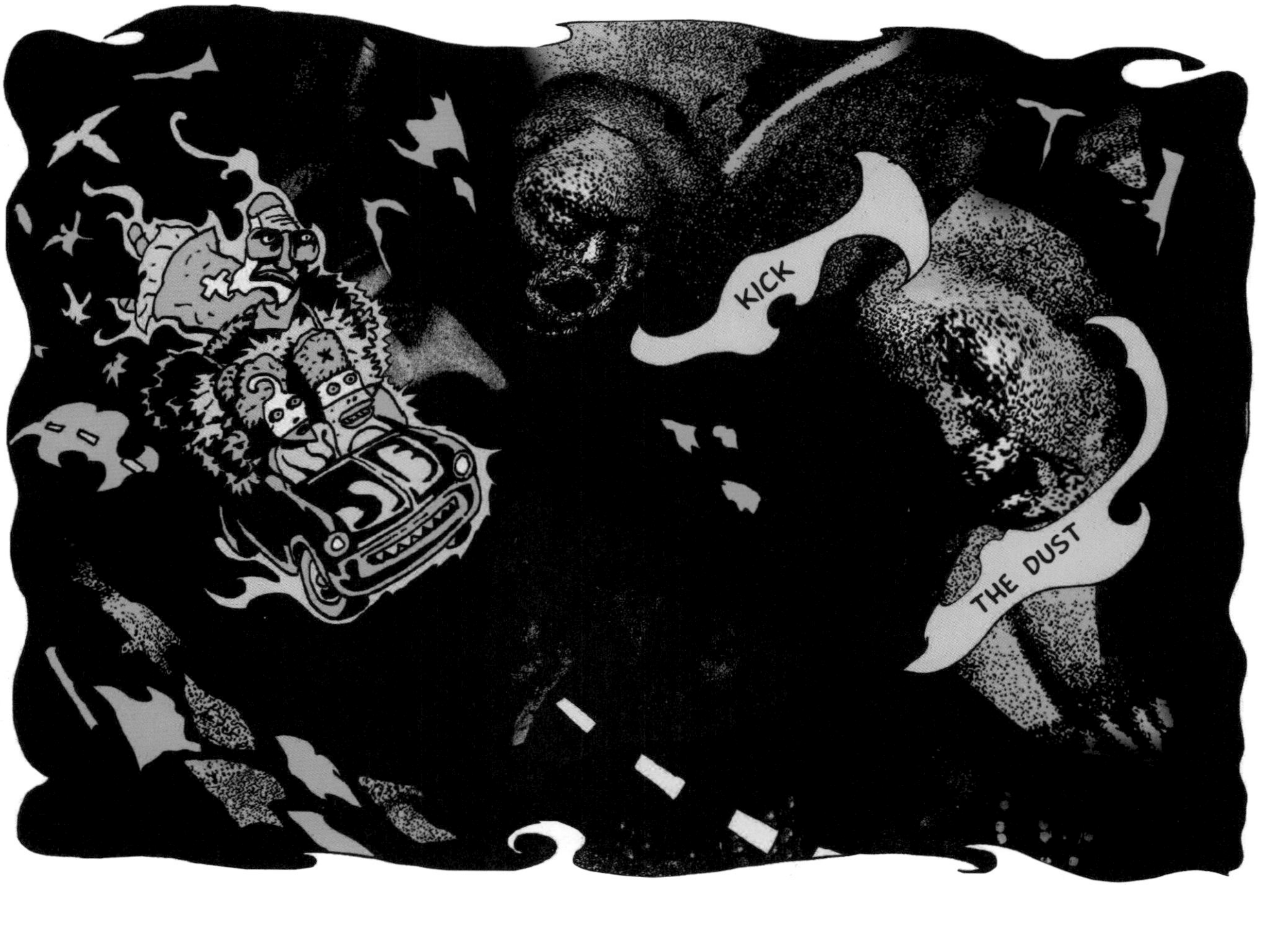
KICK
THE DUST

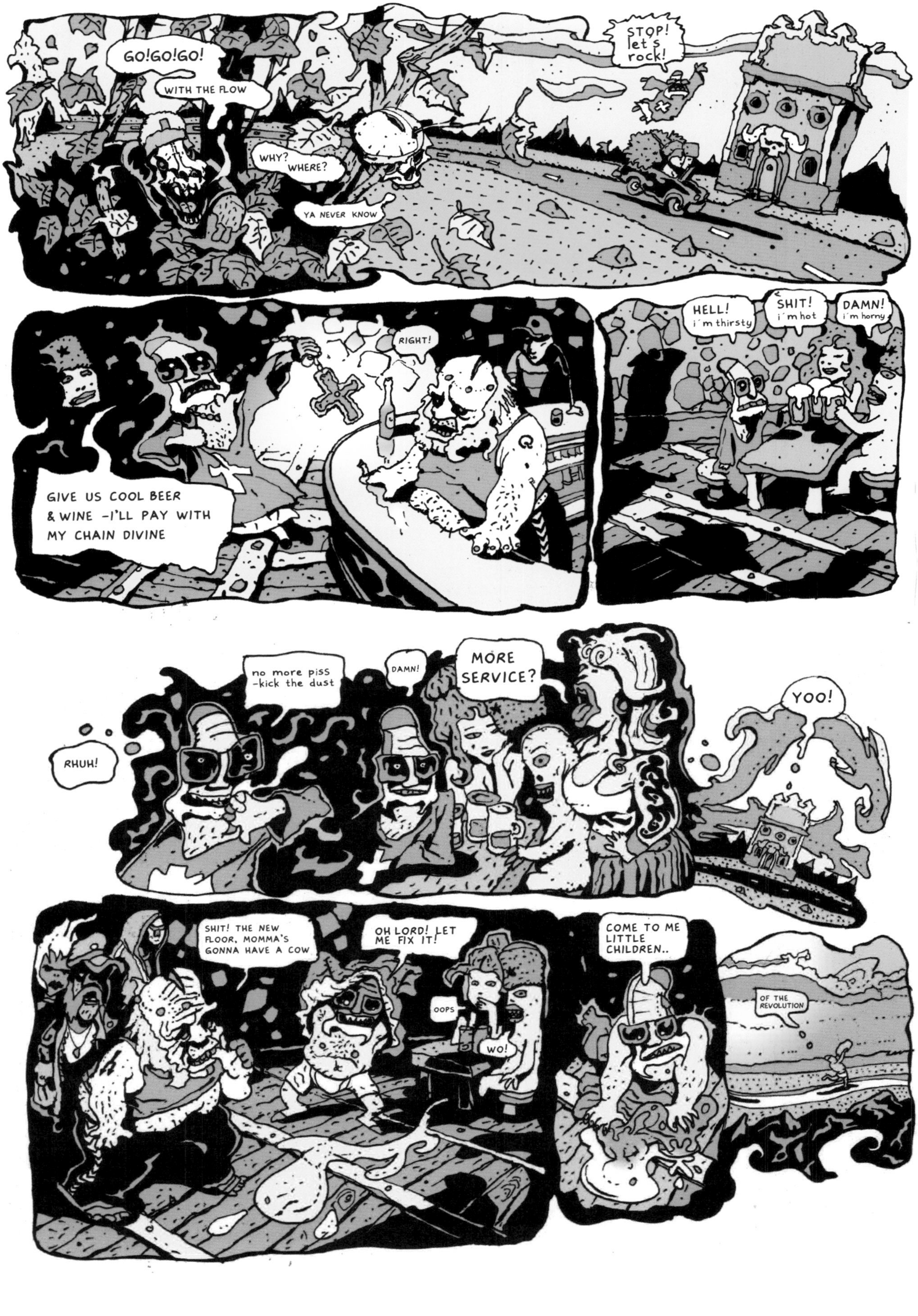
GO!GO!GO!
WITH THE FLOW
WHY? WHERE?
YA NEVER KNOW
STOP! let's rock!
GIVE US COOL BEER & WINE –I'LL PAY WITH MY CHAIN DIVINE
RIGHT!
HELL! i'm thirsty
SHIT! i'm hot
DAMN! i'm horny
RHUH!
no more piss -kick the dust
DAMN!
MORE SERVICE?
YOO!
SHIT! THE NEW FLOOR, MOMMA'S GONNA HAVE A COW
OH LORD! LET ME FIX IT!
OOPS
WO!
COME TO ME LITTLE CHILDREN..
OF THE REVOLUTION

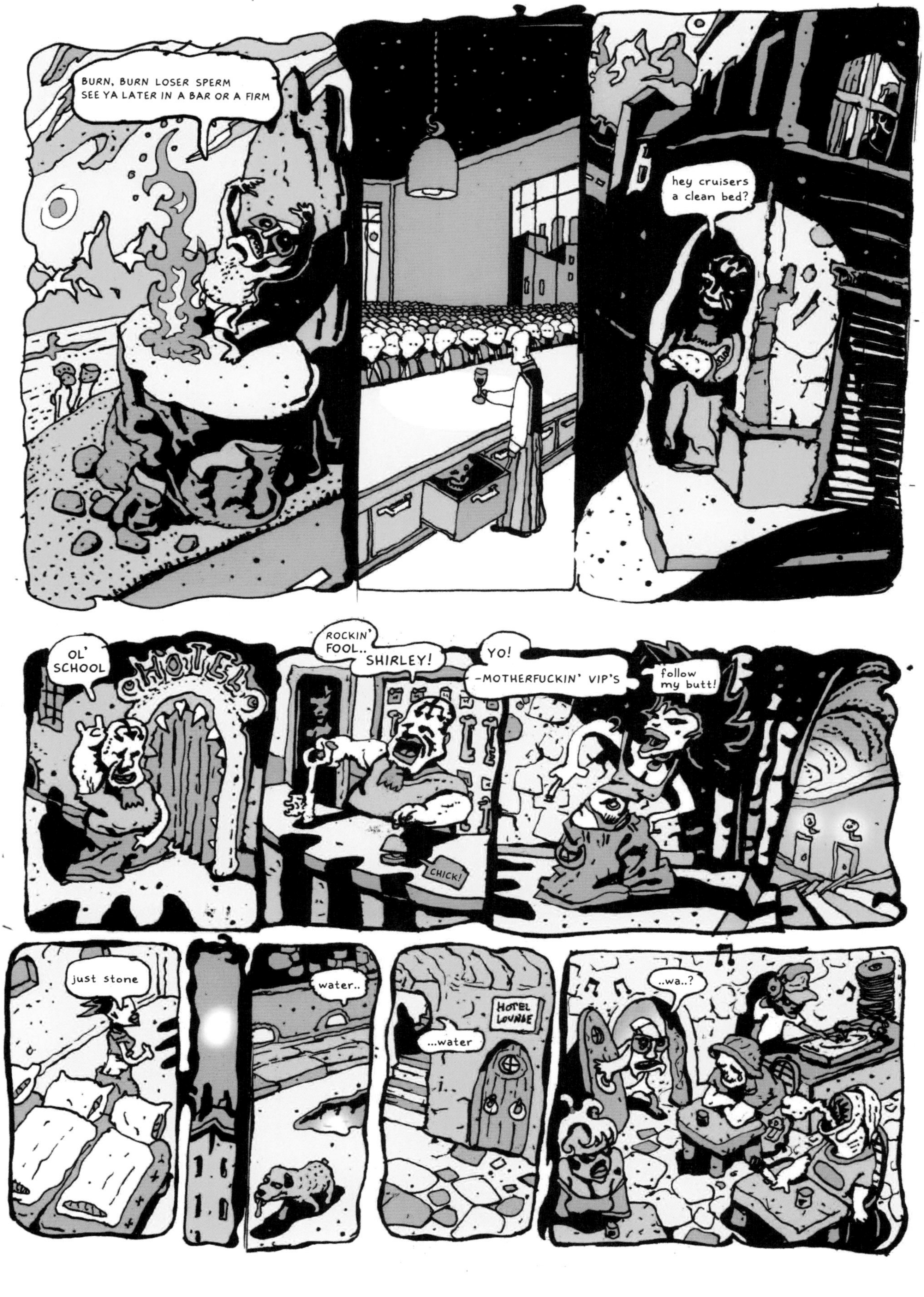
BURN, BURN LOSER SPERM
SEE YA LATER IN A BAR OR A FIRM
hey cruisers
a clean bed?
OL' SCHOOL
HOTEL
ROCKIN' FOOL..
SHIRLEY!
CHICK!
YO!
-MOTHERFUCKIN' VIP'S
follow my butt!
just stone
water..
HOTEL LOUNGE
...water
..wa..?

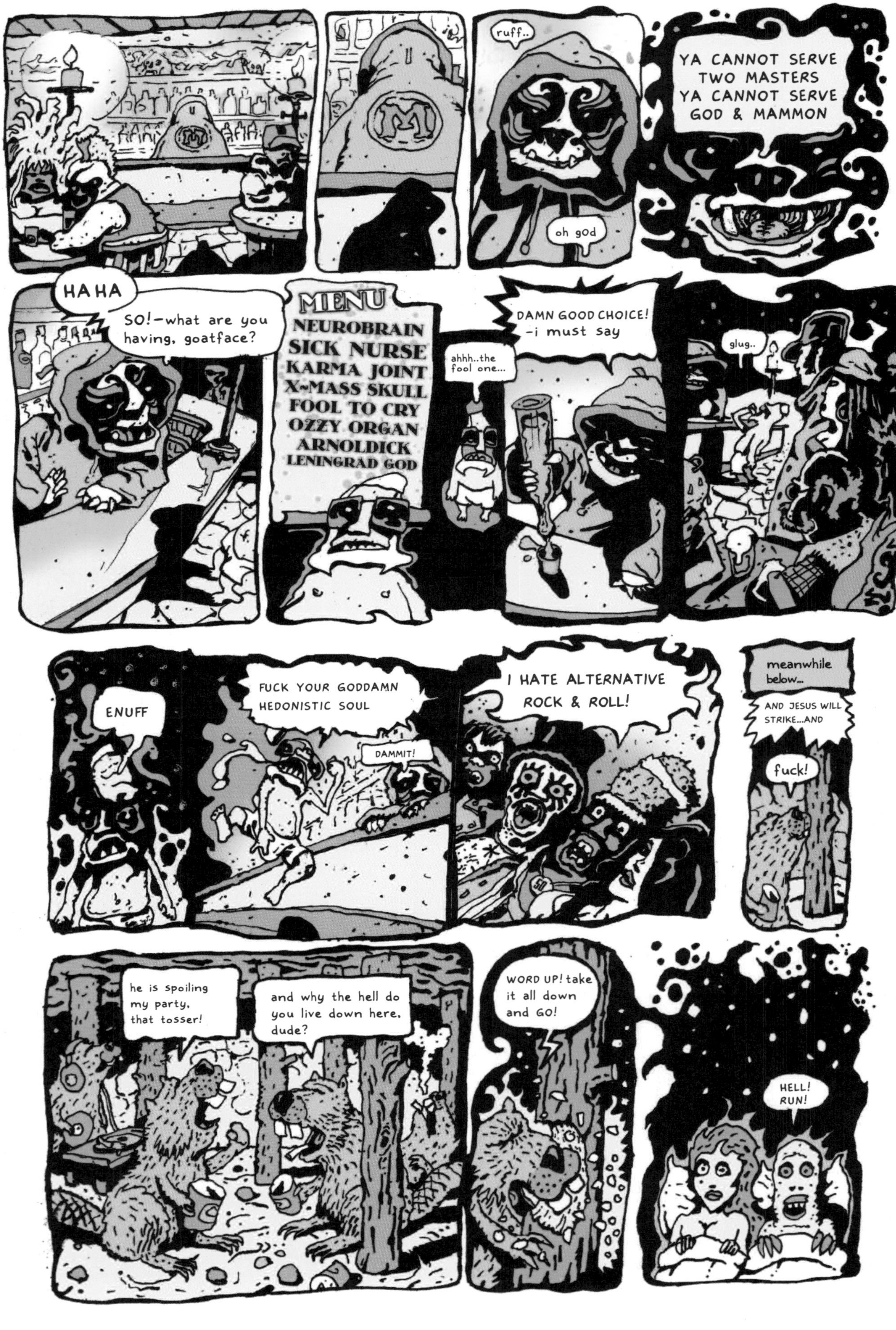
ruff..
oh god
YA CANNOT SERVE TWO MASTERS YA CANNOT SERVE GOD & MAMMON
HA HA
SO!—what are you having, goatface?
MENU
NEUROBRAIN
SICK NURSE
KARMA JOINT
X-MASS SKULL
FOOL TO CRY
OZZY ORGAN
ARNOLDICK
LENINGRAD GOD
ahhh..the fool one...
DAMN GOOD CHOICE! -i must say
glug..
ENUFF
FUCK YOUR GODDAMN HEDONISTIC SOUL
DAMMIT!
I HATE ALTERNATIVE ROCK & ROLL!
meanwhile below...
AND JESUS WILL STRIKE...AND
fuck!
he is spoiling my party, that tosser!
and why the hell do you live down here, dude?
WORD UP! take it all down and GO!
HELL! RUN!

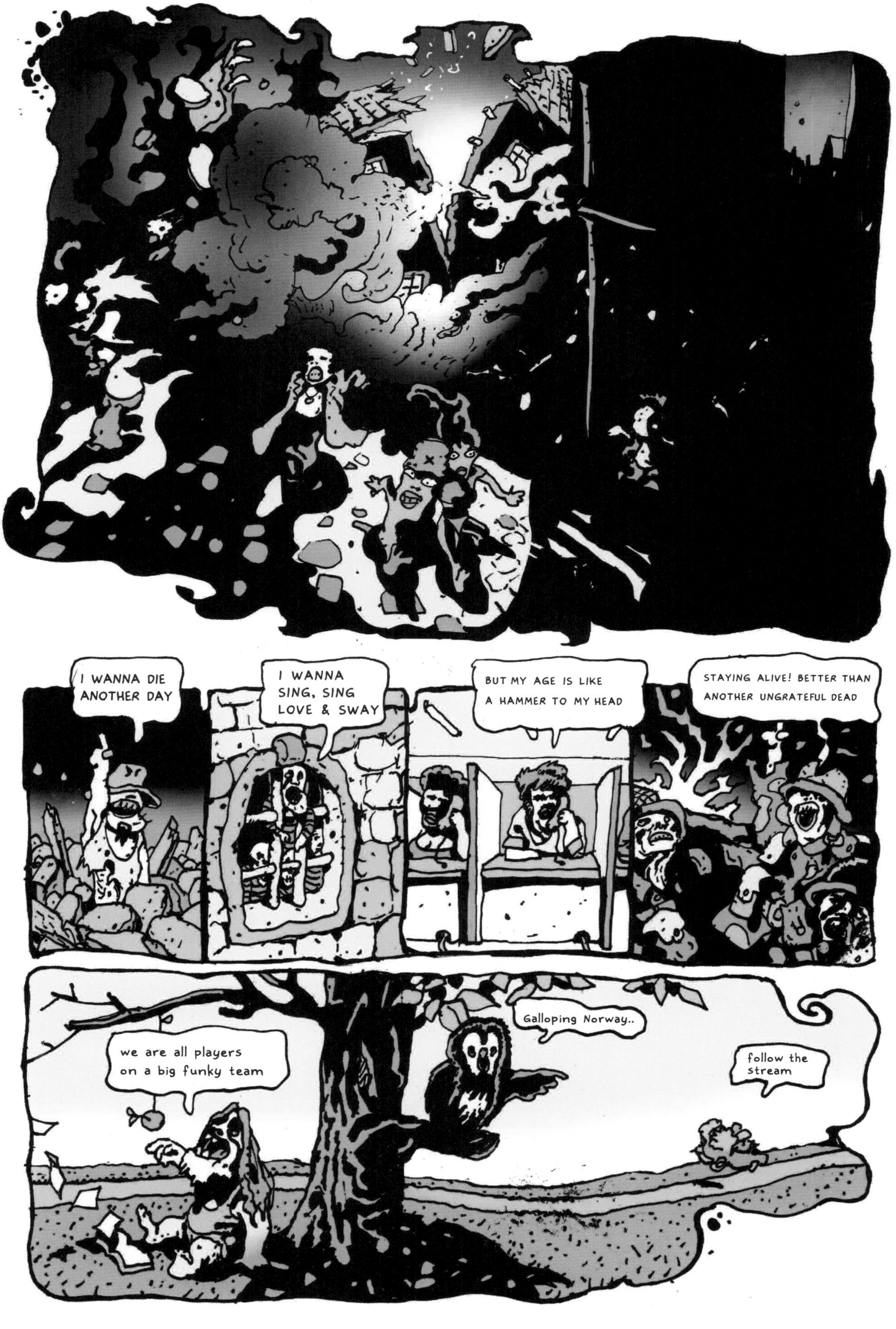
I WANNA DIE ANOTHER DAY
I WANNA SING, SING LOVE & SWAY
BUT MY AGE IS LIKE A HAMMER TO MY HEAD
STAYING ALIVE! BETTER THAN ANOTHER UNGRATEFUL DEAD
we are all players on a big funky team
Galloping Norway..
follow the stream

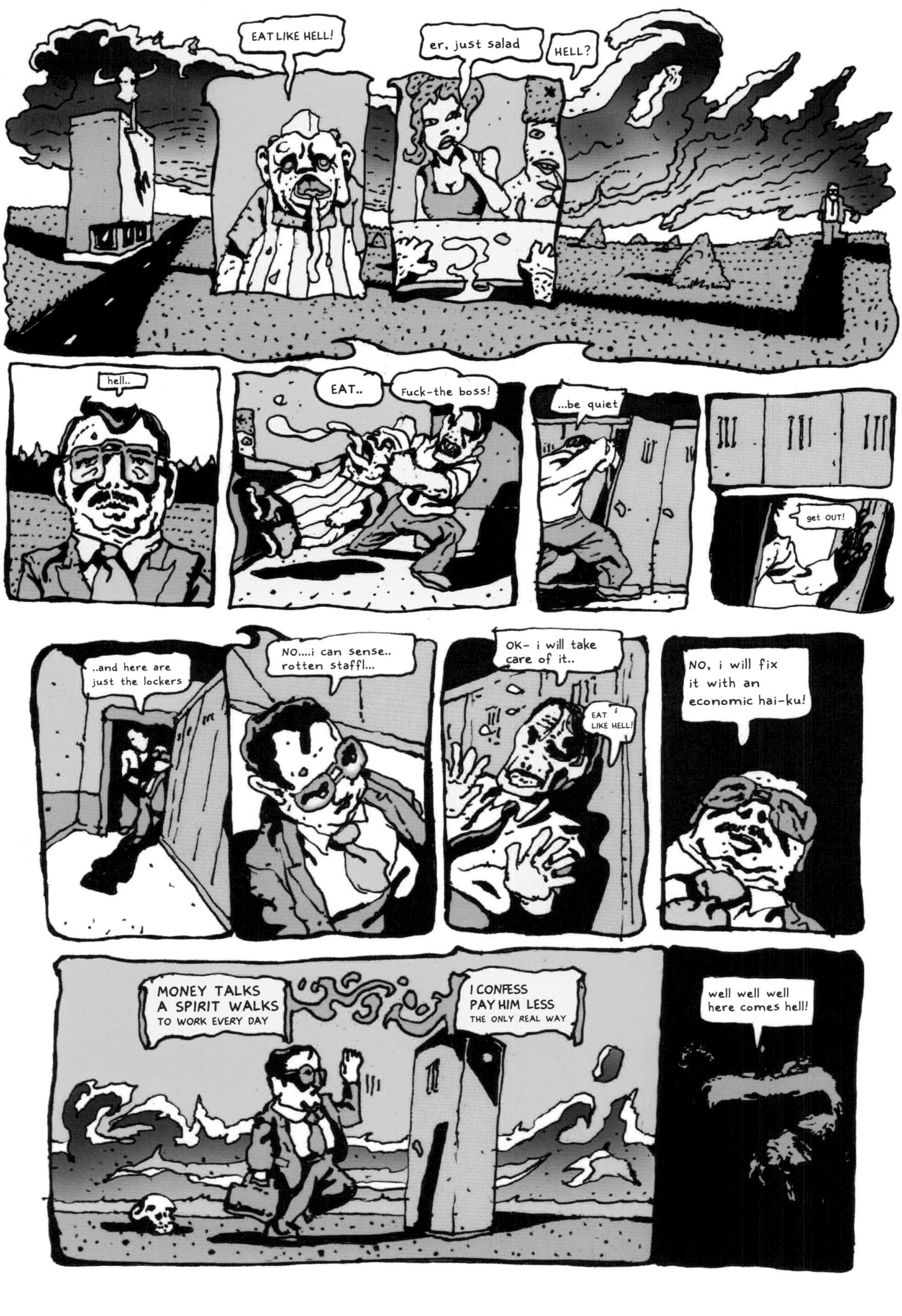
EAT LIKE HELL!
er, just salad
HELL?
hell..
EAT..
Fuck-the boss!
...be quiet
get OUT!
..and here are just the lockers
NO....i can sense.. rotten staff!...
OK- i will take care of it..
EAT LIKE HELL!
NO, i will fix it with an economic hai-ku!
MONEY TALKS A SPIRIT WALKS TO WORK EVERY DAY
I CONFESS PAY HIM LESS THE ONLY REAL WAY
well well well here comes hell!

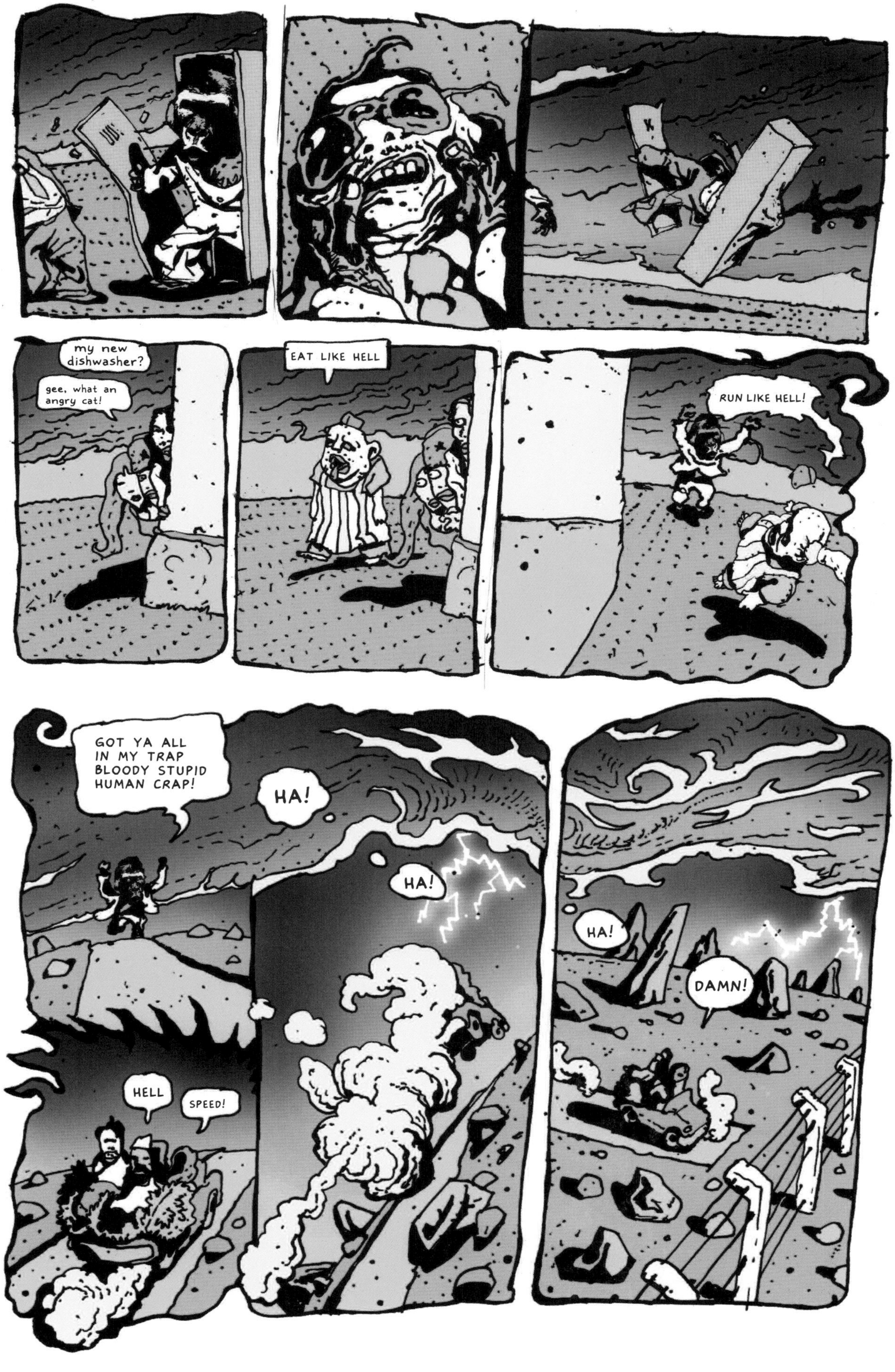
my new dishwasher?
gee, what an angry cat!
EAT LIKE HELL
RUN LIKE HELL!
GOT YA ALL IN MY TRAP BLOODY STUPID HUMAN CRAP!
HA!
HA!
HELL
SPEED!
HA!
DAMN!

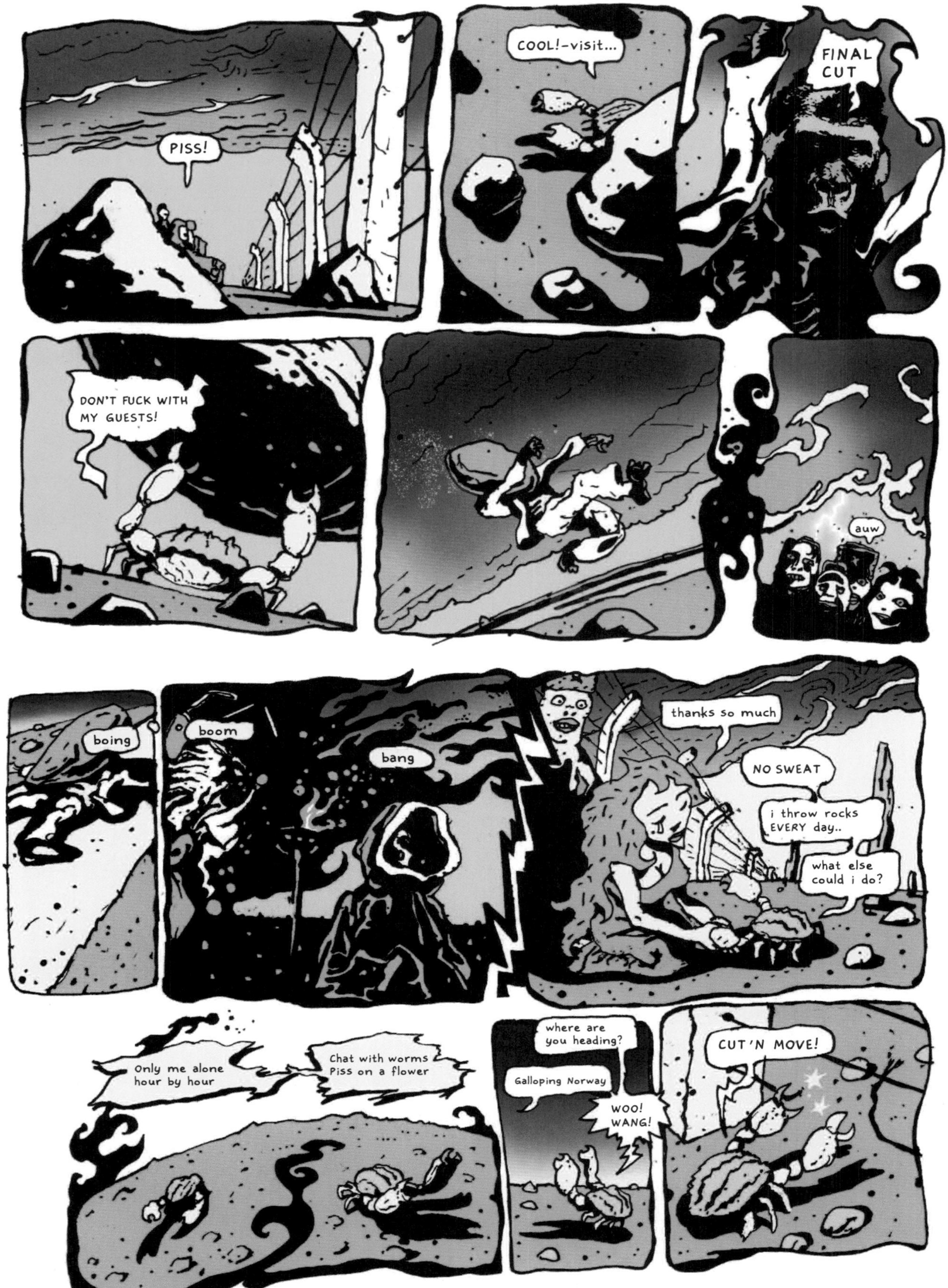
PISS!
COOL!-visit...
FINAL CUT
DON'T FUCK WITH MY GUESTS!
auw
boing
boom
bang
thanks so much
NO SWEAT
i throw rocks EVERY day..
what else could i do?
Only me alone hour by hour
Chat with worms Piss on a flower
where are you heading?
Galloping Norway
WOO! WANG!
CUT'N MOVE!

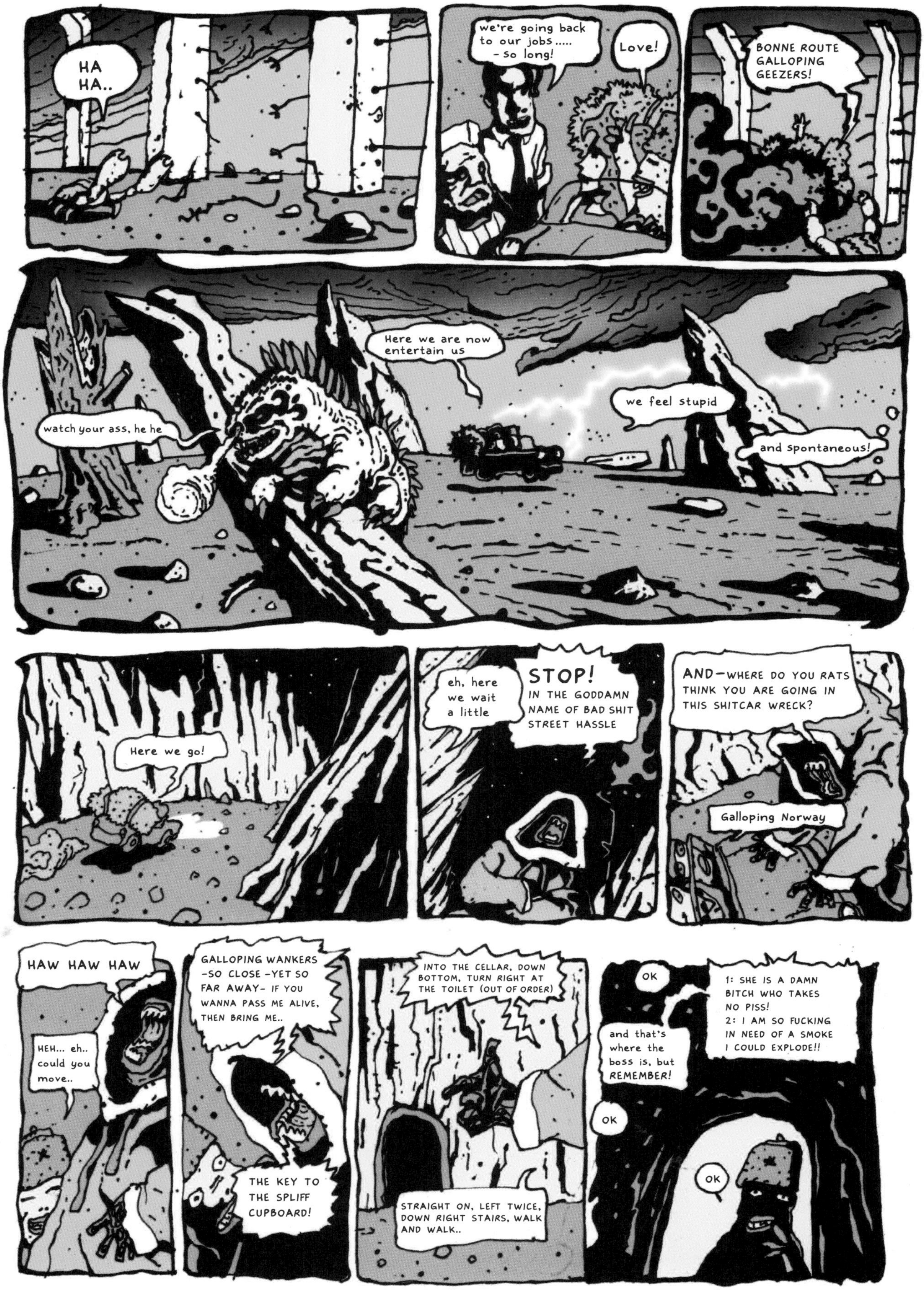
HA
HA..
we're going back to our jobs ..... – so long!
Love!
BONNE ROUTE GALLOPING GEEZERS!
Here we are now entertain us
watch your ass, he he
we feel stupid
and spontaneous!
Here we go!
eh, here we wait a little
STOP! IN THE GODDAMN NAME OF BAD SHIT STREET HASSLE
AND– WHERE DO YOU RATS THINK YOU ARE GOING IN THIS SHITCAR WRECK?
Galloping Norway
HAW HAW HAW
HEH... eh.. could you move..
GALLOPING WANKERS –SO CLOSE –YET SO FAR AWAY– IF YOU WANNA PASS ME ALIVE, THEN BRING ME..
THE KEY TO THE SPLIFF CUPBOARD!
INTO THE CELLAR, DOWN BOTTOM, TURN RIGHT AT THE TOILET (OUT OF ORDER)
STRAIGHT ON, LEFT TWICE, DOWN RIGHT STAIRS, WALK AND WALK..
OK
and that's where the boss is, but REMEMBER!
1: SHE IS A DAMN BITCH WHO TAKES NO PISS!
2: I AM SO FUCKING IN NEED OF A SMOKE I COULD EXPLODE!!
OK
OK

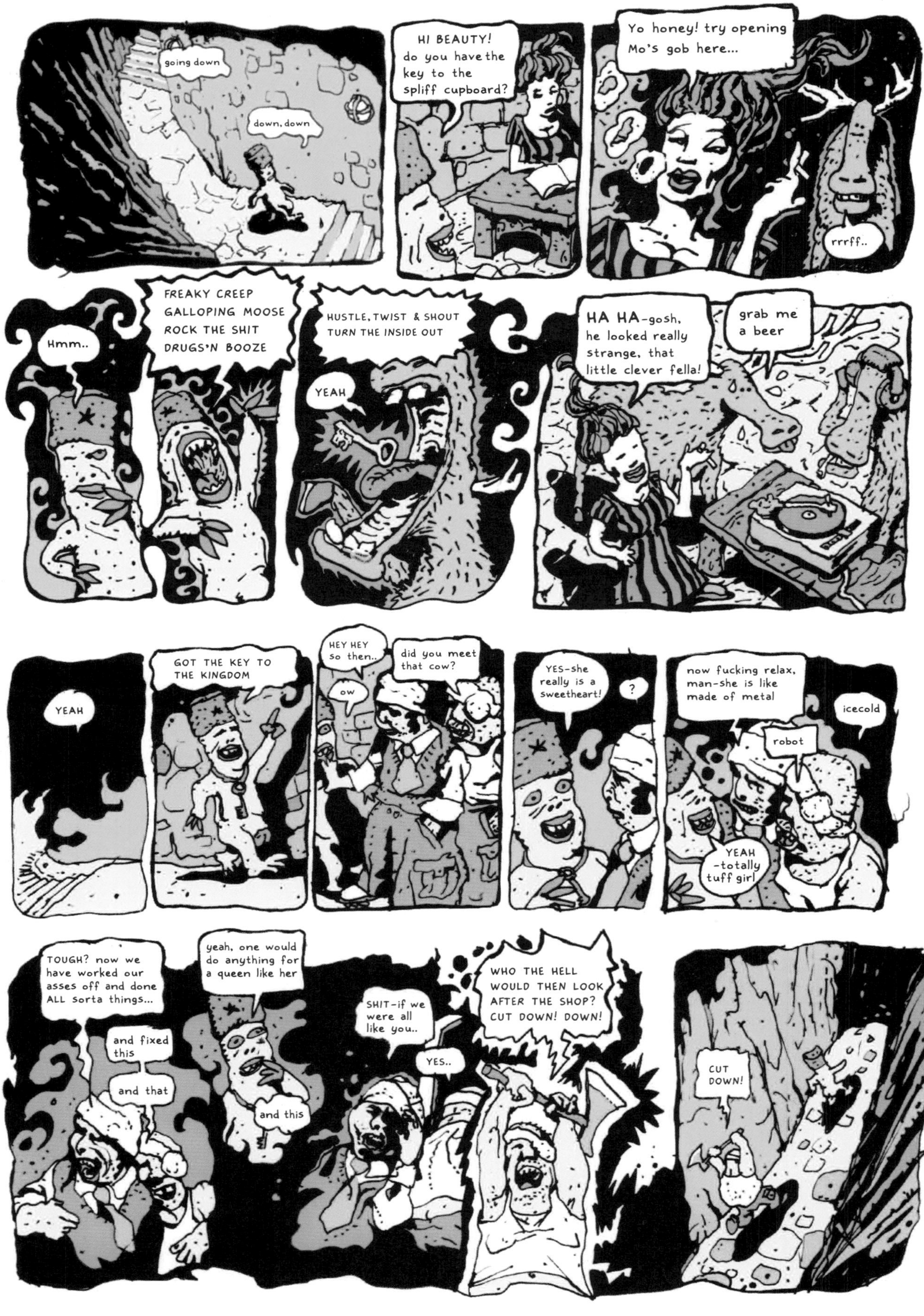
going down
down, down
HI BEAUTY! do you have the key to the spliff cupboard?
Yo honey! try opening Mo's gob here...
rrrff..
Hmm..
FREAKY CREEP GALLOPING MOOSE ROCK THE SHIT DRUGS'N BOOZE
HUSTLE, TWIST & SHOUT TURN THE INSIDE OUT
YEAH
HA HA-gosh, he looked really strange, that little clever fella!
grab me a beer
YEAH
GOT THE KEY TO THE KINGDOM
HEY HEY so then..
ow
did you meet that cow?
YES-she really is a sweetheart!
?
now fucking relax, man-she is like made of metal
icecold
robot
YEAH -totally tuff girl
TOUGH? now we have worked our asses off and done ALL sorta things...
and fixed this
and that
yeah, one would do anything for a queen like her
and this
SHIT-if we were all like you..
YES..
WHO THE HELL WOULD THEN LOOK AFTER THE SHOP? CUT DOWN! DOWN!
CUT DOWN!

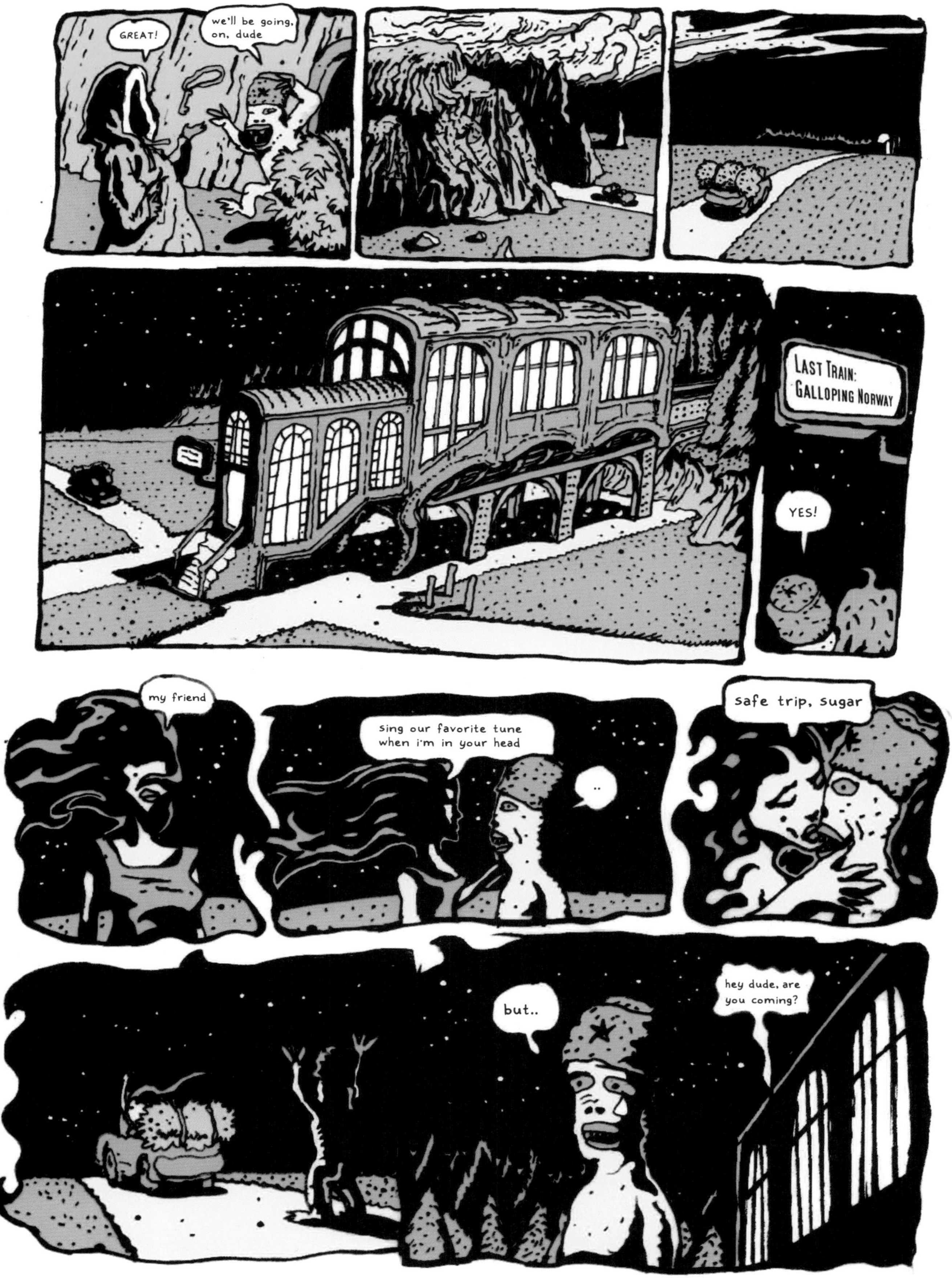
GREAT!
we'll be going, on, dude
LAST TRAIN: GALLOPING NORWAY
YES!
my friend
sing our favorite tune when i'm in your head
..
safe trip, sugar
but..
hey dude, are you coming?

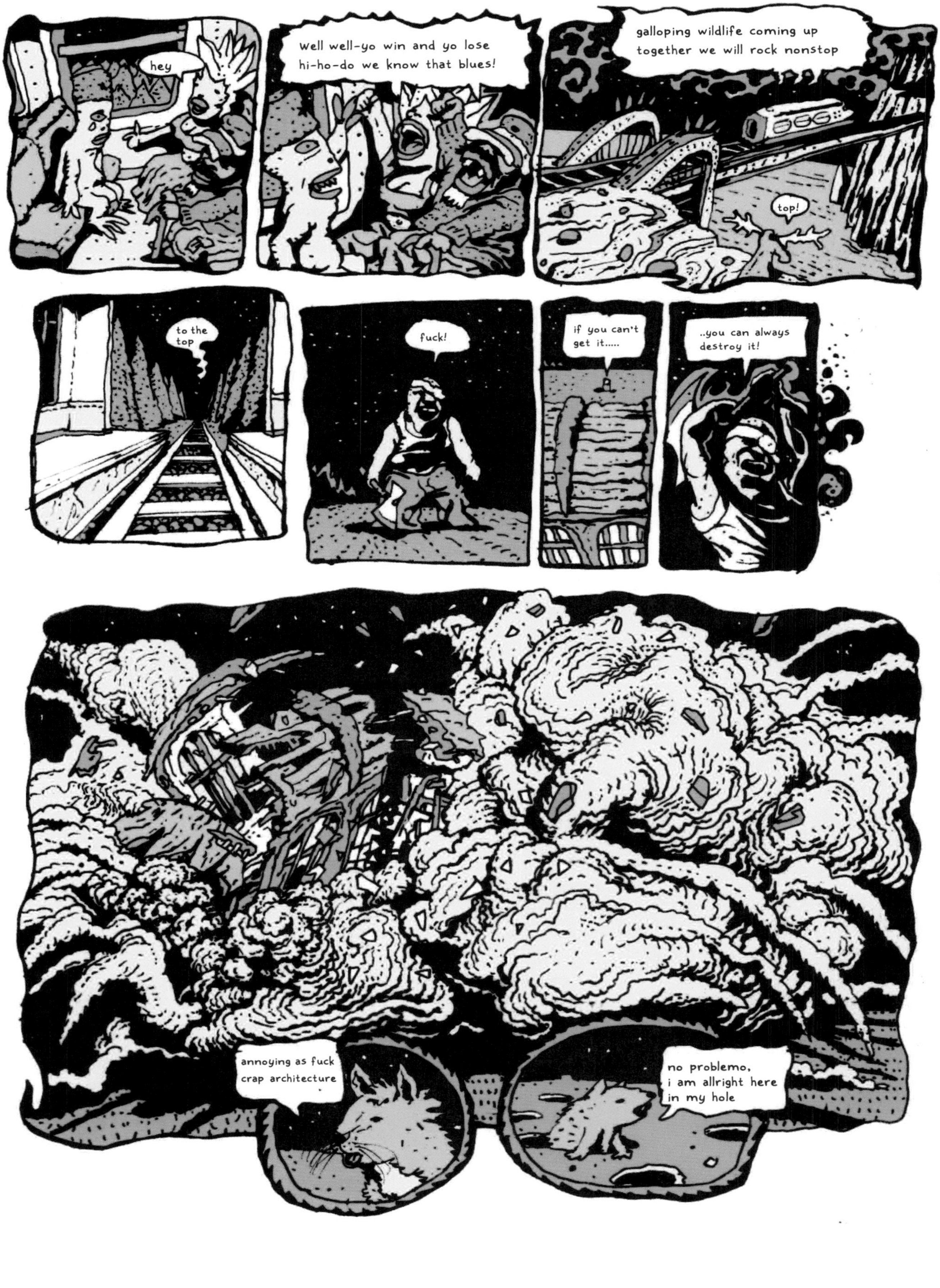
hey
Well well-yo win and yo lose
hi-ho-do we know that blues!
galloping wildlife coming up
together we will rock nonstop
top!
to the top
fuck!
if you can't get it.....
..you can always destroy it!
annoying as fuck
crap architecture
no problemo,
i am allright here
in my hole

142

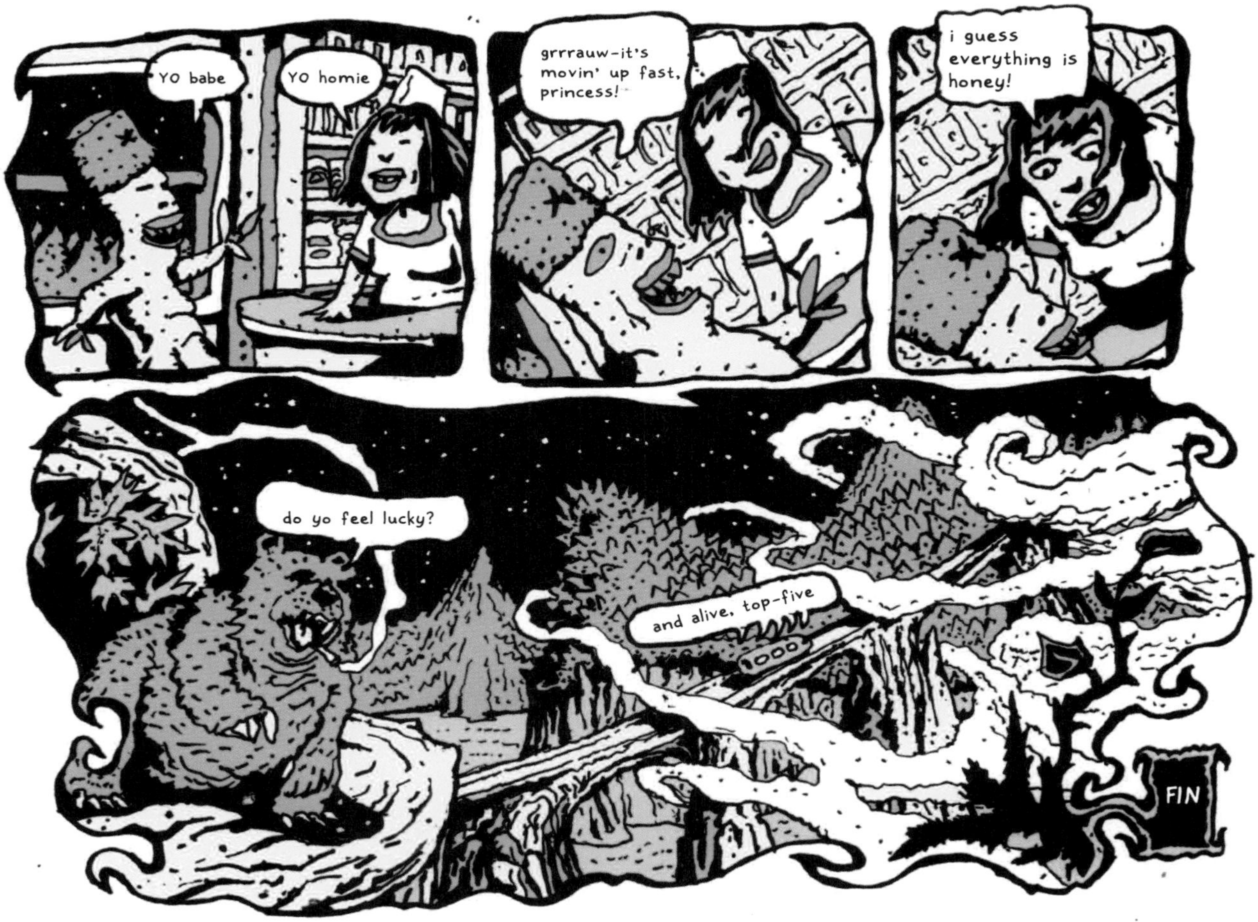
YO babe
YO homie
grrrauw-it's movin' up fast, princess!
i guess everything is honey!
do yo feel lucky?
and alive, top-five
FIN

Julie Nord

From

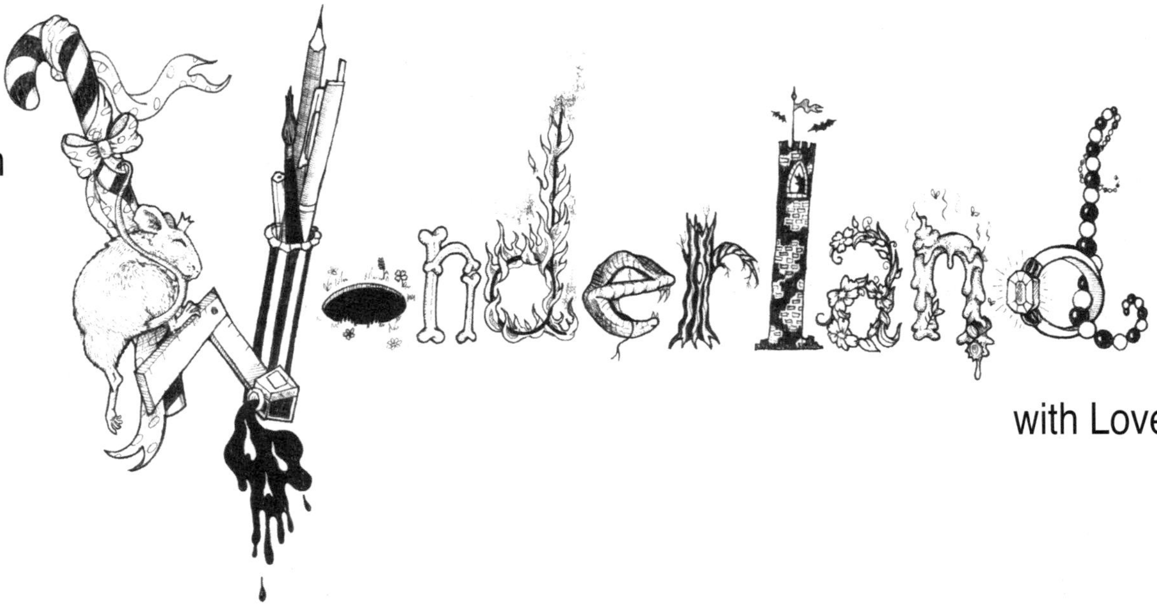
Wonderland

with Love

IN THE VANISHING OF
DAYLIGHT
THINGS BEGAN TO SEEM
FAMILIAR

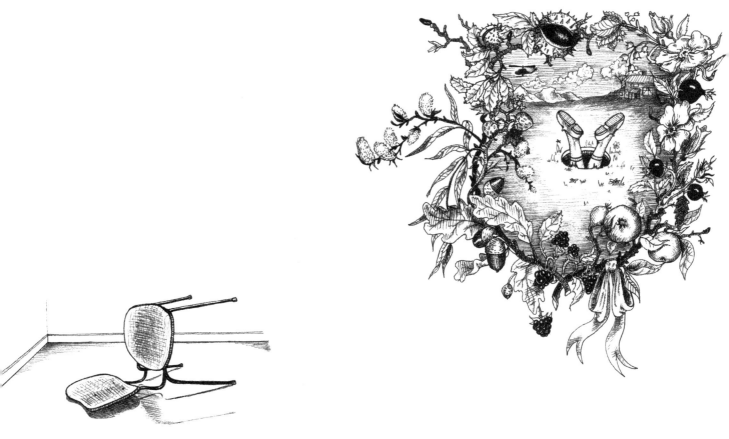

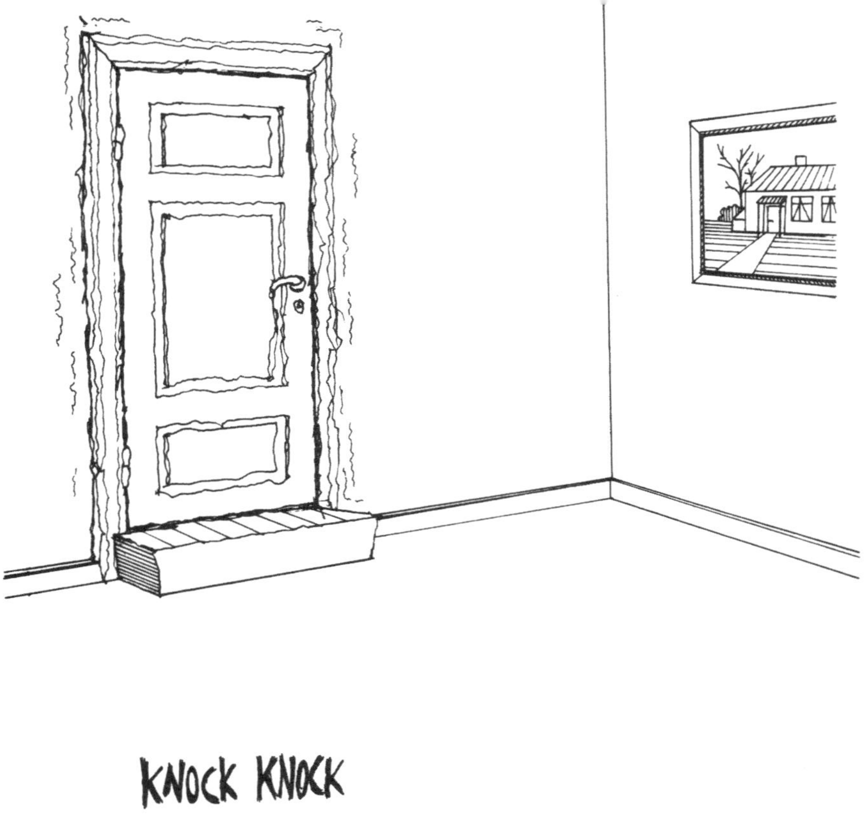
KNOCK KNOCK

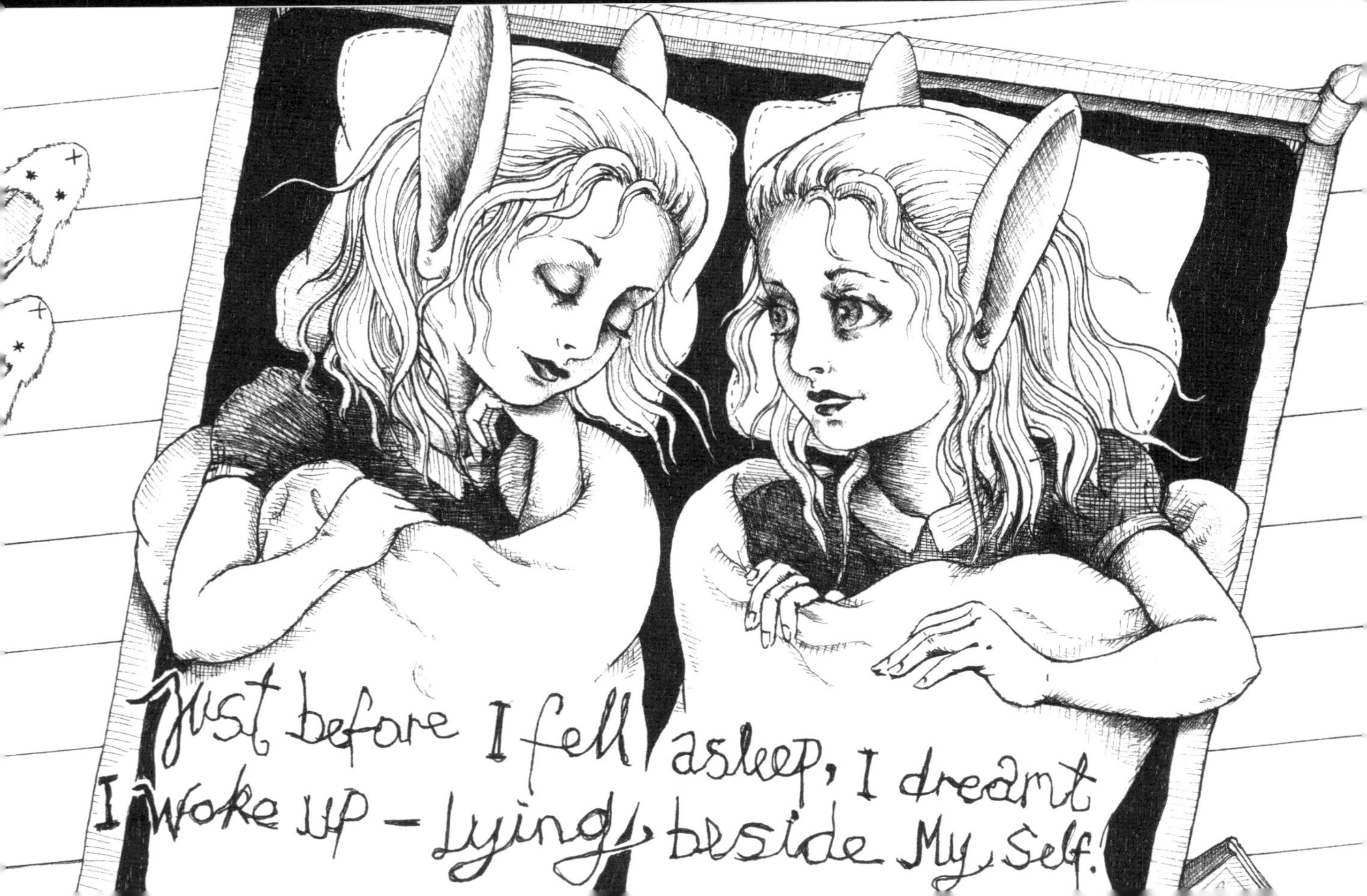
Just before I fell asleep, I dreamt
I woke up - lying beside My self.

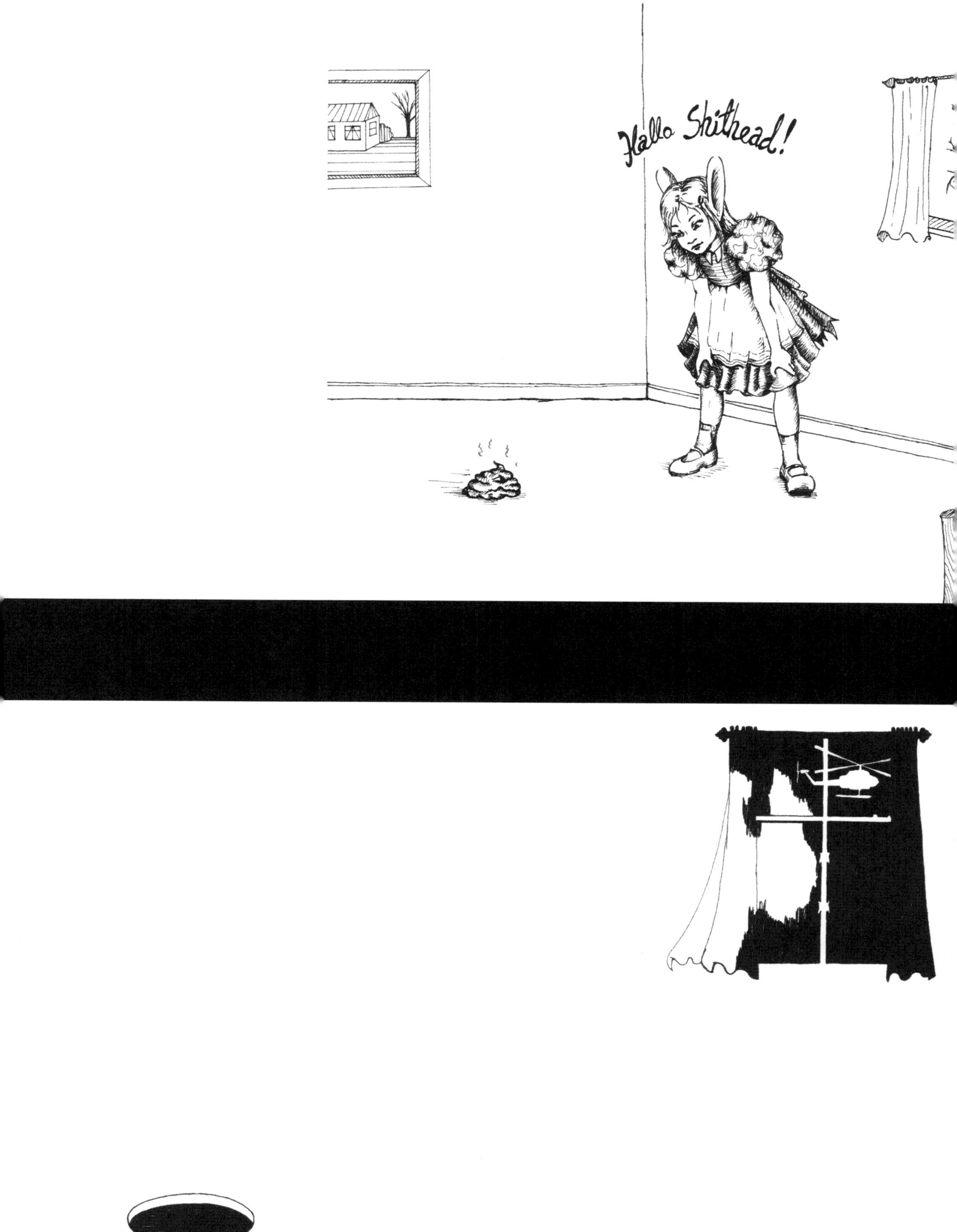
Hallo Shithead!

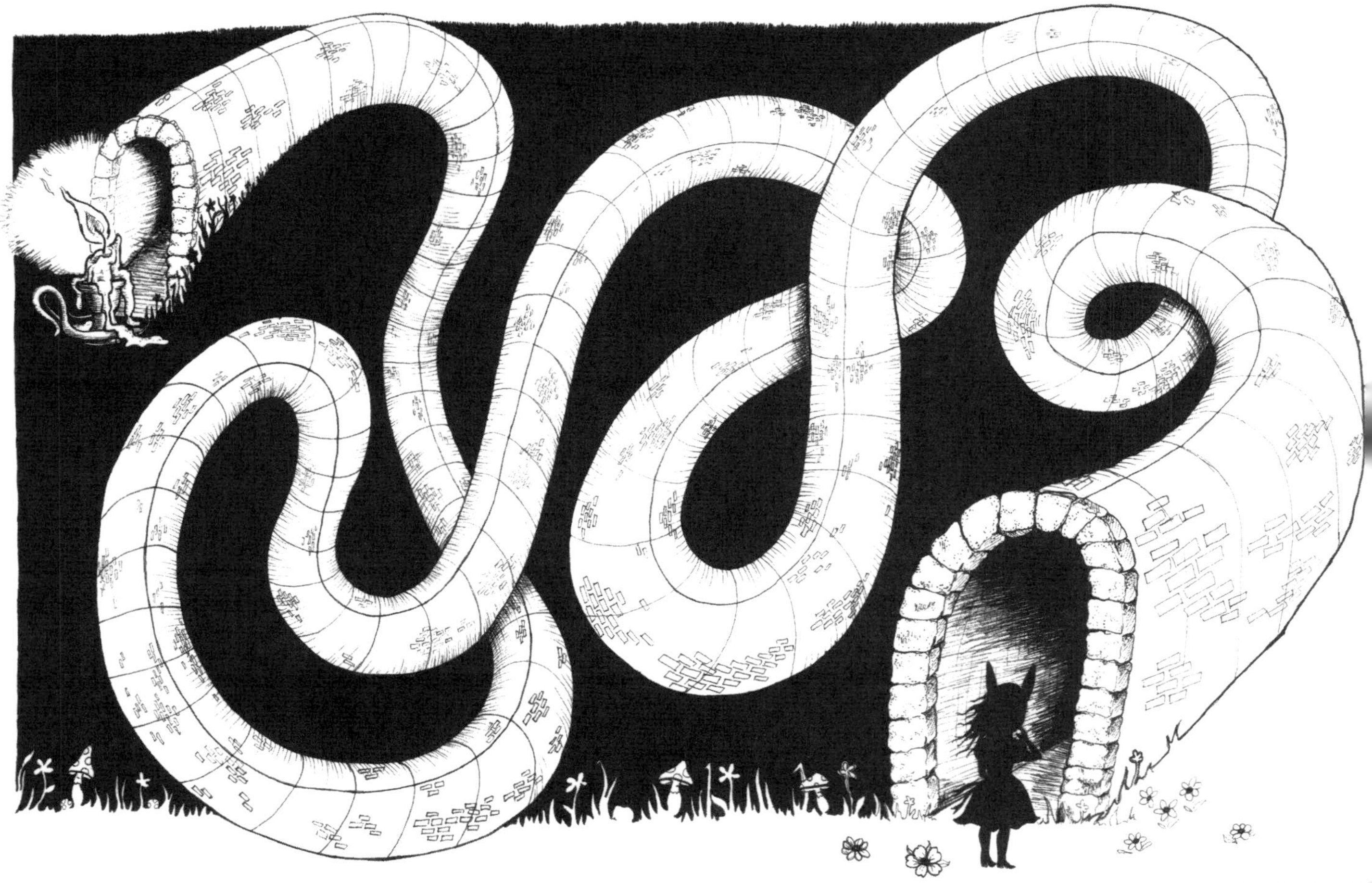

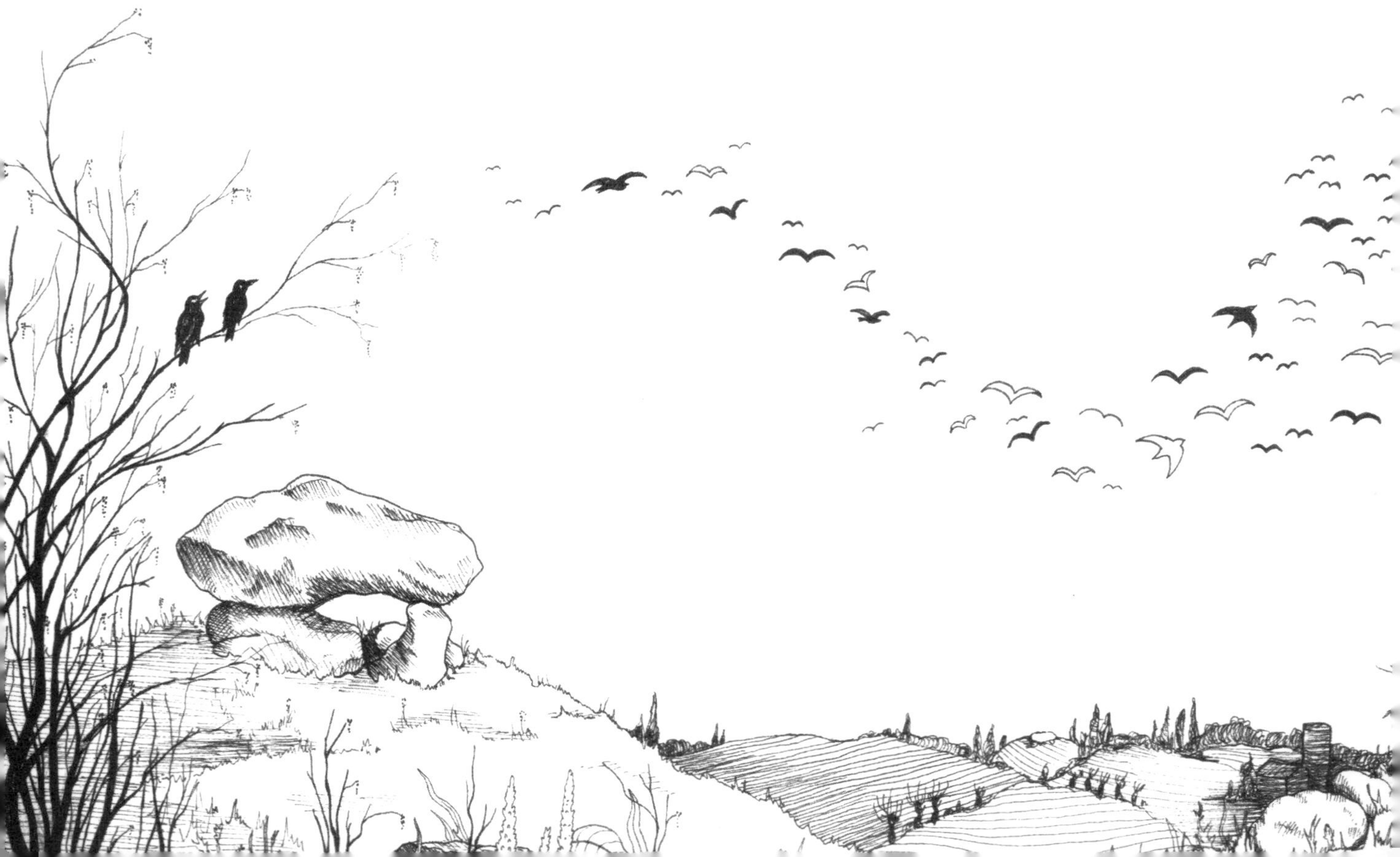

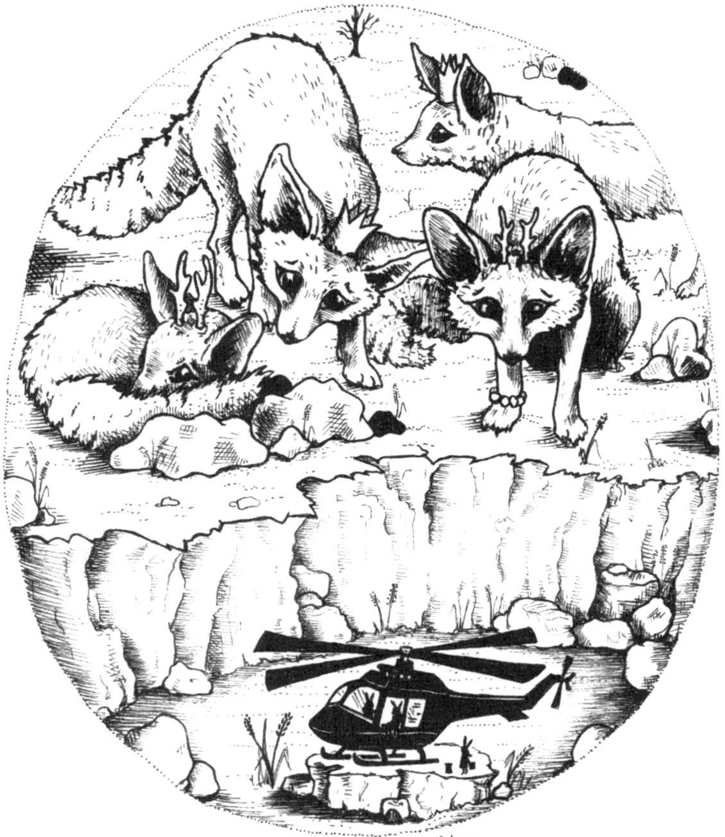

I believe in everything

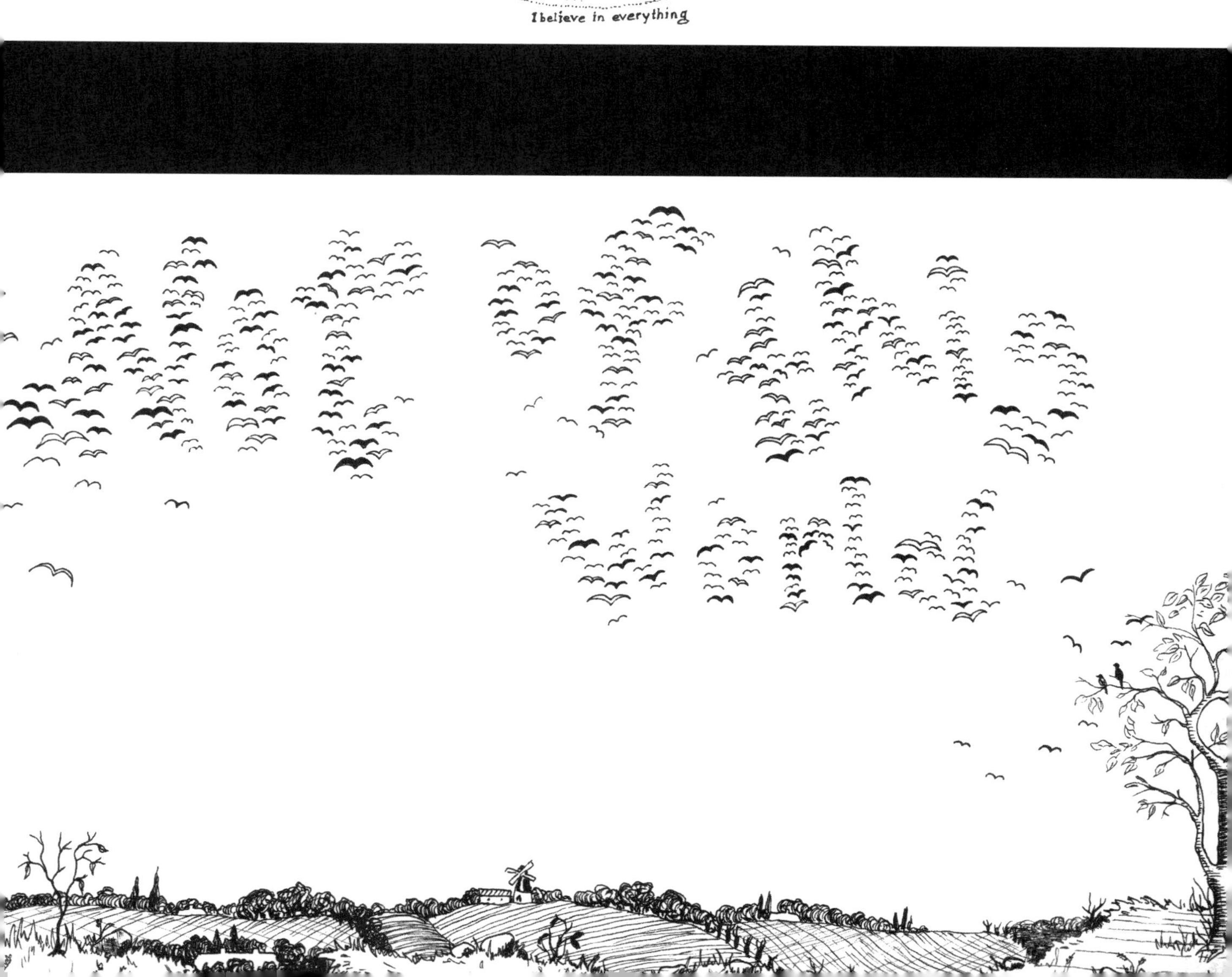
Not of this world

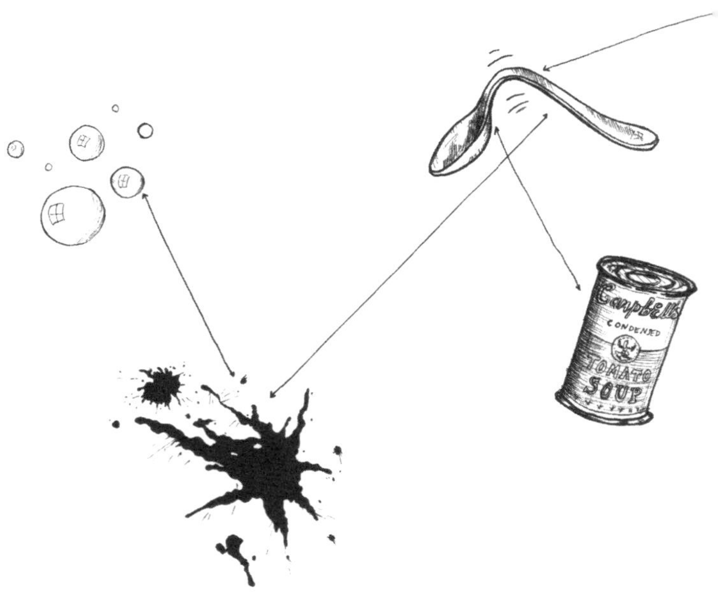
Campbell's
CONDENSED
TOMATO
SOUP

When I make a line between things – it makes me able to relax...

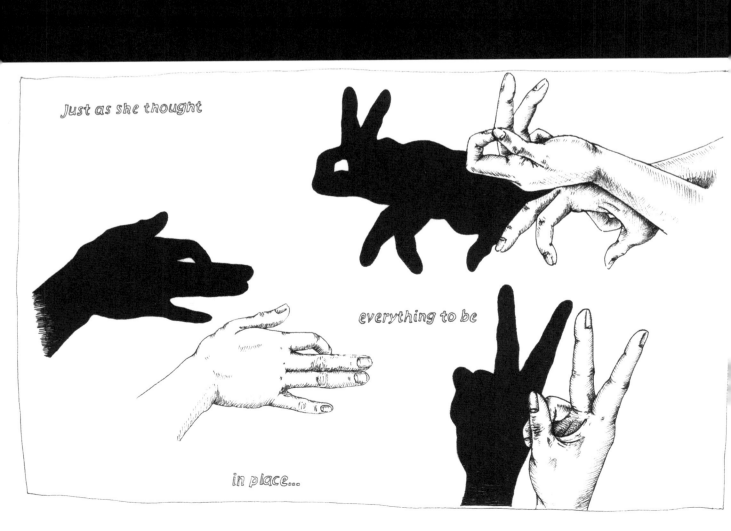

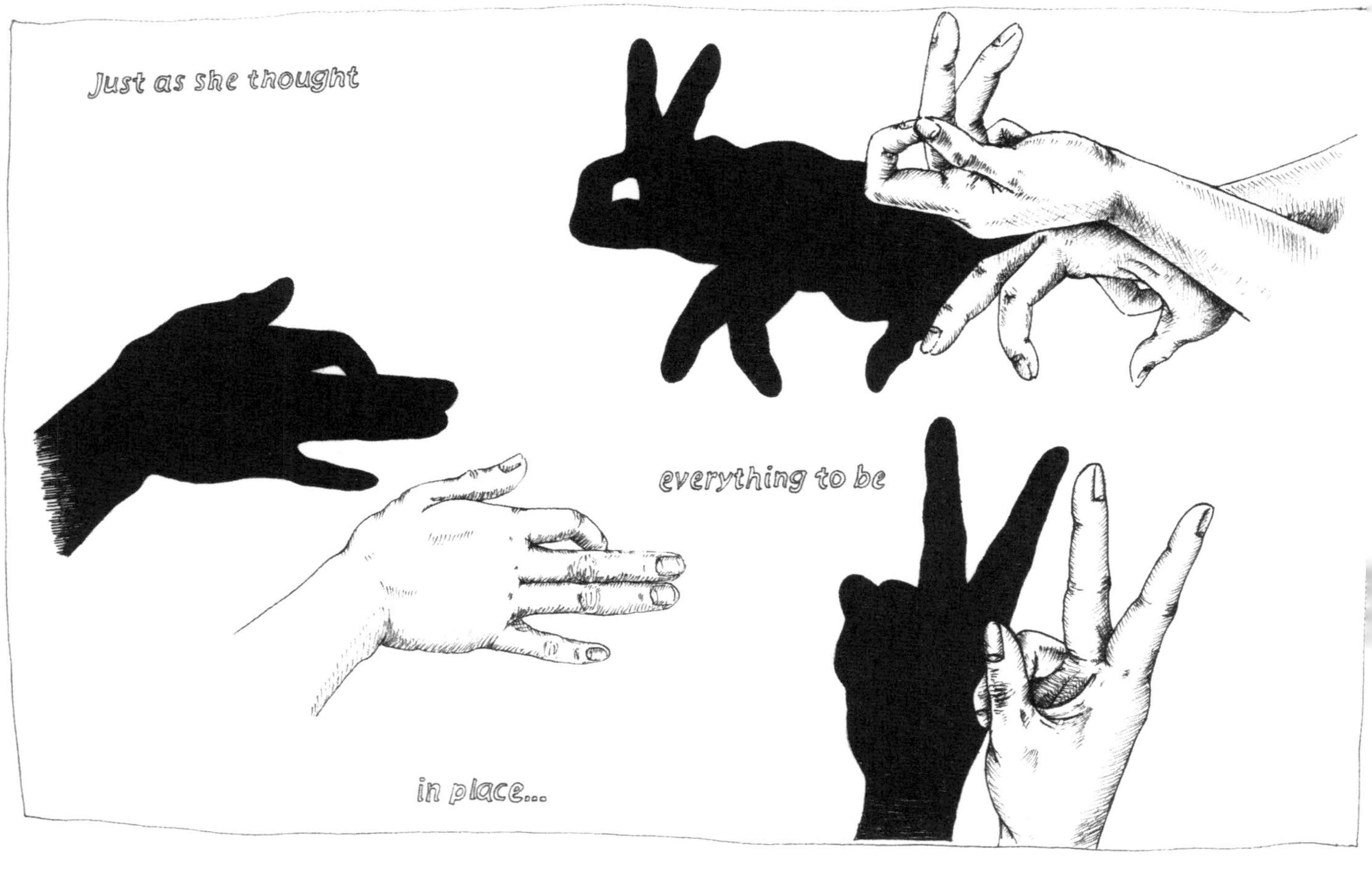
Just as she thought
everything to be
in place...

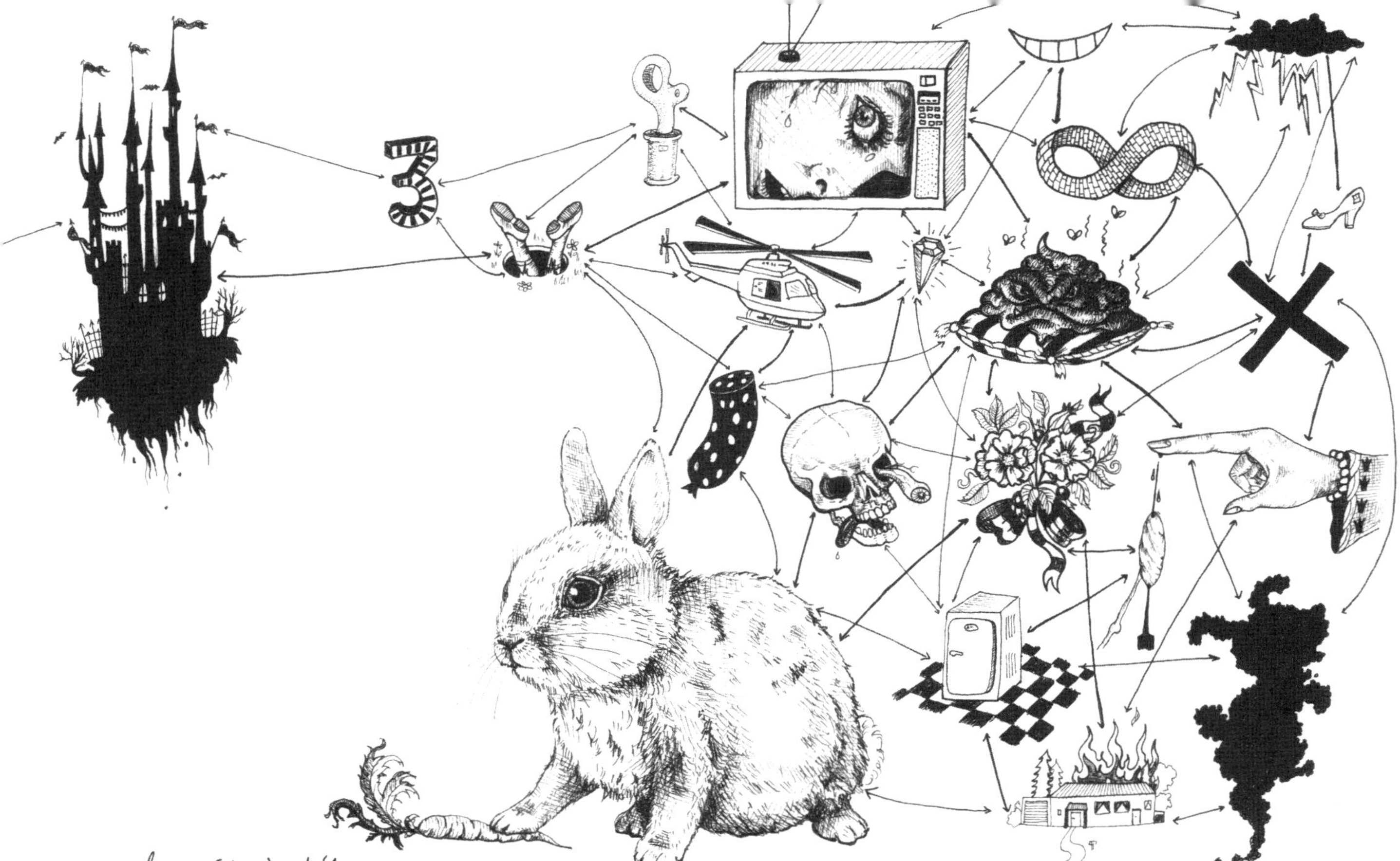

- for a (short) while.

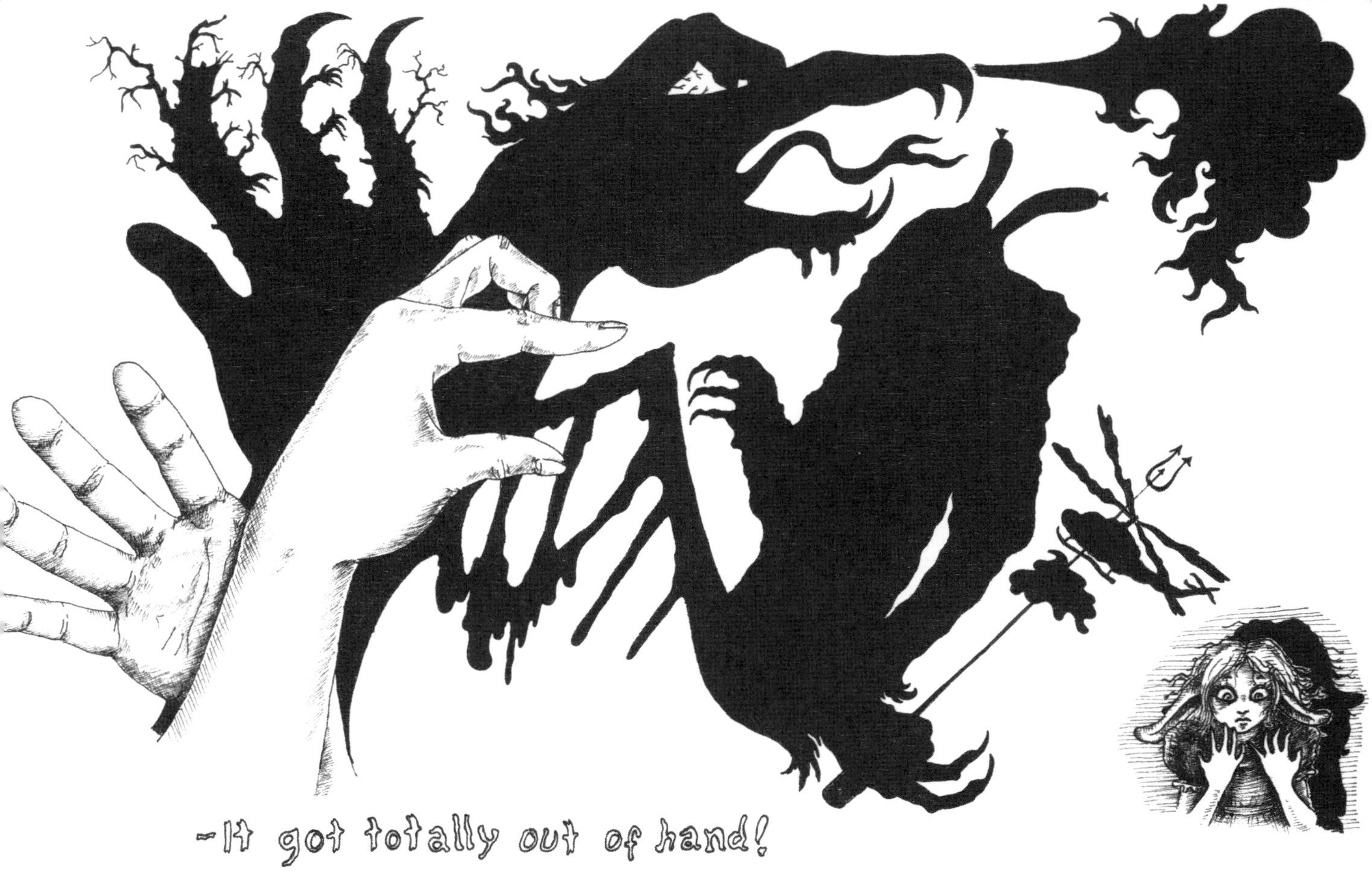

-It got totally out of hand!

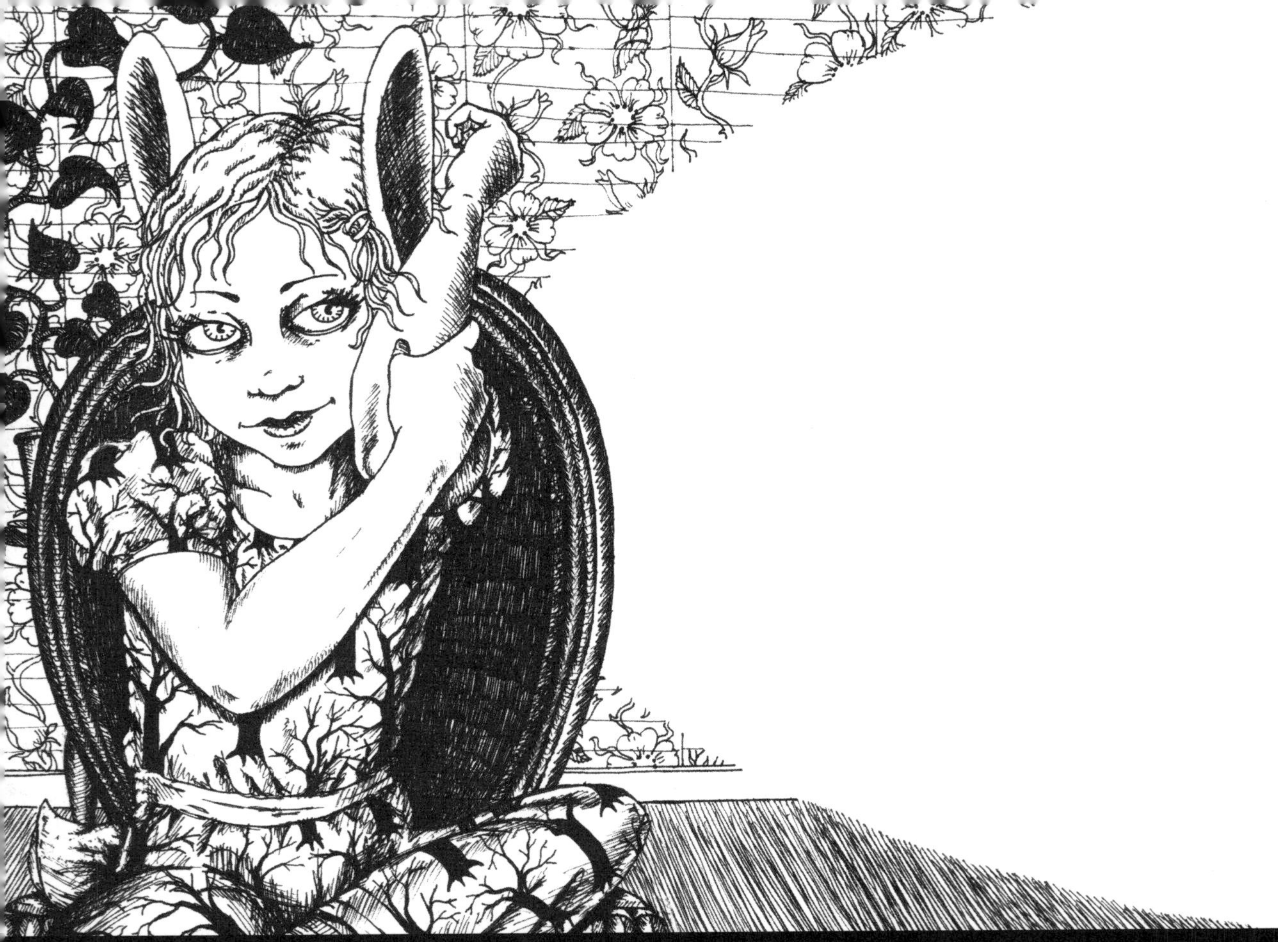

[redacted]

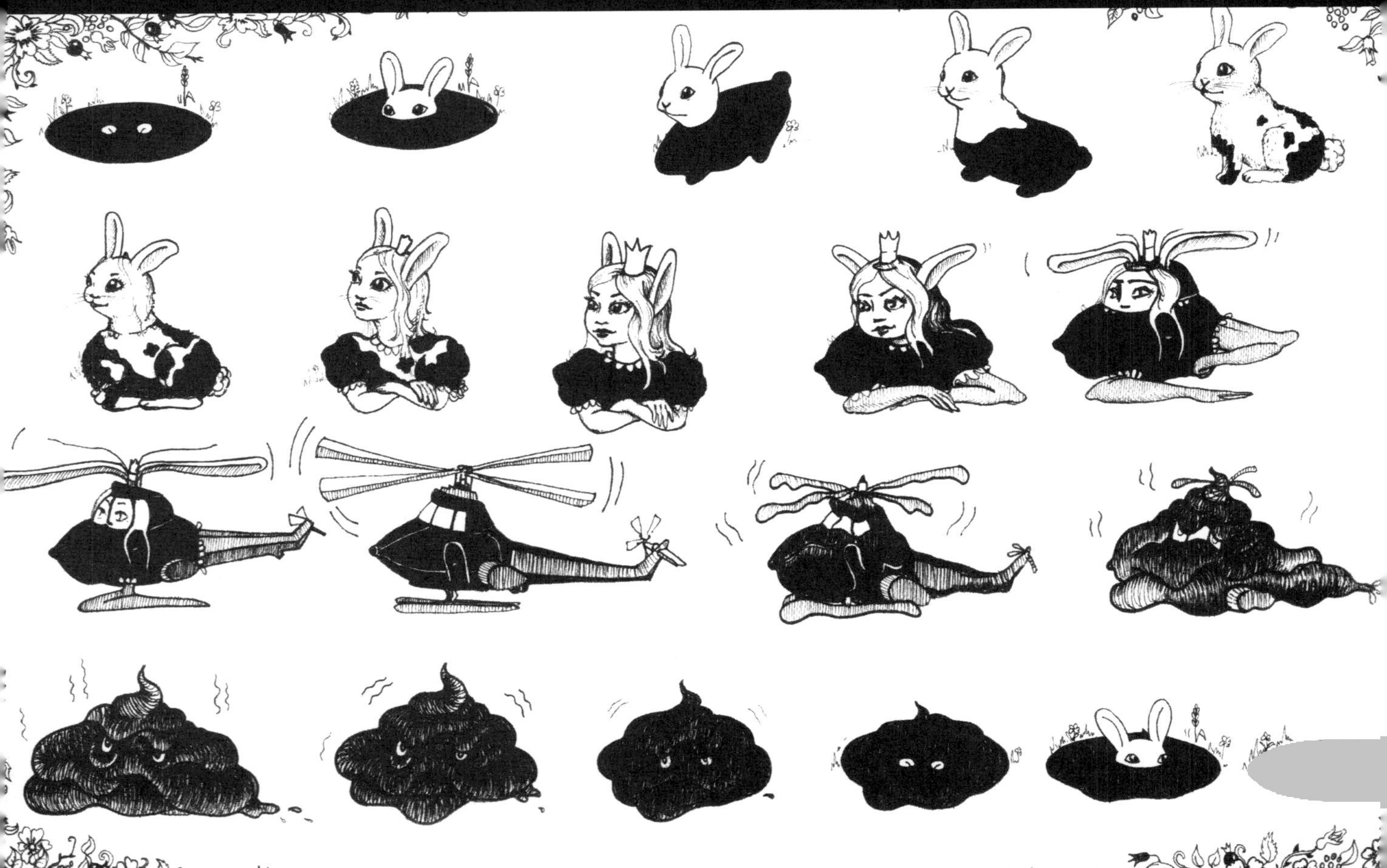

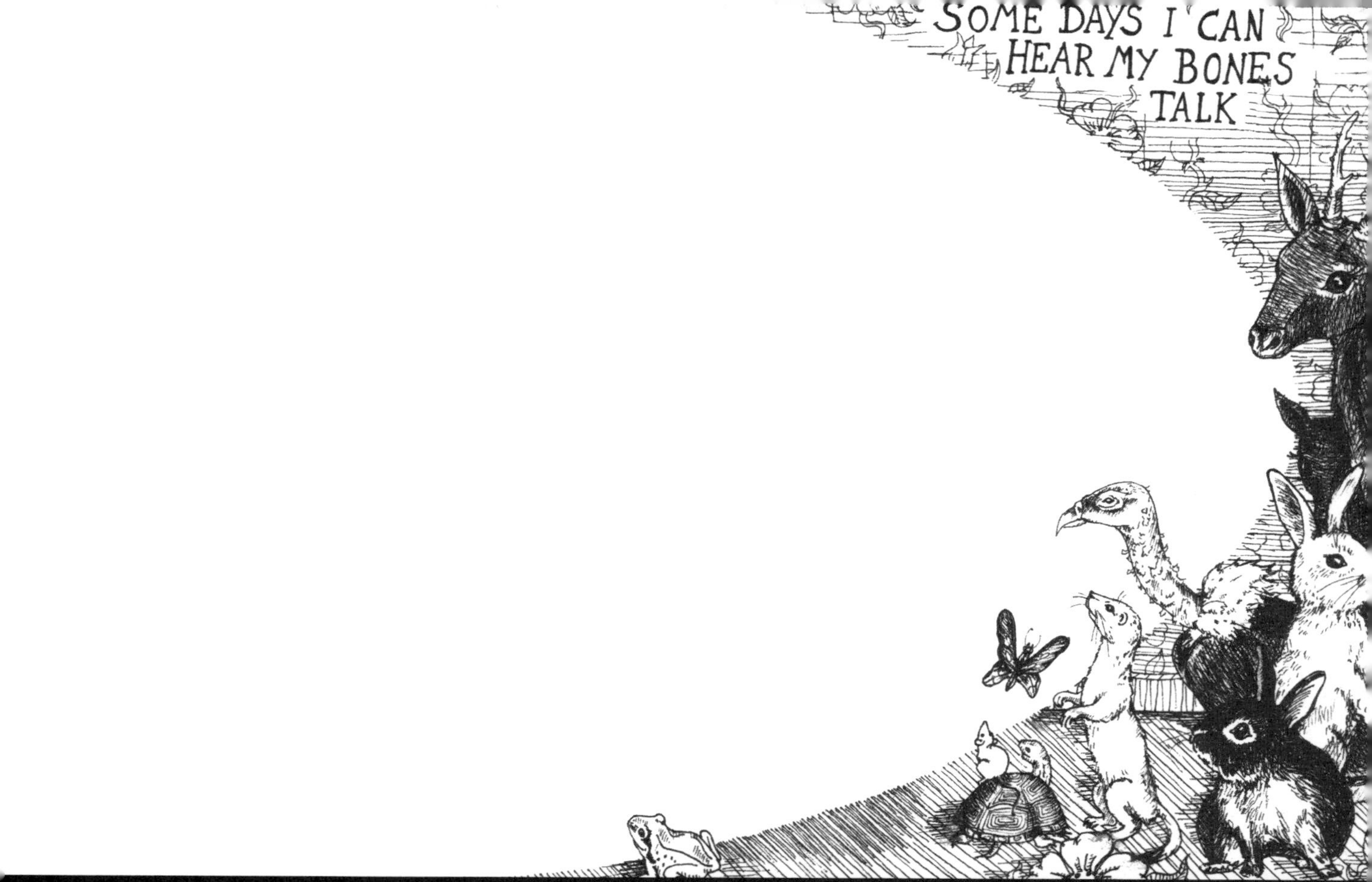
SOME DAYS I CAN HEAR MY BONES TALK

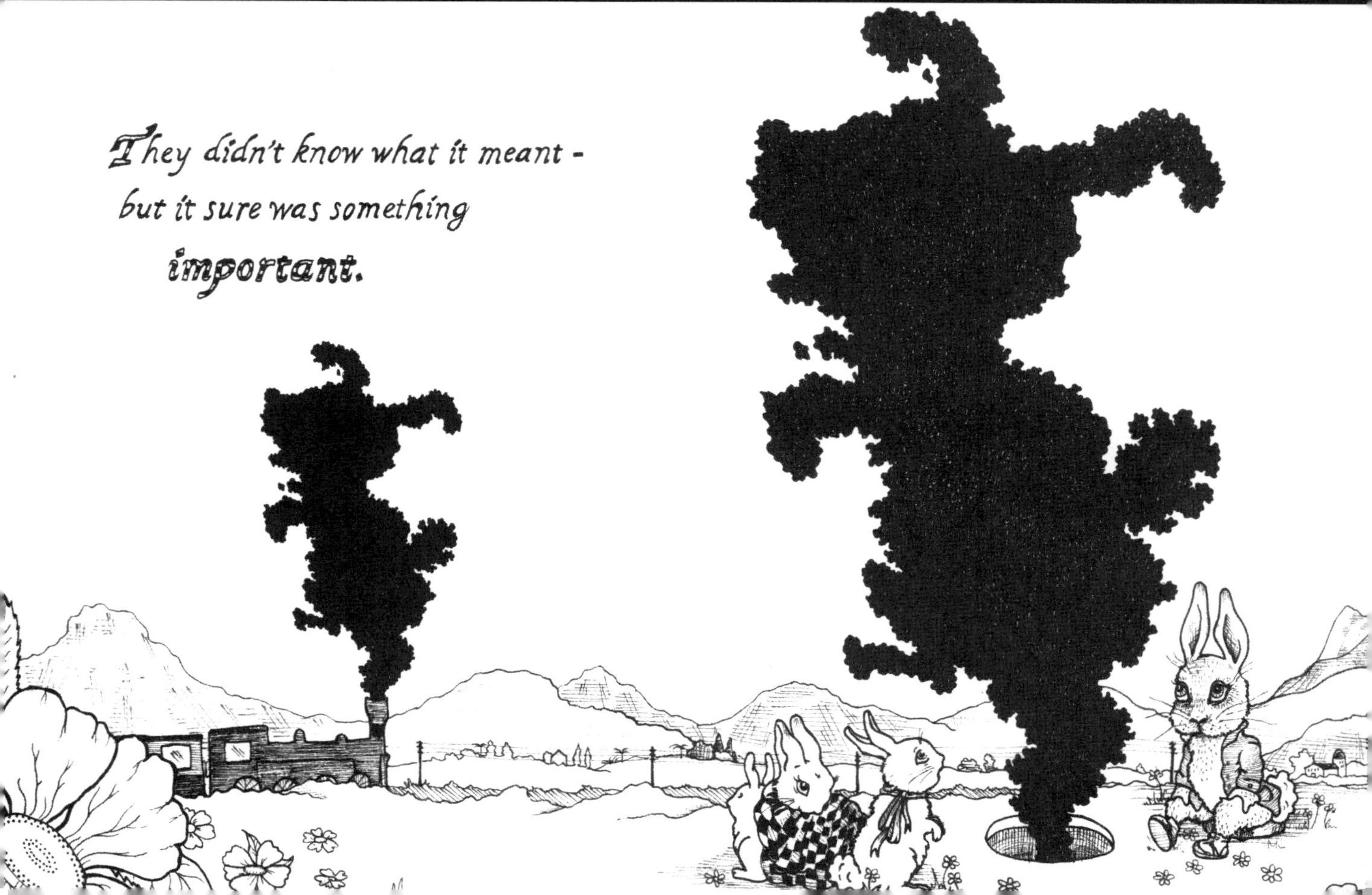
They didn't know what it meant - but it sure was something important.

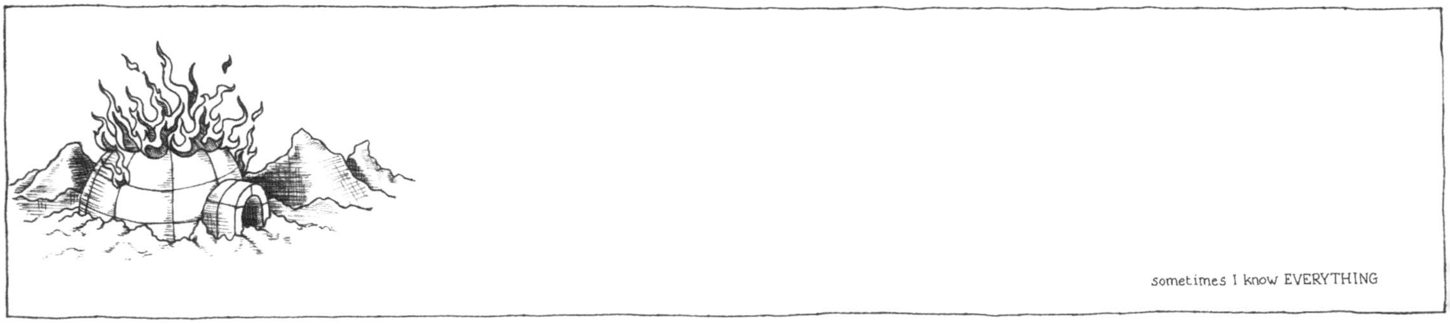
sometimes I know EVERYTHING

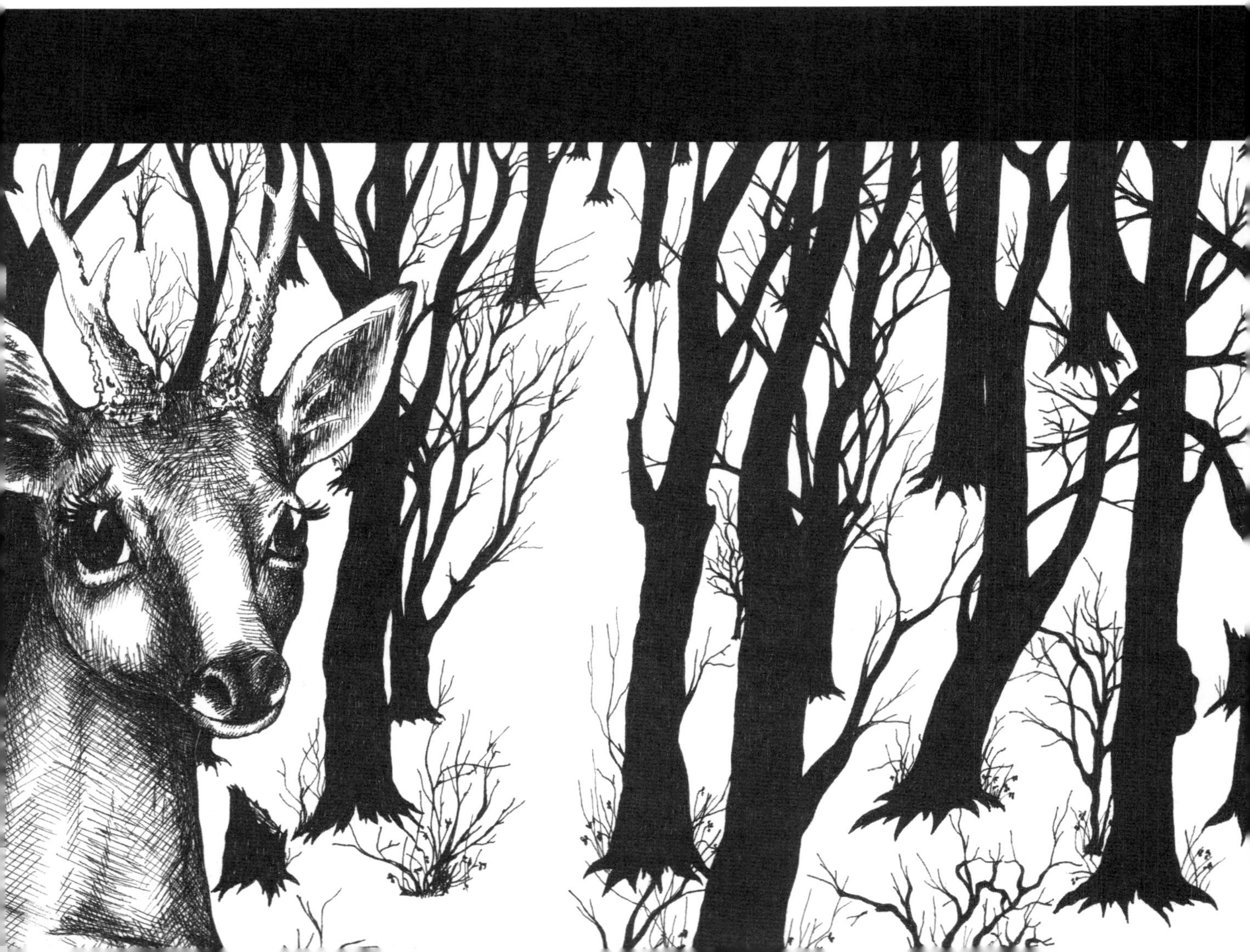

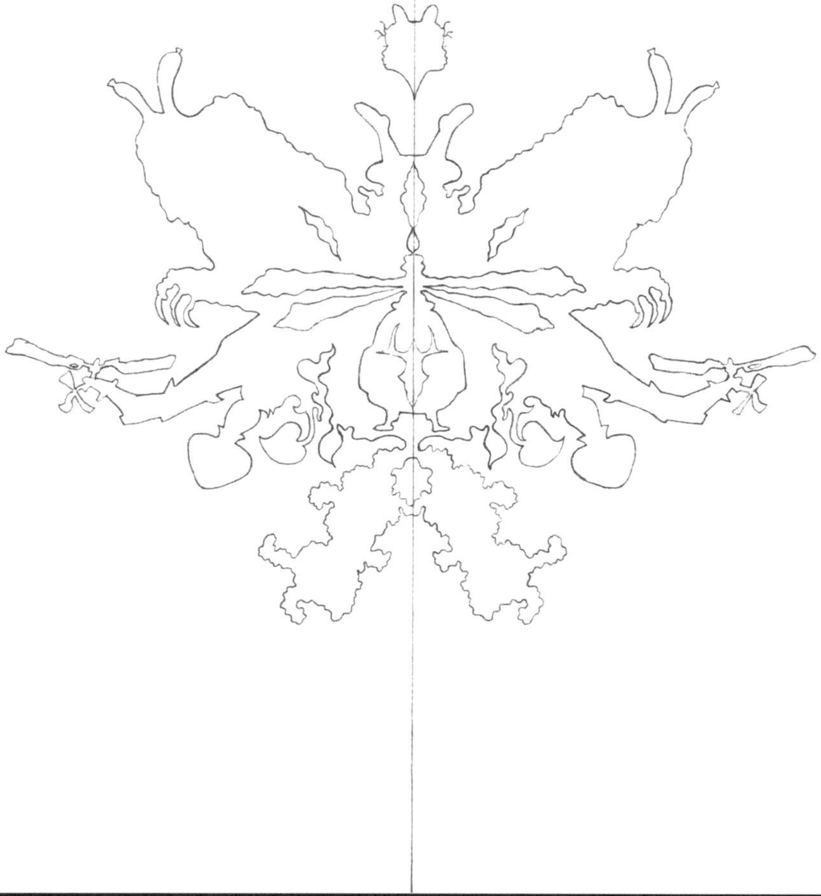

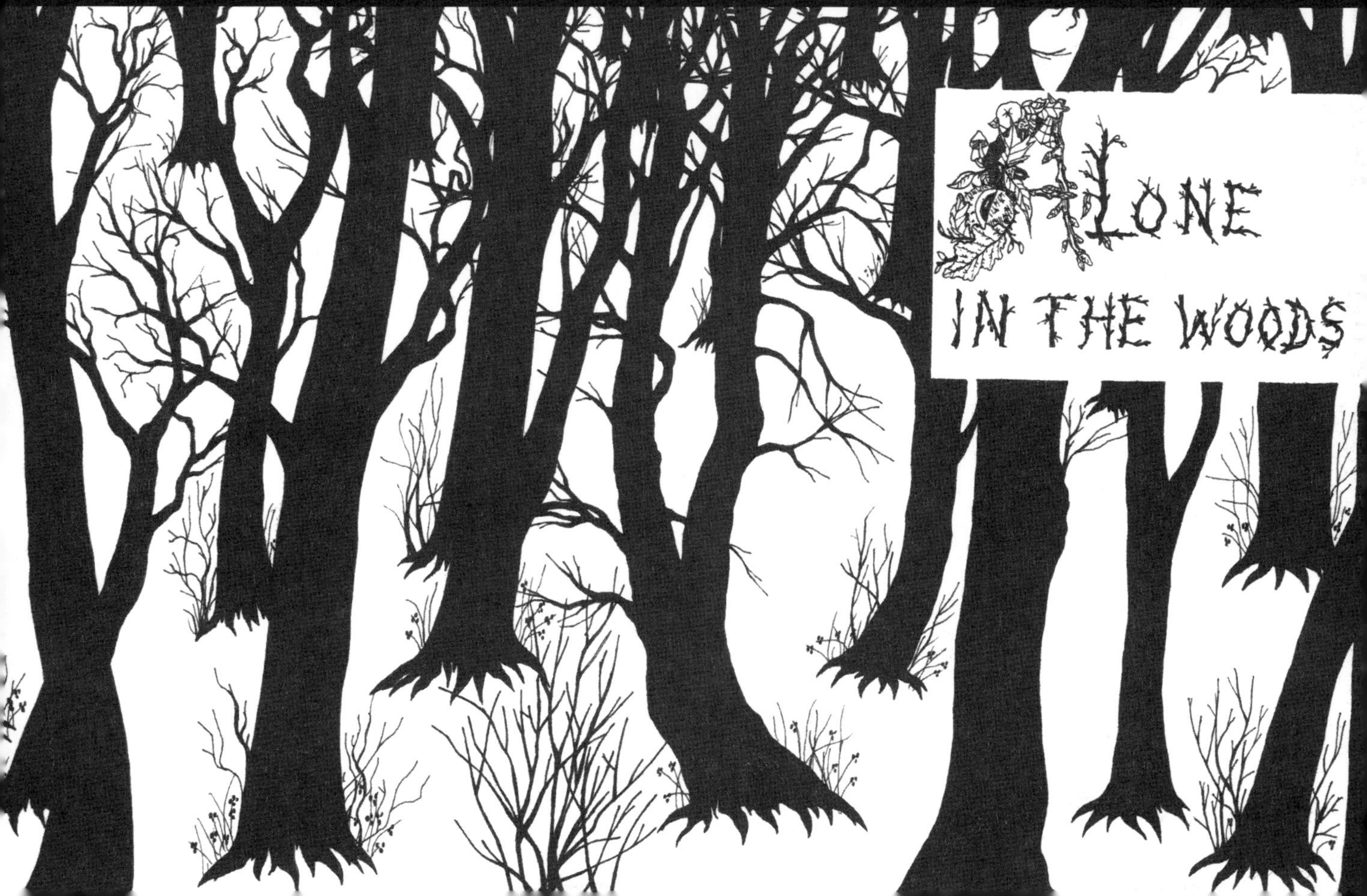
ALONE
IN THE WOODS

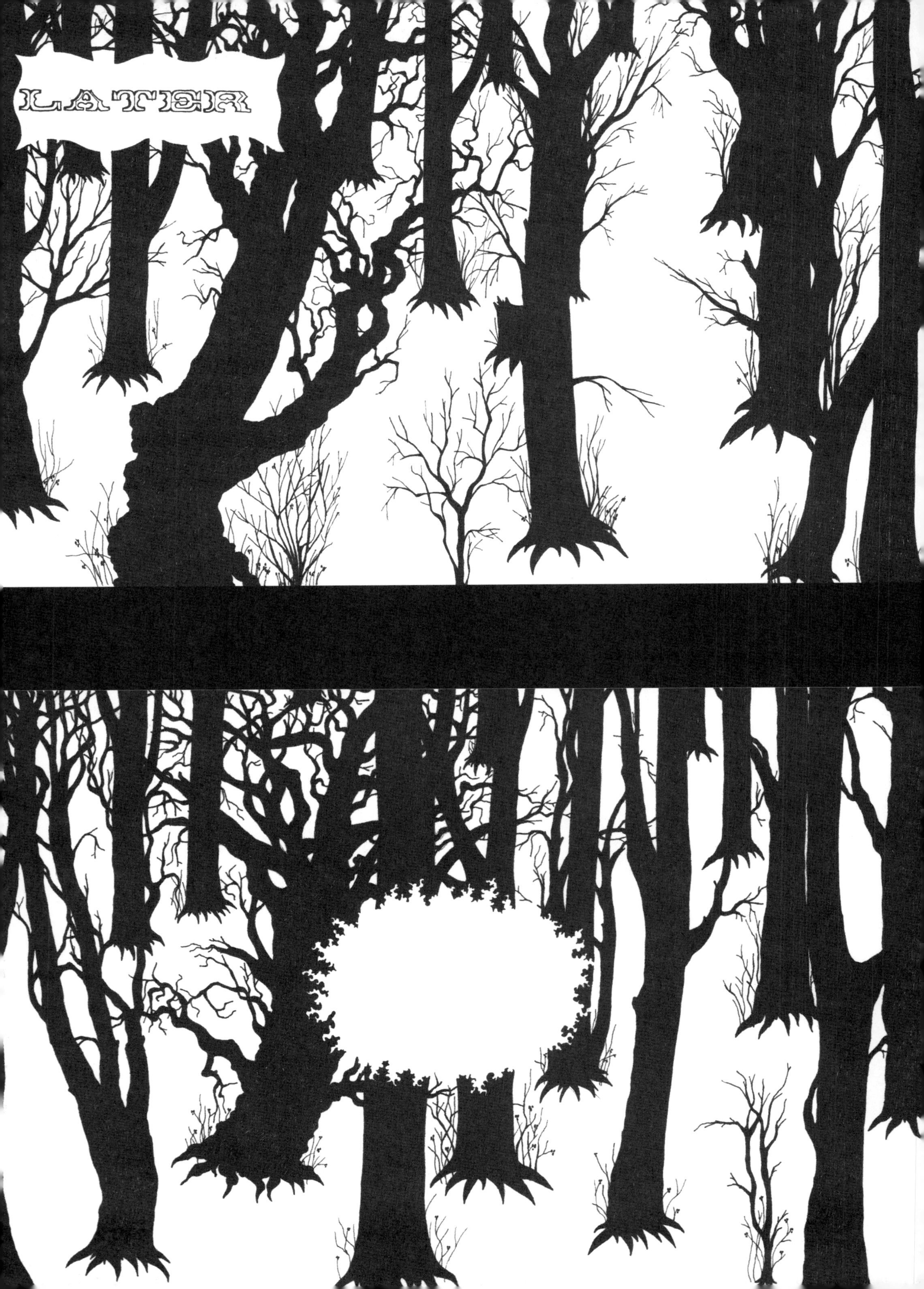
LATER

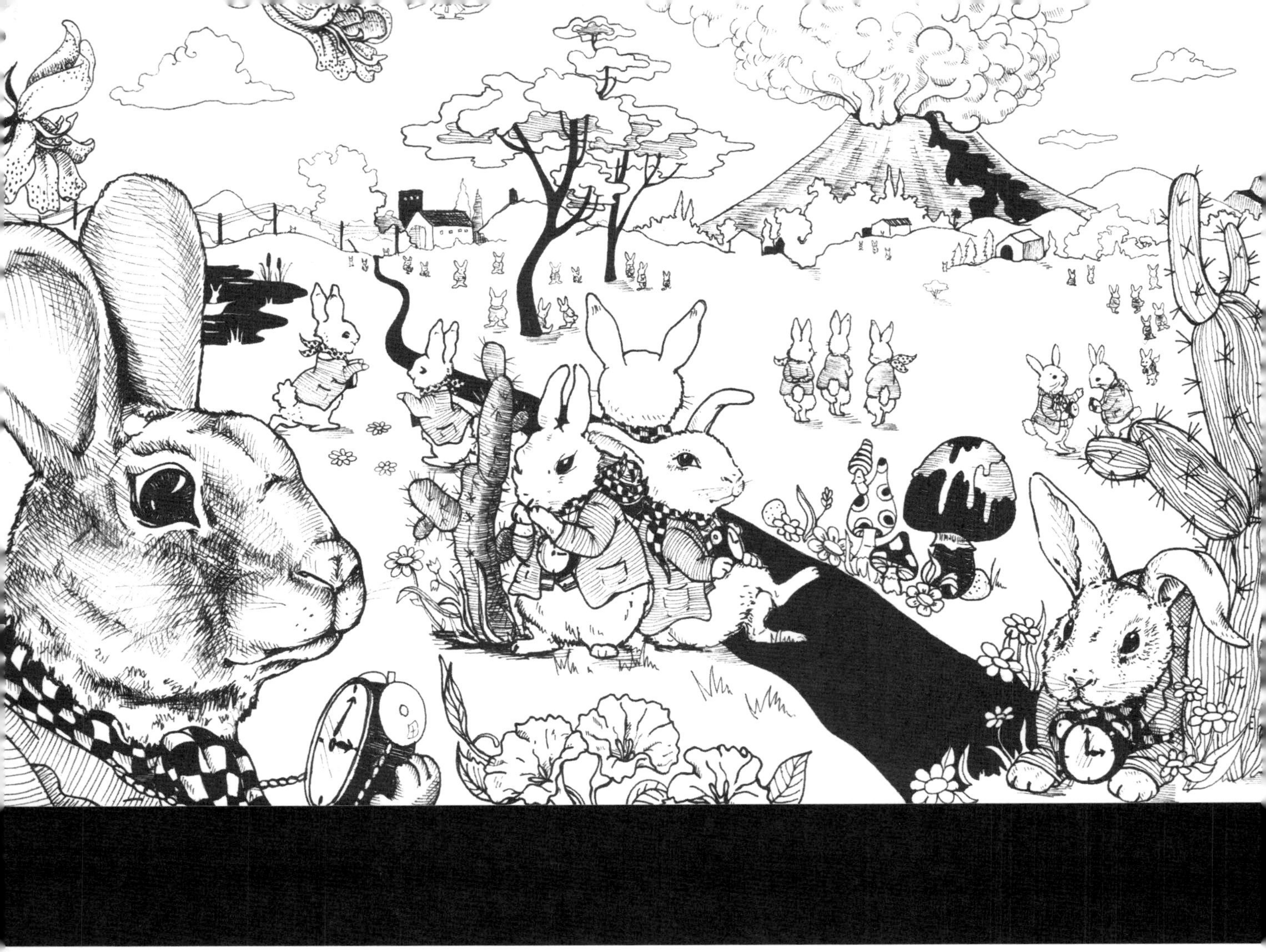

THE HORROR!
When her dream fell apart she suddenly faced it: She herself was the nightmare.

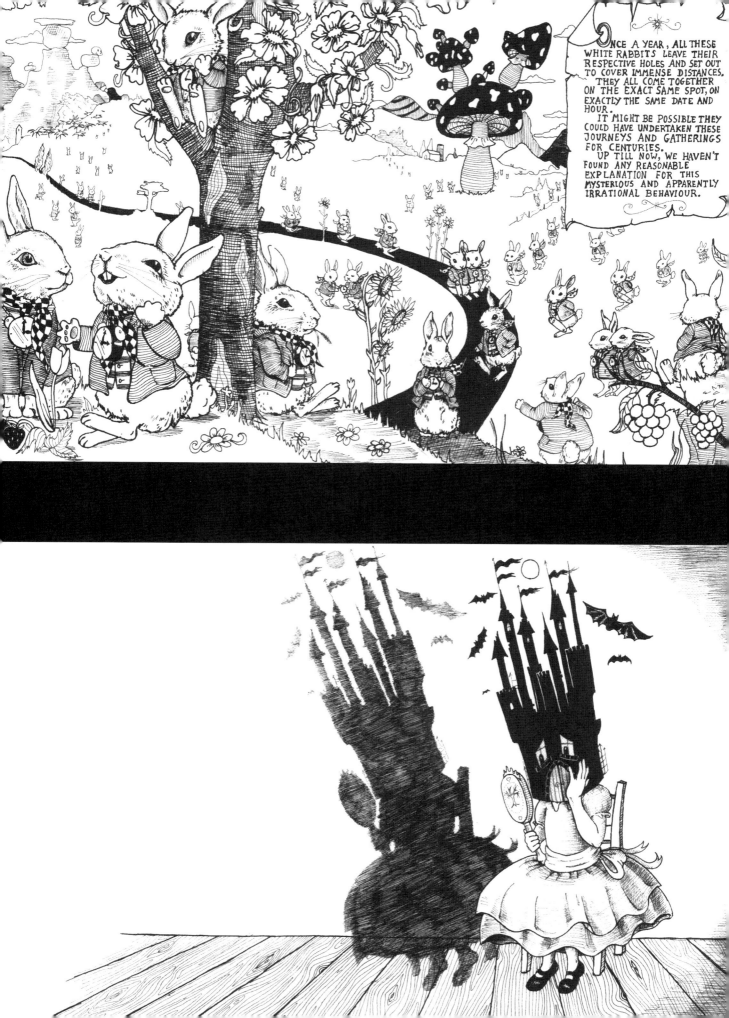

ONCE A YEAR, ALL THESE WHITE RABBITS LEAVE THEIR RESPECTIVE HOLES AND SET OUT TO COVER IMMENSE DISTANCES.

THEY ALL COME TOGETHER ON THE EXACT SAME SPOT, ON EXACTLY THE SAME DATE AND HOUR.

IT MIGHT BE POSSIBLE THEY COULD HAVE UNDERTAKEN THESE JOURNEYS AND GATHERINGS FOR CENTURIES.

UP TILL NOW, WE HAVEN'T FOUND ANY REASONABLE EXPLANATION FOR THIS MYSTERIOUS AND APPARENTLY IRRATIONAL BEHAVIOUR.

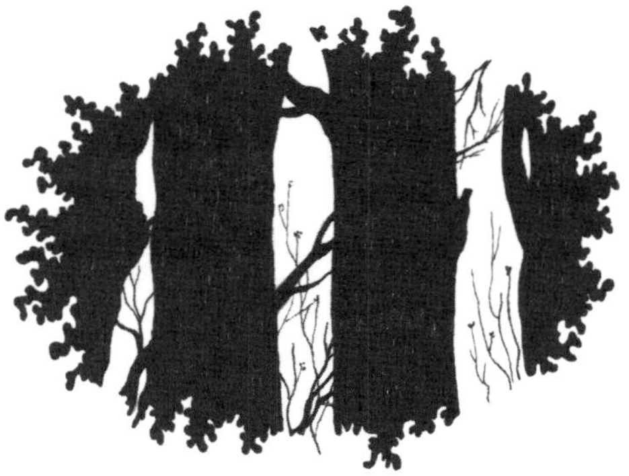

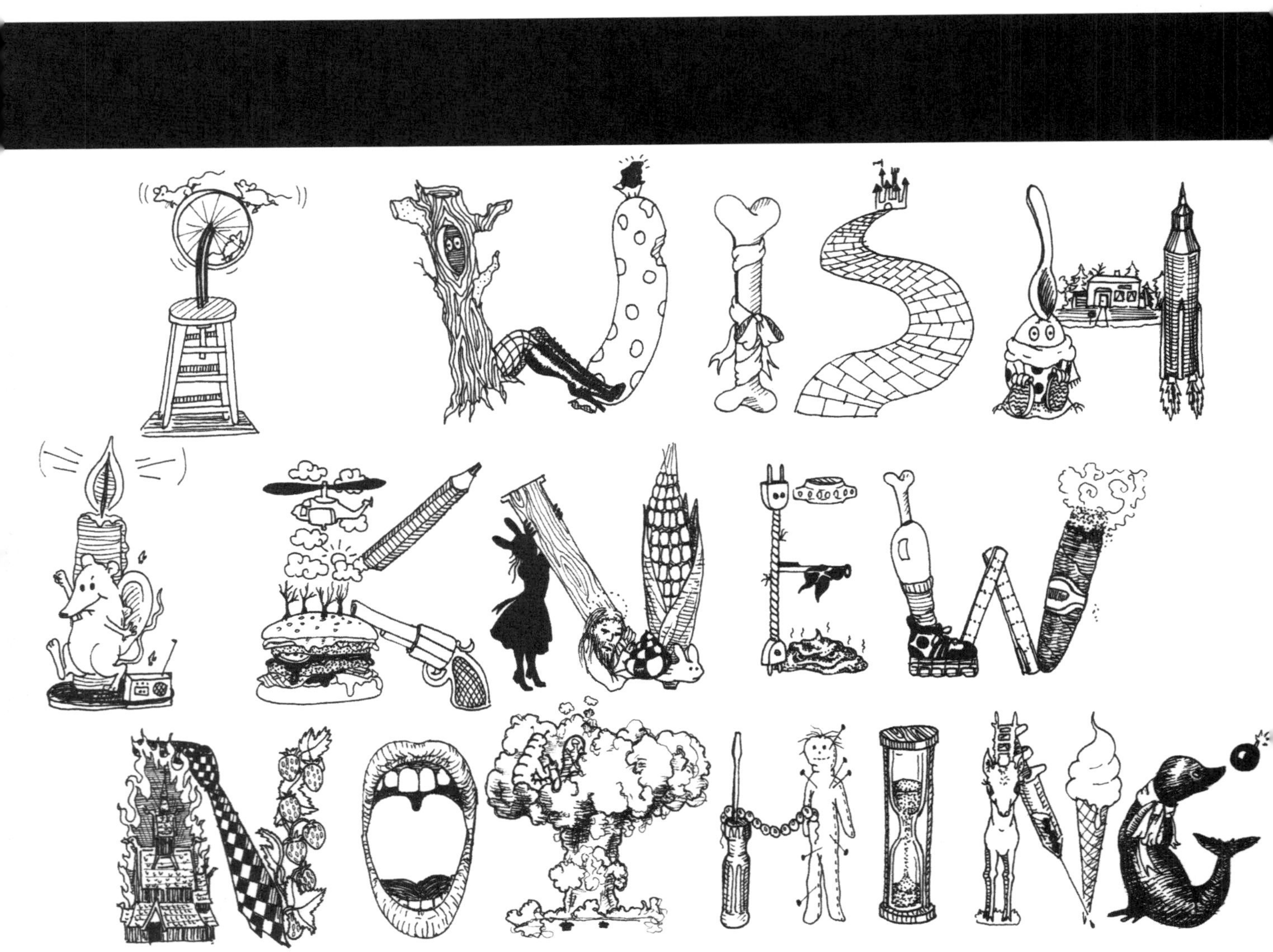
I WISH
I KNEW
NOTHING

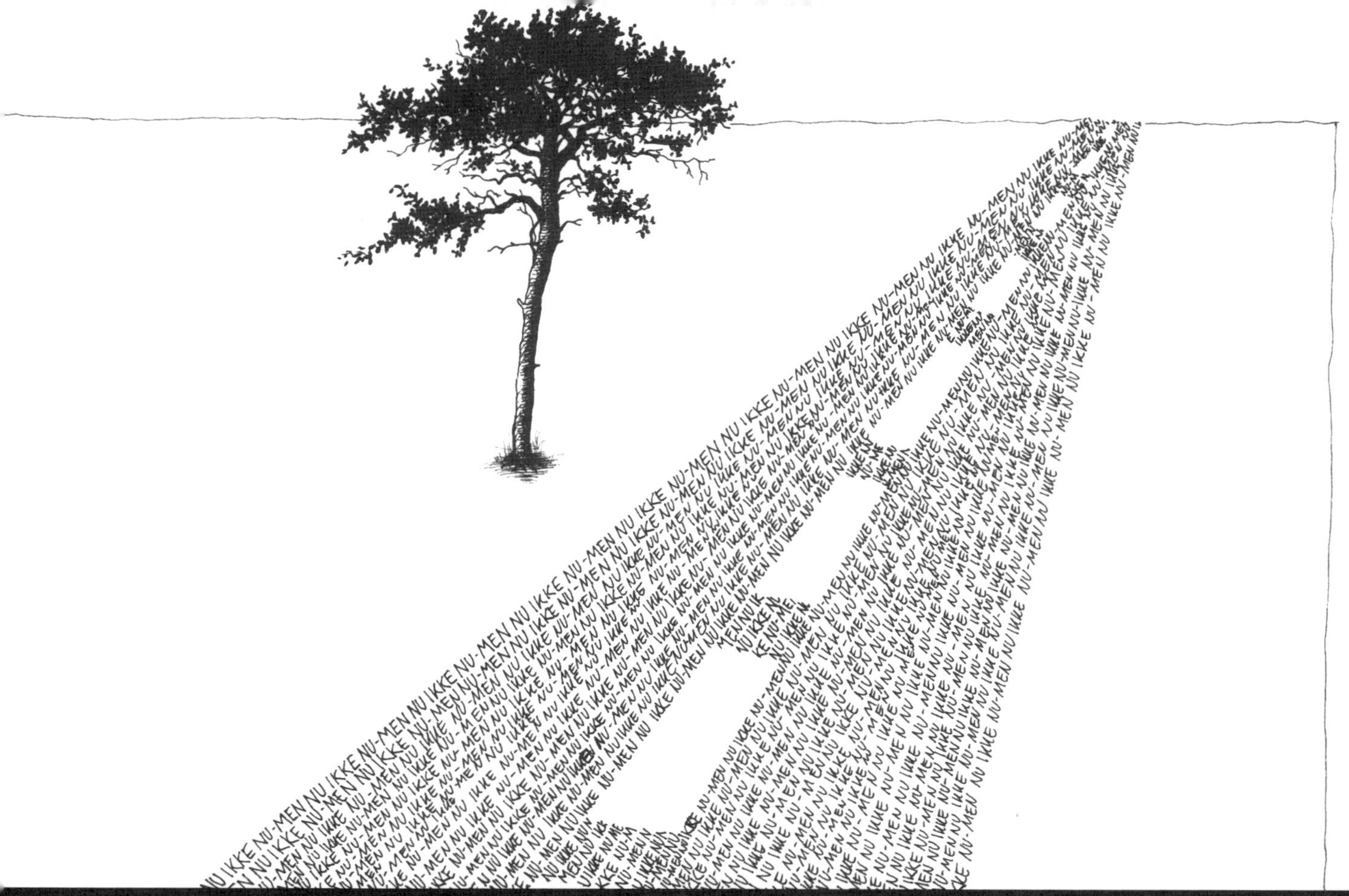
NU IKKE NU-MEN NU IKKE NU-MEN NU

[Road: not now but now, not now but now, etc.]

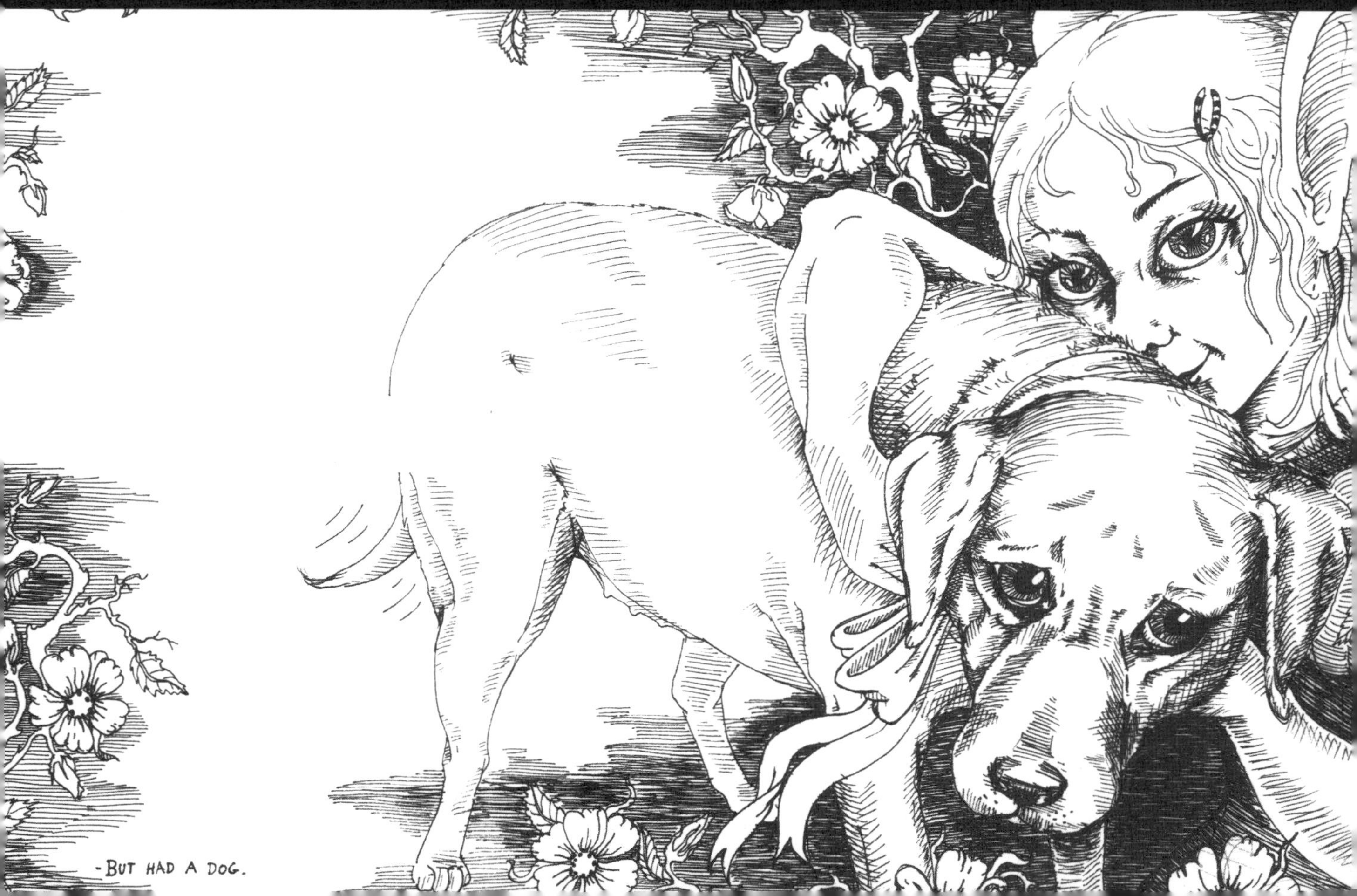
-BUT HAD A DOG.

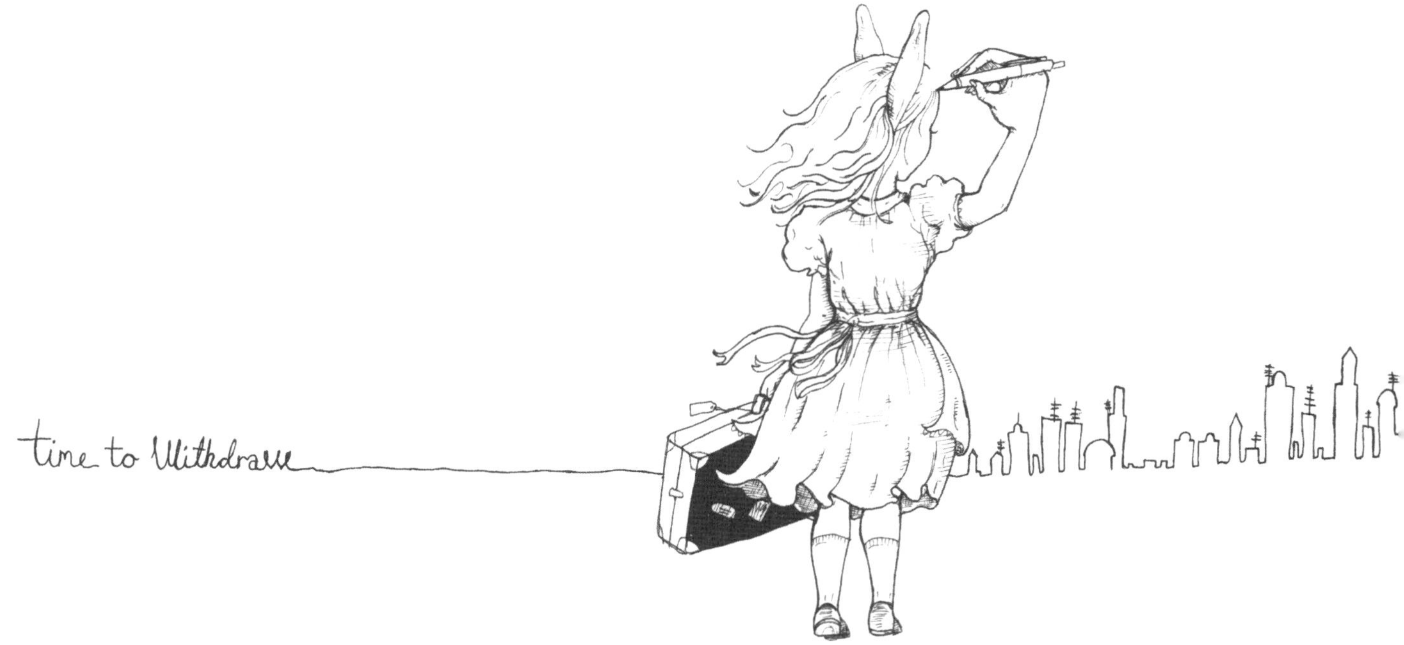
time to Withdraw

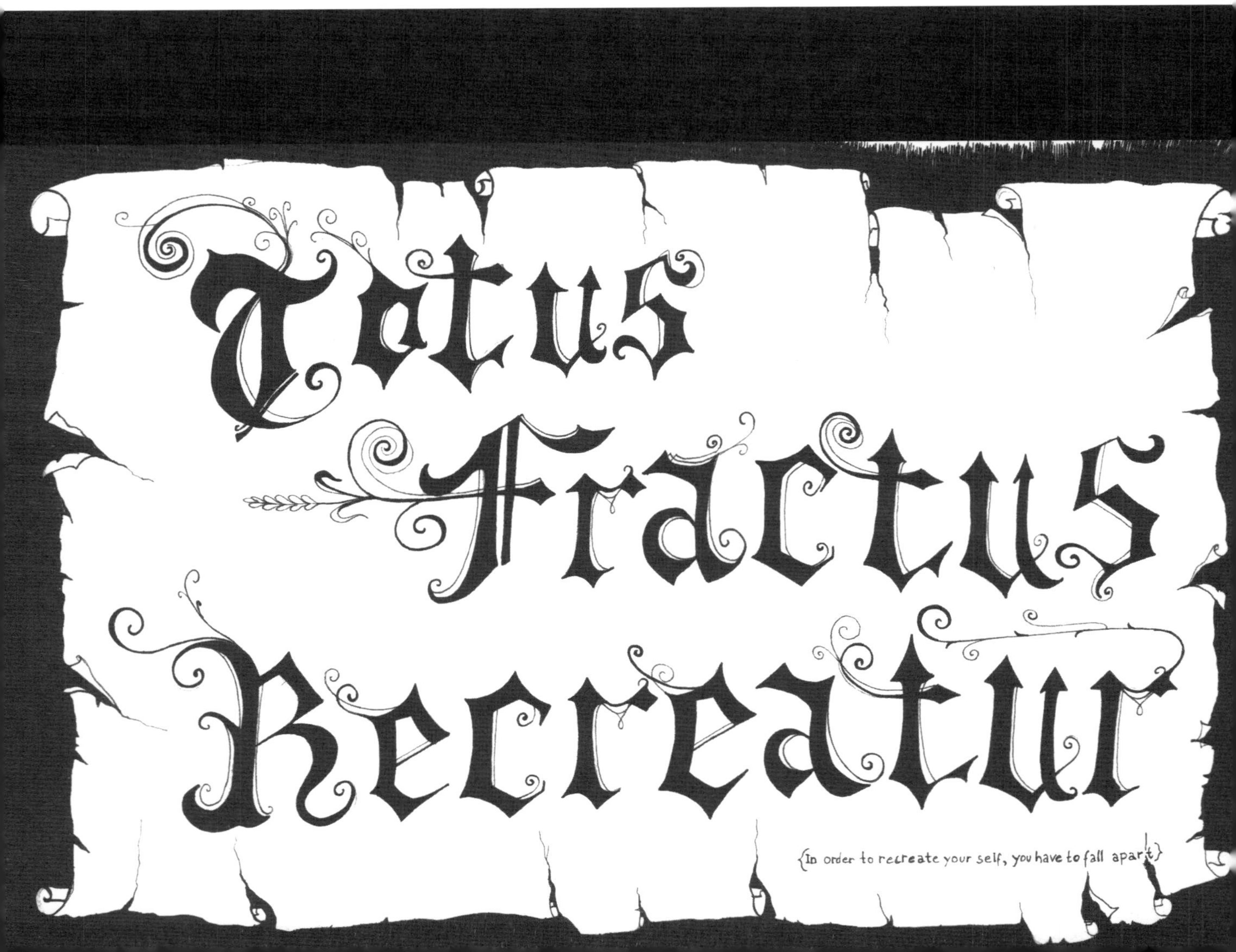
Totus
Fractus
Recreatur
{In order to recreate your self, you have to fall apart}

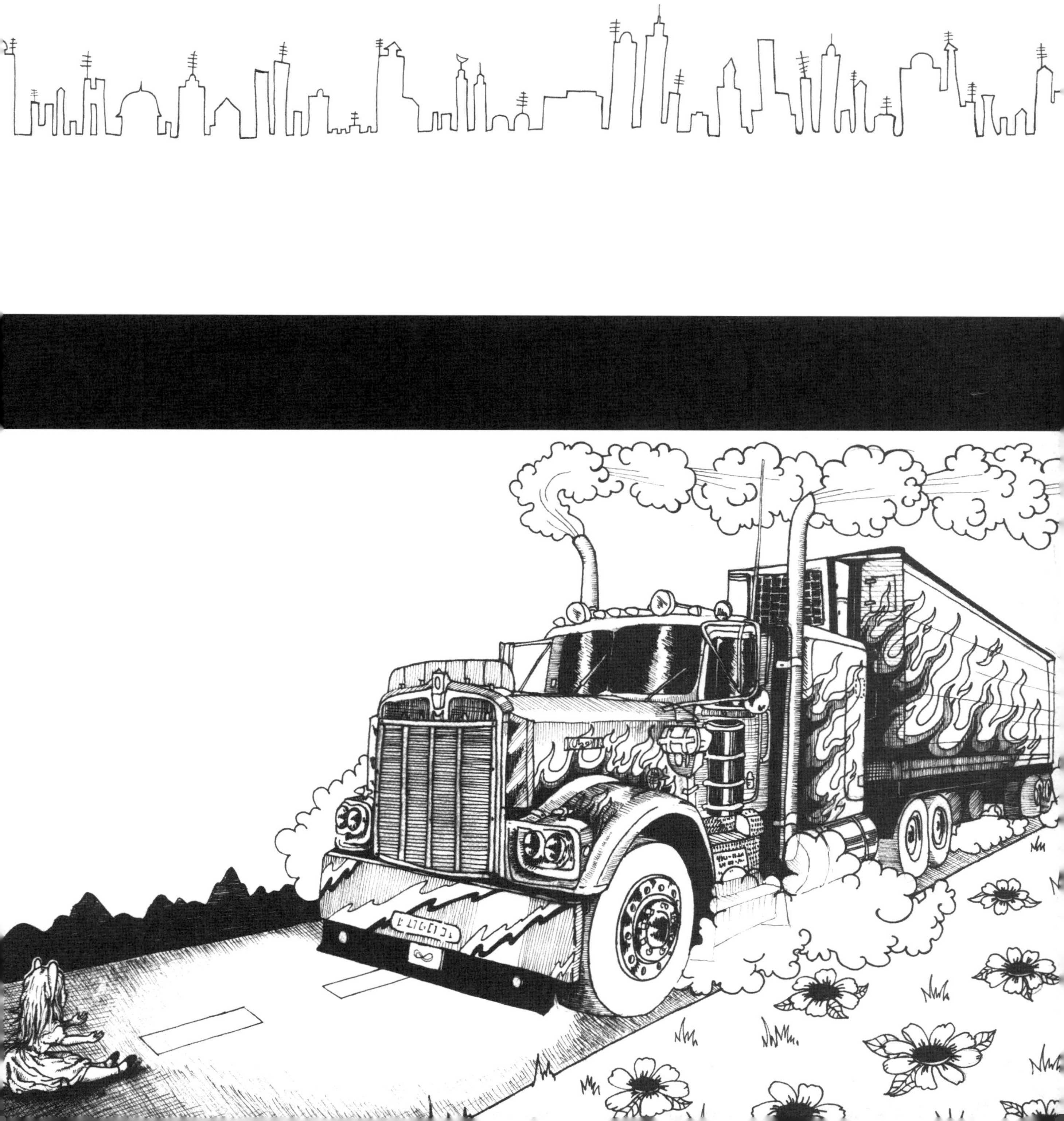

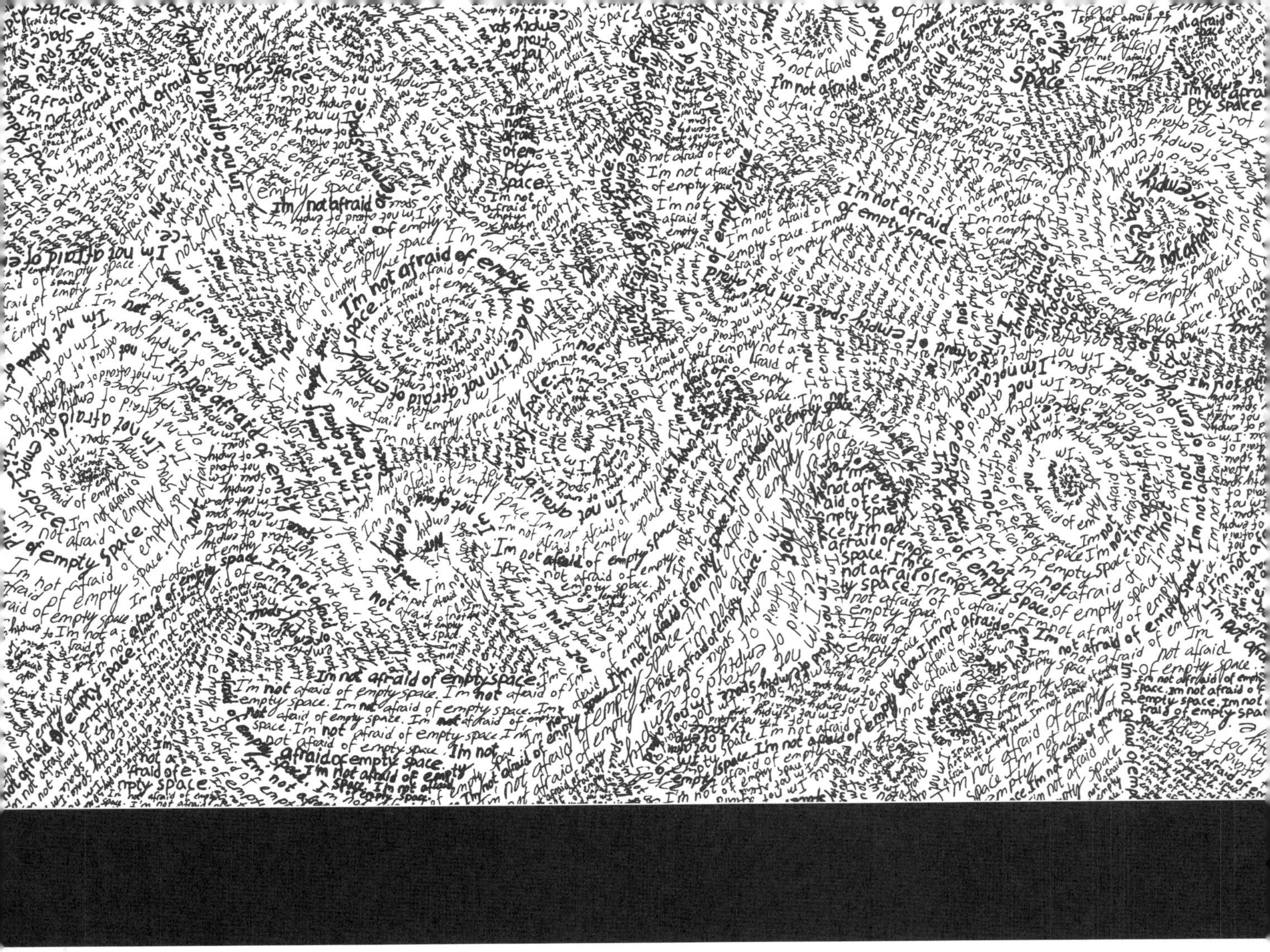
I'm not afraid of empty space.

AND TIME PASSED......

WHILE THEY WERE BUSY
DISTRACTING DEATH

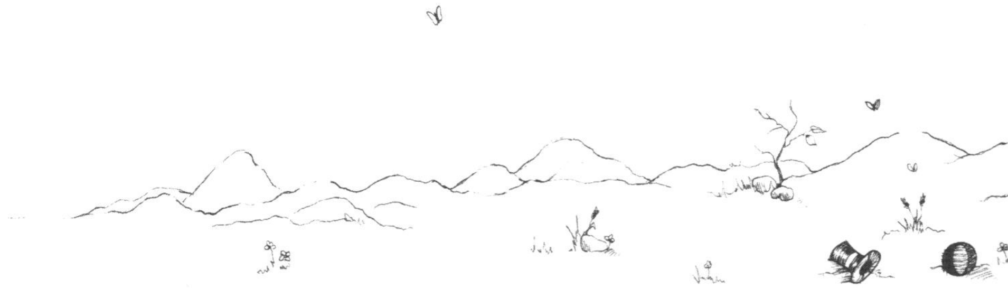

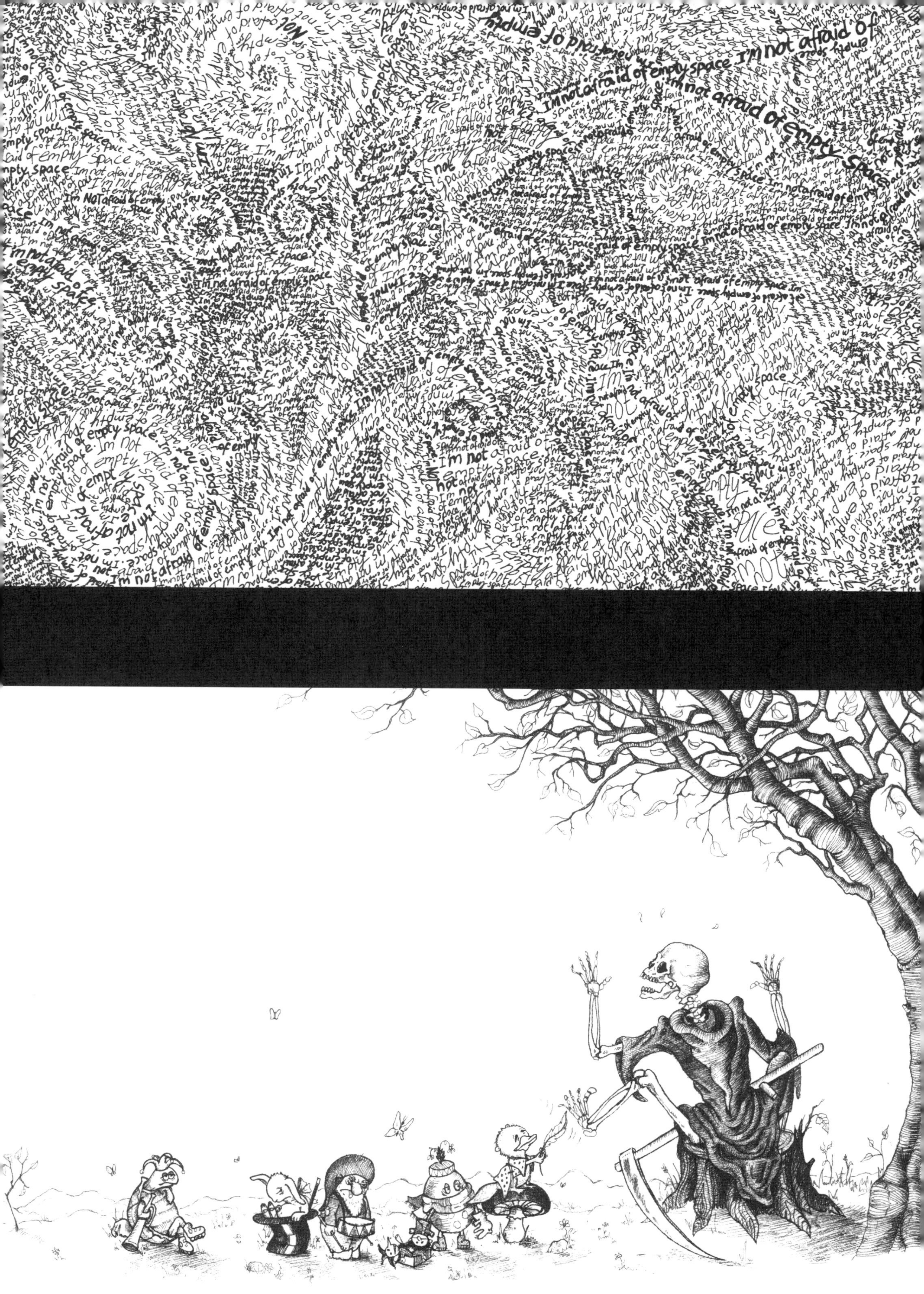
I'm not afraid of empty space.

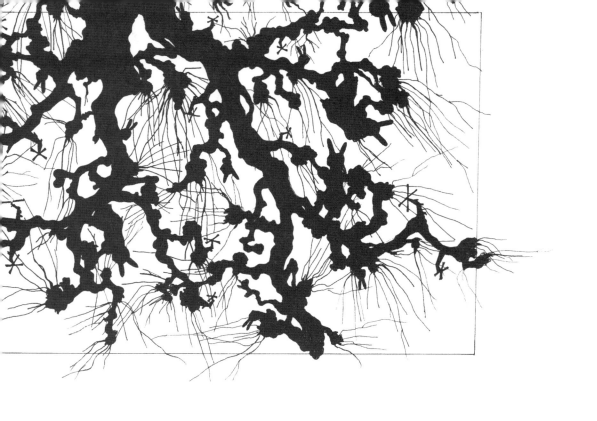

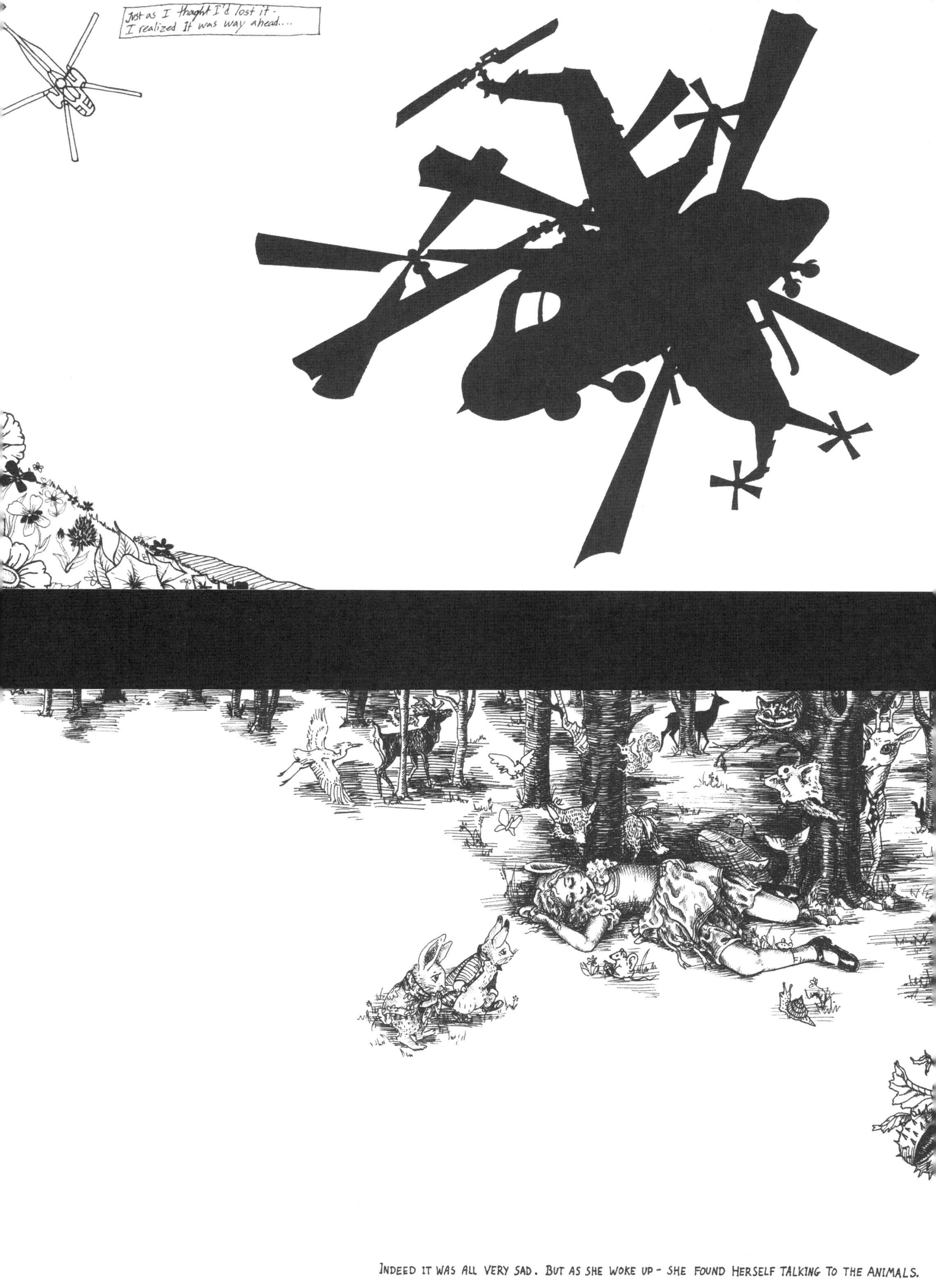
Just as I thought I'd lost it -
I realized It was way ahead...
INDEED IT WAS ALL VERY SAD. BUT AS SHE WOKE UP - SHE FOUND HERSELF TALKING TO THE ANIMALS.

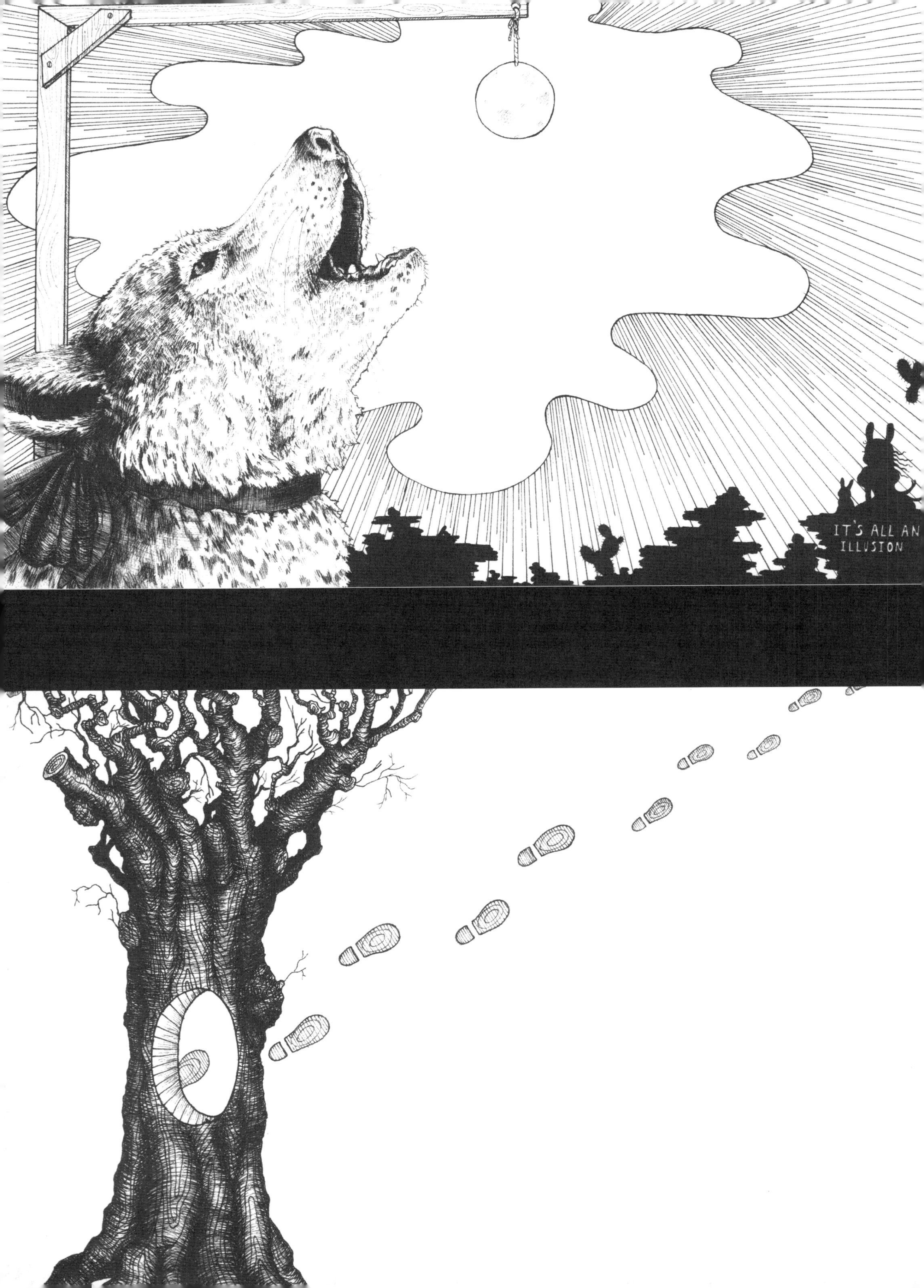
IT'S ALL AN
ILLUSION

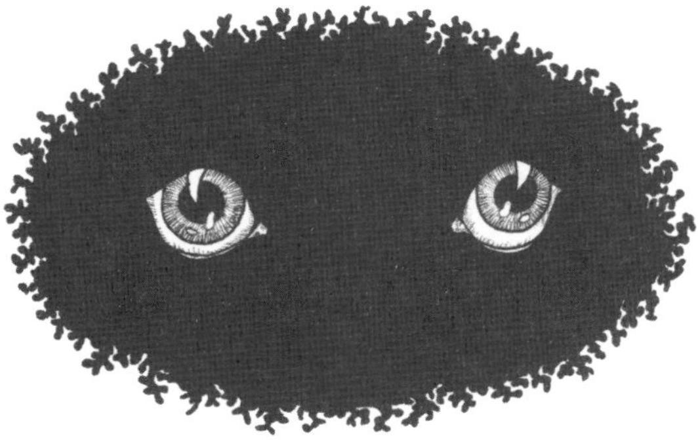

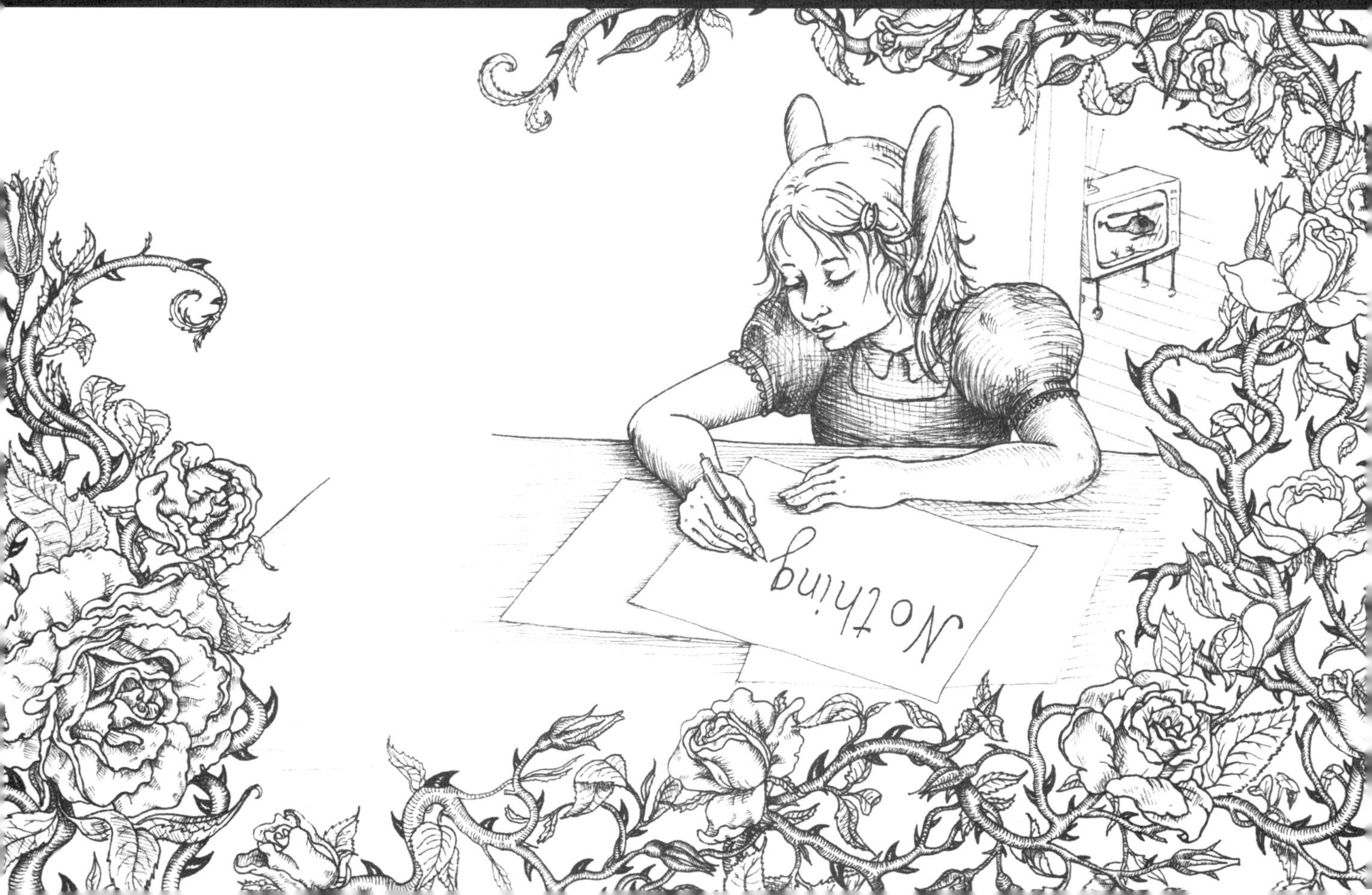
Nothing

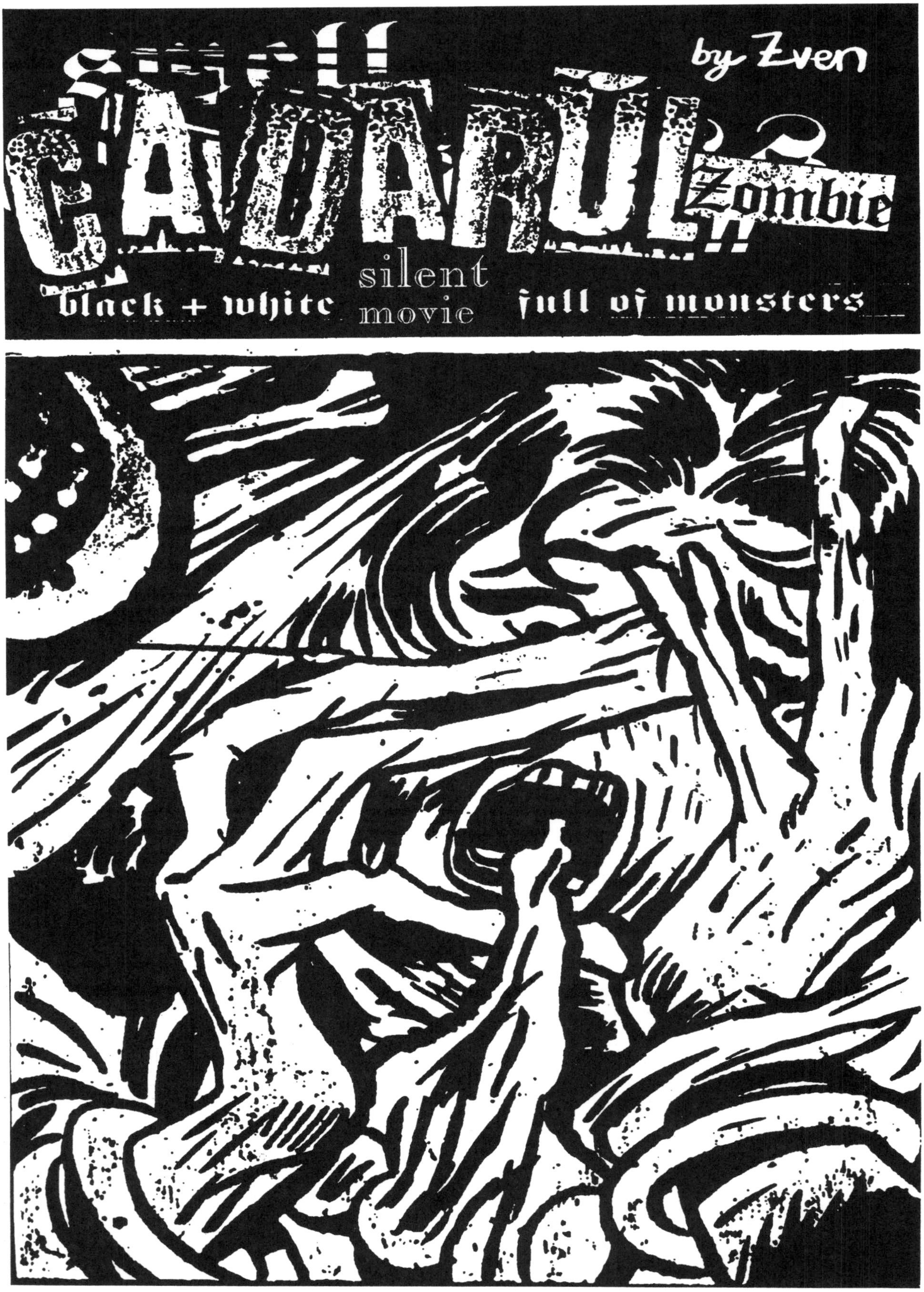
by Zven
zombie
black + white
silent
movie
full of monsters

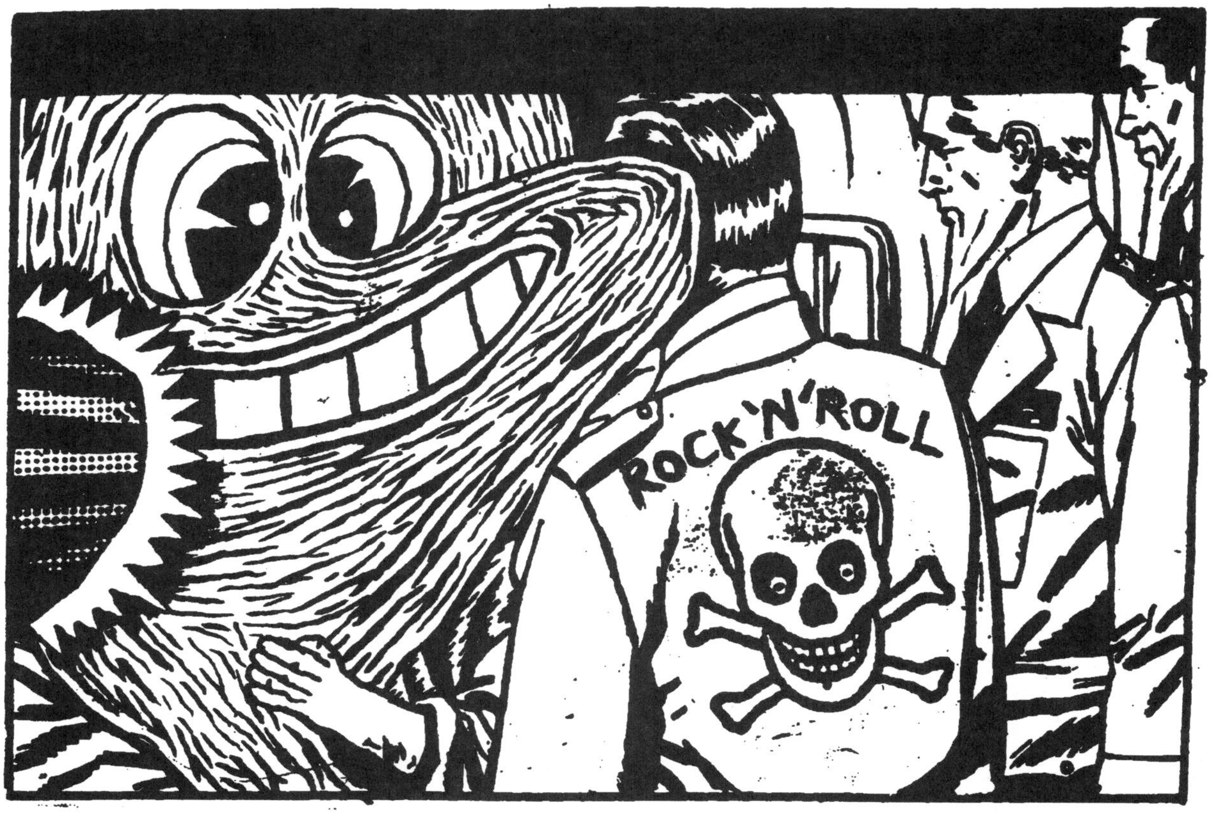
ROCK'N'ROLL

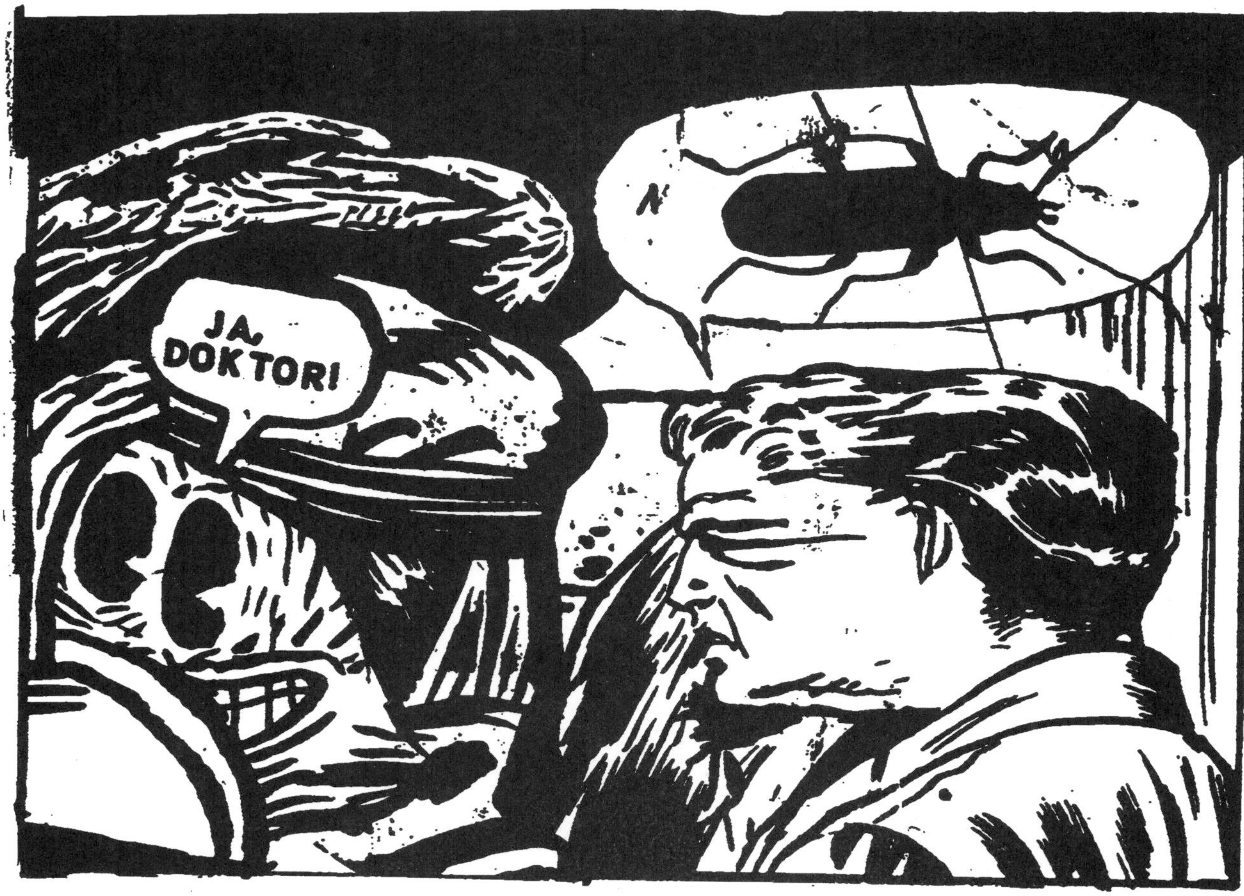
JA, DOKTOR!

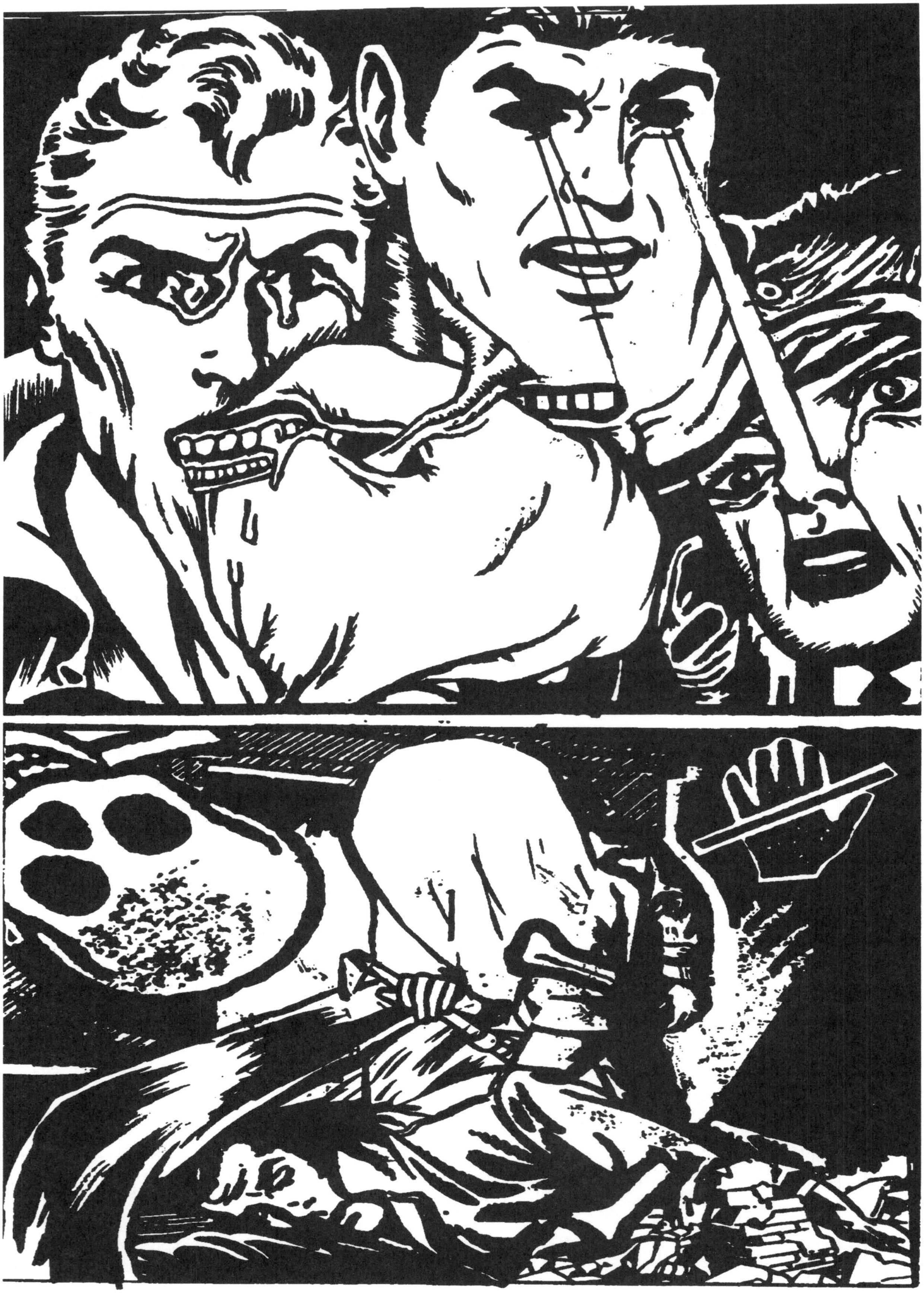

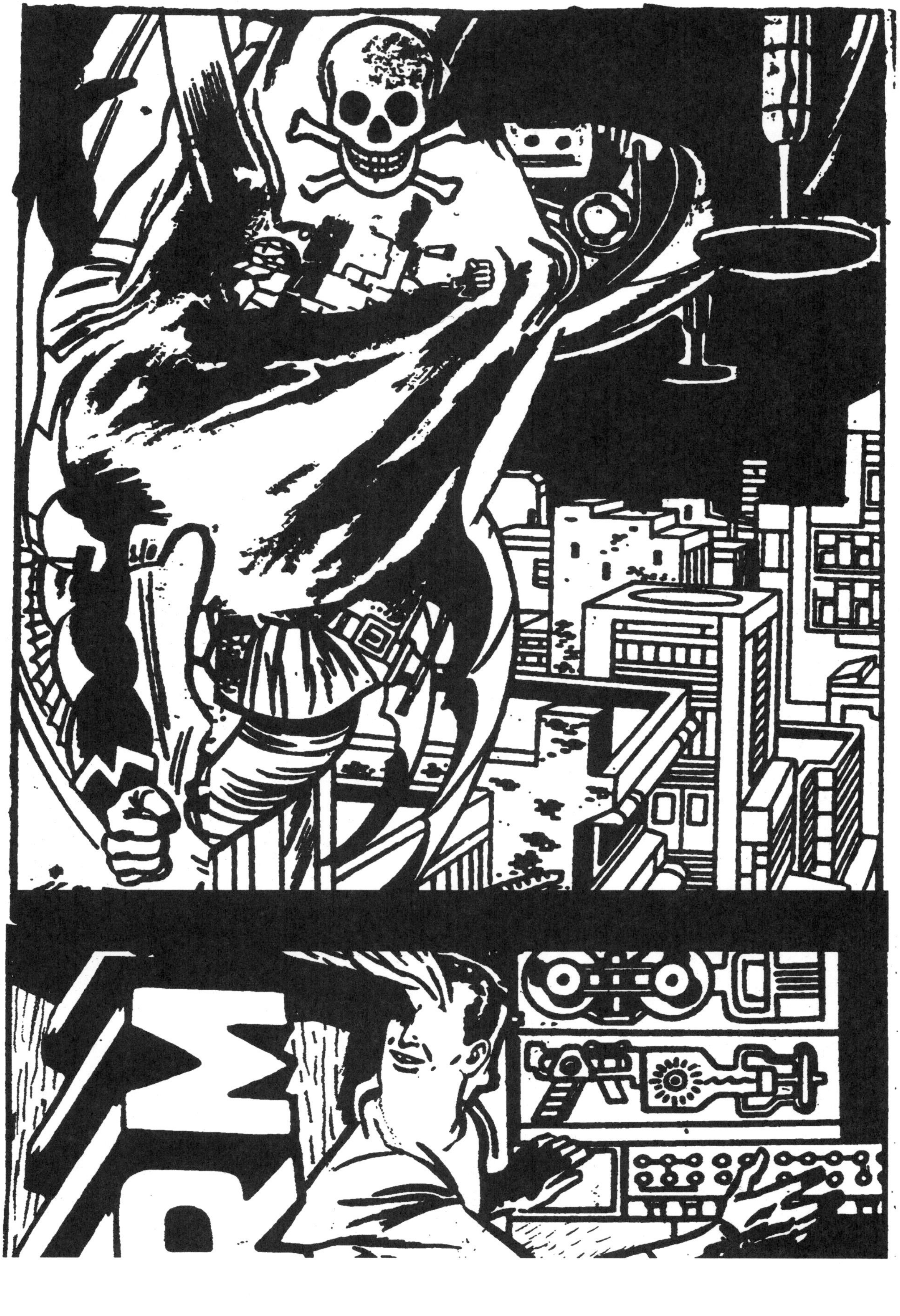

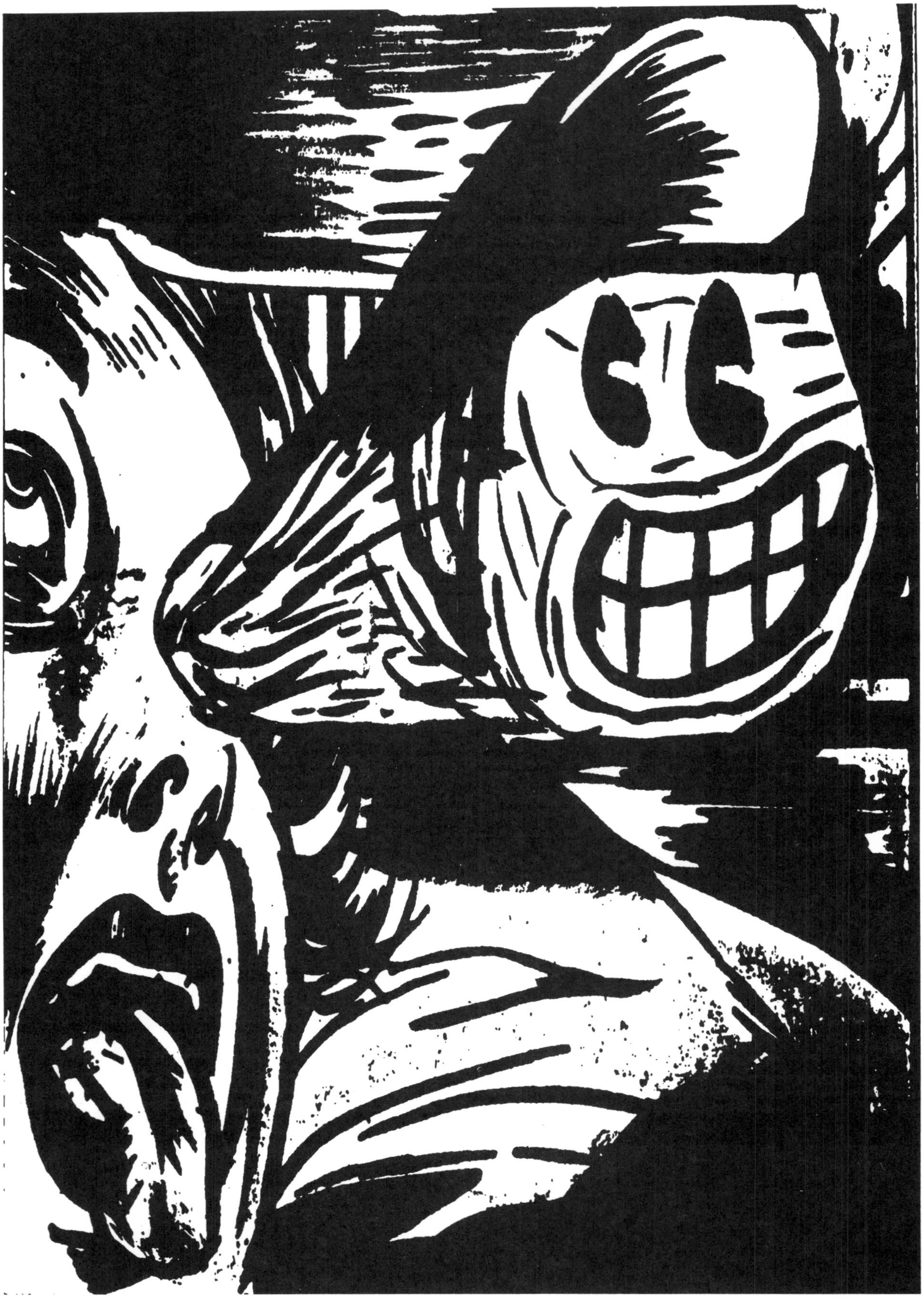

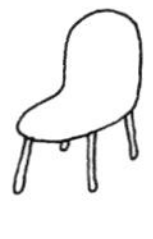

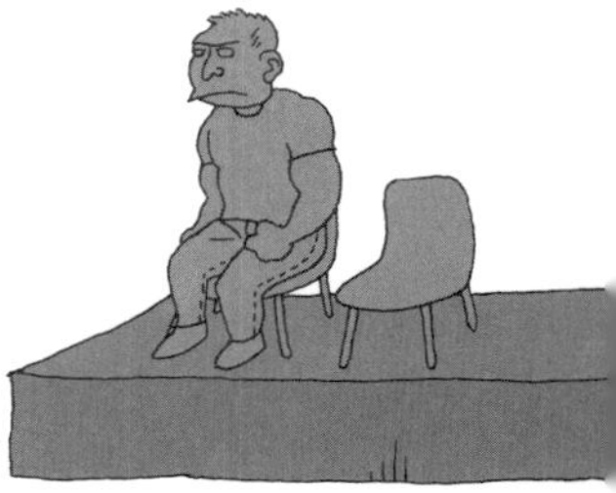

Vibe Bredahl (1974, København) vibebredahl.com
Mary's Mind Travel © Vibe Bredahl 2005.
Previously published by Hurricane Publishing.

Johan F. Krarup (1976, København)
jfkra.dk
Birte and Seven Men Practice The Art of Seduction © Johan F. Krarup 2008.

HuskMitNavn (1975, Tåstrup) huskmitnavn.com
Newspaper Cartoons © HuskMitNavn 2006 & 2007. Previously published by Politikens Forlag (2006) and Borgen (2007).

Nikoline Werdelin (1960, København)
rosinante.dk
Because I Love You So Much © Nikoline Werdelin 2003. Previously published in Homo Metropolis 7 by Rosinante.

Christoffer Zieler (1977, Århus)
christofferzieler.com
Steep Speed © Christoffer Zieler 2008.
Previously published on christofferzieler.com.

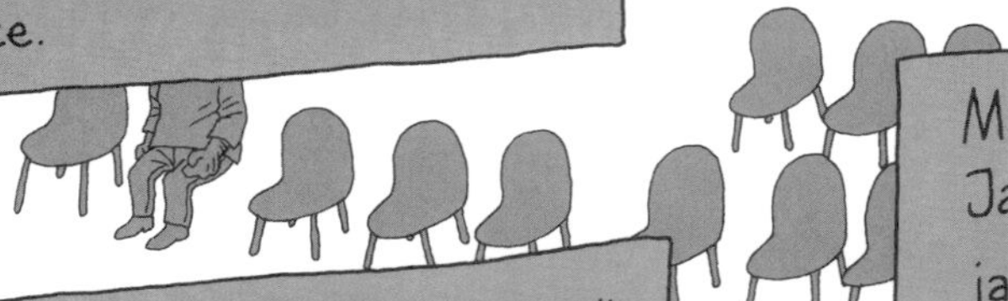

Maria Isenbecker (1973, København)
Jan Solheim (1971, København)
jansolheim.blogspot.com, solheim.dk
The Visit © Maria Isenbecker & Jan Solheim 2004. Previously published in Glömp 7 by Boing Being and C'est Bon Anthology 4 by C'est Bon Kultur.

T. Thorhauge (1973, Odder) overfloden.dk
M © T. Thorhauge 2006. Previously published in Blæk by Politikens Forlag.
Text by Albert Camus and Thomas Jefferson.

Mårdøn Smet (1961, Søborg)
overfloden.dk
Stig & Martha © Mårdøn Smet 2006.
Previously published in Blæk by Politikens Forlag.

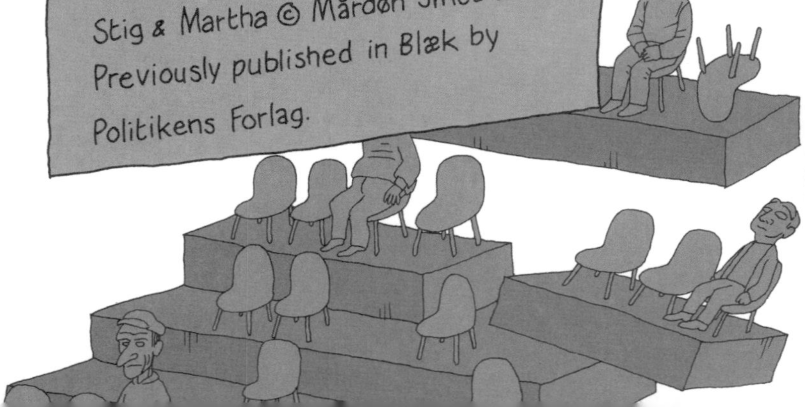

Peter Kielland (1960, Helsingør)
peterkielland.dk
Valküren Träume © Peter Kielland 2000. Previously published in Krautsalat by Jochen Enterprises.

Simon Bukhave (1978, Thisted)
simonbukhave.dk
All That I Hold in My Hand © Simon Bukhave 2006. Previously published in Blæk by Politikens Forlag.

Jacob Ørsted (1972, København) anport.dk
Søren Mosdal (1972, Nairobi) sm.anport.dk
Dog God © Jacob Ørsted & Søren Mosdal 2006. Previously published in Blæk by Politikens Forlag.

Allan Haverholm (1976, Middelfart) haverholm.com, astoria-book.net
Tomb of The Rabbit King © Allan Haverholm 2008. Previously published in Free Comics by Forlæns Publishing.

Ib Kjeldsmark (1969, København)
ib-k.dk, ib-k.blogspot.com
Sloth © Ib Kjeldsmark 2006. Previously published by Forlaget Fahrenheit.

Signe Parkins (1979, Århus)
signeparkins.com
Table Manners © Signe Parkins 2008. Previously published by Aben Maler.

Julie Nord (1970, København) julienord.dk
From Wonderland with Love © Julie Nord 2003. Previously published by Århus Kunstmuseum.

Zven Balslev (1977, Grenå) smittekilde.dk
Cadarul Zombie © Zven Balslev 2000. Previously published in Fahrenheit 68.0 by Forlaget Fahrenheit.

Giuseppe Raffael Mantard
(1964, Turin)
Endpapers © G.R. Mantard 2009

Translations: From Wonderland with Love by Julie Nord. Because I Love You So Much by Kim Thompson and Steffen P. Maarup. Steep Speed and Sloth by the artists and Steffen P. Maarup. Newspaper Cartoons, Birte, Seven Men Practice The Art of Seduction, The Visit, Dog God by Steffen P. Maarup.

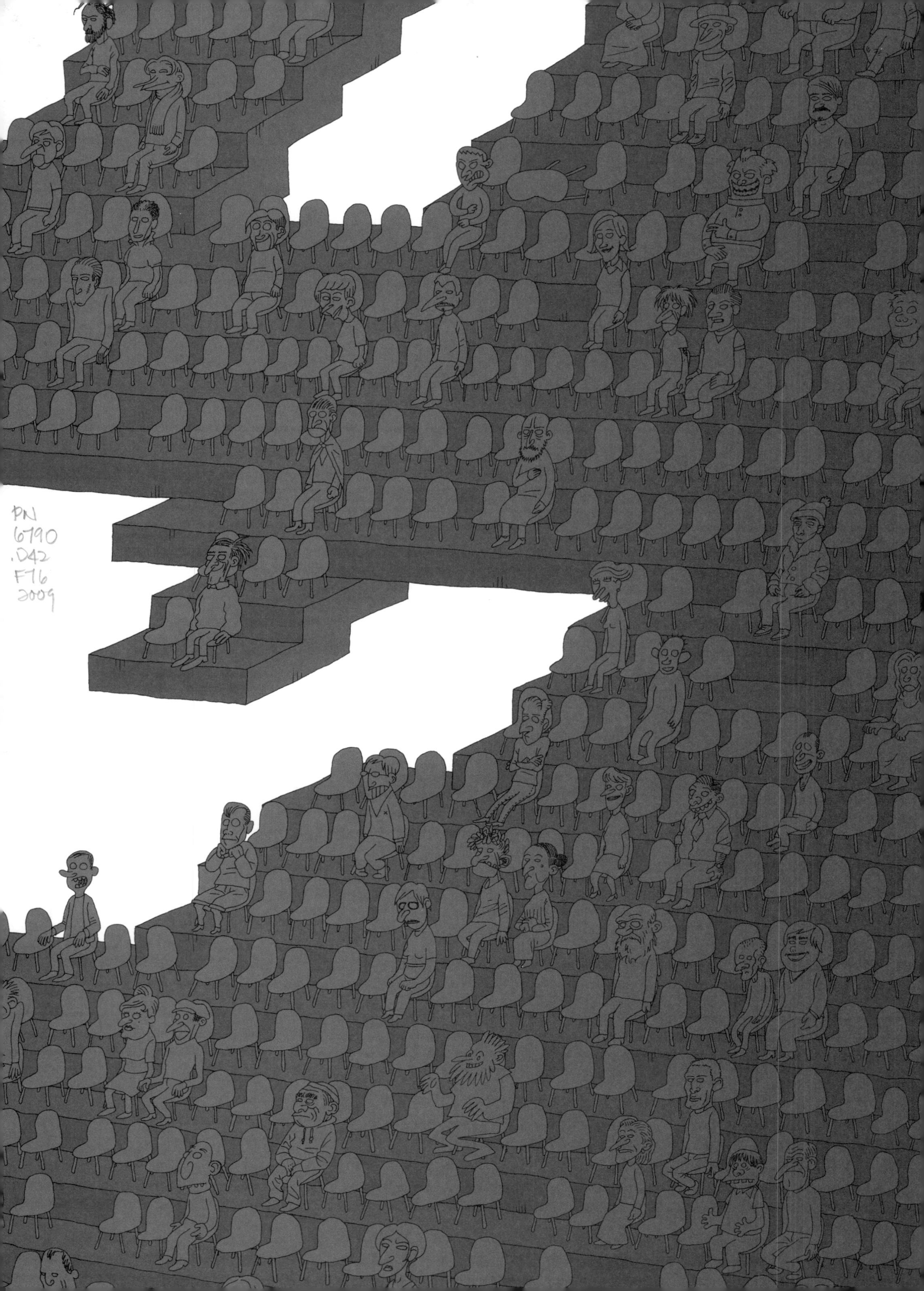